Desert in the Promised Land

Stanford Studies in Jewish History and Culture
Edited by David Biale and Sarah Abrevaya Stein

Desert in the Promised Land

Yael Zerubavel

Stanford University Press

Stanford, California

Stanford University Press

Stanford, California

Printed in the United States of America on acid-free, archival-quality paper

Library of Congress Cataloging-in-Publication Data

Names: Zerubavel, Yael, author.
Title: Desert in the promised land / Yael Zerubavel.
Description: Stanford, California : Stanford University Press, 2018. | Series:
    Stanford studies in Jewish history and culture | Includes bibliographical
    references and index.
Identifiers: LCCN 2018019361 (print) | LCCN 2018027918 (ebook) |
    ISBN 9781503606234 (cloth: alk. paper) | ISBN 9781503607590
    (pbk.: alk. paper) | ISBN 9781503607606 (ebook)
Subjects: LCSH: Negev (Israel)—Symbolic representation. | Deserts—Symbolic
    aspects—Israel. | Discourse analysis—Israel. | Semiotics—Israel.
Classification: LCC DS110.N4 (ebook) | LCC DS110.N4 Z47 2018 (print) | DDC
    956.94/9—dc23
LC record available at https://lccn.loc.gov/2018019361

Typeset by Kevin Barrett Kane in 11/13.5 Garamond

Cover photograph: View of the town of Mitzpe Ramon, Yael Zerubavel.

Cover design: Angela Moody

To the memory of Michael Feige
A missed friend and fellow traveler in the landscapes of memory

Contents

Preface

I first wondered about the meaning of the desert for Israelis when reading about the emerging tradition of trekking to Masada in the 1940s and 1950s. I already knew about the dangerous and strenuous character of those early excursions in the desert, but was surprised by participants' expressions of strong attachment to the desert landscape and admiration of its wild nature. In *Recovered Roots: Collective Memory and the Making of Israeli National Tradition* I analyzed this practice as a secular pilgrimage that enhanced the heroic interpretation of Masada and its ascent as a national myth. But I remained intrigued by the unresolved tension between the positive view of the desert articulated by some of those participants and the negative approach to it that was at the core of the Zionist settlement mission. As a child growing up in Israel in the 1950s, I learned that making the desert bloom was Israelis' national goal. On Fridays, during *kabbalat Shabbat* (the welcoming of the Sabbath), each child made a small donation to the Jewish National Fund as a personal contribution to the "redemption of the land." The performance of this ritual in the public school marked the transition from profane time to the sacred domain. Yet within this interpretive framework, which emphasized national redemption, the desert stood for a symbolic wasteland whose value appeared to be conditional on its future transformation into a settled land.

The idea that the desert might be an interesting topic for a major research project was triggered by my realization that the Israeli perception of the desert is more complex than the discourse of settlement suggests. In my earlier work, I had been fascinated by the complexities of cultural interpretations of the past, and this represented a spatial turn in my research. It also marked a move from studying what the culture consciously foregrounds to addressing a topic that has remained at the background of cultural awareness. At the same time, however, this work also reveals an important continuity with my earlier writing. The study of how Israeli Jewish society processes its relation to space is intimately connected to memory, and the analysis of discursive references to the desert in the pre-state period soon led me to explore it as a symbolic landscape rather than merely focusing on the geographical desert. In time, I realized that an underlying theme in all my various research projects on Israeli memory, identity, and space is the study of cultural ambiguities and their broader political implications.

I did not consciously focus on my own experiences with the desert until I was already deeply involved in this study. As a teenager, hiking in the desert was part of my Masada experience, though the most lasting impression that I took away from it was waking up in the predawn hours to climb up the mountain and watch the sunrise from the top. It was from that vantage point that I first remember appreciating the beauty of the desert landscape and the Dead Sea. My experience of ambivalence about the desert did not occur until my military service, a mandatory duty for Israeli Jewish men and women at the age of eighteen. Upon completing officers' training, I was given the opportunity to choose where I would serve, and southern Sinai was one of the options. I did not hesitate for a moment in selecting this destination. Southern Sinai was the farthest point from anything with which I was familiar, and I was to be the only female officer there, in charge of the female soldiers, welfare, and education. I lived in a desert area that seemed better suited to a beach resort than a military camp. I had some interaction with the Bedouins of that area, and a few times joined Israeli physicians flying to other remote sites in the Sinai Peninsula to provide medical aid to Bedouins living there. Yet at the time, it never occurred to me to reflect on the political dimension of the situation or how the Bedouins might see me, a woman in uniform who was part of a military presence that was imposed on them, even as we distributed medications to help them.

My romantic view of the desert radically changed when I moved to the middle of the Sinai Peninsula to serve as a welfare officer for a combat unit stationed there. Here the landscape was the desolate desert, with its extreme climate and difficult living conditions, and we were surrounded by sand that penetrated our clothes, food, and lodging. More than anything else, however, being there during the so-called War of Attrition with Egypt was my first direct exposure to the personal price individuals pay for participating in combat. One of my duties as a welfare officer was to visit the wounded on behalf of my unit, and it was a profoundly unsettling experience. My encounters with those young men suffering from severe burns and amputated limbs or struggling with rehabilitation shaped my later political views.

My initial idea for this book about the desert was more conceptual and textual, yet my Israeli historian colleagues insisted that one cannot discuss the tension between the desert and settlement without addressing the reality on the ground. I have followed the path they suggested in order to present a more grounded portrayal of the Negev desert, a choice that cost me a few additional years of work in reshaping the book. At times, I felt that my personal experience had become a metaphorical reenactment of the biblical wandering in the desert (though I hoped that my experience would not last as long as the biblical model). During this time, I took a few detours to work on other projects, yet eventually returned to my trek through the desert materials. This book is thus the culmination of a long journey, although relevant developments continue to unfold, defying any sense of closure.

My work on the desert is inseparable from the memory of a close colleague and friend, Michael Feige, who was killed in a terrorist attack on a Tel Aviv restaurant in June 2016. Michael and I shared our fascination with Israeli memory, memorial sites and rituals of commemoration; the intersection of archeology, nationalism, and politics; and the perceptions of the land in Israeli culture. Michael and I would meet whenever I was in Israel and spend hours discussing our current research projects, inevitably dwelling on Israeli politics and the Israeli-Palestinian conflict. When I wanted to do fieldwork in the desert, Michael, who lived with his wife Nurit and their three daughters on Ben-Gurion University's Sde Boker campus in the Negev at the time, facilitated my stay there. In our last meeting, in a café in Tel Aviv, he promised to read the final manuscript of this book before I submitted it to the press. He never got to read the entire manuscript, though he was familiar with some of its parts. The book is dedicated to his memory, with profound sadness that his life was cut short by the violence of a conflict he believed should be resolved, and appreciation for his scholarship, which will continue to benefit future generations.

Several institutions have helped me during my work on this book. The Ben-Gurion Research Institute for the Study of Israel and Zionism at Ben-Gurion University of the Negev provided me with a welcoming environment and a home base when I stayed there in the winter of 2005. I returned to Sde Boker over the years to participate in conferences and workshops, and hope to continue to do so. Residents of the Negev shared with me their thoughts about the desert and their relationship with it, and their insights enriched my study. Rutgers University, my academic home base, generously supported my research. It was at the Katz Center for Advanced Judaic Studies at the University of Pennsylvania, where I was a fellow, that the seeds of this project were planted, and the Institute for Advanced Studies at the Hebrew University in Jerusalem provided a fellowship for further research that became a part of this book. The research group on contested memories sponsored by the Allen and Joan Bildner Center for the Study of Jewish Life at Rutgers provided an enriching intellectual and collegial framework that was particularly valuable during the final phase of writing this book. My special thanks to Karen Small, Arlene Goldstein, and Sherry Endick, who have been such an important part of my work experience at the Bildner Center and have created a friendly and supportive environment throughout these years.

I am indebted to my colleagues David Biale, Derek Penslar, Galit Hasan-Rokem, Erez Tzfadia, Jonathan Gribetz, Ilan Troen, Ziva Galili, Berel Lang, Yaacov Yadgar, and two anonymous readers who helped me with insightful comments and references during various stages of this work. Ilanit Ben-Dor, who wrote her master's thesis on the individual farms in the Negev, was tremendously helpful in an early phase of this project; and Batia Donner, whose pioneering work on visual representations of Israeli culture provided inspiration for my own work, generously shared her insights and suggestions. Dvir Tzur, Lee Rotbart, and Einav Melamed assisted me in my research during early phases of this project, and Itai Artzi provided most valuable assistance during the critical phase of shaping the final manuscript. Finally, the friendship of Janet Theophano, Rivi Peer, Ilanit Palmon, and Orit Zaslavsky has helped sustain me in so many ways during this period. I am indebted to all.

As always, my family has been the most crucial source of encouragement and strength. Eviatar, my life partner, has been there as a rock through life's blessings and its challenges. His love and belief in my work, even when I myself doubted it, have been a constant support, and I have benefited tremendously from our endless conversations about ideas and insights around the coffee table and during long walks. My daughter Noga and my son Noam have been cherished sources of love, wisdom, and good humor that I can hardly take for granted; my son-in-law, Dave, extended himself well beyond the call of duty by reading an early draft of the manuscript and giving me his careful and thoughtful comments; and my future daughter-in-law, Kristin, is wisely joining our family in time to celebrate the bringing of this work to completion.

Desert in the Promised Land

Introduction

LEAVING HIS HOME IN THE SOUTHERN TOWN of Arad for an early-morning walk in the desert, Israeli writer Amos Oz notes, "The desert begins here, at the end of my street." While walking, he observes the beauty of the landscape, the fleeting figure of a Bedouin in the distance, the smell of the land that evokes the memory of biblical times. The sight of a rusty, discarded bombshell disrupts his meditative walk, but he brushes it off and continues his solitary hike in the wilderness. Upon returning to town, Oz is confronted by the din of cars, his neighbor's agitated talk about peace negotiations with the Palestinians, and a radio news report of another terrorist attack. As the day proceeds, the earlier openness of the desert gives way to its oppressive presence. The blinding light, the rising heat, and the dusty wind force Oz to shut his home's windows and pull down the shades.

Oz reflects on the achievement of establishing the town of Arad in the heart of the desert, attributing it to the town planners' vision and the successful carrying of water from the north of the country to the remote desert. His own garden, he notes, was made possible by a layer of fertile topsoil that was poured over the arid land, which he likens to the dressing of a wound.[1]

Oz's brief and evocative description of his interaction with the desert environment raises some of the central themes that *Desert in the Promised Land* sets out to explore. Arad is located in the Negev desert, but the desert and the town are constructed as distinct spatial categories—the "desert" begins where the "town" ends—and moving from one to the other introduces an abrupt shift in scenery and experience. His experience of the desert is changing and multifaceted, revealing its complex character. The desert is the open vista where one may find the serenity and solitude so missing in the urban environment, but it is also the space associated with the aggressive elements of nature that threaten to invade one's home territory. The arid desert land presents obstacles to the settlement process, yet vision, ingenuity, and persistence help transform it into an urban space and open the possibility of "making the desert bloom." The desert landscape evokes the memory of biblical times and offers a link to the ancient Jewish roots in the land; but it is also the territory where Israel has fought some of its fiercest wars and where the visible presence of the military serves as a reminder of a still-unresolved national conflict.

Desert in the Promised Land explores the complex and contradictory meanings of the desert within a broad historical framework, tracing their development in the Hebrew culture of the late Ottoman and Mandatory Palestine and, after 1948, in Israel. Following Henri Lefebvre's approach, this study examines the understanding of space through the lens of its cultural production.[2] The study's point of departure is not the geographical desert but the cultural construction of the desert as a *symbolic landscape*.[3] It therefore examines the ways in which Zionist Jews perceived, conceived, encoded, and reshaped the land they considered their ancient homeland. The study of the discourses and practices that contributed to this process highlights the interplay among the physical, mental, and social dimensions of space.[4] The analysis of the role of language and the use of metaphors further highlights the cultural foundation of the desert as a symbolic spatial category.

Studying the desert as a symbolic landscape is particularly interesting within the context of the Zionist movement and its emphasis on the vision and agenda of settlement.[5] Zionist immigrants to Palestine pursued the vision of establishing new settlements and rebuilding a new society that would develop its own national identity and culture. In the distinct "spatial code" that emerged in the Zionist Hebrew culture in Palestine, the "desert" and the "settlement" constituted key symbolic landscapes, defined by their opposition as well as their interdependence. Yet while Hebrew culture underscored the importance of the Jewish settlement, it considered the desert as the background against which the settlement was constructed. *Desert in the Promised Land* reverses this perspective. Going against the grain of the cultural emphasis on the settlement, the present study foregrounds the desert and examines the settlement in its relation to it. This perspective reveals the ambiguities and tensions that underlie the different approaches to the desert that are obscured by the traditional privileging of the settlement.

The lexical development of the Hebrew terms that designate these key categories—*midbar* for desert, and *yishuv* for settlement—reveals their intertwined meanings and supports the conceptual framework that this study presents. In the Hebrew Bible, the Hebrew word *midbar* refers to an uncultivated area that was primarily used for grazing and marked by its contrast to settled, inhabited space.[6] In modern Hebrew, *midbar* has become the standard term used to denote a highly arid land with little or no water and limited vegetation, enjoying wider use than other biblical synonyms. English editions of the Hebrew Bible have traditionally translated *midbar* as "wilderness," yet the broader semantic scope of the latter also encompasses landscapes (such as wild forests) that do not correspond to the Hebrew term. I therefore follow the translation of *midbar* as "desert,"[7] including in references to the biblical text.

The Hebrew term for "settlement," *yishuv*, originally designated space that was noted for its civilized and social order, in comparison to the desert or the sea. Medieval Jewish literature expanded the meaning of the term to refer to a *Jewish community* living among a non-Jewish population,[8] thus implying a symbolic equivalence between the desert and the non-Jewish population surrounding the *yishuv*. In modern Hebrew, the term *yishuv* refers to the process of settling the land (*yishuv ha-aretz*) as well as to the settlement as its product.[9] The significance of this concept is best evident in its use to refer collectively to the Jewish society of Palestine as *ha-Yishuv*, i.e. "the Settlement," even prior to Zionist immigration. The addition of the definite article with no further markers to describe it underscores the privileged status of this Jewish society compared to others, in the same fashion that the reference to "the Land" (*ha-aretz*) indicates the privileged status of the Land of Israel.[10] The "Yishuv period" similarly became a historiographical term referring to the period from the beginning of the Zionist immigration to Palestine in the 1880s through 1948.[11]

Desert in the Promised Land is divided into two broad parts, ordered chronologically. The first part of the book addresses the divergent interpretations of the desert as a symbolic landscape during the formative years of the Hebrew culture of late Ottoman and Mandatory Palestine, and the second part examines the construction of desert-settlement relations since 1948. The first part focuses on the perception of the landscape outside the Jewish settlement as a symbolic desert; the second part shifts the focus to the concrete desert of the Negev and explores the competing visions constructed in various discourses and practices after the establishment of the state of Israel.

Chapter 1 sets the stage for this study by exploring the interweaving of space and memory in the perception of the Palestinian landscape. This chronotopological approach demonstrates the "connectedness of temporal and spatial relations"[12] in the cultural construction of the desert as a symbolic landscape. It also reveals that the desert's multiple and contradictory meanings as a site of memory make it a particularly interesting and complex topic of inquiry. The desert plays a critical role in the biblical narrative of Exodus, relating the foundational experience of the ancient Israelites as they left Egypt for the Promised Land. The Israelites left the land of exile, representing the *counter-place*, to reach the Land of Israel, their destined *place* (*makom*).[13] Set between Egypt and the Promised Land, the desert thus serves as a liminal space that allows divine revelations and is essential for experiencing profound transitions. The Israelites wandered for forty years in the desert to prepare the way for a new generation that was born to freedom. The desert was where they received the Torah and the foundations of their distinct religion and identity as they became ready for the entry to their destined land.

Yet Jewish memory also carries a different meaning of the desert, as a symbolic landscape associated with the long period of exile from the homeland. Jewish tradition interpreted the exile as a divine punishment and Zionist memory further constructed it, within a decline narrative of Jewish history, as a regressive period.[14] Jews projected this negative view of exile onto the landscape, referring to it interchangeably as a "desert" (*midbar*) or "a desolate land" (*shemama*), or even using the hyperbolic biblical expression "desolate desert" (*midbar-shemama*)[15] to underscore the negative impact of Jewish exile on the land. Such generalized references conveyed the image of a symbolic desert and did not imply a realistic description of a concrete landscape. But they marked the land outside the Jewish settlement as the *counter-place*, the territory both representing the past destruction of the inhabited Jewish *place* and characterized by its hostility to the modern revival by Jews.[16] The construction of the desert and the settlement as opposing symbolic landscapes further highlights the redemptive value of the processes of settlement and working the land and their national and theological meanings.

The Hebrew culture of the Jewish society of Palestine articulated the duality of the desert, as both the nonplace associated with mythical origins and the hostile counter-place opposing the settlement. Chapter 2 focuses on European Jewish immigrants' fascination with the mystique of the desert.

The desert held a special appeal for Zionist Jews as the mythical site of origin that preserved their ancient spirit and national heritage, an association that was further reinforced by the symbolic status of the east (*mizrah*) in Jewish liturgical tradition and ritual practices. But the romantic approach to the desert also drew on the prevalent Orientalist notions that European Jews shared, which saw the desert as remaining outside the grip of time and resistant to change.[17] This perception reinforced the mythical view of the desert and its Bedouin inhabitants as offering a symbolic bridge to the biblical forefathers and hence as a source of inspiration for the construction of a modern Hebrew culture and identity. The discussion thus follows the impact of the nostalgic longing for the ancient past that led some of the Zionist settlers and Hebrew youth to selectively adapt various cultural idioms from Palestinian Arabs, giving rise to a hybrid "Hebrew Bedouin" identity. The romantic appeal of the desert mystique was also evident in the creation of a new Hebrew desert lore. In spite of the gradual decline of the desert mystique as the national conflict between Jews and Arabs flared up in Palestine, it has remained a continuing streak in Israeli culture.

Jews' highly ambivalent approach to the desert is evident in chapter 3, which explores the discourse of settlement and security and its competing interpretation of the desert as a symbolic landscape. The negative approach to the desert draws on its association with Jewish exile, encoding the territory outside the Jewish settlement as a symbolic desert and applying the view of it as a "desolate desert" to wide-ranging terrains that represented obstacles to the Jewish settlement process.[18] Settlement narratives alluded to the settlement as an oasis in the desert or a besieged island and described the settlement process as an uphill struggle to conquer the symbolic desert. Influenced by colonialist and Orientalist notions, the discourse and practices of Jewish settlement associated this process with the civilizing mission that would bring modernity, order, and technological progress to a backward region.[19] The frequent juxtaposition of the two symbolic landscapes in texts and images highlights the ways in which the untamed desert metamorphoses into a civilized place that becomes part of the Jewish national territory.

After 1948, the newly established state of Israel included the largely arid Negev region, which constituted more than half of its territory. In the discussion of desert-settlement relations, the desert then shifted from the symbolic to the concrete space and from the hostile counter-place that exists outside the Jewish settlement to the counter-place that has become a part of the Jewish national space. The second part of the book examines key discourses that reveal the growing complexity of desert-settlement relations and the ambiguities that this transformation introduced.

Chapter 4 addresses the Jewish efforts to settle the Negev desert starting in the 1940s. The 1948 war reinforced the besieged-island metaphor for the entire state of Israel, but the isolation of the few Jewish settlements in the Negev made their situation more acute. Following the war, when the large and sparsely inhabited Negev desert became an internal Jewish frontier, it retained the characteristics of the counter-place. Although Prime Minister David Ben-Gurion championed the national goal of "making the desert bloom" and the need for the state to transfer water to the Negev in support of this agenda, there was a limited response to this call. In the face of the massive Jewish immigration to Israel of the post-independence years, the state began to direct new immigrants to the desert, establishing rural frontier settlements and towns in the 1950s and 1960s. After the 1967 war, the Jewish settlement drive in the occupied territories—the Golan Heights, the Sinai, the Gaza Strip, and the West Bank—diminished the status of the Negev as a frontier. Following the peace treaty with Egypt and the return of the Sinai Peninsula in the early 1980s, the transfer of military and air force bases to the Negev, along with the designation of large areas as national parks and nature reserves, limited the space available for settlement. Yet new Jewish pioneers advanced experimental settlement initiatives that contributed to a growing diversity in the population of the Negev and reveal significant changes in contemporary Israeli settlement narratives.

The Negev's Bedouin population, greatly diminished following the 1948 war, is the focus of the discussion in chapter 5. The geographical extension of the desert beyond the armistice borders in the south and the state's suspicion of its Arab citizens led it to relocate most of the remaining Bedouins to a central, bounded area away from the borders, placing them (like the majority of Palestinian Arab communities) under military administration. When the state abolished these restrictions in 1966, the fast-growing Bedouin population dispersed into spontaneous settlements in the center of the Negev. The government's plan to urbanize and contain this population by relocating it to newly built Bedouin towns had limited appeal. A significant proportion of the Bedouins living in unrecognized villages refused to settle their land claims with the state by agreeing to its conditions. As a result, the unrecognized Bedouin villages have been left off of Israel's official map, embodying the continuing presence of a chaotic counter-place to the official settlements. The government's encouragement of the Jewish settlement agenda and the legal disputes surrounding the Bedouin "dispersion" living in the gray zone of a semi-permanent "temporary" state thus provide a different angle from which to examine the tensions underlying desert-settlement relations. The rise of crime in the Negev, the harsh law enforcement measures there, and the frequent demolitions of illegal structures have contributed to the perception of the desert as the counter-place and the Negev as "the wild south."

Chapter 6 examines desert-settlement relations as constructed by the environmental discourse. Like the settlement discourse, the environmental approach to the desert acknowledges the opposition between the inhabited place and unsettled space; yet, in a radical departure from the settlement discourse, the environmentalists present the desert as the open space that must be protected, assigning positive meanings to the "desert" and the "wasteland." They further criticize the state's approach to the desert as an empty space, which has turned it into a "national dump" for undesired, discredited, and dangerous elements from the populated center. Employing the rhetoric of salvage to mobilize public support for the desert environment, they reverse the roles of aggressor and victim in desert-settlement relations. The environmentalists' lawsuits defy the association of the settlement with law, order, and morality, pointing out illegal or damaging initiatives, while the proponents of the settlements attack the environmentalists' position as "anti-Zionist." The discussion highlights the contested visions of the desert and demonstrates how various coalitions are formed around particular cases and the interests of the state, local authorities, the army, the industry, and the environmental lobby.

Chapter 7 examines the discourse and practices of tourism and their eclectic approach to marketing the desert in an effort to appeal to diverse constituencies. Tourism draws on the various visions discussed in earlier chapters and provides a fluid collage with shifting emphases, ignoring the tensions between them. Like the environmental discourse, the discourse of tourism articulates the romantic vision of the desert as a mythical site associated with the Hebrew Bible and as an open space that provides an escape from the pressures of the modern urban center. After 1967, the Sinai desert and beaches became a major Israeli tourist attraction, overshadowing the appeal of the Negev desert. The Sinai embodied the romantic image of the desert as the carefree nonplace and its association with the Jewish mythical past. Sinai desert tourism continued even after the peninsula was returned to Egypt as part of the 1979 peace treaty with Israel, but declined later, in the face of growing instability in the region.

Tourist literature for the Negev also features the success of the Zionist settlement ethos and its vision of making the desert bloom. Tourist publicity highlights the mystique of the "primeval landscape," but also includes various archeological sites that provide evidence of earlier cultures. It points out the serenity of the desert landscape as an invitation to spiritual experiences and personal growth while also emphasizing the appeal of the rough terrain for adventure seekers. Whereas some sites feature simplicity and closeness to nature, others present their "pampering amenities." Jewish sites perform "Bedouin hospitality" as part of their "desert experience," but visits to actual Bedouin settlements and Bedouin-owned sites reveal a more recent, if limited, trend towards a growing diversity of tourist initiatives by Bedouins themselves.

The discussion of the multiple facets of desert tourism offers a metaphorical tour of the desert landscape as constructed in Israeli culture. In creating this complex portrait of the desert as a symbolic landscape, *Desert in the Promised Land* draws on wide-ranging sources including historical studies, educational narratives, literary works, newspaper articles, oral histories, tourist publicity, paintings, posters, cartoons, songs, and films. The analysis also draws on observations and conversations with Negev residents and visits to numerous tourist sites. This integrative approach made it possible to examine the interconnectedness of discourses and practices related to the desert and to explore the tensions and discrepancies among their approaches to desert-settlement relations.

Yet this study of the divergent visions of the desert in Israeli culture was not meant as an academic exercise in abstract distinctions. The issues explored here are directly related to Israelis' understanding of their national identity and cultural roots and reveal the ambiguities that mark Israel's vision of itself and its place in the Middle East. The epilogue extends the discussion beyond the focus on the desert, offering further reflections on the ways in which the themes discussed in the earlier chapters may shed light on Israel's position in relation to the occupied territories and the continuing conflict with the Palestinians.

Israel's experiences in the first two decades following its establishment, beginning with the 1948 war and culminating in the weeks prior to the 1967 war, reinforced the centrality of the metaphor of the besieged island surrounded by hostile Arab countries. The state's major territorial conquests resulting from the 1967 war created permeable borders with the occupied territories and a sense of openness that was dramatically opposed to Israelis' earlier sense of besiegement. The implications of this situation were highly controversial. Israelis debated Israel's policy toward the new territories that Israel had conquered and their present and future status, and promoted conflicting visions of Israeli society and its future in the Middle East.

Although proponents of the settlement and annexation of the occupied territories do not refer to these areas as "deserts" (outside the geographical areas of the Sinai Peninsula and the Judean desert), the settlement practices they have employed demonstrate continuity with the Jewish approach to settling the "symbolic desert" during the pre-1948 period. The post-1967 era gave rise to divergent visions. The first advocated a return to the pre-1967 borders in exchange for peace, following the model of the 1979 peace treaty with Egypt. It also embraced a more open vision of a shared environment that would allow Israel and its neighbors to benefit from a "cold peace," if not to actively collaborate on common interests. The other is the vision of a "Greater Israel" that identifies settlement with security and advocates a policy of expansion and besiegement. This view articulates, and ultimately reinforces, the inherently conflictual relations between Israel and its neighbors.

The epilogue examines Israel's growing entrenchment in a settlement discourse that uses a conflictual framework based on zero-sum relations and the perception of the Jewish settlement—and by extension Israel—as a civilized island surrounded by the symbolic desert. Israel's embrace of the besieged-island template has reinforced its need for territorial expansion, which in turn feeds into the continuing conflict. The centrality of this template has shaped Israel's territorial policies and practices and the trajectory of the continuing conflict. Yet *Desert in the Promised Land* also suggests that alongside the priority given to the discourse of settlement and security in recent Israeli politics, Israeli culture may also articulate the potential for alternative solutions and a more hopeful standpoint for negotiations and for Israel's future in the Middle East.

Part I

Symbolic Landscapes

1

Desert as Historical Metaphor

MORE THAN ADDRESSING THE PHYSICAL SPACE, Jewish memory has reimagined the desert as a symbolic landscape that represented the interweaving of time and space and was constructed in relation to the Promised Land. Yet in creating this chronotopological framework,[1] Jews drew on their biblical tradition and historical past to associate the desert with two different chapters of their past, thereby giving rise to divergent interpretations of its symbolic meaning. The desert plays a central role in the foundational narrative of the biblical exodus and is thus connected to Jews' mythical origins. But it is also associated with the impact of the long period of Jewish exile from the land. Both interpretations coexisted within the national Hebrew culture that emerged in late Ottoman and Mandatory Palestine and both were important and were often raised, though in different contexts. While the exodus provided a paradigm of national renewal in the homeland, the perception of the Palestinian landscape through the mnemonic lens of exile reinforced the significance of the Jewish settlement project.

The following discussion explores this dual vision of the desert and its role in relation to the Land of Israel. As the Jewish society of Palestine shaped its understanding of the desert, drawing on Jewish tradition and memory, it created a dual construct of the desert as a historical metaphor imbued with different historical, social, and theological meanings. The discussion of the redemptive meaning of the settlement is intimately linked to the symbolic role of the desert as a metaphor for exile and further illuminates the national significance attached to this interpretation.

Desert and Exodus

The biblical narrative of the exodus presents the desert as the territory that lies between Egypt and the Promised Land, between the land of exile and the future homeland, between the suffering of servitude and hopes for freedom. Within this framework, the desert is defined as the in-between space in relation to the future homeland, the destined *place*. If Egypt as the land of exile represented the *counter-place*, the desert was the liminal *nonplace* that allowed for the passages and transitions, the trials and revelations, that preceded the entry to the Promised Land.[2]

In the biblical narratives related to the exodus, the desert is where Moses encounters the burning bush and accepts the divine command to rescue his brethren from oppression in Egypt. It is the territory to which the ancient Israelites flee when they escape from Pharaoh, and where they wander for forty years on their way to Canaan. Most significantly, the desert is where the community of runaway slaves is transformed into a free people and receives the precepts of the Torah that provide them with a unifying identity, a distinct faith, and a set of laws. The story of the exodus, the Israelites' wandering in the desert, and the laws given to them there are at the center of four of the five books constituting the Pentateuch section of the Hebrew Bible; in Hebrew, one of these books is named *Ba-midbar*, i.e. "In the Desert" (though it is entitled *Numbers* in English). The Hebrew Bible and Jewish liturgical literature frequently allude to the experiences of the exodus. Biblical prophecies evoke the period of wandering in the desert as an exemplary act of faith that keeps Israel in divine favor: "I remember thee, the kindness of thy youth, the love of thine espousals, when thou wentest after me in the wilderness, in a land that was not sown" (Jeremiah 2:2, King James translation).

The historian Yosef Hayim Yerushalmi notes the prominence in the Hebrew Bible of the injunction to remember.[3] Three major biblical holidays—Passover, Shavuot (Pentecost), and Sukkoth (Tabernacles)—revolve around the remembrance of the exodus. During Passover, the elaborate ritual of the seder and the text of the Passover Haggadah provide a framework for the symbolic reenactment of the exodus. Moreover, the ritual introduces a *meta-memory* framework that highlights the direct responsibility of each Jew to perform this annual reenactment in order to comply with the injunction to remember that event: "And thou shalt tell thy son in that day, saying: It is because of that which the Lord did for me when I came forth out of Egypt" (Exodus 13:8). The Sukkoth holiday calls for the symbolic reenactment of the ancient Israelites' wandering in the desert through the recreation of temporary dwellings, while the Shavuot festival provides the annual occasion to commemorate the receiving of the Torah on Mount Sinai. Until the destruction of the Second Temple, the celebration of the three biblical holidays also called for a pilgrimage to the Temple in Jerusalem, further enhancing the centrality of the exodus within the annual calendar.

The story of the exodus presents a linear redemptive narrative composed of three phases, including the departure from exile, the wandering through the desert, and the entrance to the homeland. As the ethnographer Arnold van Gennep suggests in his study of rites of passage, the middle phase embedded within their tripartite structure offers a liminal time and space that are essential for the experience of transitions.[4] In this case, the desert provides the liminal space, deriving its significance from its structural position between Egypt and the Promised Land. The desert differs both from the land of exile, which represents displacement, oppression, and suffering, and from the future homeland, which represents permanence and security.[5] The Israelites wander in the desert, yet their wandering is part of the broader framework of their journey, which has a clear destination. The passage through the desert is thus filled with intensity and drama. It includes miraculous occurrences and harsh punishments, expressions of ambivalence and skepticism and profound revelations; it involves individual deaths and leads to a collective rebirth. The passage in the desert is therefore associated with highly positive collective memories, but also preserves the memory of regressive attitudes and subversive experiences.

The redemptive framework of the exodus narrative has been a source of hope for deliverance and redemption to both Jews and non-Jews, and it is not surprising that this foundational myth inspired the Zionist vision of the Jewish return from exile to the homeland.[6] A boat that smuggled Holocaust survivors from postwar Europe to Palestine in 1947 was named "Exodus 1947" because of this symbolic significance. When a British force seized the boat for violating the mandatory authorities' prohibition against Jewish immigration to Palestine and interned the passengers, this use of force against Holocaust survivors, combined with the symbolism of the exodus, led to a major public outcry. The event is marked in public memory as instrumental to bringing the plight of the Holocaust survivors to public awareness and mobilizing public support for the Jewish struggle for independence.[7]

Literary and cinematic depictions similarly use the exodus paradigm to portray Jews' escape from the plight of exile through a trying journey on the way to Palestine and later to the state of Israel. The experience of the Jews of Yemen, who literally had to cross a desert on their way to the Promised Land before the foundation of the state, lent itself to this historical analogy. In 1991, the writer and ethnographer of Yemenite Jewish culture Shalom Seri published a fictionalized book, based on interviews with the protagonist, entitled *By Way of the Wilderness: The Wondrous Journey to the Land of Dreams.*[8] The story describes the journey of a young Jewish man from a remote part of Yemen who sets out on the lengthy journey to Palestine at great personal risk. Facing danger as a Jew as he moves through Mecca and the Saudi desert, he hides his identity, successfully completing his personal exodus as he reaches Palestine. The young man participates in the 1948 war, and when the large immigration of Yemenite Jews later arrives in Israel by airlift, his family joins him there.

Similarly, an Israeli film made in 1956 by Nuri Habib, a first-time director who was a new immigrant from Iraq, depicts the journey of a group of Jews who made their way from Yemen to Palestine in 1926. The film presents the story as a modern version of the exodus that affirms the Zionist perspective on Jewish history. The film's Hebrew title, "Without a Homeland" (*Be'ein moledet*), emphasizes the state of homelessness that serves as the point of departure, while the English title, "The Hope," underscores the Zionist redemptive framework. The film opens with a broad statement—"our story happened many times in many places"—articulating the paradigmatic nature of its plot and the negative Zionist view of Jewish exile as defined by homelessness and persecution.[9] The film depicts two Jewish orphans who were taken to live among Muslims: a beautiful young woman, Naomi, who is a singer, and a young boy whose father was murdered when Muslims harassed Jews on the street and vandalized their synagogue. Although Naomi is initially ambivalent about the Jewish community, which, she feels, failed to protect her, her wish to save the young boy motivates her to join a group of Jews on a clandestine journey to Palestine, led by a Zionist emissary.

From this point on, the film focuses on the group's passage through the desert and out of Yemen as a modern reenactment of the biblical exodus. The long and dangerous route, the trek through harsh desert conditions, and the group's fear of their pursuers are physically and emotionally taxing. Not everyone survives the hardships. In addition, two of the men, whose resolve is undermined by the difficulties and who miss the material goods they left behind in Yemen (thus echoing their biblical ancestors who wished to return to Egypt), leave the group and die in the desert. The rest of the group is ultimately rescued by armed Zionist youth waiting for them at the border, in keeping with the predominantly secular Zionist view of the period that emphasized human agency over divine intervention.[10] The film ends with the Yemenite Jews on board a boat sailing away towards Palestine, as Naomi sings a song based on a biblical prophecy about the return to Zion. This concluding scene thus integrates the redemptive Zionist ending with the Yemenite Jews' religious sentiments and connects the Bible with this modern reenactment. Like Seri's book, *The Hope* also serves as a reminder to veteran Israelis who immigrated from Europe that some Yemenite Jews too had arrived during the early pioneering period of Israeli society, prior to the mass immigration of their community and other Middle Eastern Jewish immigrants in the late 1940s and the 1950s.[11]

The Hope is credited as being the first full-length feature film in color produced in Israel and made entirely by Israelis, and its first screening was marked by the attendance of dignitaries. Its overall reception was nonetheless lukewarm. Its failure to attract Israeli audiences may have been due, in part, to its simplistic plot and limited artistic appeal, but may also indicate the changing realities of Israeli society in the 1950s and the less receptive attitude towards Middle Eastern Jewish immigrants at the time. In this context, the story of a small Yemenite Jewish group's trek through the desert to reach Palestine would have appeared old-fashioned and evoked limited interest.[12] It is interesting to compare this film to another film that was made four years later and similarly drew on the exodus paradigm: Otto Preminger's Hollywood-produced film, *Exodus*, which was based on Leon Uris's popular novel of the same title. Preminger's film connects the Holocaust with the birth of Israel and the war experience, offering a patriotic melodrama filled with action, romance, heroic sacrifices, and a redemptive ending. With its internationally famous cast and emphasis on the plight of European Jews, it became an international success and enjoyed wide popular appeal in Israel in spite of reservations by the critics.[13]

The biblical exodus also inspired Ada Aharoni's 1983 book entitled *The Second Exodus: A Historical Novel.* The title suggests the symbolic link between the ancient and modern stories of the Jews in Egypt and their departure for the Promised Land, based on the fictionalized framework that the Egyptian-born Israeli writer presents. But Aharoni also introduces another interpretive framework in her foreword: "As a former Egyptian Jew who was a witness of the Second Exodus," she writes, "I have tried to recapture some of the essence, texture, and charm of this vanished world, in the hope that it will be kept alive, [and] not only in me."[14] The book thus serves as a literary monument to the long history and rich culture of the Egyptian Jews, which is unknown to most of her Israeli readers.

The Second Exodus attempts to interweave these two alternative interpretive paradigms, which are not necessarily compatible. The Zionist perspective conventionally casts the exilic past in a negative light, thereby enhancing the significance of leaving the diaspora for the Jewish homeland. The "salvage" approach, on the other hand, attempts to offer a thick description of a disappearing community's multifaceted life. Although the novel highlights the young Egyptian Jewish heroine's long-standing roots in Egypt and presents a brief historical review in the form of a lecture she gives to her peers, the exodus paradigm and its Zionist message play a more central role in shaping the plot. The novel dwells in great detail on the rising tensions within Egypt that force the Jews to leave their country and stresses the young protagonist's lack of a "definite identity" or a homeland, which contradicts her description of her family's deep historical roots in Egypt. Once she reaches Israel, this sense of lack vanishes: "This 'home' feeling was the primordial effect Israel had on her from the first moment she left the ship *Moledet* (Homeland) at the Haifa port."[15] The fact that her partner is a young Holocaust survivor and the young couple's choice of a new composite Hebrew last name, *Amehad* ("one people"), highlight the Zionist message that Israel is a place of refuge that unites Jews of different backgrounds. Yet unlike the film *The Hope*, which ends with the boat sailing toward an unknown future, *The Second Exodus* incorporates a brief description of the heroine's arrival and integration into Israeli society. Thus, along with the positive transformation she experiences, she also encounters the prejudices of the Ashkenazi Jews, who consider all Middle Eastern Jews as less educated, which she finds particularly misinformed in relation to Egyptian Jews. This reception may explain the author's motivation to create a literary text that would defy such stereotypes and educate her Israeli readers about her community's past.

During the pre-state and early state years the exodus paradigm also gave rise to the metaphorical reference to new immigrants as the "desert generation" (*dor ha-midbar*). The desert generation referred to the slaves who had come out of Egypt yet remained scarred by their servile mentality and were therefore unfit to reach the Promised Land. The extended wandering in the desert was designed to allow time for a collective transformation, as the older generation of slaves died in the desert and was replaced by a new generation of freeborn people prepared to enter the homeland. Thus, as mentioned above, *The Hope* features the two men who wish to go back to Yemen as a modern version of the desert generation. Like their biblical forebears, they complain about the difficulties of hiking in the desert and express their longing for the material goods they left behind. When they finally leave the group in order to return to Yemen, they are unable to find their way back and encounter their deaths in the desert.

The modern usage of the term "desert generation" also refers to those new immigrants who appear unable or unwilling to detach themselves from their exilic identity and culture. The stigmatizing label of "desert genera-tion" is, however, fluid and subjective, and is typically applied to others according to the user's expectations, ideological convictions, and historical perspective.[16] This became apparent during the 1950s and early 1960s, when veteran Israelis applied this label to Jewish immigrants, most often those who came from the Middle East and North Africa.[17]

Like other mythical texts, however, the biblical story of the exodus also contains the possibility of being read against the grain of its predominant interpretation. Such a reading can be seen in the evolving interpretation of a poem entitled "The Dead of the Desert" (*Metei midbar*)[18] by the Hebrew national poet Hayim Nahman Bialik. Once regarded as expressing a heroic call to rebellion against the oppression of exile, and to a national struggle for liberation, the words Bialik puts into the mouth of the rebelling "dead of the desert"—"the last generation of the oppressed, and the first one to be redeemed"—came to represent the Zionist redemptive paradigm. Yet as the literary scholar Esther Nathan shows, later critical readings of the poem point out Bialik's ambivalence about the Zionist call for reliance on human agency rather than divine help, as articulated by his negative portrayal of the "dead of the desert" as arrogant and of their revolt as short-lived. The poem thereby deviates from the Zionist redemptive paradigm, in which a revolt against oppression leads to liberation. Here the awakening of the dead represents a brief interlude in a cyclical narrative, which is followed by their return to their earlier state of deep slumber. Their bodies thus remain captive to the desert domain.[19]

Another counter-reading of the exodus rejects its interpretation as a linear, redemptive narrative culminating with the notion of "homeland" and instead interprets it within a mythical framework that is, as Mircea Eliade notes, essentially cyclical.[20] Indeed, the annual reenactment of the biblical exodus during the Passover holiday suggests this notion of cyclical mythical time, as implied by the Haggadah's injunction that every generation must experience the exodus from Egypt as if it were its own. According to the Egyptian-born Jewish philosopher Edmond Jabès, the desert experience is placed at the center of the Exodus narrative and its meaning. The wandering represents Jews' existential condition of being engaged in continual movement, striving to reach the homeland yet unable to strike root in any land. The desert is also the space where Jews receive the Torah, which makes an attachment to the textual tradition the foundation of the Jewish experience and establishes the book as the Jews' symbolic homeland. Jabès privileges the restless wandering in the desert in search of redemption as the core existential condition of the Jews and the source of their creativity and renewal.[21] As Gurevitch and Aran observe, the tension between process and fulfillment implies that "the Place is an object of yearning that is never fulfilled," a point that is central to their reading of the duality of the Land of Israel as an idea and a place.[22] In his novel *The Last Jew*, the Israeli writer Yoram Kaniuk echoes this perspective. Kaniuk's literary plot presents a mythical narrative of Jewish history that repeats and mirrors itself in different generations, thereby defying any sense of linear historical progression. He evokes the experience of wandering in the desert as creating a deep imprint on the Jewish psyche. "The desert is locked within the [Jews'] soul," he notes, "the wandering has become their homeland," suggesting that this experience may explain why yearning and suffering have been so deeply embedded within the fabric of Jewish culture.[23]

Another counter-reading of the biblical narrative has been offered by the literary theorist Edward Said, addressing Michael Walzer's study of the exodus as a universal liberation myth that non-Jewish communities draw on as an inspiration for their struggle for freedom and equality. Said rejects this interpretation, arguing that the modern Zionist reading of the biblical narrative has used it to support a colonialist agenda that oppresses the Palestinians and therefore subverts the message of freedom.[24] Their dialogue on the reading of Exodus has led to a further debate on the issue of Zionism and colonialism (see chapter 3).

Throughout this range of interpretations of the broader meaning of the exodus, however, the desert retains its structural meaning as the non-place located between Egypt and the Promised Land. Even though the biblical narrative has given rise to the meaning of the desert as the cradle of the Jewish people and their unique faith, Jewish and non-Jewish writers later shifted the emphasis from the desert to the Land of Israel in order to highlight the sacred status of the land as the site of monotheism and the place that shaped the distinct character of the Jewish people.[25] The Zionist focus on national and cultural renewal in the ancient homeland continued this trend. Along with its significance as a transitional phase within the redemptive paradigm of the exodus, the desert therefore assumed a competing meaning as a historical metaphor associated with the exilic past, which assumed greater weight in the Zionist settlement discourse.

Desert and Exile

Zionism constructed a decline narrative rooted in the Jewish mnemonic tradition that presented Jewish exile from the homeland as leading to a regressive period that left its negative mark on both the people and the land.[26] The symbolic void that exile represented within the framework of Zionist memory was thus inscribed onto the physical landscape of the Jewish homeland. The "desert" became a cultural trope conflating time and space to convey the ruined state of the Land of Israel as an outcome of the period of exile. Indeed, the negative view of the desert as a symbolic landscape associated with a divine punishment and the destruction of the land goes back to biblical prophecies. In the same vein, biblical descriptions of redemption refer to an inhabited and resettled land or to the rejoicing of the desert as it fills with water and blossoms.[27] The association of the desert with destruction and exile presents it as a desolate, dangerous, and impure territory and positions it in opposition to the fertile, inhabited, and cultivated land.[28] The negative portrayal of the desert is reinforced by the biblical description of the practice in which the high priest would take a young goat (or "scapegoat"), selected to represent the collective sins of the Israelites, and banish it to the desert. The Bible and later rabbinical tales thus laid the groundwork for the perception of the desert as the counterplace, the barren and chaotic wasteland that lay outside of the inhabited place and was associated with impurity, danger, and death.[29]

The European Jewish immigrants, as we shall see below, referred to the landscape as barren and inhospitable, interchangeably alluding to it as a "desert," "wasteland," or "desolate desert" (*midbar-shemama*).[30] The application of these terms to a wide range of terrains with varied physical attributes reveals that they were used as generalized references to address the state of decline of the land rather than provide realistic descriptions of particular landscapes. The "desert" therefore implied a symbolic landscape, a cultural construct in which memory and space were intertwined and projected onto the physical landscape. The early Zionist settlers' descriptions of the land illustrate the loose application of these terms to a wide diversity of landscapes. In his account of his tour of the land in 1888, the historian and writer Ze'ev Yavetz refers to the spreading sand dunes as a threat to the shore that might turn it into a "*desolate desert.*"[31] Yehudit Harari, writing about her 1904 travels as a young woman, describes a valley in the lower Galilee as "desolate and full of swamps, a *desert of white sand.*"[32] The writer Nechama Pohachevsky describes her 1908 trip in the Galilean mountains indicating that the road passes through "a *desolate desert.*"[33] A. D. Gordon, the Jewish thinker and Zionist pioneer, refers to the early settlers' perception of nature in the Land of Israel as a "desolate desert" that must be transformed into "a Garden of Eden."[34]

Zionist Jewish travelers express their anguish at seeing various parts of the land barren, noting that "*our country has been turned into a desert.*"[35] Educational brochures put out by the Jewish National Fund (JNF) continue to apply this metaphoric reference in later decades. Thus, a 1955 brochure refers to "a *desert of stones,*"[36] while a text from the early 1970s sums up the state of desolation that the Zionist pioneers encountered, indicating that "our country *was still a desert,* barren rocks on the mountaintop and stinking swamps in the valley; death-bearing mosquitoes and thorns filled the entire country."[37] Clearly, those who applied the term to such diverse landscapes were well aware that these areas did not present the physical traits that characterize actual geographical deserts, i.e. the Judean and the Negev deserts. These were generalized references to the perceived state of desolation that turned the land into a "symbolic desert" and presented a challenge to the Jewish settlement.

The newcomers explained the decline of the land from its earlier fertile state to the current state of decline as the outcome of centuries of neglect by those who had lived on the land following the Jews' exile from it.[38] An early Jewish settler in Palestine, Hayim Hissin, notes in his diary in 1882:

> The Land of Israel was once fertile, but that was back in olden times. Since then, the land has been neglected and as a result winds continued, incessantly, to carry clouds of sand from the desert and formed a layer that turned the Land of Israel, once one of the most fertile lands in the world, into a sorrowful country, with only barren hills and stretches of sand.[39]

In their 1918 history of the Land of Israel, David Ben-Gurion and Yitzhak Ben-Zvi, who would become Israel's first prime minister and second president, respectively, observe that "in every corner of the land one finds the grim signs of decline and destruction" as compared to the country's highly developed agriculture in antiquity.[40] Whatever trees remained in the country, they claim, appear to have survived from a more distant past, and they note that in Gaza "the assumption is that not a single olive tree has been planted since the Arab conquest."[41]

The perception of the country as a symbolic desert rooted in a decline narrative emerged out of Jewish mnemonic tradition and the impact of exile, but it also drew on the broader decline narrative that Europeans applied to the Middle East and North Africa. According to this narrative, these regions—once known for their advanced ancient civilizations—had turned into a desert-like land due to human neglect, deforestation, or excessive use. As Diana Davis notes, this framework established an "environmental imaginary" of a Middle Eastern landscape steeped in Orientalism and consisting of "desolate scenes of empty and parched deserts, punctuated, perhaps, with a lonely string of camels, a verdant but isolated oasis."[42] This view was reinforced by the European powers' growing involvement in the region and their emphasis on progress and modernity as part of their civilizing mission (see also chapter 3). It is not surprising, therefore, that as the geographer Yoram Bar-Gal observes, the theme of contrasting the fertility of the land during antiquity with its current state of desolation became more pronounced in Hebrew textbooks following World War I, when Palestine came under the British Mandate.[43]

A story published in a Hebrew textbook in 1934 describes a Jewish guard who wonders about the dramatic contrast between the archeological evidence of a flourishing settlement culture and the current desolation of the Negev landscape.[44] In 1953, Yitzhak Ben-Zvi reaffirmed the decline narrative: "When the land was conquered by desert tribes, camel drivers, and shepherds, the desert once more pushed back the cultivated land. The settlement shrank and the wasteland expanded."[45] The desolation of the country, therefore, was the result of the Jews' exile from the land, and David Ben-Gurion urged his countrymen to remove "the shame" of the sands that had covered the land during centuries of exile by continuing the settlement efforts during the 1950s.[46]

Zionist immigrants often resorted to anthropomorphic descriptions of the land, ascribing to it a historical consciousness and human emotions that highlighted its connection with the Jewish people. The land was described as waiting for its exiled sons to rescue it from suffering. Gordon notes that "our country, which had been a land of milk and honey, and at any rate carries the potential for high culture, has remained desolate, poorer than other civilized countries, and empty." And, he adds, "This is a sort of confirmation of our right to the land, a sort of a hint that the country has been awaiting us."[47] Harari, in writing about the state of the country before the Jewish settlement, describes the land as "waiting for Hebrew blood and sweat to redeem it again."[48] Ben-Zvi observes the neglected and desolate Jezreel valley and remarks that it "seems like it is awaiting its original owners, waiting and trusting that though they have lingered [in exile], they will surely arrive."[49] Ben-Zvi and Ben-Gurion conclude their 1918 history of the land with the following note: "The country waits for the people, its people, to return and to rebuild its ancient home, to cure its wound."[50] A children's play presents a pioneer who tells the kids that the land "weeps and cries out to you to come and redeem it from its desolation."[51] The decline and decay of the country were manifested in a range of expressions: the land was suffering from "horrible nakedness"[52]; it remained in a state of deep slumber[53]; it was deeply wounded, acutely sick, or deemed dead.[54] The settlers' mission was therefore focused on the need to "awaken" the land from its slumber[55] or cure it "from *the malignancy* that lay upon it during the period of the exile of its sons and from the *abomination of its desolation*."[56]

Such descriptions were not exclusive to Jews. The famous phrase "a land without a people for a people without a land"—often attributed to the British Jewish writer and publicist Israel Zangwill in 1901 and interpreted as articulating the Zionist perception of the land as "empty"—in fact goes back to British and American Christians.[57] It has been argued that the phrase "a land without *a* people" did not mean to imply that there were no people living in Palestine but rather to articulate the prevalent notion of the time that the Arabs living in Palestine did not have a distinctive national identity that would constitute them as "a people": at the time, they were seen as part of the greater Arab or Syrian society or as transient, and hence lacking an inherent identity connected to Palestine.[58] This notion was refuted by the historian Rashid Khalidi, who dates the early cultural and social manifestations of Palestinian identity to the late Ottoman period.[59] Yet both the phrase and arguments over its interpretation have become entangled in contemporary politics.

Accounts by clergymen and researchers of their travels to the Holy Land spurred an interest in Holy Land tours during the second half of the nineteenth century, bringing growing numbers of European and American Christian pilgrims to Palestine.[60] The American writer Mark Twain, who in 1869 accompanied a group of pilgrims and reported on their journey, often remarked that his fellow pilgrims saw the land through the lens of biblical narratives or of the exaggerated popular accounts about the land and its wild inhabitants which they had read prior to their journey.[61] Unsentimentally, he describes being "scorched to death" in a wasteland with no trace of shade. The hot, arid landscape reminds him of the biblical prophecies about the desolation of the land, and although he mentions villages and cultivated fields in the Jezreel valley and the orange groves in the surroundings of Jaffa, he observes that the country as a whole is hopelessly barren.[62] At the conclusion of their pilgrimage, Twain summarizes his view of the landscape:

> Of all the lands there are for dismal scenery, I think Palestine must be the prince. The hills are barren, they are dull of color, they are unpicturesque in shape. The valleys are unsightly deserts fringed with a feeble vegetation that has an expression about it of being sorrowful and despondent.[63]

Other travelers similarly noted the visible gaps between past descriptions of the Holy Land and the present reality they observed. The American biblical scholar Edward Robinson underscores this contrast in his description of Bi res-Seba, the biblical Beer Sheva: "Here then is the place where the Patriarchs Abraham, Isaac and Jacob often dwelt. . . . Over these swelling hills, the flocks of the Patriarchs once roved by the thousands; where now we found only a few camels, asses and goats."[64] The Scottish-born Presbyterian minister and writer John Cunningham Geikie noted the desolation of the land, especially in the arid southern part of the country, and concluded that even if one took into account the deterioration of the land over time, the biblical descriptions of the Promised Land must have been shaped by the oriental tendency to embellish.[65]

Yet these travelers' descriptions were also countered by other evidence. Jews clearly saw the Arab towns and rural settlements in Palestine and their cultivated land. Jews lived among Arabs in mixed towns (such as Jerusalem, Safed, Hebron, and Tiberias), their rural settlements existed near those of the Arabs, and Arabs and Jews living in proximity interacted with each other. Moreover, the views of some western travelers and European Jewish settlers cited above were not necessarily shared by the Sephardic and Middle Eastern Jews who were familiar with the physical landscape and better integrated into the local society and culture.[66]

Thus, for example, the account of Rabbi Rahamim Yosef Oplatka, who traveled from Jerusalem to the Galilee in 1876, includes information about the state of Jewish communities in Arab towns as well as his impressions of the abundance of olive groves and the cultivation of crops he saw in certain areas on his way.[67] Other Jewish travelers similarly marked the diversity of fruit trees, including olive, palm, citrus, pomegranate, almond, and fig trees, in various parts of the land.[68] Zalman David Levontin, the leader of the Zionist group "The Lovers of Zion" (*Hovevei Zion*), who founded the agricultural colony Rishon LeZion in 1882, pointed out the cultivated land in Palestine as evidence of the potential for new Zionist settlements.[69] Ben-Gurion and Ben-Zvi referred to areas covered by olive trees around Lod and Ramla and describe Gaza as "surrounded by large gardens, vineyards and orchards on all sides," even as they attributed these plantations to Alexander the Great's vision.[70]

The Zionist settlers' tendency to highlight the Jewish Yishuv and the Jewish settlement process while belittling or ignoring the Palestinian Arabs and their settlements—an attitude articulated in the imagery of the Palestinian landscape as a symbolic desert—became the subject of internal Jewish critique. The famous Jewish thinker and writer Ahad Ha'am addressed this issue, pointing out the gap between Jews' perception of the land and the reality on the ground, following his visit to Palestine in 1891:

> We are used to believing abroad that the Land of Israel is now in almost total desolation, a desert of a wasteland, and that anyone who wishes to buy land can come and buy as much as he desires. But the truth is that this is not so. In the entire country it is difficult to find land for cultivation that is not cultivated, only fields of sand and mountains that are not fit for planting without an extensive work and at a high cost.[71]

Ahad Ha'am went on to refer to the development of Palestine and evidence of its modernization, including methods of transportation, such as the introduction of a railroad. Other Jewish writers in the Jewish society of Palestine also questioned the predominant Jewish view of the Arab presence in the land. In 1907, Yitzhak Epstein, a Hebrew teacher, published an article entitled "A Hidden Question," in which he addressed this issue and insisted on Jews' obligation to respect Arabs' history and presence in the land.[72] A few years later, the farmer, writer, and Zionist leader Moshe Smilansky wrote:

> From the beginning of the Zionist idea, the Zionist propaganda described the country to which we arrived as a deserted and a desolate land

that longs for its redeemers. . . . And thus, during the first Zionist years we developed the conviction that the Land of Israel is a virgin land, and this conviction served as the foundation for the Zionist methods that have everything in them except for one component: attention to those people who settled in our country before us.[73]

In chapter 3, I shall return to the discussion of the perception of the reality in Palestine and how it was reconstructed within the Hebrew settlement discourse of the late Ottoman and mandatory periods. Not surprisingly, however, diaspora Jews who did not have to face the complexities of life in Palestine but were exposed to publications by the Zionist organizations that emphasized the desolation of the land were more easily inclined to relate to the Land of Israel as a symbolic desert. Yoram Bar-Gal's study of Zionist textbooks of "homeland geography" (*moledet*) demonstrates that the textbooks that were published in Europe in the 1920s and 1930s presented a more selective view of the landscape than those written and published in Palestine.[74]

History, space, and national ideology were thus interwoven in the construction of the desert as an "environmental imaginary" that was rooted in Jewish mnemonic tradition and the popular perceptions of the Orient that flourished during the nineteenth and early twentieth centuries (see chapter 2). The reference to the country as a desert reflected a focus on the importance of the Zionist return to the land and its settlement mission. As a symbolic landscape, the desert provided the historical and ideological context for enhancing the significance of the Zionist settlement as a step toward a redemptive vision of the land and the Jews. Translated into this environmental imaginary, the Jewish settlement represented a way to overcome the regressive state of the country and turn the symbolic desert into its former state as a Jewish place.

Settlement and Redemption

The perception of exile as a symbolic lack and the deserted homeland as a symbolic desert was closely linked to the Zionist vision of return to the homeland and its redemptive meanings. The interweaving of national ideology and religious concepts in the Zionist discourse of the early-state and state periods is articulated through the use of the traditional Hebrew concept of *aliyah* (ascent, and by extension, pilgrimage) to characterize Jewish immigration to Palestine before 1948 and Israel since then.[75]

The settlement process was the means to achieve both the "redemption of the people" (*ge'ulat ha-am*) and "the redemption of the land" (*ge'ulat
ha-aretz*). Zionism was influenced by the Jewish Enlightenment and its
critique of the traditional Jewish society of exile, by European romantic
nationalism and its attachment to land and nature, and by the prevailing
socialist ideologies of the importance of labor and productivity. As a result,
farming emerged as an important process for introducing critical changes in
Jewish society. These ideas led to experiments in establishing Jewish farming
communities at the end of the nineteenth century and the first half of the
twentieth century not only in Palestine but also in Eastern Europe as well
as the United States, Canada, Argentina, and Brazil.[76]

Highlighting the primordial link between Jews and their homeland,
the Zionist movement advanced the centrality of settling and working the
land as the means to transform exilic Jews into productive farmers and to
free the country from the hold of the desert. Jewish leaders in Europe called
upon Jews to buy lots in their ancestral land and to establish new settlements
as a way to redeem the Land of Israel.[77] Jewish groups from Romania, Russia,
and Yemen arrived in Palestine during the 1880s and 1890s to fulfill this
vision. Retrospectively identified as the First Aliyah within Zionist historiography, this immigration gave rise to a new form of Jewish agricultural
settlement, the *moshava*[78] (plural *moshavot*), based on individual ownership.
Within the traditional Jewish community of Palestine, a new initiative to
settle outside of the urban spaces and work the land was driven by economic
needs as well as the importance attributed to the religious commandments
related to the Land of Israel.[79] In 1876, a new association Farming and the
Redemption of Land (*Avodat Ha-Adama Ve-Ge'ulat Ha-Aretz*) was formed in
Jerusalem, and the establishment of a small agricultural settlement, Petach
Tikvah, soon followed.[80]

When the Zionist Organization established the Jewish National Fund
in 1901, it served as the primary Zionist agency for promoting land pur-
chases and Jewish settlements in Palestine. The significance of working the
land informed its publicity and educational materials, and its donor certifi-
cates featured images of farmers working and biblical verses that underscored
the links among land, settlement, and redemption.[81] A drawing by the artist
Ephraim Moses Lilien for the Fifth Zionist World Congress in Basel featured
an old Jew, or perhaps the wandering Jew, as a gloomy and dispirited figure
constrained by barbed-wire fencing (figure 1). A sympathetic young angel
gently touching his shoulder shows him a vision of awakening in the east,
featuring a robust Jewish farmer (perhaps his own future image) plowing

FIGURE 1. Ephraim Moses Lilien, "From Ghetto to Zion" [*Von Ghetto nach Zion*], 1902.

a field while facing the rising sun. The Hebrew verse from a Jewish prayer that alludes to the prophecy of a Jewish return to Zion is inscribed below the drawing and reinforces its redemptive Zionist message.[82]

Those members of the so-called Second Aliyah (1904–14) and Third Aliyah (1919–23) who subscribed to Socialist Zionism and to the ideological emphasis on working the land played a key role in developing the Zionist pioneering ethos. The *halutz* (pl. *halutzim*), the iconic "Zionist pioneer," emerged during the first decades of the twentieth century. The Socialist Zionist *halutzim* emphasized the value of labor and direct engagement in working the land as part of their redemptive Zionist vision and agenda. They were critical of the bourgeois lifestyle of the settlers of the First Aliyah, who were landowners but relied on hired Arab help. The Socialist Zionist pioneers developed new forms of settlement such as the egalitarian farming commune, the *kvutsa* or *kibbutz*, and the small farming village, the *moshav*, which unlike the First Aliyah *moshava* was based on cooperative organization.[83] Although the *halutzim* made up only a small segment of the Jewish immigrant population in Palestine at the time,[84] they are credited with shaping the social, cultural, and political foundations of the new Jewish society.[85]

The importance of labor and the ideal of working the land resonated powerfully in the pioneering ethos that developed in Hebrew culture during those formative years. Although the Socialist Zionists were motivated by secular ideology, their attachment to the land was rooted in Jewish tradition, and they frequently used religious terms to underscore the value of settlement and work for the land and the Jewish people. The influential thinker A. D. Gordon highlighted the spiritual and redemptive qualities of the physical engagement in working the land, an ideology that prompted the concept of "the religion of labor." For Gordon, direct contact with the Land of Israel and its nature was the way to achieve personal and collective renewal.[86] Yet his attachment to and appreciation of nature also led him to doubt the impact of settlement on the natural landscape, especially if it was achieved through the employment of others. Calling that kind of settlement process "a vulgar creation" that claimed to have "turned the desolate desert into a Garden of Eden," Gordon criticized such an approach as "desecrating the desolate land" and saw it as a missed opportunity to morally engage with the meaning of the destruction (*hurban*) of the land.[87]

The sanctification of labor and the analogy of the pioneers' work with divine creation are themes that appear in the literature of the pre-state and early state periods, when the ideology of labor and the pioneering ethos were predominant. An analysis of two poems, written in the mid-1920s by two young poets, Avraham Shlonsky and Rachel Bluwstein, suggests the different ways in which the pioneers expressed these ideas.[88]

In Avraham Shlonsky's poem "Toil" (*Amal*, published in 1927),[89] the male speaker asks his mother to dress him "in a glorious robe of many colors" and take him to perform his labor duties at dawn. Like the biblical Joseph's robe, his dress indicates his privileged status as the favorite son.[90] At dawn, when traditional men typically perform their morning prayers and children are taken to religious school, he leaves home to perform his settlement work. The poet draws on analogies to sacred objects (the prayer shawl, the frontlets, and the phylactery straps) to describe the fruits of the pioneer's labor:

> My land is wrapped in the light as in a prayer shawl.
> The houses stand forth like frontlets,
> And the roads paved by hand, stream down like phylactery straps.
> Here the lovely city says the morning prayer to its Creator.
> And among the Creators is your son Abraham,
> A road-building bard of Israel.

Shlonsky not only assigns sanctity to the work of building a new settlement; he goes further by addressing the pioneers as "Creators." The poem conveys confidence in the power of their labor to bring about a new dawn, as the last stanza alludes to Ezekiel's prophecy of resurrection (37: 1–14):

> And in the evening twilight, father will return from his travails
> And like a prayer, will whisper joyfully:
> My dear son Abraham, skin, sinews and bones
> Hallelujah.

Labor is thus suffused with religious meanings, and the biblical prophecy further highlights the settlement work as leading to redemption.

The poet Rachel Bluwstein (more widely known by her first name Rachel) is one of the few female poets of the early settlement period[91] whose work became widely recognized. Rachel presents the perspective of the *halutzah*, the female pioneer, in her poem "To My Country" (1926), which provides an interesting counterpart to Shlonsky's poem. The pioneers in both poems engage in transforming the landscape and describe their activities in doing so, yet whereas Shlonsky's approach is triumphant and even aggrandizing, Rachel uses a minor key to describe the female pioneer's activities. The female *halutzah* emphasizes the modesty of her contribution and underscores its mundane character as contrasted with men's grander and more public patriotic acts: "I have not sung to you, my country / not brought glory to your name / with great deeds of a hero / or the spoils a battle yields." Instead of paving a road and building a city with the heavy tools and machines that Shlonsky's male *halutz* describes, she alludes to her bodily imprint on the landscape: the tree that she planted by her own hands, the path that her feet formed in the fields.

Whereas the male *halutz* places himself at the center of the work and asks his mother to take care of him as a chosen child, the female speaker expresses her concern for the land in the same way that a daughter would worry about her ailing mother, and belittles her own contribution: "Modest are the gifts I bring you, I know this, Mother. / Modest, I know, the offerings / of your daughter." She describes the tear she sheds as she silently shares her mother-country's pain facing its current poor state, and the outburst of joy on the day the light appears.[92] The *halutzah*, a doting daughter who identifies with her mother, addresses the land in an intimate voice, as if they were engaged in a private conversation. The contrast in tone between the two poems, which were written around the same period, is quite striking.

Yet the *halutzah*'s strategy of belittling her gift to the land also masks her recognition of the true value of her activities. In Hebrew culture, walking the land was a ritual reenactment of ownership, and planting trees was seen as a symbolic act of renewal.[93] And in referring to her labor as a "sacrificial offering" (*minha*) to the homeland, Rachel's pioneer shifts from the secular to the sacred sphere and discloses the true nature of her contribution.[94] Thus, in spite of the major differences in style and tone, the two pioneers, female and male, share a goal and an understanding of the importance of the settlement process for transforming the country's landscape from a desolate desert to a cultivated land, and through this process promote the redemptive vision of national renewal.

In some texts, the land itself assumes human agency, as it partners with the pioneers to help bring about its own redemption. In 1958, a children's story published in a fourth-grade textbook described four anguished springs that vowed to turn their water into malaria-spreading swamps following the Jews' exile from the land; yet upon learning of the Jews' return, they lifted their self-imposed curse in order to help the Zionist pioneers make the valley flourish again.[95] Another children's story of the same period describes how the Zionist hero Yosef Trumpeldor plows the field holding the plow in his single arm. When two lumps of soil witness his dedication, they voluntarily jump into the plow in an act of self-sacrifice to help him perform this task.[96]

Zionist pioneers describe the deeply moving and spiritual experiences of working the land as a symbolic partnership in the act of creation.[97] This idea also appears in Rabbi Z. Gold's brief entry in the catalog of Israel's international exhibit on *The Conquest of the Desert*:

> I ask myself in Talmudic vein, "On the Conquest of the Desert," what blessing should one pronounce? And I answer: on the "Conquest of the Desert" one proclaims the blessing, "Blessed be the Maker of the Creation." Because those who engage in this important activity become partners of the Holy One Blessed be He in acts of Creation.[98]

The Hebrew poet Nathan Alterman goes a step further in comparing the urgency of the pioneers' efforts to that of God: "It took the Creator a week to do it, and for us, perhaps, it presents an even more urgent task."[99]

The idea of comparing the pioneers' accomplishments with the divine creation, which is an expression of their predominantly secularist stance, can easily be read as sacrilegious. But it also reveals how the secular Socialist Zionists, who rebelled against the exilic world of tradition that they had left behind, also drew on it for the cultural reservoir and vocabulary that supported the redemptive vision of the settlement.[100] The borrowing of terms and symbols from the religious domain conveys the pioneers' connection to the world of Jewish tradition as well as their desire to enhance the sanctified character of their work.

The epiphany that the Zionist pioneers experienced in farming the land emerged as a cultural trope. After being sick with malaria on the first day of his stay in a new colony, a newcomer is finally able to join those working in the field. "I too filled my hand with seeds and forgot my weakness. . . . My eyes shed tears of joy, tears of happiness, on the ground. My heart was filled with awe and excitement."[101] The first act of plowing the land became a transformative experience. Yehuda Raab, one of the founders of Petach Tikvah, describes the first time he and a few older men plowed their land in 1878. The first person to handle the plow, Raab made the historic first furrow; the others (including his father), took turns following him. Moved to tears by this experience, one of the men recited a blessing: "Blessed are we to be the first ones as we walk behind the first furrows that a Jewish plow makes in the land of the prophets." Raab's reference to these rounds as *hakafot* (the Hebrew term for the rounds made in the synagogue while holding the Torah scroll) redefines the plow as a sacred object, and the blessing underscores the ritual character of introducing the first furrow.[102] The symbolism of the first furrow was internalized by school children, as a student's story in a school newspaper demonstrates.[103]

The impact of the first experience of cultivating the land may be so overpowering that the newcomers feel that in performing this sacred act they shed their exilic identity and experience the budding of a new self. A young female pioneer writes:

> The day I took up a hoe to work [I felt] as if I had been born again, and since that day I count the years of my real life. Whatever had happened before I cast behind me, as if it had never occurred, and I actually live and exist from that day forward."[104]

In 1914, in a letter to his parents, who had remained in Europe, my own grandfather, Yaacov Patt, described his first experience plowing the land and his exhilaration at reconnecting with "the land that our ancestors plowed and cultivated":

> Today I made a covenant with our land, the first time that I plowed the Land of Israel. There is no happiness equal to mine. And you, my parents, get ready to come to the country and be as happy as I am.[105]

His use of the biblical term "covenant" suggests that beyond his individual rite of passage, he experienced the plowing of the first furrow as a reenactment of the ancient bond between Jews and their land, one that tied him, the modern Zionist pioneer, with his biblical ancestors. Rachel Yanait, a leading Socialist Zionist pioneer and later the wife of Yitzhak Ben-Zvi, describes having seen Jewish pioneers plowing the land with two oxen in the Galilee in 1909 and sensing it as affirming a symbolic continuity with the ancient past, "as if the Hebrew farmer had never ceased [to work] in the fields of the Galilee, as if he had never let down his plow."[106]

The desert played a major role as a mythical space associated with the biblical patriarchs and the origins of the Jewish people, and as such it held positive connotations as a symbolic link to the ancient past. The following chapter will continue to explore the cultural strategies of reenacting that sense of continuity through the discussion of the desert mystique. But the centrality of the settlement as a vehicle for achieving the Zionist vision of the "redemption of the land" was intimately linked to the Zionist decline narrative, which constructed the country's landscape as a symbolic desert that represented the pathological impact of exile. Within the context of the settlement discourse, the desert therefore serves as the counter-place, the desolate, uncultivated, and neglected land that poses challenges to the settlement yet must be conquered and transformed into a cultivated Jewish place, as discussed in chapter 3. The Hebrew culture that evolved in Yishuv society thus developed this dual perception of the desert that focused on different aspects of its meaning in Jewish collective memory and its contribution to promoting the Zionist national agenda.

2

The Desert Mystique

JEWISH LONGING FOR THE ANCIENT HOMELAND and the reimagining of the Holy Land in Western culture contributed to its idealization and its association with the desert landscape. European writers and artists depicted the Holy Land as a mythical oriental landscape infused with Orientalist tropes, including palm trees and flocks of sheep, camels and tents, and people dressed in ancient-looking garments.[1] Jewish writers drew on a long Jewish tradition to present idyllic descriptions of the land, detached from its present state, a trend that continued into the beginning of the early twentieth century.[2] Thus, during the early decades of Zionist immigration to Palestine, the romantic approach to the East as the place of origins highlighted the desert mystique as a source of inspiration for the creation of modern Hebrew culture.[3]

"My Heart Is in the East"

Zionism drew on Jews' strong attachment to "Zion," the idealized homeland that had been the object of longing and hopes for redemption over centuries of Jewish life in exile. Its unique sacred place in Jewish memory was articulated in prayer and ritual and embodied in the physical orientation toward Jerusalem during prayer—and for the majority of Jews living in Europe, this direction implied facing east. A special decorative sign called *mizrah* ("east") therefore marked the eastern wall of synagogues and Jewish homes to note its elevated status.[4] Jewish liturgical texts and poetry articulated the pain and sorrow of living in exile and the longing for Zion. The famous

verse by the renowned twelfth-century Spanish Jewish poet Yehuda Halevi—
"My heart is in the East and I am at the edge of the West"[5]—expressed the
duality of Jewish exilic experience and the sense of displacement. Toward
the end of the nineteenth century, the young Russian Hebrew poet Hayim
Nahman Bialik similarly expressed his profound yearning for the warm,
beautiful country away in the East, where "spring lasts forever."[6]

The desert embodied the most direct connection to antiquity and
nativity and was a source of inspiration for the revival of native Hebrew
identity and culture. The desert was where the shepherd patriarchs wandered
with their herds, where the Israelites received the Torah, and where their
collective identity as a people was formed. And the Bedouins, who likewise
roamed the desert landscape with their herds, appeared to embody the
biblical Hebrews. This strategy of archaizing[7] the land and its inhabitants
presented them as relics from a distant past and obscured the diversity and
details of present-day life in the Middle East. Although this perception had
its roots in Jewish memory and the veneration of the Bible and antiquity, it
was reinforced by the Western Orientalist approach to the east, which, as
Edward Said points out, was pervasive in Europe at the time. This Western
view of the Orient presented it as a backward region that had remained
outside of historical time and resistant to modernity and the ethos of progress. Introducing a mythical perception of the Orient and its inhabitants,
Orientalism constructed an idealized image of the "native" as the "noble
savage" but also presented negative stereotypes that portrayed the locals as
lazy, impulsive, and immoral.[8] And while the construction of the desert
mystique in Hebrew culture articulated a similar exoticizing approach to
the landscape and the Arabs, the negative stereotyping was clearly evident
there as well. The Jews' layered origins nonetheless present a more complex
case that challenges Said's construction of a clear-cut East/West dichotomy
based on monolithic identities, as will be further discussed below.

The desert mystique was also linked to another important European
trend, articulating deep-seated concerns about the future of the West. A
growing anxiety about the dehumanizing impact of technology and the
destructive power of modern warfare regarded them as indicative of the
degeneration of the West. This anxiety was paired with a fascination with
the East and its traditional societies, which were seen as living in greater
harmony with nature. The East thus appealed to Westerners as a place of
refuge from the excessively technologized modern West, a view that contributed to the appeal of the desert. As the historian Priya Satia writes about

the British perceptions of Iraq prior to and during World War I, "it was not merely orientalism that shaped prewar British imaginings of a desert utopia but the particular cultural anxieties of the early twentieth century," including the concerns over the degeneration of the West and the destructive power of modernity.[9] These ideas were prevalent among the British and the French and famously embodied in the iconic figure of T. E. Lawrence. Similar concerns about the degeneration of the West contributed to Zionist Jews' disillusionment, reinforced the Jewish decline narrative and the portrayal of the European Jew as feeble and aging (see figure 1), and made the East appear a more promising environment for restoring the Jewish people to an earlier and healthier state.[10] The national trope of the sunrise, or "dawn," as representing national awakening was not unique to the Jewish national movement, but it was particularly resonant for Hebrew speakers given the shared linguistic root of "east" (*mizrah*) and "sunrise" (*zeriha*).[11]

As the discussion below illustrates, these approaches and ideas resonate in the ways in which European Zionist settlers used the symbolic desert to reimagine and reconstruct their native identity and culture, interchangeably emphasizing their historical and cultural roots in the East and articulating their European notions of cultural and moral superiority toward the region and its inhabitants. The following discussion therefore focuses on the Jews who arrived from Europe and experienced the East as an unfamiliar territory; it does not pertain to Sephardic and Middle Eastern Jews who had previously lived in the Ottoman Empire or adjacent countries.

In Search of the Native

The idea of a return to the homeland, entailing the recreation of a new kind of Jewish society that is closer to its ancient spirit and cultural heritage, drew on a romantic belief in the organic bond between a people and a land that provides the foundation for their national identity and the link between the group's ancestors and their contemporary descendants.[12] The creation of a new "Hebrew" man and the revival of a national Hebrew culture turned the process of "becoming Hebrew" (to borrow Arieh Saposnik's suggestive title) into a deliberate act of identity-fashioning undertaken by the immigrant Jewish society and the youth growing up in Palestine. The construction of a new type of Jew was most clearly defined by the powerful negative model of the exilic Jew as effeminate, weak, and excessively spiritual, and an emphasis on the strong, resourceful, and youthful image of the new

Hebrew.[13] Yet Jews' search for a positive model posed a particular difficulty. European national movements often identified the peasants as the carriers of their earlier heritage, which had declined among other segments of their societies. Unlike the Germans, the Finns, or the Russians, however, the Zionist movement lacked any peasant class that could serve as such a link to a remote Jewish past. Instead, it was the Hebrew Bible that played the critical role in producing the foundational ancient-modern axis of Zionist memory. Biblical ancestors and post-biblical heroes therefore emerged as the model for the shaping of the new Hebrew identity. Hebrew educational, literary, artistic, and performative texts often used the complementary mnemonic strategies of archaizing the Zionist Jews and contemporizing the ancient Hebrews in order to reinforce that ancient-modern axis.[14]

And yet, although these biblical and post-biblical figures originated in Jewish memory, they lacked the concrete immediacy of a living model. Zionist immigrants therefore searched for alternative models to further support the reshaping of Jewish native identity. The European (Ashkenazi) Jews who had been living in Palestine prior to the Zionist immigration largely followed the enclave lifestyle of their European communities and shunned Zionism as a form of heresy; to the newcomers, they represented an extension of exilic Jewish culture. The Sephardic Jews in Palestine, including those whose ancestry went back to Iberia as well as those of Middle Eastern and North African origins, appeared to the newly arriving European Jews as closer to the ancient Hebrews. During the Ottoman period, the Sephardic Jewish population of Palestine was an integral part of the multiethnic and multi-religious fabric of Ottoman society. Middle Eastern and North African Jews were familiar with Arab culture and local ways of life, and the educated Sephardic elite represented its own hybrid culture that blended traditionalism with Western education. Whereas some of the Palestinian Sephardic elite were open to the Zionist immigrants and acted as cultural interpreters to help them navigate the unfamiliar Middle Eastern environment, others opposed the newcomers' nationalist and secularist ideology on political and religious grounds. Those Sephardi critics regarded the Zionist immigrants as destabilizing Sephardic Jews' position within Ottoman Palestinian society and, like the anti-Zionist Ashkenazi critics, they believed that secular nationalism was a subversive ideology that contradicted the precepts of the Jewish faith.[15] As the immigration of European Jews shifted the demographic balance of the emergent Yishuv society during the pre-state period, the Sephardic Jews were turned into an increasingly marginalized minority.

Among Middle Eastern Jews, the Yemenites, who had lived for centuries in remote and relatively isolated communities and who immigrated
to Palestine in small numbers, stood out by their distinct look and dress,
Arabic dialect, and adherence to old customs.[16] The European Zionist immigrants regarded these Yemenite Jews as the best living model among the
Jews for reimagining their biblical forefathers and as a source of inspiration
for the construction of Hebrew culture. Thus, when Boris Schatz founded
the new Bezalel School of Arts and Crafts in Jerusalem in 1906, he recruited
Yemenite artisans to his school to help with the effort to create "a specifically
Jewish Palestinian style, which reflects the beauty of the Biblical age and
the fantasy of the Orient."[17] Other prominent European artists involved
with the Bezalel school, including Ze'ev Raban and Abel Pann, used Yemenite and other Middle Eastern Jews as models to depict biblical figures
and highlight symbolic continuities between the ancient and the modern
Hebrew cultures.[18] Similarly, Shlomo Dov Goitein, who was a scholar of
Islamic and Jewish history, drew on his ethnological research among his
contemporary Yemenite Jews for his study of the Bible.[19]

The Russian-born dancer and choreographer Rina Nikova, who
founded the Yemenite Biblical Ballet in 1933, explained her motivation
for sponsoring and training female Yemenite dancers to realize her vision:

> My education was rooted in the European ballet tradition but my heart
> belonged to the Bible and the East. I posed the question: How does one
> create something that belongs here, to this place? How does one shape
> an indigenous Semitic dance?[20]

Nikova's troupe, which used a variety of names, including the "Biblical and
Oriental Ballet from Palestine," went on to perform for Jewish audiences
in Palestine and abroad. Later, her lead dancer, Rachel Nadav, formed her
own Yemenite dance troupe, which likewise drew on the Yemenite Jewish
tradition and highlighted biblical and pastoral themes.[21] Another dancer,
Yardena Cohen, whose roots in the land extended over six generations, drew
on Palestinian dances and biblical narratives to create new dances that were
accompanied by Middle Eastern Jewish musicians.[22] More widely known is
Sara Levi-Tanai, the Yemenite Jewish dancer and choreographer whose early
dance compositions were featured at the first Dalia Dance Festival in 1944
and whose Yemenite dance troupe evolved into the Inbal Dance Theater.[23]
Though she was born in Jerusalem, Sara Levi-Tanai described her personal
ties to the desert landscape as being part of her Yemenite heritage and a

major source of inspiration for her work, echoing the romantic constructions of a symbolic desert landscape typical of pre-state Hebrew culture:

> I feel our landscape strongly from all directions. For me, the desert is a
> basic fact and it is part of my consciousness. I see the desert when the
> Yemenite men dance in their special way, shaking up and down as if they
> were riding on camelbacks. . . . The origin of the people as a community
> was molded in the desert. I have never seen myself as cosmopolitan,
> European, or Western.[24]

The Zionist immigrants saw the Arabs living in Palestine, and especially the Bedouins, as the most striking living model of those who appeared
to adhere to centuries-old customs once shared by the ancient Hebrews.
The Bedouins regarded themselves as the authentic sons of the desert and
as direct descendants of the original Arabs, and had long been the inspiration for European images of the Bible and the Holy Land.[25] Early Zionist
iconography thus featured biblical figures as Bedouins and contemporary
Bedouins as "relics" of the past, and the Bedouins' traditions were observed
as a way to learn about the biblical period.[26] When the theater director
Moshe Levi was preparing for the performance of a biblical play on Jacob
and Rachel, he took his Jewish actors to visit the Bedouins to learn about
their culture.[27] This view of the Bedouins produced a tendency among
Jewish artists such as Raban and Pann to create prototypical portraits of
local people that lacked specificity and ignored the cultural and historical
variations of their models.[28] Later modernist Jewish artists, such as Reuben
Rubin and Nahum Gutman, reacted against this trend by shifting toward
primitivism and portraying local scenes with earthy and sensual figures of
Arabs and Middle Eastern Jews. Although their style differed significantly
from the ornamental Bezalel style, it too was marked by the Orientalist
view of the "native" as simple, sensual, and close to nature, reinforcing the
stereotypical portrayal of these figures.[29]

The European immigrants displayed an ambivalent attitude toward the
Arab peasants or *fellahin*. The early Zionist immigrants to Palestine drew on
the Arabs' farming experience, and the First Aliyah settlements relied heavily
on hired Arab work to maintain their farms. Yet the European newcomers
also considered the Arabs' cultivation methods antiquated and the Arabs
to be ignorant of modern technology and cultivation methods. In spite of
this attitude, the Arabs' influence on Jewish farming is linguistically evident.
Hebrew incorporated the Arabic term for farmer, *fallâh* or *fellah* (plural *fel-*

lahin), creating the Hebraized *fallah* (plural *fallahim*), as well as the word *falha* to designate the cultivation of field crops. These terms were widely used during the pre-state period, and *falha* is still in use today.[30] Thus, for example, the 1908 mission statement of the association of Jewish agricultural workers describes its goal as creating "a new brand of worker-farmers who are healthy in body and spirit," using both the Hebraized *fallahim* and the biblical term *ikarim* to denote "farmers" throughout the document.[31]

The use of the Arabs as a model for the native Hebrews was supported by the premise of their common descent from Abraham the Patriarch, whose sons, Ishmael and Isaac, are considered the respective ancestors of Arabs and Jews. This framework of a joint origin offered the genealogical model of a family, defining the Jewish-Arab affinity as that of cousins.[32] A more radical Jewish theory of common descent maintained that the Galilee's Arab *fellahin* were the descendants of Jewish farmers who had remained on the land and, following the Muslim conquest, converted to Islam. Their remote Jewish origins had been preserved, so the theory went, in certain linguistic expressions and customs that revealed their earlier Jewish roots. This theory gained popularity during the first two decades of the twentieth century and was embraced by well-known Zionist figures, including the Hebrew educator and writer Israel Belkind, as well as David Ben-Gurion and Yitzhak Ben-Zvi.[33] The idea of shared distant origins also implied the possibility of a future reintegration. The well-known Jewish writer and essayist Ahad Ha'am alluded to this possibility in 1912: "After we become a cultural force in Palestine in the spirit of Judaism, the Arabs may be assimilated in our midst; they are age-old residents of this country and some of them may be fellow Jews, i.e. descendants of Jews forcibly converted to Islam."[34]

Another theory of common descent advanced the notion that some Bedouin tribes were the descendants of the ten lost tribes of Israel. That theory led the writer Hemda Ben-Yehuda to compose a short story entitled "The Farm of the Sons of Reikhav" in 1903, describing a young Jew's search among the desert people for the lost Jewish tribes. When the young man reaches his destination, he points out the Bedouins' familial ties with Jews and admires the strength of their attachment to the land: "Here we are among our ancient brethren for whose descendants I have been searching for some time! Can there be any doubt about this? These *savage brothers* of ours have preserved our land for two thousand years. . . . Their feet did not touch foreign lands and they have kept our language alive. . . . *Loyal sons*!"[35] Similarly, the Socialist Zionist activist Rachel Yanait Ben-Zvi describes the excitement that she and her comrades felt upon learning that some Bedouin families from the Haibar region believed themselves to be descendants of Jews.[36]

The emphasis on a common descent shared with the "lost brethren" contributed to the desert mystique and supported efforts to recover Hebrew native identity and culture by observing the Arabs' culture. But the belief that Arab peasants or Bedouins were descendants of Jews also had obvious political ramifications, since it implied a continuous Jewish presence in the land that minimized the rupture of Jewish exile and reinforced Jews' historical right to the land.[37] This theory may have also raised hopes for possible return of those Arabs to the fold of the Jewish people. The assumption it involved that the Jews had preferred conversion to leaving the land was quite plausible to the Socialist Zionists, who saw the bond with the land as a more important historical force than religious observance.[38]

The "Hebrew-Bedouin"

In 1903, the Kishinev pogrom sent shock waves through Russian Jewry and Jewish communities elsewhere. The publication of Bialik's detailed report from Kishinev following the pogrom and his powerful poems heightened public awareness of this violent event. Russian Zionists organized a group of Jewish orphans, and the Zionist educator and First Aliyah leader Israel Belkind brought a group of them to Palestine to launch a Jewish agricultural boarding school, with the goal of educating them to become Hebrew farmers. In the following year, a group photo featured these boys in Palestine, each of them wearing a white *kaffiyeh* held in place by a black cord (*igal*) and holding a shepherd's stick in his hand.[39] The boys' appearance does not reflect the children's ordinary clothing but is designed to impress the viewer with their transformation from exilic orphans, embodying Jewish victimhood, to free-spirited natives in their own homeland.

The display of an identity change from exilic Jew to modern Hebrew became an early Zionist trope. In 1907, Itamar Ben-Avi, the eldest son of Eliezer Ben-Yehuda, who was nicknamed the "first Hebrew child," noted this change among the youth of the First Aliyah, and in 1911 the Second Aliyah writer Meir Wilkansky observed it among his fellow immigrants.[40] The photo of the Kishinev orphans in Palestine was obviously posed according to the conventions of the period, and their appearance in hybrid dress was a deliberate performative act articulating the Zionist Jewish immigrants'

FIGURE 2. Boris Schatz in Jerusalem, circa 1910. The Collection of The Israel Museum, Jerusalem.

preoccupation with their native identity. During these early formative years, certain items of clothing emerged as symbolic markers of the "transformed Jew." Among these popular items were the Arab overcoat, the *abbaya*, and the Arab headdress, the *kaffiyeh* (also *kúfiya* in Arabic; pronounced *kafiya* in Hebrew), most typically in its white variety known as *hatta*, which was popular among the local *fellahin* and Bedouins. The writer and educator Ze'ev Yavetz often described his literary heroes as young Jewish men wearing an *abbaya*, and the artist Ze'ev Raban featured Hebrew youth wearing a *kaffiyeh*.[41] Boris Schatz, the founder of the Bezalel School of Arts and Crafts, appeared in the streets of Jerusalem wearing a long white gown or an *abbaya* (see figure 2).[42]

This kind of hybrid dressing was most popular in the first decades of the twentieth century, among those who considered themselves the vanguard of the New Jews, including Hebrew youth who had grown up in the settlements of the First Aliyah and activist Socialist Zionist immigrants.[43] As is typical of cultural transitions, the experimentation in hybridity drew on a diversity of available resources, combining Eastern European elements with features of the new Middle Eastern environment. Indeed, the practice of integrating European and Middle Eastern clothing was quite common among urban Arabs, who wore Western suits along with the Ottoman hat known as a *fez* (or *tabush*).[44] Moreover, as the literary scholar Itamar Even-Zohar points out, the idea of Jews turning to non-Jews for a model of identity change was already familiar in Eastern Europe prior to the Zionist immigration to Palestine, and Yishuv society simply continued this trend: "The 'heroic Bedouin robber,'" Even-Zohar observes, "replaces the Cossack, and the fellah the Ukrainian *kulak*. The *kafiyeh* takes the place of crude *galoshes*."[45] The historian Israel Bartal analyzes the hybrid model of the "Cossack-Bedouin" further, focusing on the appeal of the Cossack's popular image as warrior-settler for those Eastern European Jewish activists who wished to combine Jewish farming with Jewish self-defense.[46]

The early Zionist settlers' fascination with the Cossacks and then the Bedouins led Michael Halperin, a Russian Jewish Zionist activist and a romantic, to establish the People's Legion in 1903. This was a group of armed horsemen wearing hybrid clothing styles freely borrowed from the Cossacks, the Circassians, and the Bedouins. Although the group's role was mostly ceremonial, it embodied the desire to cultivate a new kind of Jew who was daring, feisty, and ready to fight for Jewish self-defense. Later organizations, such as *Bar-Giora* (named after an anicent Jewish hero in the revolt against the Romans) (1907) and its offshoot, *Ha-Shomer* (The Guard), founded in 1909, continued to similarly display their transformed identity.[47] The latter's passion for horse riding and hybrid dressing became part of their iconic representation (figure 3), as seen in a display of the history of Jewish defense and on a 2007 commemorative stamp.[48]

During the 1940s, members of Zionist youth movements and the *Palmach* underground, both male and female, often wore the white or checkered *kaffiyeh* as a head covering or a scarf, even as the *kaffiyeh* was emerging as an Arab and Palestinian national icon.[49] The *kaffiyeh* became part of the iconic representation of the *Palmach* as seen in photos and films, and was displayed in the *Hagana* Museum exhibit.[50] Young people continued to wear the *kaffiyeh* on field trips and for outdoor activities through the 1950s and 1960s, and even the elderly David Ben-Gurion could be spotted with a *kaffiyeh* wrapped as a scarf with his khaki uniform. A photo of a young woman wearing the red-and-white-checkered *kaffiyeh* also appeared on greeting cards put out by kibbutzim (figure 4).

FIGURE 3. *Ha-Shomer* Members (1910). Reproduction by Dan Schaffner, The KKL/JNF Photo Archive.

Horseback riding was another marker of an identity change that followed the Cossack-Bedouin model and articulated the Zionist preoccupation with the male body as the locus of the transformation into a native Hebrew. Far beyond its practical value, the mastery of horsemanship represented the embrace of new masculinity, gallantry, and power that was part of the Zionist revival. During the early years of Yishuv society, the public display of Jewish horsemanship became an important feature of festive cel-

צברית' עם גדי

לשנה טובה תכתבו

A Happy New Year

FIGURE 4. New Year's Greeting Card from the kibbutz. Courtesy of Yitzhak Grossman/Isranof; Yad Yaari Research & Documentation Center.

ebrations, following the Arab custom.[51] When Hebrew youth performed a display of horsemanship during Theodor Herzl's visit to Palestine in 1898, Herzl described in his diary how moved he was to see their performance.[52] Halperin, whose *People's Legion* advanced the idea of horseback riding, was reported to have said to a local Bedouin sheik:

> One day, *Hebrew Bedouins* will put up their tents near the Bedouins' tents. . . . In this place where free Arabs now ride their well-bred horses, our ances-tors used to ride their horses. And who knows if the sheik himself is not one of the twelve tribes of Israel, many of whom stayed in the country after we had been exiled from our land.[53]

The *Ha-Shomer* members' love of horses was part of their public image. A humorous illustration by the painter Nahum Gutman, who grew in the Hebrew culture of the Yishuv, features a Hebrew child with a *kaffiyeh* enthusiastically riding a rocking horse.[54] The child's appearance echoes the iconic representation of *Ha-Shomer* members as an inspiration to a new generation of youth, while the rocking horse adds a playful frame that redefines the riding as a form of child's fantasy.

While for Sephardic and Middle Eastern Palestinian Jews, speaking Arabic was already a way of life during the Ottoman period, for Zionist Ashkenazi immigrants and their children the use of Arabic idioms within Hebrew speech emerged as another feature of an identity change. This practice, which persisted into later decades among Hebrew youth, did not necessarily imply competence in colloquial Arabic, although there were European Jews who acquired conversational Arabic to be able to communicate with Arabs in the marketplace or as employers.[55] Like the hybrid dressing, the incorporation of Arabic terms was a performative act to display familiarity with the local culture. The First Aliyah farmer, Zionist activist, and writer Moshe Smilansky describes his literary hero as a transformed Jew whom the Arabs admiringly nicknamed Hawaja Nazar, for his "heroism, for learning how to speak fluent Arabic so quickly, and for knowing how to ride a galloping horse like one of them. And more than once or twice, he would compete with young Arabs in horse races; dressed like them in *abbaya*, *kaffiyeh*, and *igal*, and fully armed like them."[56] Michael Gluzman points out the remarkably similar themes in a description of an early Zionist immigrant, Sender Hadad, who was likewise admired by the Arabs for his physical strength and given an Arabic last name.[57]

The incorporation of Arabic terms in colloquial Hebrew speech continued to be an important practice among members of the youth culture. In her memoir of her experience as a female fighter with the *Palmach*, Netiva Ben-Yehuda describes its members' fascination with Arab culture:

> From the days of *Ha-Shomer* to the *Palmach*—we were dying to be like them, only this preoccupied us: to talk like them, to walk like them, to behave like them. . . . We regarded them as the model of the native. . . . The more familiar one was with Arab customs—with how to mingle with them, behave like them, foster a common language with them—the more Godlike one appeared to us."[58]

Ben-Yehuda's account may be somewhat exaggerated, but it points out a familiar trend among the youth of the 1940s. In his portrait of the Sabra, the native Hebrew of the *Palmach* generation, the sociologist Oz Almog calls this collective figure "Uri of Arabia," weaving together the two figures of Lawrence of Arabia and Moshe Shamir's famous literary hero Uri.[59] The display of Arabic terms and knowledge of Bedouin customs continued to be a way to show native know-how even after the foundation of the state.[60] As we shall see below, these demonstrative gestures stand in dramatic contrast to the low status associated with Arabic-speaking Jews within Yishuv society and in post-1948 Israeli society, in spite of Arabic's status as an official language in Israel until July 2018.[61]

An important facet of the desert mystique was the portrayal of the ancient Hebrews and the contemporary Arabs as close to nature, a quality that had been lost to Jews during centuries of life in exile. Within this context, the figure of the shepherd emerged as a major trope of Zionist renewal. The shepherd served as a direct link to the biblical ancestors who had held the same occupation, and the biblical allusion to God as a shepherd foregrounded the positive qualities associated with this figure: The shepherd projected simplicity, harmony with nature, guidance, and protection. In her extensive study of the image of the shepherd in Hebrew culture, Michal Sadan points out its prominence in the literature and art of the Jewish Enlightenment and in the Hebrew fiction, poetry, art, songs, and dance that were produced in Palestine in the first decades of the state. The figure of the shepherd calmly playing the flute as he watches over his herd has often been reproduced in artistic, popular, and educational materials.[62]

The desire to become a Hebrew shepherd appealed to some young members of the Socialist Zionist pioneers. In 1914, *Ha-Shomer* members formed a special group whose goal was to learn the necessary skills to become shepherds so that Jews would be able to raise herds on their own rather than depend on hired Arab help. During the following years, several individuals and small groups lived among Arab shepherds as apprentices to acquire these necessary skills.[63] One of these individuals was Pesach Bar-Adon (formerly Panitsch), who had left Poland for Palestine as a young man in 1925. After a brief engagement in Jewish and Middle Eastern studies at the Hebrew University, he went to live among the Bedouins as a shepherd apprentice, assuming an Arabic name and dressing like the Bedouins. When tensions flared between Jews and Arabs in 1929, Bar-Adon returned to Jewish society for a short period, but he later joined another Bedouin tribe to continue his training. His memoir of his experiences—*In the Desert Tents: Notes of a Hebrew Shepherd with the Bedouin Tribes*—was originally published in 1934. When it was reissued in 1981, the new edition introduced the author with his dual Hebrew-Bedouin identity: his adopted modern Hebrew name Bar-Adon as well as his adopted Arabic name Aziz Effendi.[64] When the Association of Hebrew Shepherds (*Agudat Ha-Nokdim Ha-Ivri'im*) was formed, in 1930, and a new publication, *The Shepherd* (*Ha-Noked*), subsequently appeared in 1939,[65] the association's choice of the archaic biblical term *noked* rather than the modern Hebrew term *ro'eh* highlighted this occupation's evocation of the biblical period.

In spite of its romantic aura, the path to becoming a shepherd entailed a long period of apprenticeship and difficult work in challenging conditions. Such experiments therefore were often short-lived. A member of the Shepherd Association later admitted: "It never occurred to us that this was just a beautiful dream. We didn't ask ourselves how European men would be suddenly transformed into Bedouins." Ultimately, he added, "we gave up the glory of the shepherd who leads the herd while playing the flute, and the dream of becoming a Bedouin, like the Bedouins who live in the desert, faded."[66] That reality, however, did not affect the emergence of a rich shepherd lore in Hebrew culture.

In a short story by the writer Yosef Luidor, written in 1912, a native Hebrew boy rebels against school and adult authority, preferring to ride his horse and spend time with the Bedouins. His affinity with the world of nature and open spaces makes him a part of the symbolic desert. This observation is confirmed by his immigrant Jewish friend, who sees him as "a desert figure whose black eyes burn with a strange, wild fire."[67] A similar theme is presented in a short story entitled "The Loyal Shepherd," written in 1928 by the writer and educator Eliezer Smoli. The story describes a ten-year-old boy who does not know how to read and write, yet finds his fulfillment in accompanying the shepherds and their herds. One day, when he is out in nature with the herd by himself, a sheep has difficulty in giving birth; the boy stays with the herd, even past nightfall, not willing to abandon the suffering sheep until adults are able to locate them.[68] The story, reminiscent of tales about righteous simpletons, praises the nature-loving boy and his courage. The cover of Smoli's short-story anthology *The Loyal Shepherd* features a picture of the shepherd boy wearing a white *kaffiyeh* with an *igal* and carrying a flute in his hand, providing a visual representation of the early image of the Hebrew-Bedouin.[69] Both stories build up these child protagonists as noble savages admired for their independence, courage, and love of nature, as free agents free of supervision by parents or schools. In the spirit of the time, they offer these literary heroes as a counter-image to the exilic Jewish child immersed in religious studies from an early age.

Smoli's young-adult novel *Frontiersmen of Israel*, which was published in 1933 and became a canonical work of the period, highlights the transitional role of the Hebrew-Bedouin identity in the transformation of a Jewish guard into a farmer. The protagonist, a European socialist pioneer, associates his past life as a wandering guard with being a "Hebrew-Bedouin"[70] and defines his goal as becoming a *fallâh*. The novel portrays him as being more comfortable among the Bedouins than among other Arabs or even urban Jews, and as a novice farmer, it takes him time to learn how to control the plow, to the amusement of Bedouin onlookers.[71] His children, growing up in the wilderness and away from other Jews, are more familiar with the Arabs' ways of life than with Jewish religious practices. Seeing a Jew wrapped in a prayer shawl (*tallit*) for the first time, the daughter asks her father why that man is wearing an *abbaya*, thus relating to the unfamiliar Jewish ritual through the lens of local Arab culture.[72]

The variants of this hybrid identity[73] (referred to variously as Hebrew-Bedouin, Jewish-Bedouin, Jewish-Arab, or Hebrew-Arab) emerged when the recreation of a native Jew was a deliberate, involved process, and in a period in which the identities of Jews and Arabs did not represent an obvious dichotomy within a shared, multicultural environment. As Jonathan Gribetz observes, "in late Ottoman Palestine, ethnic, racial, national and religious categories were all in some degree of flux."[74] The new hybrid identity departed from the familiar mode of diasporic Jewish identities (i.e. "German Jews" or "Arab Jews"[75]) by making the Bedouin the unmarked component.[76] And unlike the "Young Hebrews" movement of the 1940s and early 1950s (better known as the "Canaanites"), this identity did not collapse the two components into a single category that privileged one over the other.[77] Indeed, the Hebrew-Bedouin identity served as a transitional phase in the process of becoming native Hebrews and was discarded once the transition was deemed to be complete.

The public display of this Hebrew-Bedouin identity, whether performed on the street or on stage or featured in literary or artistic works, was designed first and foremost for internal consumption by Jewish society, as a reassuring gesture that the desired identity change was indeed taking place. Yet the coveted validation of this process by others further enhanced its value. Two significant "others"—diaspora Jews and local Arabs—fulfilled this role. As the literary historian Yaffa Berlovitz notes, the witnessing of the newcomers' identity change was a recurrent theme in narratives of the First Aliyah. Ze'ev Yavetz describes how an exilic Jew visiting Palestine is shocked to discover that an approaching Arab riding his horse turns out to be a Hebrew-speaking Jew. "Had someone told me back home that a person can be transformed to such an extent, I would have found it incredible," he admits.[78] Arabs too are cast in the role of the astonished witnesses, affirming the transformation of exilic Jews into Arabized natives riding their horses.[79] Other sources, however, suggest that the hybrid dress and horseback riding may have fooled fellow Jews more easily than Arabs. Thus, for example, the *Ha-Shomer* member Gershon Fleisher, who apprenticed with the Bedouins, notes that even though Jews could not tell the Jewish shepherds apart from their hosts, Arabs could distinguish them from afar by observing their riding style.[80]

As national tensions between Arabs and Jews flared up in 1929 and, more intensely, during the Arab Revolt of 1936–39, the escalation of the national conflict in Palestine diminished the appeal of theories of a common descent or hybrid identities. By this time, the image of the new Hebrew was better formulated, and the foundations of Hebrew culture had become progressively stronger. Reliance on the desert mystique as an important facet of the recreation of a symbolic continuity with the ancient Hebrew identity and culture weakened but did not disappear, and has remained part and parcel of Israeli culture since 1948.

Desert Lore

Among the European immigrants eager to create a new Jewish society in Palestine, artistically inclined pioneers, writers, and educators contributed to the emergence of Hebrew poetry and short stories, songs and dances, visual and performative arts, and new rituals. New cultural forms created by grassroots activities often spread across the small Yishuv society and were further disseminated through schools and youth movements. The desert mystique inspired the creation of a diverse Hebrew desert lore that articulated the romantic view of its landscape through various themes including the camel, the well, the importance of water, and the connection to the biblical past.

During these early formative years, the camel was featured prominently in Hebrew literature and art and became, as the literary scholar Uri Cohen noted, a "Zionist animal."[81] A popular Hebrew song, "Carry us to the Desert" (La-midbar sa'enu), was based on a poem by Alexander Penn, who was close to the Hebrew shepherds of Sheik Abrek.[82] The lyrics express deep longing for the desert and a wish to return to it on camelback and experience the profound tranquillity and serenity of the desert in the stillness of the night. The melody, inspired by a Bedouin folksong, introduces the camels' slow and rhythmic movement, and the repeated trilling adds to the Orientalist depiction of the symbolic desert. The song "A Caravan in the Desert," inspired by a poem by Yaacov Fichman and adapted and set to music in 1927 by the young David Zehavi (who was a high school student at the time), offers another example of the new desert lore. Here too, the lyrics emphasize the vastness and stillness of the desert landscape through which the caravan passes:

> Right and left only sand and more sand,
> A yellow desert with no mark of a trail.
> A caravan passes by, soundlessly moving on,
> As an enchanting apparition within a dream."[83]

The slow melody rises and sinks, thereby reproducing the camels' walk, and the sound of the bells enhances the repetitiveness of this movement. With its dreamy atmosphere, monotonous pace, and depiction of a vast space devoid of any clear paths, the desert appears as a metaphoric bubble, a mythical space or fantasy that conveys no goal or sense of purpose.[84] These Orientalist depictions reappear in Israeli culture. The choreographer Sara Levi-Tanai echoes a similar vision of the desert in describing her sources of inspiration:

> The yellow desert landscape, the capricious climate, the vision of the dunes next to the seashore, the veils of sand that are carried by the southeast winds, the camels' steps, their proud necks held high, their bells ringing, the horses' galloping hoofs have all influenced me.[85]

These descriptions also reproduce the desert as a gendered landscape, marked by its feminine qualities. The soft, curved outlines of the desert dunes and the silhouette of the camel, the caravans' slow movement, the stillness of the night and the enchanted atmosphere contribute to the feminized portrayal of the desert and its marked contrast to the straight, masculine lines associated with the Jewish settlement, as the discussion in chapter 3 reveals.

FIGURE 5. The Flying Camel—The Levant Fair, Tel Aviv. The Central Zionist Archives (KRA\4301).

Perhaps the most interesting adaptation of the camel in Hebrew culture emerged in the emblem of the Levant Fair (*Yerid Ha-Mizrah*), which was established in Tel Aviv in the 1930s. Drawing on the camel as an iconic representation of the desert, the emblem transformed it into a symbol of change, creating a new hybrid creature in the form of a flying camel.[86] Equipped with two large wings that represent the advance of technology, the flying camel soars up and forward, leaving the desert and its culture behind. This flying camel, designed in 1932 by the Israeli architect Aryeh Elhanani, represents the impact of Western technology and the ideology of progress on a centuries-old tradition and way of life, reorienting it toward the future (figure 5).

The popular association of the figure of the shepherd with antiquity and with the desert made this figure another productive part of the renewed lore, and the kibbutzim provided a fertile ground for its further development. The creation of new festivals such as the water festival (*hag ha-mayim*) and the shearing festival (*hag ha-gez*) provided occasions to create new songs and dances by members with an artistic drive. This was the case with the collaboration between two creative members of kibbutz Ramat Yochanan, the songwriter Matityahu Shelem and the choreographer Lea Bergstein. The songs and dances they composed for the shearing festival and other communal celebrations in their kibbutz, drawing on their experiences (Shelem had worked as a shepherd), soon spread to other kibbutz settlements and beyond.[87] Dances composed by another amateur choreographer, Rivka Sturman of kibbutz Ein Harod, similarly contributed to the development of Israeli folk dance. Inspired by a traditional Arab dance, she composed "The Shepherds' *Debka*" and "I'm a Zionist Shepherd" (*ani ro'eh tsiyoni*) among her earliest creations. Sturman describes the influence of Arab dance on her work:

> At Ein Harod, I could watch the Arabs as they led their sheep down into the valley where the well lay. As they danced on the path, playing their *hallil* [flute], their steps and behavior were of intense interest to me. . . . These observations gave an Arabic color to my earliest dances.[88]

Sturman was further inspired by the traditional dances of the Yemenite Jews, and she introduced into her dances the "Yemenite step," which became one of the cornerstones of Israeli folk dance.[89]

This experimentation with creating hybrid cultural forms, drawing selectively on imagined ancient forms, local traditions, and Western images of the Orient, was also manifested in the domain of costumes. The new kibbutz festivals and holiday celebrations incorporated costumes that projected an ancient look, along with Eastern European folkloric clothing. Women dressed in long gowns, carrying pitchers and gourds on their heads or on their shoulders or holding tambourine drums in their hands, became an iconic component of holiday festivals and dance performances designed to invoke the ancient past and desert lore.[90]

Other iconic representations associated with desert lore were springs and wells, which like the camel and the shepherd became symbolic bridges to the ancient past. In the song "To the Water Spring" (*El ha-ma'ayan*),[91] composed in the late 1920s, the speaker addresses a young white goat that has arrived at the well, inquiring about its origins. Upon hearing that the goat is from Haran, the place where Abraham's family stopped on the way to Canaan and where Jacob met Rachel and was introduced to Laban's family, the speaker further inquires about the biblical figures' well-being, as though they were still alive now.[92] The songwriter Emanuel Zamir, an important contributor to shepherd lore, elaborated on the role of the well in his song "A Well in the Field" (*Be'er ba-sade*). The lyrics describe an ancient well that the shepherds had dug, which sealed off its water when they went away, refusing to give water to foreign herds. Upon hearing that the shepherds had returned, however, it renewed its water supply and called to the returnees to bring their herds to drink from its water.[93] The song thus attributes agency to the ancient well and describes it as actively disapproving of Jewish exile and supporting Zionist national revival. The calm melodic tune enhances the pastoral ambiance associated with shepherd lore.

The discovery of water was another important theme in desert lore as represented in song and dance. This lore often drew on biblical verses as seen in examples such as "God Makes the Desert into a Lake of Water" (*Yasem midbar la-agam mayim*), based on Psalm 107:35, and "Water, Water" (*U-she'avtem mayim be-sasson*), based on Isaiah 12:3. The first Dalia Folk Dance Festival prominently featured dances composed to these songs, and the cover of the third record of the "Palestinian Folk Dance Series" featured the "Water, Water" dance.[94]

In spite of the growing gaps between the romantic vision of the desert and the reality of the Jewish experience in Palestine, the desert and shepherd lore continued to play a visible role in Hebrew culture, a trend that extended into the early decades of the state. Examples included new works such as Lea Bergstein's 1951 dance "The Shepherd and the Shepherdess" and the song "Night Falls" (*Erev ba*), a pastoral depiction of herds returning to a village at twilight, which was the winner of the 1960 Israeli Song Festival. Similarly, the kibbutzim's New Year's cards included pastoral images depicting youth as young shepherds.[95] The mystique of the desert generated a trove of romantic songs, dances, and popular images that became part of the Hebrew culture of the Jewish society of Palestine, even though by the 1940s the reality they depicted had become increasingly distant from the actual reality of the Yishuv.[96] In later years, this lore remained part of nostalgic Israeli memory, representing the Hebrew folklore of the society in its more idealistic formative years.[97]

At Home in the Orient?

The European Zionist immigrants considered themselves the "lost sons," returning to their ancestral land, but their encounter with the realities of life in Palestine was often alienating and challenging and made them aware of their cultural difference. Some of the Zionist immigrants articulated the shock of their first encounter with the land. Eliezer Ben-Yehuda revealed his initial shock at experiencing his foreignness upon arrival, his fear of the unfamiliar people, and the emotional numbness that he felt in response to the land and its sights, about which he had dreamed in Europe.[98] Ben-Zvi recalled his first impression of the Jezreel valley shortly after his arrival: "How strange and foreign this environment appeared to me."[99] An immigrant from the Ukraine remembered with longing "the large open space, the green meadows, the limitless view of fields with crops" he had left behind, and confessed to experiencing "difficult and depressing feelings."[100] A. D. Gordon wrote that he could not forget the landscape of the Russian countryside where he grew up and that he loved, confessing that he did not have the same sentimental attachment to the nature of his new environment.[101] Poems by Avraham Shlonsky and Yitzhak Lamdan allude to a sense of detachment from the new environment, where the heat is suffocating and "hunger and malaria await us."[102] Indeed, it was the gap between the idealized Land of Israel and the reality they encountered that had contributed to the conception of the country as a symbolic desert.

The European Jewish settlers also relegated the Arabs to the symbolic desert and its nature. The Hebrew word *pere*, which was applied to the Arabs to describe them as wild or savage, was the word used in the Bible to refer to a wild donkey.[103] Thus, for example, the writer Moshe Smilansky, whose work typically provides romantic representations of the Arabs, describes his tour of "a semi-wild region" and refers to the "wild" or "savage" Bedouins living there.[104] Yosef Weitz of the Jewish National Fund alludes to the challenges faced by the First Aliyah settlers as "a struggle against nature and the savages around them,"[105] and Yitzhak Ben-Zvi mourns the two men who were killed by "the Arab savage's arrow" when serving as guards.[106] Such allusions to the Arabs as "savage" or "wild" echo the Western colonialist discourse about indigenous populations in non-Western countries and reveal the influence of the American frontier on the discourse of the Hebrew settlement, themes that will be further explored in the following chapters.

The multilayered meanings of the term *pere* reveal the newcomers' view of the Arab as uncivilized, and therefore as part of nature. The Jewish immigrants saw the rural Arab settlements in Palestine as primitive, dirty, noisy, and chaotic. This is how the writer Hemda Ben-Yehuda describes her impressions of Palestine in 1892, shortly after her arrival:

> I was shocked by the Arab village I saw: houses made of mud, window-less, housing both men and animals. Piles of garbage everywhere and half-naked children, their eyes sick and flies sucking the pus. . . . In front of the houses blind old women and dirty young girls sit and work, grinding wheat as was done thousands of years ago.[107]

Ben-Yehuda frames her description as evidence of the local Arabs' lack of knowledge or ability to separate hygiene and dirt, home and yard, and humans and animals. Yitzhak Ben-Zvi, who first notes the beauty of Nazareth from a distance, describes his disappointment upon approaching it and realizing that "its streets are narrow and dirty, filled with mire and garbage, like all Arab towns. And the dust-filled air is even worse than the filth."[108] A Jewish resident of Tel Aviv describes a local Arab market as "Asian in the full sense of the word, with its filth, its congestion, its rough manners, and its Levantine cries."[109]

Local Arab culture appealed to some of the newcomers and Hebrew youth, but for others it evoked deep anxiety over the potential impact of Middle Eastern culture on the European foundations of the new Hebrew culture. Although the multiethnic Ottoman society presented a greater flexibility of hybrid identities and cultural forms, those who viewed the local culture as inferior, among them some leading European Jewish intellectuals, warned their brethren against the dangers of flirtation with the desert mystique, which could undermine the foundations of their Jewish culture and identity. A. D. Gordon was outraged at seeing a younger Zionist pioneer wearing a *kaffiyeh* in the streets of Jerusalem,[110] and Yosef Aharonowitz, the prominent editor of a major Socialist Zionist newspaper, *Ha-Poel Ha-Tsair*, criticized the trend of adopting local cultural expressions as "revolting."[111]

These warnings against the lure of the desert mystique echo similar warnings to American pioneers to beware of the "wilderness temptation" that might pull down the level of American civilization.[112] The historian Yosef Klausner wrote in 1907 that "we Jews have been living for more than two thousand years among cultured people and we cannot and must not descend once more to the cultural level of semi-savages."[113] In 1914, the Socialist Zionist writer Yaacov Rabinowitz denounced those who looked to the Bedouins as a model and advocated the creation of a European-style Hebrew model "that is cultured and civilized."[114] Ze'ev Jabotinsky, the Revisionist Zionist leader, emphatically noted in 1926:

> We, Jews, have nothing in common with what is denoted "the East," thank God for that. To the extent that our own uneducated masses have traditions and spiritual prejudices which are reminiscent of the East, they must be weaned away from them. . . . As for the Arabs of Palestine, that is their own affair, but there is one favor we can do them: to help them free themselves from "the East."[115]

Other Zionist leaders and intellectuals, however, criticized the stereotyping of the Arabs and the negative approach to the East. Ahad Ha'am, in
his famous essay "The Truth from the Land of Israel," writes,

> We abroad are accustomed to believe that the Arabs are all desert savages,
> people who are like donkeys who neither see nor understand what goes
> on around them. But this is a big mistake. The Arabs, like all Semitic
> people, are intellectually sharp and cunning. All the towns in Syria and
> the Land of Israel are filled with Arab merchants, . . . and things are
> done here as they are in Europe.[116]

In his critical 1907 essay "A Hidden Question," the teacher and writer
Yitzhak Epstein, who had settled in Palestine in 1886, addressed the attitude
of his fellow settlers toward the Arabs. Epstein focused on the need to pursue
a policy of coexistence with the Arab majority in Palestine and to respect
their history in the land. He criticized the alienation of Arabs as a result
of the purchase of land cultivated by Arab workers and offered a vision of
mutual benefits from close cooperation between Arabs and Jews.[117] In 1923,
the head of the Palestine office of the Zionist Organization, Arthur Ruppin,
wrote in his diary, "Once again, we must integrate among the peoples of the
East, and create, together with our brothers of the same race, the Arabs (and
the Armenians), a new cultural community in the Near East."[118] In 1925,
embracing the integrationist approach, Ruppin and other Zionist leaders
founded *Brit Shalom*, which advocated the creation of a bi-national state.
Although it was just a small group on the margins of the Yishuv's political
spectrum, *Brit Shalom* included major figures and prominent intellectuals, including the professors Hugo Bergman, Ernst Simon, and Gershom
Scholem. The integrationist orientation, however, remained marginal and
Brit Shalom was criticized by other Zionist groups. In the aftermath of
1929, with the further radicalization of the national conflict, this approach
lost a great deal of ground, and by 1933 *Brit Shalom* had ceased to exist.[119]
    When the Jews, who were often seen as Oriental in Europe, arrived
in Palestine, they in turn regarded both the local Arabs and Middle Eastern
and North African Jews as Oriental. The duality of Jews' relation to the East
accounts for the inconsistencies and contradictions underlying the European
Jews' views of the Middle East. Indeed, the issue of Jews and Orientalism
has occupied and continues to occupy scholars, to a large extent in response
to Said's monolithic construction of the East/West dichotomy and to the
rise of global interest in hybrid identities and multiculturalism.[120] As Julie

Kalman suggests, Jews occupy a "middle space" between the "Orientalizing" and the "Orientalized." "The figure of the Jew in the history of Orientalism," she concludes, "disrupts categories and boundaries in productive messy ways: here and there, us and them, powerful and disempowered, and even East and West."[121] Although European Jews assigned a special niche to Sephardic and Middle Eastern Jews as models for new Hebrew cultural forms that represented a continuity with the ancient past, the roots of those "models" in Arab and Middle Eastern cultures marked them as occupying a lower status within the Jewish society of Palestine.[122] It is quite telling that warnings about the dangers of traversing the boundaries between Jews and Arabs peaked in the 1950s and 1960s, in the face of the mass immigration of Jews from Middle Eastern and North African countries.[123]

The public response to Middle Eastern performers and their cultural traditions reveals this deep ambivalence toward the East and the rejection of an unfiltered representation of Jewish-Arab culture by European Jewish audiences in Palestine. Rina Nikova's Yemenite dance troupe was criticized in the mid-1930s for singing in Arabic during its performances, and it later shifted to Hebrew songs.[124] The Yemenite Jewish singer Bracha Zefira performed songs of Yemenite, Bedouin, and Sephardic traditions both in Europe and in Palestine, but was accompanied by her partner, the Russian-born pianist Nahum Nardi, who helped adapt her singing to Western audiences. In later years, she introduced orchestral arrangements that would make her Middle Eastern singing more accessible to European Jewish audiences that were unaccustomed to her repertoire.[125] At the same time, performers also felt the pressure to accommodate their European audience's expectation of Middle Eastern culture. Thus, Yardena Cohen insisted that the Middle Eastern professional musicians who accompanied her replace their European clothes with white tunics.[126] Clearly, Middle Eastern artists internalized the European vision of the desert mystique that was accepted by their predominantly European audience and required "staged authenticity"[127] to meet those expectations.

Although European Jews came to Palestine with a desire to put the history of exile behind them, their experiences in Europe were projected onto their reality and minority status in Palestine. References to Jewish-Arab relations in terms that were borrowed from their past sometimes made this explicit. Thus, the Second Aliyah writer and critic Yosef Hayim Brenner described the Arabs as "the Poles of the East,"[128] and the editor of the Socialist Zionist newspaper *Davar*, Moshe Beilinson, noted that he felt more alienated from the Arabs than he had ever felt from Polish and Russian peasants.[129] As we shall see at various junctures, rising tensions in Palestine and Israel's continuing conflict with the Palestinians contributed to the forging of lines of continuity, within the Israeli discourse of settlement and security, between Jews' past exilic experiences and the present.

Indeed, the appeal of the desert mystique to *Ha-Shomer* members, the *Palmach*, and members of the youth movement did not necessarily imply a closeness to the Arab society in Palestine. *Ha-Shomer* members, who were famous for their hybrid dress, horsemanship, and adoption of Arabic expressions, were also known for their militant approach to the Arabs. Their strong advocacy of self-defense as a way to protect Jewish property rights and their insistence on promoting Jewish labor were often criticized as escalating the tensions with local Arabs.[130] Others criticized *Ha-Shomer* members for their apparent fascination with Arab culture, which they explained by pointing out the pragmatic benefits of acquiring those skills that would assist them in carrying out their mission as guards. In the same vein, some of the shepherds who had lived among the Bedouins highlighted the benefits of their occupation to Jewish security. Their knowledge of Arabic and ties with Arab shepherds were instrumental to information gathering, and being out in the fields they could serve as scouts to detect the movements of the Arabs in open spaces.[131] It is quite possible that the growing conflictual relationship between Arabs and Jews also led to the justification of a genuine earlier interest in the Bedouin culture by reframing it within the more widely accepted security discourse. A similar duality was apparent in the *Palmach*, whose members' fascination with Arab cultural idioms was driven in part by the desire to cultivate a local native identity, but also encouraged by the imperative to "know your enemy," in preparation for a future military confrontation with the Arabs.[132] This approach thus fed into the settlement and security discourse and its emphasis on the conflictual relationship between desert and the settlement.

It is interesting to note, then, the impact of renewed encounters with Palestinians, Druze, and Sinai Bedouins in a later period, following the 1967 war, on the re-embrace of some of the pre-state practices associated with the desert mystique, albeit in a radically different political constellation. In the late 1960s and the 1970s, the ease of movement across previously sealed borders evoked a desire on the part of many Israeli Jews to travel to the occupied territories and interact with their inhabitants. There they discovered new markets in Palestinian towns where they could purchase lower-priced produce, food products, household items, and other consumer goods. The trend of decorating homes with furniture and objects bought in the territories popularized such items as wicker furniture, brass trays, clay jars, and decorative tiles, as well as artifacts made of Hebron glass and Armenian ceramics. The *kaffiyeh*, worn as a scarf or head covering, reappeared as a popular item among Israeli Jews, who preferred the white *kaffiyeh* to avoid the political and nationalist connotations of the red-and-black-checkered ones. The *galabiya*, the long Middle Eastern gown (also worn by more traditional North African Jews), became popular mostly as a women's dress item. Yet the writer and artist Dahn Ben-Amotz famously wore a white *galabiya* in Tel Aviv in the post-1967 years, evoking the memory of Boris Schatz, who had walked the streets of Jerusalem dressed in an *abbaya* in the early twentieth century. The refound sense of openness and fascination with Arab material culture of the early post-1967 period declined again, however, as the occupation became more entrenched and the conflict with the Palestinians intensified.

High fashion's interest in Middle Eastern styles is, perhaps, even more indicative of the desert mystique. The Maskit Company, which was established in 1954 to provide employment to immigrant Jewish craftsmen and developed a line of handmade Israeli crafts and garments, expanded its high-end fashion in the post-1967 era, inspired by traditional folk art

FIGURE 6. "Desert coat" designed by Finy Leitersdorf for the Maskit collection. Photograph by Ben Lam 1970; courtesy of Thomas Leitersdorf. Published in the catalog of Tel Aviv Museum's exhibit on Finy Leitersdorf (1983).

and Middle Eastern crafts. Ruth Dayan, its founder, recalled that "after the Six-Day War, Arab-Israeli coexistence became one of Maskit's major sources of inspiration. All the embroideries were made in Bethlehem, Beit Jala, and Gaza; the mother-of-pearl and olive wood buttons were created in Bethlehem, the wicker furniture and some of the rugs in Gaza."[133] Among Maskit's fashionable items were the desert coats designed by its lead designer, Finy Leitersdorf (see Figure 6), and described in the 2003 Maskit exhibit catalog as Maskit's flagship garment.[134]

In the early post-1967 period, Israeli fashion also introduced desert-colored garments and "*kaffiyeh* dresses" designed by Rosie Ben-Yosef, who considered her designs to be part of the trend toward developing an Israeli style that would connect Israelis with the Middle East.[135] Later, the global interest in innovative *galabiyas* and *kaffiyeh* dresses received wide coverage in Israel[136] and led to the opening of a *galabiya* store in the chic historic neighborhood of Neve Tzedek in Tel Aviv and the reopening of Maskit.[137]

Palestinian and other critics object to this phenomenon, which they regard as the co-optation and exploitation of Palestinian heritage by Israelis and hence as another facet of their occupation.[138] Articles in the Israeli media raise questions about the issue of cultural ownership but do not necessarily present a uniform perspective.[139]

Liron Ohana notes that while the Israeli-Arab conflict intensifies on the street, Israeli designers display new collections adorned with *kaffiyeh* patterns, *galabiya* gowns, and Arab embroidery, and questions if this is a disconnect from the reality, a global trend, or an attempt to shape a local style. Featuring a sample of photos displaying this fashion trend, Ohana concludes that "one can speak about the Orientalist aspect of this choice—to coopt the esthetics of the Arabs without addressing their meanings. But the designers' attempt to create clothes that fit the local climate, combining local techniques and inspiration from their natural environment, the Middle East, is praiseworthy."[140] Similarly, most Israeli designers interviewed refute the accusation of cultural co-optation, claiming that their work is apolitical or pointing to its ancient and contemporary Middle Eastern Jewish roots.[141] Some Israeli scholars interviewed nonetheless observe the impossibility of separating this Israeli trend from the current political situation.[142]

In some cases, artists deliberately wish to explore Israelis' attitudes through their work. Thus, for example, the Israeli artist Tsibi Geva is known for his use of such iconic Arab forms as the *kaffiyeh*, backgammon, and ceramic tiles. His work is interpreted as articulating the tensions between

East and West and, as the art critic Yigal Zalmona notes, a desire for dialogue.[143] The designer label Threeasfour provides an example of fashion that explicitly delivers a political message of peace and coexistence through its transnational team, the interweaving of Jewish and Palestinian heritage, and its concept of "InSHALLOm," combining the Hebrew *shalom* (peace) with the Arabic *inshallah* (God willing).[144] At the other extreme, however, the creation of so-called "Jewish *kaffiyeh*" appears to have been politically motivated, as a way to offer a counterpart to the use of the Arab *kaffiyeh* by pro-Palestinian demonstrators.[145]

The debate about fashion products illustrates the complexity of the broader questions regarding Israeli society's historical and cultural roots and its own understanding of its place in the Middle East. Israeli literature, art, theater, and film continue to probe these issues, both within the context of Israeli society and in terms of Israel's relation to its broader environment. Whereas the issue of the representation of Mizrahi Jews in various Israeli cultural spheres recently led the government to pursue initiatives to enhance the representation of the history and culture of Middle Eastern and Northern African Jewish communities in school and university curricula and to provide greater representation to Mizrahi artists,[146] these changes are mostly defined as intra-Jewish issues and do not extend to the history of the Arab minority, nor do they imply a closer identification with Arab culture.

FIGURE 7. Poster for the 1935 film *Terre promise* (*The Land of Promise*). The Central Zionist Archives (KRA\792).

3

Desert as the Counter-Place

A HEBREW NEW YEAR'S GREETING CARD features the traditional saying, "Let a year and its curses end and a new year and its blessings begin," along with images that reveal the ways in which time and space are interwoven to underscore this opposition. The right panel of the card (which is where a Hebrew reader starts) introduces an Orientalist representation of the country's landscape, with a mosque, some ruins, tents, a camel, and a swamp. This landscape illustrates the first part of the inscription that appears above, "let a year and its curses end." On the opposite end, the left panel presents a Jewish settlement, with its iconic water tower, trees, and farmers plowing the swamp-free land, under the inscription, "and the new year and its blessings begin." In between the two panels, the central panel features a photo of the family sending the greeting, wishing the recipients "a happy New Year" and indicating the time and place: "Tel Aviv, the Land of Israel, 1929."[1] The greeting card associates the symbolic desert with the curse of the past and contrasts it with the cultivated Jewish place and the blessings of the future, thus affirming the Zionist redemptive narrative. Like this greeting card, the poster for Judah Leman's 1935 film *The Land of Promise*, which was produced to represent the achievements of the Zionist settlement, juxtaposes the two symbolic landscapes. The prototypical Orientalist "desert" landscape features vistas of sand, a camel turning the wheel of an old well, and herds of sheep; below it, as if growing from below to replace the desert, we see the urban landscape of the young Tel Aviv with its tall, modern houses, wide boulevards, and trees (see figure 7).[2] These visual representations capture the contrast between the symbolic desert and the settlement that is deeply entrenched in the Zionist settlement discourse that developed in the Hebrew culture.

Settlement and Progress

The Zionist decline narrative, which was discussed earlier in terms of its development within the Jewish mnemonic tradition and historical past, resonated with the European colonial discourse and coincided with its expanding presence in the Middle East and North Africa. The British and French decline narratives compared contemporary Egypt to its ancient Pharaonic past, modern Iraq to ancient Babylon and the civilization of the "Fertile Crescent," and the modern Maghreb to the Roman past. Blaming the decline on the inhabitants' neglect and abuse of the land, the colonial powers legitimized their military, political, and economic control in the name of progress and restoration. Within this comparative perspective, then, the Zionist settlement discourse on awakening the land, reviving it, removing its shame, and returning it to its earlier glory and blissful state conforms to the rhetoric of restoration and redemption of the European colonial discourse. Similarly, the dual vision of the landscape in the Hebrew culture of the late Ottoman period—representing it both as a state of blissfulness in accordance with the biblical portrayal and, conversely, as a barren and desolate desert—resonated with the Western imagery of the Middle East.[3]

A study of pre-1948 settlement discourses and practices also reveals the influence of European colonial ideas on the discourse and practices of Jewish society in Palestine. Zionist European immigrants were largely the agents of change that developed modern Jewish settler society in Palestine from the late 1880s to 1948. Yet, as Derek Penslar notes, in spite of discernible traits of an Orientalist mentality, the Zionist civilizing mission during the pre-state period was primarily self-directed.[4] Jews defined their move to Palestine as a "return" to their homeland that was inherently different from "immigration" to other places. This ideological framework was lexically marked by the use of "Aliyah" as a special term for Jewish immigration to Palestine prior to 1948 or to Israel after 1948. As we saw earlier, the Zionist decline narrative and the redemptive vision of national renewal were largely motivated by the desire to correct the impact of exile and centered on Jews' relation to the land. Unlike colonial powers, Jews did not represent a European "mother" state searching for new territories and markets, nor did they settle on land acquired through military force during this period. The Jewish settlers in Palestine first lived under Ottoman and then British rule and had no administrative or political power over the Arab majority or other minorities. Within this framework, they developed their own institutions and political leadership, as well as paramilitary organizations, on the basis of civic participation.

The Hebrew settlement discourse that developed in the Jewish society of late Ottoman and Mandatory Palestine was nonetheless heavily influenced by Western Orientalism and colonial conceptions. Jews' identification with Western civilization, technology, and progress was a central theme that highlighted the contrast between their settlements and those of the Arabs. Zionist immigrants expressed their belief that they served as the carriers of modernity to Palestine and suggested that their settlements would contribute to the economic, technological, and cultural development of the country in a way that would benefit the Arab population as well. In his 1902 utopian novel *Altneuland*, Theodor Herzl expressed this view, and it was reiterated by Max Nordau and others during the early decades of the twentieth century.[5] Ben-Gurion and Ben-Zvi, writing to a Jewish audience abroad, emphasized that the Zionist immigrants' workmanship and entrepreneurship had transformed Jaffa and its surroundings above "the general backwardness of the country."[6] Jews saw the Arabs' use of homemade implements such as a light nail plow, a sickle, a threshing board, and two sieves as similar to the implements used in biblical times. They looked down on the Arab *fellahin* (farmers) as practicing old, primitive cultivation methods, and Jewish experts dismissed Arab agriculture as irrational and inefficient. Yet Jews also watched Arab farmers and learned from their practices, as well as from the experience of the German Templers who arrived in the late 1860s in fulfillment of their religious beliefs and established several colonies, combining European cultivation methods with local practices in their rural settlements.[7]

Descriptions of the Palestinian landscape outside the Jewish settlements as barren and neglected and the dismissive attitude toward existing Arab agriculture are examples of the selective representation of the reality in Palestine. The historian Beshara Doumani demonstrates the existence of developed economies of cotton and olive oil in Jabal Nablus that led to export and trade connections in the region as well as with Europe during the eighteenth and nineteenth centuries.[8] Other studies show that in the late Ottoman period, when the first waves of Zionist immigration to Palestine took place, the cultivation of citrus expanded along the entire coastal plain from Gaza to Haifa and into the Jordan Valley, and in 1915 Jews owned only about a third of the area planted in citrus groves.[9] Exports of oranges and other fruit made up close to half of the total value of exports from Jaffa, Palestine's principal port, and the large majority of the orange export (72%) drew on Arab groves.[10] The noticeable expansion of citrus growing and of agricultural production during the British Mandate led to the expansion of olive, orange, and grain exports from Palestine to Britain and Europe, as well as to northern Syria.[11] Studies indicate that both Arabs and Jews contributed to this development, and it was only in the 1930s that the Jews' citrus groves slightly surpassed those of the Arabs in size, while the Arabs' grain cultivation continued to exceed that of the Jews.[12]

Land purchase provided a legal foundation for the establishment of Jewish settlements in Palestine, which were led by Jewish agencies and through private acquisition.[13] Yet when the land was purchased from absentee landowners, that meant that the Arab *fellahin* who lived on that land and cultivated it were displaced by the Jews who were intent on settling there and working the land themselves. The historian Rashid Khalidi regards the peasants' resistance to the Jewish settlement as an expression of Palestinian identity and national consciousness.[14] While Jewish settlers of the First Aliyah, who arrived in the late nineteenth century, employed Arab laborers in their colonies, as was the traditional practice of landlords in Palestine, the Socialist Zionist Jewish workers of the Second and Third Aliyot promoted a campaign for "Hebrew Labor," directed against the hiring of Arab workers by Jews. The advocacy of Hebrew Labor, which was integral to the Socialist Zionist ideology of self-reliance and a direct physical engagement with the land, meant reduced opportunities for Palestine's Arabs of employment by Jewish land owners.[15] The campaign to buy only "Hebrew products," although not altogether successful, similarly worked to the economic detriment of the Arabs.[16] As the sociologist Gershon Shafir argues, the seeds of the Israeli-Palestinian conflict can be found in those labor policies that contributed to the formation of parallel Arab and Jewish economies.[17] Even in the area of citrus exports, where more collaboration had once existed between Arab and Jewish owners, they went separate ways in the 1930s.[18] Furthermore, some critical assessments of the impact of Jews' technological advantage over Palestinian Arabs note that the Jewish settlers' technological innovations did not necessarily help the Arab *fellahin* and that the development of Arabs' crop cultivation was, rather, a result of projects and reforms introduced by the British government.[19]

Although rural settlement remained a key trope of Hebrew settlement discourse, most Jewish immigrants to Palestine chose to settle in an urban environment. Among those who arrived from 1905 to 1913, 38% lived in Jerusalem and Hebron, 36% in Jaffa, and only 16% settled in the Jewish colonies.[20] By 1931, only 19% of the Jews in Palestine lived in agricultural settlements,[21] most of those in privately owned settlements.[22] Jewish immigration made a most significant contribution to the development of urban life in Palestine, yet Hebrew culture emphasized Jews' rural settlements. Zionist iconography, influenced by European conceptions of rural landscapes, displayed the iconic rural settlement marked by its red-roofed white houses and the water tower and surrounded by plowed fields, orchards, or blossoming gardens (see figure 10, later in this chapter).[23] The "greening" of the landscape, which emerged as a central trope of settlement discourse, was used to indicate the success in restoring the country's desolate desert landscape to a healthier state. An upbeat song thus hails the pioneers' labor and cultivation of the land as lightening up the landscape with a "green flame."[24] A 1938 story, reprinted in a geography textbook from 1945, compares the Arab and Jewish landscapes:

> Our fields are cleared of stones, fertilized, plowed in depth, and theirs are covered with many stones and their soil is used up. Our village is green with trees, surrounded by a strong fence, and built of concrete. Their houses are gray, without windows, and colorless, and only dusty olive trees can be spotted in the village.[25]

Other narratives similarly compare the earlier symbolic desert, which was embodied by barren land, swamps, and sand dunes, to the cultivated Jewish settlements, where "hundreds of houses and thousands of trees cover the land, and thousands of people . . . are living, working, building, and creating."[26] A later poem about the Negev desert depicts the working hands of young men and women as "weaving a green carpet to cover the naked desert."[27] A settlement novel similarly provides the idyllic vision of a rural settlement in the Negev: "We'll have plenty of trees here, and grass, and houses, with red roofs, and you know, green fences, and the sprinkler will spin, and birds."[28]

The nature-culture dichotomy that was often applied to the opposition between the symbolic landscapes of the desert and the settlement was clearly formulaic and fraught with internal contradictions. Eliezer Smoli's 1933 novel *Frontiersmen of Israel* provides an example. The novel describes the Jewish guard's vision of his future farm: "we'll plant figs and vines here in the winter, and turn this *barren countryside* into a *Garden of Eden*."[29] This vision is particularly striking given the earlier description of the lushness of the forested landscape in that area, which he now redefines as "barren," and given the existence of fig trees in that landscape before their arrival, the fruits of which the family has already enjoyed. The new farmer elaborates on his plans:

This is the kind of life we'll make for ourselves. . . . We'll turn these *barren valleys* into *gardens of Eden.* They'll be covered with corn and barley, oats and hay, and we'll plant vineyards and orchards on the hillsides in place of these thorns and thistles. We shall have to drain the marshes to get rid of the mosquitoes and then turn them into vegetable patches.[30]

The settler's vision of his future farm thus focuses on the very process of cultivation, the act of planting and seeding that transforms the same plant or tree from part of wild nature into part of the civilized land. Friends who visit the family on their isolated farm similarly refer to the wild nature of the area as a "desolate desert."[31] In using this idiom, they are not implying that the land is arid and unfit for cultivation, but rather use it rhetorically to underscore their concern about a single Jewish family living in the wilderness and away from other Jewish settlements.

The planting of forests emerged as an early instrument of the settlement mission and as an icon of national renewal. The multivalent symbolism of trees further supported their use as a fund-raising tool and a marker of ownership. Tree planting thus embodied the ideal of putting down roots in the land and the vision of regeneration, but it was also tied to the symbolism of the forest as a living memorial, which was popular in European cultures and embraced in Zionist circles abroad and in Hebrew culture in Palestine.[32] Indeed, Theodor Herzl, the leader and first president of the Zionist Organization, planted a tree near Jerusalem as a symbolic gesture of renewal on his visit to Palestine in 1898.[33] The Jewish National Fund (JNF), which the Zionist Organization established in 1901, at its fifth congress, to promote the purchase of land in Palestine, began a tree-planting campaign for its fund-raising efforts. The planting of "Herzl Forest" in 1908 and "Balfour Forest" in 1928 are prime examples of the memorialization of prominent figures in Zionist history during the early Yishuv period, and the practice of memorializing individuals or entire communities has continued. The association of trees with renewal was central to the JNF's publicity and visual representations. Thus, its Hebrew book series for youth, *La-No'ar*, featured a tree stump sprouting new growth; and in the aftermath of the Holocaust, a JNF poster for the "Forest of Martyred Children" featured the fading images of the dead children hovering above the trees that represent them.[34] Another poster, for the Zionist Federation, presents a more optimistic image, of a full tree with one dead branch, and the inscription reinforces this message: "Branches of our people are chopped down and fall off, but the tree is alive and well. Give your hand to our national renewal. Be a member of the Zionist Federation."[35]

The afforestation mission was linked to the Zionist decline narrative and the notion that the Land of Israel had once been covered by forests that were later destroyed by the Arabs and the Turks. Within this view, forest planting implied "reforestation" and contributed to the mission to restore the landscape to its earlier, greener state. Afforestation also had an important pragmatic legal value: Ottoman laws recognized trees as markers of land ownership, and in the face of limited resources and where settlement conditions were most challenging, forests provided a quick and relatively inexpensive means to claim Jewish ownership over purchased land.[36] Afforestation was a known means of land reclamation in colonial and nation-building projects in the twentieth century, and the British mandatory authorities similarly advanced afforestation initiatives in Palestine.[37]

The JNF promoted the significance of planting forests and of the settlement agenda more broadly, and was particularly keen on developing educational materials that supported its mission.[38] During the pre-state period, Zionist educators and mnemonic agents employed the cultural strategy of inventing new holiday traditions in order to advance their national-historical or symbolic value,[39] and in a similar vein, the celebration of a minor Jewish festival, Tu Bishvat (the fifteenth of the Hebrew month Shevat), shifted toward tree-planting as its major ritual.[40] The JNF's educational materials presented planting as a patriotic ritual that advanced "the redemption of the homeland," and children's lore for Tu Bishvat further highlighted the close symbolic link between trees and children as representing the ideal of a national rebirth.[41]

As Penslar's *Zionism and Technocracy* shows, theories of human progress and technocratic visions that were popular in Europe at the end of the nineteenth century, as well as projects of internal colonialism and nation-building, influenced Zionist leaders and shaped the Zionist Organization's policies and practices in Palestine in the late Ottoman period. The modernist discourse of progress, with its emphasis on the power of technology and machines, the importance of industrialization, and the role of experts in engineering these projects, became more pronounced in the era following World War I; it was used in support of European colonialism but also Fascist and Soviet ideologies.[42] Experts played an important role in advancing the Zionist settlement agenda and in establishing training farms in accordance with the need perceived by the Palestine Office of the Zionist Organization, directed by Arthur Ruppin, to prepare newcomers for engaging in agriculture from the earliest phases of Zionist settlement in Palestine, although the European ideas and methods imposed by expert agronomists did not always fit the local conditions and sometimes clashed with the settlers' convictions or needs.[43]

These themes emerged more fully in Hebrew settlement discourse after the 1920s. Socialist Zionist immigrants, most notably those of the Third Aliyah who had participated in the Russian revolutionary movement and experienced the early years of the Soviet Union before their arrival in Palestine, advanced the ideology of labor, the formation of "workers' battalions," and the admiration of technology.[44] The kibbutzim, the Federation of Workers' Unions (*histadrut ha-ovdim ha-kelalit*), youth movements, and Hebrew schools participated in the production of educational materials and expressive forms that articulated these ideas as part of the settlement vision. The Hebrew settlement lore of that period glorified the pioneers who toiled on the land and engaged in construction projects.

Like the land, work tools and machines were anthropomorphized and presented as willing participants in the settlement mission. A popular song of the 1930s addresses "the shovel, the pickaxe, the hoe, and pitchfork" and calls upon them to "unite in a storm,"[45] as if they were active agents of progress. Other texts address hammers and nails, sprinklers and water pipes, tractors and bulldozers, cranes and drilling machines, or sing the praises of construction materials such as bricks, cement, and concrete.[46] Nathan Alterman, a prominent Hebrew poet of the late pre-state and early state periods, wrote the lyrics for "The Road Song" (1934), focusing on the intensive labor of road construction and its role in combating the desert.[47] The speaker, a road builder, first addresses his work instrument, the hammer, and encourages its participation in the physical task of constructing the road: "Hit hard, hammer, rise up and go down / As we stretch roads of concrete in the sand." The speaker then turns to the wasteland (*shemama*), using the feminine form of the desert: "Wake up, wasteland, your verdict is decided / We are coming to conquer you!"

The harsh-sounding Hebrew words and the staccato-like rhythm reproduce the controlled and powerful movements of the worker's hand that holds the hammer. The poem goes on to describe the hot asphalt, the heavy machinery, and the demanding physical effort of performing this task that has made the worker's hand bleed. The speaker's voice becomes belligerent as he announces the goal of conquering the wasteland. The poem shifts its focus from the individual worker and his tool to the collective character of the action ("we are coming") and ends with a sweeping statement about mankind's struggle against the desert. Similarly, song lyrics by the poet Lea Goldberg focus on the building of the Tel Aviv port in the mid-1930s. The "Port Song" she wrote alludes to the collective effort of "thousands of hands" engaged in "the conquest of the shore and the wave" and highlights the materials (the concrete) and machinery (the crane) employed in this process. The lyrics praise the workers, their tools, and the construction materials as participants in the building of the port.[48]

The veneration of the construction process and materials went even farther in Nathan Alterman's lyrics for "Morning Song," composed in 1933. This song addresses the homeland and describes the various types of settlement activities performed for its future, ranging from plowing and planting to building and road construction. The speaker defines these activities as expressions of patriotic love and reassures the homeland that "Even if the road is difficult and treacherous / If more than one dies on the way, / We will love you forever, the homeland / We're committed to you in the battle and in labor." The speaker then poses the workers' promise to the homeland that "We'll dress you in a gown of concrete and cement,"[49] turning these mundane substances into beautifying agents that adorn the landscape.

"Morning Song" belongs to the canonic repertoire of the "songs of the Land of Israel" characteristic of the pre-state and early-state periods.[50] Yet as we shall see in chapter 6, supporters of the environmental discourse later rejected its glorifying reference to "a gown of concrete and cement" as symbolic of the excesses of the settlement ethos in Israeli culture. At the time, however, the glorification of mundane building materials and work tools was as central to the settlement mission as marking Jewish agricultural produce as "Hebrew," a term that transformed fruits and vegetables "from everyday objects to national symbols."[51]

Hebrew grade-school textbooks highlighted settlement as advancing the national goal of redeeming the land.[52] The Hebrew school curriculum included "knowledge of the land" (*yediat ha-aretz*, the Hebrew expression for homeland geography), nature, and agriculture, all considered subjects that promoted "love of the country" (*ahavat ha-aretz*).[53] Beyond their academic content, these classes also involved hands-on experiences for students, including educational trips, hiking expeditions, and the cultivation of the land through seeding and planting in school yards or nearby lots. The Zionist youth movements, which were highly popular during the late pre-state and early state periods, similarly promoted their members' commitment to establishing new kibbutzim or joining struggling settlements. The socialization and mobilization of youth in support of the settlement agenda thus advanced the Yishuv's nation-building efforts and settlement work.

The Desert, the Oasis, and the Island

The symbolic desert encompassed a vast array of landscapes, such as sand dunes and swamps, barren mountains and arid land, terrain filled with rocks, and wild nature that undermined or threatened the settlement process. The discursive act of addressing a specific terrain as a "desert" did not describe its physical conditions but rather related to it symbolically as a synecdoche,[54] a part that represents the country's broader state of desolation and decline. On the opposite end from the desert, symbolically, each new settlement (*yishuv*) constituted a building block in the process of reviving the Jewish homeland and a synecdoche that represented the larger Yishuv (the Settlement). Tel Aviv's mythical origin story provides a fascinating example of the role of the symbolic desert in settlement discourse. As the cultural geographer Maoz Azaryahu shows, the mythical narrative highlights Tel Aviv's emergence from the "sea of sand" as an act of creation ex nihilo. In Azaryahu's words, the story marks "the victory of civilization and progress over the desert that represents the combination of wild nature and backwardness."[55]

As we saw above, the settlement narrative constructs a zero-sum relationship that leaves the boundaries between settlement and desert inherently in flux and subject to opposing pressures. Yitzhak Ben-Zvi presented the decline narrative in these terms: "When the land was conquered by desert tribes, camel drivers, and shepherds, the desert once more *pushed back* the cultivated land. Settlement *shrank* and the wasteland *expanded*."[56] Similarly, a Hebrew geography textbook refers to the conflict between the desert and the settlement but also notes the positive implications for the settlement process: "The boundaries of the desert are never fixed since an industrious people would enlarge and expand its settlement and turn the desolate desert into a flourishing garden."[57]

After the Ottoman authorities had evacuated the Jews from Tel Aviv during World War I, Rachel Yanait Ben-Zvi sadly noted that the city was overrun by stray cats and jackels and covered by sand. "The new, polished Tel-Aviv with its clean streets and green gardens," she laments, "seemed as if it had been deserted for generations, appearing like a desert."[58] The desert is thus portrayed as an aggressive force of nature that can always retake the settlement. But when the settlement aggressively pursues its goal to colonize the desert, the process is defined in positive terms. Tel Aviv's houses are thus described as the "walking camp of a conquering army" that made the wasteland withdraw and the jackals retreat, and the city is described as an ever-expanding island that extends into the sea of sands.[59] The fluidity of the boundaries between the desert and the settlement thus requires the settlers to remain vigilant in order to protect their achievements and prevent a potential reversal, making the city's residents highly aware of "the last houses" that demarcate its border with the sands.[60]

The visual and literary representations of settlement reveal the use of different strategies to enhance its achievements. A major strategy presents the settlement within an environment of symbolic absence, obscuring neighboring Arab neighborhoods or cultivated land. Avraham Soskin's canonical photograph of a lot-drawing meeting of the founders of Ahuzat Bayit, later renamed Tel Aviv (figure 8), shows them standing huddled together in the sand and surrounded by sand dunes, with nothing else on the horizon. The sand was undoubtedly there, but so was the town of Jaffa with its major port,

יסוד תל-אביב - טקס הגרלת המגרשים. כ' ניסן תרס"ט (11 באפריל 1909)

FIGURE 8. Tel Aviv founders' meeting in the sand dunes (April 11, 1909). Photo by Avraham Soskin, the Soskin Collection; Collection © Muza, Eretz Israel Museum, Tel Aviv.

neighborhoods, and commercial institutions. Ahuzat Bayit was founded as a Jewish neighborhood of Jaffa, and not even its first one. Only in the 1920s and 1930s did Tel Aviv shape its distinctive identity and culture as the first Hebrew city.[61] The photo, however, became a mnemonic tool that helped to define this meeting retrospectively as marking "the birth of Tel Aviv," and its visual framing affirms the theme of "a city built on the desolate desert sand."[62] The image of Tel Aviv surrounded by sands also reveals the "rules of irrelevance" that defined the space outside the Jewish settlement as a symbolic desert. This tunnel vision,[63] focusing on the Jewish settlement, brackets out the vibrant urban life of nearby Jaffa, the citrus groves and cultivated land, as if they were irrelevant to this framework. A recent cartoon demonstrates the imprint of this image, as further discussed in the epilogue (see figure 32 in the epilogue).

A similar tendency to focus attention on the Jewish settlements and obscure the Arab villages or towns coexisting in that space may be found in Zionist anthologies of the time and in settlement museums.[64] In the same vein, the JNF directs the writer of a settlement narrative to emphasize the desolation and neglect prior to the arrival of the Zionist pioneers and to highlight the quick change that the Jewish settlement produced.[65] Alternatively, Arabs and their spaces are presented as a framing device to compare and enhance the achievements of the Jewish settlements.[66] Early Zionist films show the Arabs working in the background, as if they were part of the natural landscape. Helmar Lerski's *Avodah* (Labor), the first feature-length Jewish film produced in Palestine, in 1935, presents Arabs riding donkeys or working in the fields at the beginning, yet they soon fade out as the film shifts its focus to the building of the Zionist settlement. The film *The Land of Promise*, mentioned above, similarly focuses on the Zionist settlement process.[67]

The use of the oasis and the island as metaphors for the settlement underscored its contrast with the surrounding desert. Hebrew settlement narratives depict the settlement as embedded within a large desert or "sea of sands" that surrounds it. This metaphor also appears in Theodor Herzl's fictional description of a visit to the Jewish colonies:

> The next morning Kingscourt and Friedrich . . . drove out to the colonies. They looked at Rishon Le-Zion, Rehobot, and other villages that lay like *oases* in the *desolate countryside*.[68]

The writer and publicist Ahad Ha'am, who visited Palestine in 1891, later described the Jewish visitor's tour of the Jewish colonies with a note of irony, pointing out the perception of these new Jewish settlements as islands surrounded by the desert:

> This Jew moves from one *moshava* [colony] to another, and at times those are separated by a journey of many hours, and fields and villages of non-Jews fill all that space, but he sees this in-between space *as if it were an empty desert* devoid of human beings. And after that "desert," the settlement appears, and he can breathe again the national Hebrew air that revives his soul.[69]

A geography textbook published in Europe in 1918 refers to Tel Aviv as "the jewel in the crown of the new Jewish Yishuv, a European oasis in an Asian desert."[70] "Like an oasis, the scores of eye-pleasing Jewish colonies appeared amongst the hundreds of Arab villages," Aharon Ever Hadani writes.[71] A kibbutz member in the Jezreel Valley notes in 1936 the feeling of being on "a desert island in the hateful sea of the desert tribes," and another kibbutz member refers to the early Jewish settlements in the Negev desert as "tiny islands" within a "sea of Bedouins and Arabs."[72]

The use of "oasis" and "island" as spatial metaphors dramatizes their structural resemblance. Both represent a relatively small territory that is distinguished from a seemingly vast and open space surrounding it, be that the desert or the sea.[73] Furthermore, both the island and the oasis provide a refuge from the potential threat to one's survival, yet the state of being encircled by the desert or the sea might produce an experience of isolation or besiegement. The analogy between the ocean and the desert also underlies such expressions as the camel's nickname as "the ship of the desert" or references to the "sea of sand." In spite of these commonalities, however, there is a critical difference between the two metaphors. While an oasis presents a certain continuity with the desert terrain, an island carves out a distinct entity of land that is dramatically different from the water that surrounds it. The island therefore provides a sharp contrast with the forces of nature that surround it, and its insularity allows it to develop its own identity and culture independently of other places. This may explain why islands have been seen as idyllic territories, the places to rediscover the lost Garden of Eden, and why the English philosopher Thomas More chose to place his utopian society (*Utopia*, 1516) on an island.[74]

This difference may account for the greater frequency of use of the island as a spatial metaphor for the Jewish settlement. The island underscores the theme of its distinctiveness from its Middle Eastern environment and evokes its inhabitants' dual experience of refuge and besiegement. Literary allusions to Robinson Crusoe, Defoe's famous castaway Englishman who found refuge on an untamed island, reveal both the interpretation of the Land of Israel as a place of refuge and the Orientalist perspective that defines the European castaway as culturally superior to the local native he finds on the island and includes the desire to introduce civilization to the island. Moshe Smilansky, thus, refers to the early settlers' "oppressive Robinsonian feeling . . . that they were cast away on a desolate and isolated island";[75] and in *Frontiersmen of Israel*, the visiting friend of the settler family observes that they live "just like Robinson Crusoe."[76]

Literary and artistic representations of the Zionist settlement articulate the settlers' sense of besiegement by the desert and its natural and human agents such as the sand, the heat, the jackals, and the Arabs. As night falls and darkness envelops the settlement, the sense of besiegement by the surrounding desert forces may become more acute. Amos Oz depicts a kibbutz settlement surrounded by a fence behind which the jackals, the vicious agents of the desert, lurk:

> Round about they creep, . . . a ring of tremulous jackals circling at the edges of the shadow, closing in on the island of light. Until morning they fill the air with wailing, and their hunger shatters in successive waves upon the shores of the fenced, lighted island.[77]

In Smoli's *Frontiersmen of Israel*, jackals are similarly described as encircling a family's wagon during their first night on the frontier, as the father remains awake and watchful to prevent them from breaking into the wagon.[78] Years later, the poet Hamutal Bar-Yosef writes about her memories of besiegement by the destructive agents of the symbolic desert: "The jackals of my childhood return to surround / The thin shutters of the old shackle / With the poisonous malaria and overflowing fury / An endless circle of desolation and destruction."[79] The specific home may be seen as standing in for the besieged settlement and the Yishuv as a whole, surrounded by the agents of the desert and the dark forces of the counter-place that threaten the home's safety. The literature of the Israeli frontier thus echoes the cultural trope of an island of light that stands in marked contrast to the dark forces surrounding it, a recurrent theme in the literature of the American frontier as well.[80]

During the late Ottoman period, new Jewish settlements were built with a growing awareness of security issues, but they were not typically surrounded by a defensive wall.[81] The increased instability in the aftermath of World War I and the escalation of national tensions during the British mandatory period enhanced the security concerns of Yishuv society, leading to the organization of the Labor-affiliated *Hagana* (The Defense) underground in 1920. The concentric layout of the first cooperative *moshav*, Nahalal, which was established in the Jezreel valley in 1921, was noted for its "clear defensive design."[82] The Zionist leader Ze'ev (Vladimir) Jabotinsky's essay "On the Iron Wall (We and the Arabs)," published in 1923, advocated that the Jews of Palestine rely more on the use of force. "Settlement can develop under the protection of a force," he argued, "which is not dependent on the local population, *behind an iron wall* which they will be powerless to break down."[83] Like the "island" metaphor, his use of the "iron wall" was a figure of speech that articulated his demand for greater emphasis on military power. Jabotinsky's position, which was radical at the time, clearly shaped his followers' views, but it may have also influenced the views of other Jewish leaders.[84]

Starting in the 1930s, in response to the 1929 riots and to the Arab Revolt of 1936–39, the discourses of settlement and security became more closely intertwined and their agendas more urgent, staking out territory in frontier areas to ensure the best position possible for a future partition of Palestine. Although frontier settlements largely pursued the vision of establishing agricultural communities, security needs played a critical role in determining their location, and turned these rural settlements into "military outposts."[85] In a quasi-military operation, sixty new settlements were established in frontier areas during the Arab Revolt of 1936–39. Most of the new settlements followed the "tower and stockade" (*homa u-migdal*) model, which consisted of a core settlement made out of prefabricated structures, including a watchtower surrounded by a wooden fence with double walls reinforced with small stones and sand and an additional barbed fence.[86] The new model thus enhanced the island metaphor, highlighting the settlement's need to protect itself from possible attacks from the outside. The duality of work and defense was preserved in the mission of the Labor-oriented *Palmach* underground of the 1940s, whose members lived and worked on kibbutzim, partly as a suitable cover for their military activities.[87] Following the establishment of the state, this dual emphasis led to the formation of *NAHAL* (an acronym for "pioneering combat youth") as a distinct framework within the Israel Defense Forces (IDF) that combined combat training with building (or joining) a frontier settlement.[88]

FIGURE 9. *Eretz* by Pessach Irsai (1930s). © Copyright Istvan Pessach Irsai. All rights reserved to the Irsai Estate and his daughter Miryam Sommerfeld; photo from the collection of David Tartakover.

Gendered Landscapes

A painting by Pessach (Istvan) Irsai from the 1930s (figure 9) presents a layered landscape: in the foreground it features the outline of a camel's head and long neck; behind that, a barren, transparent hill; and in the back, behind both, a modern building created in the international style of the 1930s. Next to the building, the Hebrew word "*Eretz,*" an abbreviated reference to *Eretz Israel* (the Land of Israel), is written in boldly stylized geometrical letters.

The outline of the camel's neck and head stretching along the front of the painting represents the domain of the symbolic desert, while the massive building at the back represents the modern Jewish settlement. In between, the silhouette of the barren hill, with its tiny Oriental structure, a palm tree, a cactus, and angular tents typical of the Zionist pioneering period, represents the transition between the two.[89] The delicate outline of the camel and the smooth round hill with its domed structure invoking the image of the female breast highlight the effeminate features of the Oriental landscape. By contrast, the modern building, positioned at an angle that accentuates its straight lines and geometrical shapes, projects the power and potency associated with masculine forms. The light projected onto a part of the building pulls the eye toward it through the transparent images. While the transparency of the camel and the hill suggests their ephemeral quality, the massive building projects solidity and durability and implies its continuing presence into the future.

One of the iconic markers of the Jewish settlement is the straight lines or geometrical forms that govern its houses, planted trees, and roads. These formations represent the cultivated place that introduced order, rationality, and advanced technology into the chaotic desert environment and its curved, feminine lines.[90] Ze'ev Yavetz notes how easy it was to spot a Jewish settlement from a distance thanks to its "two lines of snow-white houses with bright red roofs, seen among the green trees planted in front of them in a straight line."[91] A visitor to the early colonies similarly describes the contrast between "walking in this desolate land . . . with no paved roads" and sighting "the paved paths and the striking colonies with their beautiful houses and wide, straight streets."[92] The straight boulevards of Tel Aviv emerged as a source of pride for the city's "European look."[93] A novel about the industrialization of the desert (to which I will return below) notes the introduction of a network of straight lines into the open landscape as a measure of progress,[94] and settlement images often featured the straight lines of the plowed fields. A JNF poster (figure 10) further accentuates the straight lines of the field, featuring a pipe bringing water to the Negev in the foreground. The inscription refers to "the fulfillment of the vision of the Negev" that brings "redemption and water for the desolate land."

The planting of orchards in straight lines also had practical value, since it provided easier access for machines,[95] but the imposition of straight lines on a supposedly wild landscape also carried a moral value, as Isaiah's prophecy

notes: "A voice cries in the wilderness, prepare ye the way of the Lord, make straight in the desert a highway for our God" (Isaiah 40:3). The leveled plane and the straight line thus serve as visual emblems of a moral order that transforms the symbolic desert and its chaotic character. It also reinforces the positive connotations of technological progress that the Jewish settlement represents.

The gendered landscapes of the Jewish settlement and the symbolic desert articulate the Zionist focus on the male Jew: the New Hebrew was constructed as a male figure endowed with a strong, muscular body, compared to the effeminate stereotype of the exilic Jew.[96] The conflictual desert-settlement relations placed men at the center, as those who engage in the war against the desert, positioning females in support-

FIGURE 10. "The Negev Vision," 1948, Poster by Franz Krausz. Courtesy of Michael Krausz. The Central Zionist Archives (KRA\65).

ing roles. Although women joined pioneering groups and participated in the settlement process, the male *halutz* occupied center stage as the potent agent of change.[97] The visual image of Zionist laborers marching forward shouldering their work tools as one would shoulder weapons highlights the symbolic framework of a battle against the desert (figure 11). Such representations, also typical of Soviet art, were common during the 1930s and the 1940s and continued to be prominent in the early decades of statehood.[98]

The male engineer emerged as a heroic figure, leading the industrialization of the country, which was part of the settlement's struggle against the desert. Pinchas Rutenberg, who built the Jewish electric company in

Palestine in the early 1920s, inspired "The Network Song" (1934), which praises "the old man of Naharayim" as a visionary who transformed the symbolic desert space "where there was nothing" into a place where "there is

electricity."[99] Rutenberg also inspired the writer Ever Hadani (Aharon Feldman) to write a two-volume novel, *The Arava Project*, constructing the heroic character of the engineer.[100] The novel presents its protagonist as a prophet of industrialization, a charismatic figure, and a strong-willed leader who is determined to build a new industry in the desert against all odds. *The Arava Project* describes the construction work in the Dead Sea region as an attack on the desert and "a ruthless war," in which the engineer's employees are called "the workers' army."[101] In spite of the challenges of working in the extreme heat and difficult conditions of the desert terrain, as well as others' failure to appropriately support his work, the engineer ultimately prevails.[102] Aharon Megged's story "The Abyss on the Way to Sodom" returns to the character of the charismatic engineer whose vision and strong personality guide the construction of a new road to the Dead Sea. The project, first dismissed as sheer "craziness," ultimately becomes a reality.[103]

FIGURE 11. "Mobilize to Labor" poster designed by Rudi Dayan. Courtesy of The Rudi Dayan Collection and The Neri Bloomfield Haifa School of Design & Education, and the Netanya Municipal Archive; photo from "Time Travel," Ephemera Collection at The National Library of Israel.

The Hebrew language also contributed to the emergence of a gendered settlement discourse. The grammatical identification of man (*adam*) and pioneer (*halutz*) as masculine, and country (*eretz*), land or soil (*adama*), and homeland (*moledet*) as feminine introduces gendered relations that evoke sexual allusions.[104] Analyzing pioneers' descriptions of their personal encounters with the land and its soil, the historian Boaz Neumann demonstrates this dimension of the *halutzim*'s discourse. The pioneers allude to their desire to penetrate the virgin land and describe how their bodily fluids pour into the soil as they passionately engage in working the land.[105] When the Hebrew poet Esther Raab writes about her father's first experience of plowing a field, she refers to him as the one "Who plows the furrow in spite of the desert / Who is first to *break open the virgin land*."[106] A pioneer of the Third Aliyah describes his longing, "almost a physical desire," to experience "the feeling of *conquest*, and the *plow penetrating the virgin land*."[107] Yet another settler notes that "the land lay in its virginity. For dozens of years the pin of a plow had not penetrated it."[108] The writer Moshe Smilansky offers an analogy between the desire to know the land and the desire for an intimate relationship with a woman, and a kibbutz founder refers to the establishment of a new settlement in terms of "becoming engaged" to the land.[109] The multivalent expression *yediat ha-aretz* (literally, the knowledge of the land), mentioned earlier, encompasses the biblical connotation of the verb "to know" as having sexual relations.[110] The frequent references to the land as "virgin," to the settlement process as "conquest," and to the settlers' work as "penetrating" and "awakening" the land reveal the gendered and sexual dimensions of the settlement discourse.

The identification of the land as a "desert" nonetheless changes the gendered framework, since the most common Hebrew term for desert, *midbar*, is grammatically marked as masculine, and the same applies to its more literary synonym, *yeshimon*. The conflict between the settlement and the desert is therefore portrayed as a conflict between males and involves an unmasked power struggle and aggressive use of force. Other Hebrew nouns referring to the "desert" or "wasteland" (such as *arava*, *tsiya*, and *shemama*), however, are feminine, and their use opens a space for introducing an alternative gendered framework. Thus, for example, the allusion to barren hills as a woman's breasts or to dunes and smooth rocks as invoking the curves of a female body introduces an erotic dimension into the perception of the desert.[111] In the novel *The Arava Project*, mentioned above, a bourgeois woman falls for the male engineer and sees the *arava* as her competitor in attracting his attention; she ultimately feels defeated by it. The novel also refers to a male worker who "opens the lock" of the *arava*, invariably suggesting a sexual allusion to this act of conquest of the desert.[112] Avraham Shlonsky's 1929 poem "Facing the Desert" illustrates the conflation of a gendered relationship with the theme of conquest and subordination. The poem refers to a male Jewish worker who triumphantly confronts a camel caravan, announcing to it, "I've overpowered you today." He further warns that the caravan is going to be mobilized to help the Jewish workers construct their settlement.[113] The framing device of placing the Arabs at the margins of the pioneers' settlement work as passive or fearful bystanders, mentioned earlier, also highlights the dynamism associated with the Zionist male figure and the Jewish settlement in relation to them.[114]

Settlement Narratives and War Rhetoric

Hebrew settlement narratives highlight the conflictual framework that marks settlement-desert relations, depicting the settlement process in terms of a struggle to transform the counter-place into a cultivated Jewish place. Settlement discourse used Hebrew vocabulary that denotes a state of conflict and struggle and alludes to its outcome as a victory or defeat. During the early decades of the twentieth century, a favorite expression of the Socialist Zionist pioneers was *kibbush*—a multivalent term that implied success in overcoming a challenge, restraint of a negative urge, or military conquest.[115] The success of the Jewish settlement was defined in terms of "the conquest of the desert" (*kibbush ha-midbar*) or "the conquest of the wasteland" (*kibbush ha-shemama*), and a range of challenging landscapes were seen as obstacles to the settlement process and hence belonging to the symbolic desert: the barren mountains, the poisonous swamps, and even the sea.[116] The concept of "conquest" similarly appeared in relation to labor, guarding, and shepherding, to denote Jews' mastery of challenging tasks in the process of promoting the settlement agenda, and was similarly applied to the cultural domain.[117] The term did not literally imply a military conquest but it provided the template of struggle and victory, and the frequency of these expressions within the settlement discourse of the early decades of the twentieth century contributed to the development of the conflictual framework of settlement-desert relations.

As the national tensions in Palestine built up, it became common for the discourses of settlement and defense to be merged.[118] Proto-military expressions used by the Socialist Zionist pioneers included "conquest groups" (*kvutsot kibbush*) and "work battalion" (*gedud ha-avodah*), as well as the "conquest points" (*nekudot kibbush*) and "observation outposts" (*mitzpim*) that marked an early phase of settlement.[119] The military rhetoric of the settlement narratives was manifested in such concepts as war, battle, struggle, assault, retreat, yielding, conquest, victory, and defeat. A *Ha-Shomer* member reflects: "from the beginning, our goal was *the war against the desert*," and then adds: "we were confident that we would *win* in spite of all obstacles; that building and creating would ultimately *prevail over* the desert and the desolate land."[120] The predominant Socialist Zionist ideology advanced the image of the *halutz* holding the plow and the gun as complementary tools in the war against the desert. In the 1930s debate over the legacy of Yosef Trumpeldor, who had died in the defense of a Jewish frontier settlement in 1920, the Socialist Zionists emphasized his double commitment to work and defense, while the Revisionist Zionists highlighted his military heroism and leadership.[121]

Like the narratives of the American frontier that emphasize the conflictual relationship with the wilderness, Hebrew settlement narratives fight the symbolic desert in the name of progress, morality, and civilization. As the historian Roderick Nash notes,

> In the morality play of westward expansion, wilderness was the villain, and the pioneer, as hero, relished its destruction. The transformation of a wilderness into civilization was the reward for his sacrifices, the definition of his achievement, and the source of his pride.[122]

The Hebrew settlement narrative of the pre-state and early state periods typically depicts a long and continuing struggle against the desert and its hostile natural and human agents. The settlers suffer from the lack of experience and inadequate resources, the scarcity of water, attacks by insects and animals, illnesses, and death. In spite of these challenges and repeated setbacks, however, they manage to make progress, thanks to their persistence and resourcefulness. The ability to survive those challenges and accomplish the settlement mission provides a personal and collective triumph and reaffirms the Zionist redemptive paradigm. The settlement narrative begins a process of confronting obstacles and overcoming challenges on the way to achieving success, thus echoing the deep structure of a heroic tale and positioning the settler as a hero.

The narrative presents the very decision to settle in a desolate and dangerous site as courageous, revealing the settlers' determination to face the battle against the desert forces. The centrality of the malarial swamps in the settlement narratives stands as a central icon of the counter-place. Thus, Shmuel Dayan describes how he and his friends scouted an area of the Jezreel valley in 1921 for their new settlement and were shocked to see the many graves of Germans and Arabs who had died of malaria there: "Death swarmed everywhere around us," he notes, "and down, around the hill, were the dark, cruel, and threatening swamps." In spite of this grim evidence and in defiance of the doctor's stern warnings not to pursue this venture, the group was determined to carry out its plan.[123] Nahalal became the first *moshav*, a cooperative agricultural settlement, and its founders' determination to proceed against all odds augments the narrative's moral lesson that courage, willpower, and persistence ultimately prevail in the war against the desert. Along similar lines, Yehudit Harari recalls the stories that she heard in her childhood from Hadera's founders about the difficulties and subsequent deaths brought by malaria, which they eventually overcame. She compares their unswaying resolve to stay on in spite of the risks with the attitude of the German settlers who had fled from that area.[124] In a similar spirit, Moshe Smilansky describes a Zionist pioneer who settles next to the ruins of a village north of the Sea of Galilee where earlier residents had died of malaria. The narrator marvels at the newcomers' decision to settle in that place: "How do these people have such courage and devotion?"[125]

The swamps became an iconic representation of the history of the settlement's battle against the hostile and destructive symbolic desert, along with other challenging terrains that the Jewish pioneers encountered. As summarized by a text from the early 1970s, which I quoted earlier, "our country *was still a desert*, barren rocks on the mountaintop and stinking swamps in the valley; death-bearing mosquitoes and thorns filled the entire country."[126] The swamps belonged to the "pathological landscape"[127] of the symbolic desert and as such were seen as the outcome of the abandonment and neglect from which the country suffered:

> In the ancient past, the valley was the storehouse of crops for the entire country, yet when the Jewish people were exiled from the country the land became deserted and the fertile valley was transformed into the site of poisonous swamps.[128]

As the literary scholar Eric Zakim points out, Hebrew settlement narratives demonstrate "the poetics of malaria" that highlight its "psychic condition of oppression" but also represent it as a transformative experience: Jewish settlers who recovered from malaria describe their experience as a rite of passage leading to their symbolic rebirth as natives of the land.[129]

Another major recurrent theme in the settlement narratives is the scarcity of water. Early settlement films of the 1930s, such as Alexander Ford's *Sabra*, Helmar Lerski's *Labor*, and Judah Leman's *Land of Promise*, feature the importance of the discovery of water, which ensures the future of the settlement. *Labor* further highlights this theme by dramatizing the impact of the lack of water on the members of a new Jewish settlement, and their growing despair following the failure of multiple drilling experiments. When their efforts finally succeed and water gushes out of the ground at a drilling site, men, women, and children run to the site to drink the water, singing and dancing with overwhelming joy. The discovery of water thus represents a critical turning point in the history of the settlement and highlights the importance of science and technology for its success. The film then features the Jewish settlers engaging in agricultural work, their cattle drinking water, and fields with ripe crops, underscoring the settlement's victory over the desert.[130]

The significance of water is also a recurring theme in songs and dances of the pre-state and early state periods. The highly popular song, based on Isaiah's verse "with joy you will draw water," and the dance "Water, Water" that was later composed for it, were among the iconic forms of this lore and are still central to Israeli culture.[131] A popular 1946 song, "You, the Land" (*At adama*), written by a member of kibbutz Revivim, an early settlement built in the Negev, addresses the desert land and its malaise: "You, the land / At the heart of the desert / Without the shade of a tree / Without rain." The monotonous melody, with its slow, heavy beat, augments the sense of immobility and lack of hope. The second stanza breaks through with a sudden burst of energy and an upbeat tune, as the speaker announces to the desert land: "We are coming to you, going southward," and leads to the description of the revival of the land, alluding to the workers' sweat as a metaphoric rain that awakens it.[132] The allusion to raindrops recaptures the meaning of the kibbutz's name, Revivim, and highlights the association of water with the promise of renewal.

In the context of an uphill struggle against multiple challenges, every step along the way represents a small victory that contributes to the settlement's success. A popular children's song about the JNF's mission of redeeming the land underscores the importance of proceeding step by step or, in the words of the song, "a clod after a clod" (*regev ahar regev*).[133] Another settlement narrative notes that "every portion of land from which stones are removed, every field that is plowed, implies a great achievement."[134] The birth of children, and most particularly of the "first son" of a new settlement, becomes another turning point that highlights the theme of growth and the future trajectory of the settlement.[135]

The novel *Frontiersmen of Israel*, mentioned earlier, is constructed as a sequence of tasks and challenges, with two strands interwoven into a single narrative. The first strand addresses the various phases of work and construction, including building a home, raising animals, plowing a field, seeding and planting, giving birth, and imposing a social order onto a wild and chaotic spaces as the settler attempts to colonize nature and transform it into a civilized place. The second and opposite strand highlights the obstacles and setbacks that the family experiences, which appear in the form of successive invasions of its space. The invading agents include forces of nature such as thunderstorms and wild animals, insects, and rodents that prey on their stock or damage their home and fields. The invasion also includes a range of people, such as Bedouin shepherds who enter the land with their herds, Arabs who steal wood from the forest, Ottoman government officials, and unsympathetic Jewish bureaucrats. But when a visiting friend appeals to the father to leave this dangerous outpost for the sake of his family, the latter dismisses his concerns. "I'm a soldier and the battle doesn't scare me," he answers. "On the contrary, it adds to my courage—and [what's more,] we'll win."[136]

Settlement narratives nonetheless disclose the toll that such hardships took on the settlers. Loneliness, frustration, and despair pushed many of the settlers to leave the struggling settlements for more secure urban environments or even to return to the Diaspora or, in the most radical cases, to commit suicide. Despite the Yishuv's overall demographic growth during the first decades of the twentieth century, the rate of Jewish emigration from Palestine was high and at times exceeded that of Jewish immigration to the country.[137] Works of fiction describing the early settlement process often include the despairing voices of those who give up, echoing the complaints of the "desert generation" in the biblical narrative. Aharon Ashman's 1942 play, "This Land," presents the drama of building a new settlement that includes the negative voice of a character who wishes to go back to Europe, though he dies of malaria before he can carry out this plan.[138] In the film "Sabra," a man complains that "it wasn't worthwhile to come here, to a land of desert and desolation and with no water," while another reaches the anguished conclusion that "the desert will never bloom" and proposes to others to run away from it, admitting that "I can't tolerate this anymore. . . . How much longer shall we suffer?"[139] The Nobel Laureate S. Y. Agnon, in his novel *Only Yesterday*, about the Second Aliyah period, describes a young man who gives up on the effort to find a job as an agricultural laborer and then chooses to work in an urban clothing shop, thereby regressing to his exilic occupation as a prelude to his subsequent return to Europe. Agnon's narrator ironically remarks that the young man left the Land of Israel as "others had done before him, and as others do after him, arriving as dreamers and departing as doers."[140]

In the overall redemptive framework of the Zionist settlement narrative, however, those failures are constructed as temporary setbacks that ultimately serve to augment the perseverance and determination of those who remained, as the key to the settlement's victory. In Baruch Agadati's 1935 film *This Is the Land* (*Zot hee ha-aretz*), when a pioneer dies while plowing the field, a fellow pioneer simply takes his place and resumes his activity. This continuing chain demonstrates that an individual's death does not represent a deterrent in the collective fulfillment of the settlement mission.[141] In the novel *Frontiersmen of Israel*, when Arabs destroy the family's farm by setting it on fire, the settler who witnesses the ruins of his hard work is overcome by grief and despair, which almost lead him to suicide that night. But when his elder son joins him in the morning and they tour the burnt grounds, the settler regains his resolve at the sight of his plow, and father and son begin to plow the burnt field in a symbolic act of renewal: "Slowly the plow moved forward, churning the black soil over and leaving behind a trail of freshly-turned earth. 'There, Eitan! We've opened a new furrow,'" the father says to his son, and the book ends with his final words: "*We should always begin from the beginning*".[142]

Beginnings and endings play a critical role in shaping the interpretation of narratives, and the meaning of historical events may vary significantly depending on where the narrative boundaries are placed.[143] The ending of the novel, with these highly resonant words, redefines the destruction of the farm as a temporary setback and replaces the sense of ending with a symbolic act of renewal. Eliezer Smoli, the Socialist Zionist author of the book, was a teacher in kibbutz Kfar Giladi, on the far northern frontier, when he composed his narrative, and his key protagonist, the Jewish guard who becomes a farmer, was inspired by the Second Aliyah pioneer Alexander Zeid, one of the founders of Kfar Giladi.[144] A deeply committed Zionist writer and educator, Smoli constructs the novel to highlight the themes of dogged persistence in carrying on the settlement process as the educational legacy of the pioneering ethos. It is possible, however, to interpret the ending of the novel differently. In that counter-reading, "*we should always begin from the beginning*" may suggest a cyclical trajectory that implies a continuing battle that defies any sense of closure. Such an ending would imply that the settlement's victory over the desert is always incomplete and fragile, introducing the possibility of having to return to the beginning.

Clearly, this alternative interpretation does not convey the author's intention or his contemporaries' understanding of it. *Frontiersmen of Israel* was met with enthusiasm by its readers and won critical acclaim, and when it received an important literary award in 1936, the committee's report noted that the book "presents to the youth an important chapter in the history of conquest and pioneering that . . . provides an accurate description of the heroism of a Jewish family struggling to survive with faith and perseverance in the face of afflictions and obstacles and to put down roots in the homeland."[145] The novel, a canonical work of the settlement period, remained popular reading for youth during the late Yishuv and early state periods. However, its emphasis on the conflictual relationship between the settlement and the symbolic desert reinforces the besieged-island metaphor and the fear of recurrence that locks the settlement narrative into an unresolved tension between its overt linear structure and implied cyclical ending.

The legacy of the settlement narratives and the centrality of the concept of "the conquest of the desert" nonetheless remained at the heart of the national discourse after the establishment of the state of Israel in 1948. When the young state organized its first international exhibit in Jerusalem in 1953,[146] the exhibit's official English title was *The Conquest of the Desert*, while its Hebrew title, *kibbush ha-shemama* ("the conquest of the wasteland") indicated that the exhibit addressed the symbolic desert. The exhibit logo, featuring a robust hand holding a blooming flower with a straight stem that doubles as a ruler, implied that cultivation and technology serve as complementary icons of the settlement's battle with the desert. The exhibit, following the tradition of the earlier Levant Fairs, displayed Jews' agricultural, technological, and industrial accomplishments in promoting progress in the region, but also tied that into an international context of land reclamation, desertification, and the impact of technology. The overall universalist message was thus, in the words of Avraham Granott, the chairman of the directorate of the JNF, "man's incessant grappling with the powerful elements for survival and development"; and more specifically, it highlighted Israel's contribution to the global effort "to harness the desert in the service of mankind," as the chief of Israel's Food and Agriculture Mission, A. G. Black, stated.[147]

On September 22, 1953, the official opening of this first international exhibit was marked by the attendance of prominent Israeli leaders, among them President Yitzhak Ben-Zvi, Deputy Prime Minister Moshe Sharett, cabinet ministers, Knesset members, top government officials, heads of national agencies, and religious leaders. Five hundred companies from fourteen countries, and four United Nations agencies, participated in the exhibit, contributing to its international scope.[148] The plan to hold the exhibit in Jerusalem at that time also had a political goal, to advance international recognition of the city as Israel's capital. In this respect, however, the exhibit did not achieve its goal, as only three countries—Finland, Belgium and Luxemburg—officially took part.[149] But in spite of this setback, the large participation by international companies and the representation by the United Nations were considered a success, and the fact that the exhibit drew a half million Israeli viewers exceeded expectations. The ministry of tourism responded by turning the exhibit into a permanent feature, and *The Conquest of the Desert* became a part of the official face of the state of Israel in the 1950s.[150]

At the macro level, the establishment of a sovereign Jewish state within the broader space of the symbolic desert could be seen as the attainment of "the conquest of the desert." Yet the conflictual settlement-desert framework also required the maintenance of a vigilant attitude toward the desert to deter its forces from reversing the balance of power. Furthermore, the desert, which had been used primarily as symbolic of the landscape outside of the Jewish settlement, was increasingly identified in the 1940s with the southern Negev region, as the major last frontier prior to the establishment of a Jewish state. Following 1948, the Negev became the concrete representation of the desert landscape, which shifted its position from an external to an internal frontier.

Part II

Shifting Landscapes

4

The Negev Frontier

THE ZIONIST SETTLEMENT DISCOURSE of the formative years of the Jewish society of Palestine articulates its members' perception that the territory that lay outside of the Yishuv's space was desolate, unproductive, and uninhabited. Jews' allusion to the various landscapes in the country as a "desert" was designed to convey those qualities rather than provide a description of their specific geographical traits. The use of the desert as a symbolic category highlighted its contrast to the Jewish settlement, but it also implied that the territory outside the Jewish settlement served as an *external frontier* that could with time be developed, inhabited, and transformed into the Jewish national space. During most of this period, the actual geographical areas associated with the physical desert—the Judean desert east and south of Jerusalem and the Negev region in the southern part of Palestine—remained outside the scope of the Jewish settlement, as potential frontiers. As we shall see below, a significant change in this view occurred in the late 1930s, as the Negev assumed greater significance as a southern frontier, first focusing on the territory that stretched down to Beer Sheva and ultimately extending farther south, to Aqaba Bay.[1]

A New Frontier

From the 1940s to the 1960s, the desert became identified with the concrete, physical landscape of the Negev region, as a challenging frontier that had been transformed from its initial position as external to the Jewish settlement into an internal frontier, contained within the borders of the state of

Israel. Yet in spite of the political and military developments that determined its inclusion in the Jewish national space, this open and scantly settled desert landscape, inhabited by Bedouins and a small Jewish population, continued to represent the counter-place to Israeli Jews. David Ben-Gurion, Israel's first prime minister, was the most powerful proponent of the need to make the settlement of the Negev the young state's top priority. The post-independence decades were therefore characterized by the need to address the precarious position of the desert as an internal frontier that was a part of the Jewish national space yet retained the qualities of the counter-place.

The term "*negev*" appears in the Hebrew Bible (deriving from the linguistic root n-g-b, which means to dry or to wipe dry), where it refers to the area known today as the northern Negev and where it is also used to designate "south."[2] The geographical boundaries of the Negev have fluctuated historically, yet today the Negev region includes the northern Negev (roughly from the 300-mm average annual rainfall line to south of Beer Sheva), the Negev plateau, and the Arava Valley from the Dead Sea all the way down to the southern tip at Eilat/Aqaba Bay. Its triangular shape was created by the political boundary to its west, separating it from the Sinai Peninsula, and by the Jordan Rift Valley to its east.[3]

Although Jews had purchased some land in the northern Negev prior to World War I, the few attempts to settle in the Negev failed, discouraging further initiatives.[4] The southernmost Jewish settlement, Beer Tuvia, which was established in 1888, experienced faltering beginnings and population turnovers until it was reestablished as an agricultural *moshav* in 1930.[5] The first settlement established in the northern Negev, in 1912, was Ruhama, located more than 19 miles south of Beer Tuvia. During World War I, the Turkish army's use of the farm as a military station drained its meager resources, and following the arrest of members suspected of supporting the British army, Ruhama was evacuated in 1917.[6] In 1936, Jews owned only 19,000 acres (40,000 dunams) in the Negev yet there was no active Jewish settlement south of Beer Tuvia.[7] Doubts about the viability of settlements in the desert persisted, given the lack of water, harsh climate, physical and social isolation, and tense relations with the Bedouins. Land acquisition presented a major challenge due to the British restrictions on land purchase in the Negev area and the Zionist organizations' budgetary constraints and preference for focusing on more promising areas.[8]

It was only in the late 1930s that the settlement of the desert in the Negev began to attract more focused attention as part of the drive to expand the Jewish territorial base and counteract Britain's plan to assign the Negev to the Arabs and guarantee its own interests there. The Jewish National Fund (JNF) now attempted to advance land purchase wherever possible, often involving a third party to evade the British restrictions.[9] In 1939, toward the end of the massive "Tower and Stockade" settlement project, a new kibbutz named Negba was established in the Negev. Its name articulated its geographical location but also underscored the symbolic move southward that identified the Negev as a new frontier. From 1941 to 1944, three "observation outposts" (*mitzpim*) were established as experimental agricultural stations, and seven small settlements were founded in the northern and western Negev. On October 5, 1946, the settlement drive culminated in the overnight construction of eleven new Jewish settlements, in a carefully orchestrated operation.[10] By 1947, the number of Jewish settlements and outposts in the Negev had reached twenty-five.[11]

The military character of the settlement operation and the use of outposts as a venue to test the plausibility of future settlements and to establish a presence in the desert became the hallmark of settling the Negev frontier. These small, new settlements were typically surrounded by fences and ditches and had watchtowers, and security concerns played a critical role in determining their location, taking priority over concerns about their sustainability in the desert environment. As Yosef Weitz of the JNF explained that approach, making sustainability the measure would have ruled out any possibility of building a Jewish settlement in the Negev at the time and this was not the Yishuv's main goal: "We essentially deal here with conquest, with increasing the number of our settlements in the Negev, and from this perspective, one does not examine the agricultural potential of the land."[12]

Security considerations led to the choice of elevated grounds close to main roads to allow accessibility and for defense purposes. Given the precarious situation of these outposts, women and children stayed behind during the early phases of the settlement process, until conditions appeared safe enough for them to join the men.[13] The construction of a pipeline to carry subterranean water from the northern Negev to the new Negev settlements was a most critical and major undertaking in 1947 to ensure the future survival of the new settlements in the desert conditions, and a special patrol was assigned to guard the water pipes from thefts or sabotage by the Bedouins.[14]

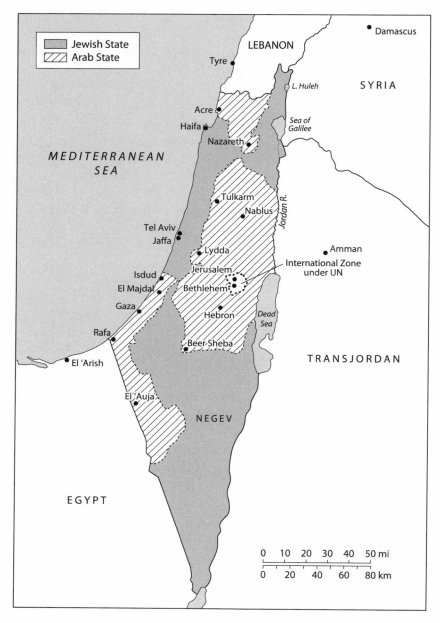

MAP 1. The 1947 UN Partition Plan.

MAP 2. Israel, 1949–1967.

The Negev had great value to Jews because of its size and the geopolitical advantages it offered, as a potential wedge to protect the relatively small and populated Jewish territory at the center of the country. The settlement strategy was therefore designed to stake a claim to it and redefine the desert as part of the inhabited Jewish territory. Following the visit of the United Nations Special Committee on Palestine (UNSCOP) and its recommendations earlier in 1947, the United Nations' vote on the partition of Palestine in November 1947 included a large portion of the northern and central Negev and the entire southern part of the Negev within the future Jewish state (see map 1). The Arab state received an extended portion of the western Negev, along the coast from Rafa to north of Isdud and east of Beer Sheva and toward Hebron.[15]

The escalation of hostilities between Arabs and Jews following the United Nations vote enhanced the isolation of the small frontier settlements in the Negev, with a population that was estimated at around 1,200 residents and 1,300 *Palmach* recruits.[16] Doubts about the feasibility of the survival of the Jewish settlements in case of an Arab attack led to calls for their evacuation, yet David Ben-Gurion rejected the idea, insisting on their critical significance for the future of the Jewish state. "In any other place in the country we need to defend existing settlements," he noted, "but in the Negev, *we need to defend the desert, the non-settlement.*"[17]

The settlements' situation became more acute after the state of Israel declared its independence on May 14, 1948, and Arab forces attacked it on various fronts. Egyptian forces advanced into the Negev region and attacked the isolated Jewish settlements along their way to the north. When they stopped their advance, about twenty miles from Tel Aviv, they created a blockade that prevented Jews' access from the center of the country to the northern and western Negev.[18] In response, a small, makeshift Israeli air force operated mostly by foreign volunteers, both Jewish and non-Jewish, provided critically needed supplies to the settlements that remained beyond the enemy lines. The fate of the Negev remained in doubt because of the presence of Egyptian forces and competing Jordanian claims as well as international pressures to disengage the Negev from Israel in light of Israel's military gains in the Galilee.[19] The situation changed during a later phase of the war, in October 1948, after additional troops and supplies had been transferred south by air. The Israeli army succeeded in breaking through and moved on to conquer Beer Sheva and open the way to the northern Arava and the Dead Sea. When Egypt and Israel signed another cease-fire agreement, in February 1949, it left the larger part of the northern and western Negev in Israel's territory. Finally, in a last effort to gain control over the entire Negev and guarantee access to the Red Sea, the Israeli army pushed its way toward Aqaba/Eilat Bay, which the Negev Brigade reached on March 10, 1949.[20] Israel thus emerged from the 1948–49 war with the entire Negev region included within its territory, with the exception of the coastal Gaza Strip (see map 2).

For Israeli Jews, the collective memory of the 1948 war revolves around the themes of besiegement, the fight of a few against many, and readiness for sacrifice and endurance, ultimately leading to victory.[21] The war accentuated the earlier theme of the Jewish settlement as an island besieged by the desert and its forces, which was now extended to the entire state of Israel. The Arabs' collective attack on Israel following its declaration of independence—enhanced by the experience of siege by individual settlements, most acutely Jerusalem and the Negev settlements—reinforced the themes of besiegement and survival. The war ultimately led to a victory for Israel, yet the experience of individual settlements did not always match this larger commemorative narrative. While most Jewish settlements in the Negev desert were able to hold out during the war in spite of their isolation and losses, about a third had to be evacuated during the war or in its immediate aftermath. In some cases, the residents were soon able to return to their settlement, but in others, residents moved to alternate locations in the Negev or in other parts of the country.[22]

The 1948 war further dramatized the close connection between the discourses of settlement and security that had developed during the pre-state period. The film *Pillar of Fire* (*Amud ha-esh*), directed by the young Zionist American director Larry Frisch in 1959, was shot in kibbutz Revivim and visualizes the drama of the Jewish war experience in the Negev desert. It opens with long shots of the open desert landscape before the camera zeroes in on a small group of people in an isolated outpost.[23] The opening accentuates the contrast between the tiny Jewish outpost and the vastness of the desert environment, and the view of enemy tanks advancing in the distance sets the stage for the unfolding fight of a few against many. The film portrays a diverse group of people who defended the settlement, including an older commander, Holocaust survivors, a young American Jewish volunteer, and a young female Sabra nurse. In spite of the differences in age, gender, origin, and life experiences, they are ready to join the struggle and fight to the bitter end.

A shelling of the outpost leaves one person dead and several others wounded, and the Jewish defenders realize that the military headquarters in Beer Sheva cannot provide assistance. The complaint by the single woman in the group articulates the key themes of the settlement narrative: "It's not fair, they are destroying everything. We've worked so hard. . . . There was nothing here when we came—just sand and stones. Now they bring them back again." The war thus aligns the Egyptian army with the sand, the stones, and the destructive forces of the desert environment that are set to destroy the Jewish settlement. Following a confrontation with the Israelis, the Egyptian tanks move on, leaving four of the six defenders, including the group's commander, dead. The two survivors, namely the female nurse and a wounded American volunteer, get out and manage, after a trying journey through the desert, to reach the Jewish military headquarters and deliver the warning about the enemy's further advance.

The story of the outpost may be interpreted as an allegory for the state of Israel and its struggle for survival during the 1948 war. The song "He Was Gray," performed by the Israeli singer Nehama Handel, playing the lead female role in the movie, focuses on the patriotic sacrifice made by "the living dead" that was a prominent theme in the commemoration of the 1948 war. The song became part of the canonical repertoire of Israel's Memorial Day for fallen soldiers.[24] Like other Israeli and Hollywood films about the 1948 war (e.g. *Hill 24 Doesn't Answer*, *Exodus*, and *Cast a Giant Shadow*), *Pillar of Fire* introduces a non-Israeli (or non-Jew) who first expresses doubts about the viability of the Zionist cause, only to be transformed into an ardent Zionist who is ready to fight and die for the cause of the Jewish state. At the end, the budding romance between the transformed American Jewish volunteer and the committed Israeli nurse represents the trajectory of survival, hope, and future continuity for the Jewish settlement.

Following the 1948 war, the incorporation of the Negev region turned the physical desert into an internal frontier and introduced new ambiguities to the desert-settlement relationship. While the cultural construction of the desert and the settlement as oppositional landscapes continued to mark the Israeli settlement ethos, the changing sociopolitical reality gave rise to alternative discourses. The Negev, Israel's sizable southern region, occupied 4,700 square miles (or 13,000 square kilometers) and constituted about 60% of its territory. But the temporary character of the armistice borders, the lingering disputes over the interpretation of the armistice agreements, and the continuing state of war between Israel and its Arab neighbors undermined any sense of security associated with established borders. The open character of the desert environment and the fragility of the borders led to frequent border crossings and hostile encounters that further highlighted the porousness of the borders and the lack of stability in the region. When Palestinian refugees who had escaped across the border or been expelled from areas under Israeli control attempted to return to their homes, harvest their fields, or retrieve belongings they had left behind, Israeli authorities defined them as enemy "infiltrators" (*mistanenim*) whose illegal entry posed a direct challenge to the state's sovereignty and threatened the security of its citizens. Frequent reports of infiltrators entering frontier settlements at night and stealing property, at times involving injury or murder, produced an atmosphere of fear in Israel, experienced most acutely by the residents of the desert settlements. The situation further deteriorated when the Egyptian army trained Palestinian fighters, the *fedayeen* (in Arabic, "those ready to sacrifice themselves"), who crossed the border to gather information and performed numerous acts of terrorism and sabotage within Israeli territory.[25]

Israel, too, used the fragility of the borders to initiate border crossings in the reverse direction. During the early 1950s, the Israel Defense Forces (IDF) entered enemy territories to target Arab settlements as "reprisal operations" (*pe'ulot tagmul*) for hostile actions performed by Arab infiltrators. These operations, designed as deterrents to the *fedayeen* and morale boosters for the Israeli public, became more frequent when Moshe Dayan became the IDF's chief of staff in 1953. The response of the Israeli public to these military reprisals across the border was mixed, and the public debates about them reached its peak following the extreme action undertaken by the commando "Unit 101" in Qibya in 1953. As a reprisal for the killing of a Jewish family in Yahud, the commandos entered the village of Qibya, in Jordan, and killed sixty of its residents. The harsh criticism and international outcry in response to this incident put pressure on the IDF to limit the scope of such actions.[26] Border crossings on both sides nonetheless continued in subsequent years, until the 1956 Sinai campaign, when Israel, in collaboration with Britain and France, moved into the Sinai Peninsula but was later forced by international pressure to return this territory to Egypt.

The state of being surrounded by hostile Arab countries, with porous borders between them, enhanced Israelis' sense of besiegement and vulnerability and further reinforced the view of the settlement as an island surrounded by the dark desert forces. Amos Oz's 1962 short story "Before His Time" suggests an analogy between jackals wailing outside the kibbutz's fence and the threat of the *fedayeen*. The description of the key protagonist, Dov, a kibbutz founder, and his need to protect his family home at the edge of the kibbutz from the surrounding danger, echoes these themes:

> In days gone by Dov would bar the shutters of the little room at the edge of the kibbutz, close the window and the curtain, envelope the room with calm, and keep away the night and its darkness. . . . Lean, very lean are the jackals, bleary-eyed and drooling. . . . Their eyes glint with sparks of cunning, their ears perked in expectation, their mouths always open, their teeth shining hate. The jackals circle around on tiptoe . . . round about they creep . . . a ring of tremulous jackals circling at the edges of the shadow, closing in on the island of light.[27]

The metaphor of the home as an island of light stands in dramatic contrast to the massive forces that besiege it: the night, the desert, the Arabs, and the jackals. The fate of Dov's son, the fearless military hero who participated in all the reprisal operations and was killed on his way back from one of them, after which the jackals destroyed his face, discloses the ambiguous outcome of the struggle between the settlement and the desert forces. Dov's reflections at the end of his life, while sitting in his enclosed apartment at night and listening to the jackals' wails, further affirm that he no longer has his earlier assurance about who will have the last laugh in this conflict.

The theme of Israel's military reprisals across the border returned to the center of attention in 1967 in the film *Scouting Patrol*, a drama directed by Micha Shagrir, where the desert environment again plays a central role. A small IDF patrol that discovers mines hidden by the *fedayeen* receives an order to cross the border, capture the *fedayeen*'s commander, and bring him back to Israel alive. The film follows the four commandos, who hike through the desert terrain, wait for night to fall to cross the border into an Arab town, and capture the sleeping Arab commander in his home. When another middle-aged Arab man, whom one of them releases, summons others to chase after them, the retreating Israeli commandos must choose a longer and more challenging path through the desert on their way back.

The sweeping views of the open desert landscape at the beginning of the film serve to foreshadow the central role played by the desert in this film, much as it did in *Pillar of Fire*, discussed above.[28] The open desert landscape through which the commandos begin their heroic venture shifts to wilder and more dramatic desert scenery on their way back. In scenes that borrow heavily from the American Western, the film shows the Israeli commandos escaping through a hidden canyon, climbing rocks, and engaging in shooting exchanges with those who track them. Throughout this excursion through the desert, they display their daring and resourcefulness. Yet at the point when they believe that the danger has been averted and they lower their guard, the captive Arab commander, attempting to run away, kills one of them.[29] The last scene depicts the three remaining commandos and their captive returning to their base, carrying the body of their dead comrade, while his image accompanies them, suggesting that he continues to be part of the group and its mission to the very end.[30]

The alluring openness of the desert environment, the sense of being restricted within the newly imposed political borders, and the adventurous character of crossing the border became more clearly evident when Israeli youth embraced this practice beyond its military context. Hiking through the desert was a way to follow the legacy of pre-state Hebrew culture, and youth movements, army units, orienteering groups, and other adventurers would hike through the desert for days at a time. For Israeli youth, the desert represented "an unusual combination of danger and a sense of freedom . . . absolute freedom: no law, no police, nobody would reach you here and tell you what to do. You could go wherever the wind carried you."[31] Field trips to the desert were considered a daring, patriotic activity that symbolically reenacted the "conquest" of the desert. The popular custom of ending these excursions by climbing up to the top of the Masada mountain and reconnecting with the heroic legacy of its ancient history, as it was interpreted at the time, added another dimension to this multilayered experience.[32]

The Negev was still considered a dangerous territory in the early 1950s, and school field trips to this destination required special permission.[33] But in time, Hebrew youths grew more familiar with its topography, and hiking in its desert landscape no longer presented a sufficient challenge for the more adventurous among them. The search for new heroic adventures led some to cross the border on their own, in direct violation of Israeli law and at enormous personal risk. The most famous destination for such border crossings was Petra, the ancient Nabbatean city in Jordan that was built into the red rock. Its relatively short distance from the border with Jordan and the physical continuity of the desert landscape made this adventure appear doable, but the danger of being discovered and shot by Jordanian guards or armed Bedouins was imminent and real: of the fifteen known hikers who attempted to reach Petra, only three made it back alive.[34] The possibility of reaching Petra fired the imagination of Israeli youth in the 1950s. When the song "The Red Rock" was performed and broadcast in 1958, it became an immediate hit. The lyrics, written by Haim Hefer, a popular songwriter of the 1948 generation, describe the allure of the legendary city that lies "across the mountains and the desert" and from which "no one came back alive." Alarmed by the song's impact on young people and its glorification of the dangerous fad, the government censored its broadcast on Israeli radio, but thereby only further contributed, inadvertently, to Petra's mystique.[35]

The post-1948 reality triggered a sense of besiegement and confinement within the country's borders that evoked a desire to test boundaries and defy these political constructs. The generation that came of age in the 1950s and was brought up by the *Palmach*'s heroic ethos and the image of the adventurous, defiant, and daring Sabra, looked for new venues in which to experience their legacy, outside the bounds of the familiar landscape. In this spirit, a famous Israeli hero, Meir Har-Zion (b. 1934), noted his immense dislike, as a young adult, of walking in line or following an established path, as motivating him to pursue such adventures as a solo climb through an unexplored path to the top of Masada. Har-Zion describes the close call he had during the climb when he found himself hanging over the abyss, as well as his epiphany when he reached the top:

> An amazing feeling, a crazy joy mixed with a happy sense of victory comes over me, I get wild with excitement and run around on the elevated peak like a crazy man. What touched me so? The wild desert that surrounds me? The victory? The daring? I stand there bewitched by this strange, barren landscape as the shadows of the evening fall. I look around and there is no sign that any man has ever visited this elevated peak.[36]

Rachel Savorai (b. 1926), who accompanied Har-Zion on the hike to Petra and back, offers a retrospective accounting for the urge to defy the borders: "We wanted to reach those places that had become unavailable because of the Green Line [i.e. the armistice borders]. For us, the Green Line was not a border. . . . For my generation, the Green Line did not define the homeland."[37]

In the same vein, the writer Naomi Frankel, who wrote the introduction to Har-Zion's published diary, notes the gap between "the vast landscapes" and "the narrow borders closing in on [the youth]."[38] And in Ehud Ben-Ezer's novel *The People of Sodom* (1968), a fictional officer describes his decision to hike alone across the border, explaining that he was aware that this was "a crazy thing to do," but he felt his need for solitude, and was also driven by his love of adventure and his desire "to prove something to himself."[39]

It is important to note that in spite of the obvious differences between such illegal excursions across the enemy lines, initiated by individuals, and the military operations performed by IDF soldiers, both forms of border crossing share the tripartite structure of rites of passage: beginning with the departure from the home territory, they lead to a stay in a liminal space, where one experiences a personal transformation, which is followed by a return and reintegration into the home sphere in a transformed state.[40] Like the adventurous military operations across the border, the forbidden hikes across the border to Petra manifested the readiness to risk one's life; yet unlike actions performed by the army, they were acts of daring and defiance by individuals, and fell short of the expectation that they would advance collective goals.

A few examples illustrate the ease with which youths transitioned from one type of border crossing to the other. In an interview, Micha Shagrir, the director of *Scouting Patrol*, recalled his personal venture across the border after being wounded in military action in 1956. Similarly, Ram Pargai, who was later killed on an excursion to Petra, had started practicing for that forbidden trip after recovering from an injury in a military reprisal operation.[41] In both of these cases, the personal challenge became a way for the men to feel self-motivated and to reassure themselves that they were able to perform the daring act of crossing the border on their own. The excursions to Petra nonetheless drew public criticism for the senseless loss of human lives, which could not be justified in the name of patriotic sacrifice, and the government therefore moved to curb this phenomenon.

The border crossing to Petra inspired the making of the film *Blazing Sands*, directed by Raphael Nussbaum in 1960, in which the crossing is thinly disguised as a fictional excursion to an ancient desert city named Sitra.[42] The film revolves around the clandestine mission to rescue a young Israeli man who was wounded during an excursion to Sitra, where he discovered ancient scrolls in a cave and remained in hiding in the cave. A female friend of his receives the news of his fate from the only person who made it back to Israel from the expedition, before that person dies in the hospital. She recruits four men to join her and, disguised as Bedouins, the five set out for the desert, cross into Jordan, reach Sitra, and locate the wounded friend and the scrolls. At this point, however, greed and the pursuit of personal interest pull the group apart. One of the men escapes with the scrolls and encounters his death, while the critically wounded man dies on the way home. Two of the other men are later killed in a firing exchange with Bedouins, and the heroine is wounded. The only person to survive intact, an archeologist, crosses the border carrying the wounded woman in his arms, as the scrolls are blown away by the desert wind. The film articulates the disapproval by authority figures of young people's illegal and irresponsible border crossings, referring to this fad as a misguided "national sport" that "puts the entire country at risk."

Blazing Sands is a melodrama that suffers from a weak script and mediocre acting, and as one would expect, it received a negative critical response, addressing its artistic shortcomings. Yet the film has also evoked a less predictable negative response from those who disapproved of its portrayal of the excursion to Petra.[43] This response came not only from the families of those killed during those forbidden border crossings but also from prominent politicians and writers who, like the well-known writer of the 1948 generation, Aharon Megged, found fault in the film's "groundless misrepresentation of Israeli youth."[44]

These responses reveal the blurred line in public memory between the two kinds of border crossings, emphasizing their shared heroic legacy in spite of their distinct difference within official memory. More broadly, the pervasiveness of border crossings during the 1950s reveals Arabs' and Israelis' difficulties in accepting the boundaries around the state of Israel. The earlier associations of the open desert landscape with a sense of freedom and adventure, as well as defiance of the law, that inspired the youth hiking tradition in the pre-state period also fed into the continuing excursions across the border in the early post-1948 period. These border crossings highlighted the duality of the desert, as both an internal frontier contained within the state and part of an enemy land extending beyond the border within what appears as a contiguous landscape. This ambiguity contributes to the fragility of the political borders and the blurring of lines between "inside" and "outside," "place" and "nonplace," soon after the official establishment of the state.

"Making the Desert Bloom"

During the 1950s, the Israeli government, Jewish national agencies, and schools continued to emphasize the pioneering Zionist ethos and the national value of the settlement agenda. Israel's first prime minister, David Ben-Gurion, famously defined the Negev desert as Israel's most important frontier, and stated: "The state of Israel cannot tolerate the existence of a desert within it." Invoking the conflictual framework of the desert-settlement relations, he went on to warn his fellow countrymen: "If the state is not going to destroy the desert, the desert might destroy the state."[45] He objected to the conventional Hebrew reference to "going down" to the southern region and insisted instead on the biblical expression of "going up" to the Negev, underscoring its association with the symbolic meaning of *aliyah* (literally, ascension) as a patriotic, Zionist act. Emphasizing the pioneering value of settling the desert, he issued a public call to young people to go "southwards," but his call failed to bring about the anticipated response (see figures 12 and 13).[46]

In a gesture that stunned the nation, Ben-Gurion announced in 1953 that he was stepping down from his positions as prime minister and minister of defense and moving to the Negev desert. His decision, at the age of sixty-seven, to join Sde Boker, a small cooperative commune in the heart of the Negev that was not affiliated with any of the established kibbutz movements, was designed to demonstrate his personal commitment to the old pioneering values of Labor Zionism. His choice of this settlement was also interpreted as a sign of his disapproval of the kibbutzim movements'

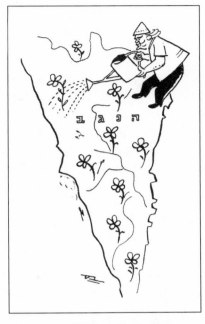

FIGURE 12. "I Have a Garden," cartoon by Joseph Mordechai Bass. Courtesy of Yona Spiegelman, Yael Haen, and Rephael Bass. Copyright © "HA'ARETZ" daily newspaper LTD.

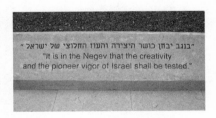

FIGURE 13. Engraving of David Ben-Gurion quotation at Sde Boker. Photo by author.

lack of response to his call to settle the Negev, relinquishing their earlier leadership in carrying out the settlement mission.[47] Ben-Gurion's move to the desert and short-lived engagement in physical work drew public attention but failed to produce any significant change. For a short period, his humble home in Sde Boker emerged as an alternative site of power to the official government in Jerusalem, inadvertently recreating the subversive character of the desert as the counter-place.

Following the extended period of struggle and nation-building efforts, culminating in a war that took a high toll, Israelis felt the need to return to their everyday life and attend to their families and personal needs. This trend was also true for members of the kibbutzim, who had taken a leading role in new settlement initiatives but wished to return to their homes when the war effort was over. The existing Jewish settlements in the Negev, mostly kibbutzim and a few *moshavim*, similarly turned their energies inward in the postwar years to strengthen their agricultural foundations. As the historian Orit Rozin notes, the shift from collectivism toward an individualistic ethos can be traced back to the decade following the establishment of the state, although it became more widely acknowledged in the 1960s.[48] Nevertheless, in spite of this general climate, several core communes were established in

FIGURE 14. The Yarkon-Negev water pipeline (1950). Photo by Zoltan Kluger, courtesy of the KKL/JNF Photo Archive.

the desert in the 1950s, mostly by youth movement members who combined their military training with settling in the frontier; the more successful of these later developed into full-fledged kibbutzim.[49]

To advance the possibility of turning the Negev into an active frontier, the government focused on expanding the water supply allocated to the desert region. The water pipeline that was hastily constructed in 1947 to bring water to the Jewish settlements in the Negev was critical to their survival, but could not support any further expansion of the settlement of the new frontier. The installation of the Yarkon-Negev pipeline (completed in 1955) was therefore designed to transfer water from the center of the country to the Negev to support the vision of making the desert bloom. The new pipeline increased the amount of water available to existing Negev settlements and supported the plan for new settlements (figure 14).[50]

The politically charged issue of the use of water from the Jordan River and its tributaries was negotiated by an American team that introduced the Johnston Plan for a water-sharing regime among Jordan, Israel, Syria and Lebanon. Although never officially ratified, the plan provided a workable framework for the countries involved. Israel then began to develop its own more ambitious project to transfer water from the Jordan and the Sea of Galilee to the Negev to establish "the optimum combined utilization of the land and water resources."[51] In 1964, it completed the long and complex construction of its National Water Carrier, which provides about two-thirds of the country's water. A banknote commemorating the carrier marks it as a national achievement, and its symbolic and practical significance made it the target of the Fatah movement's first attack in Israel, in 1965.[52]

In spite of the government's failure to mobilize a massive movement of volunteers to settle in the desert, the identification of the Negev as the new frontier and the national goal of making the desert bloom featured prominently in Israeli culture of the 1950s and early 1960s. Israel's aforementioned international exhibit featured the conquest of the desert in broader terms, but Hebrew books of the early state period focused more specifically on the Negev,[53] and titles such as *The War between the Cultivated Land and the Desert* or *Man Subdues the Desert* reproduced the conflictual framework of the settlement discourse.[54] The latter textbook explains to students that "the desert had conquered the Negev and didn't want to abandon it" and emphasizes the need to learn about the desert as a strategy to win this conflict: "the desert is facing us as an enemy, and you cannot assault the enemy without knowing its nature and power."[55]

The new desert lore demonstrated a thematic continuity with the pre-state settlement lore, presenting the desert land as waiting to be redeemed and glorifying the efforts to settle in it. The dire need of water to ensure the success of the settlement process is a major theme in Hebrew desert lore from the late 1940s on. Some popular Hebrew songs drew on biblical visions describing redemptive visions of the desert.[56] A popular "Water Song," based on a poem by Avraham Shlonsky, portrays the arid Negev's land praying for water. Typically for the secular, collectivist ethos of the time, it is not a divine power that answers these prayers but the settlers, who are represented through an anonymous "we," pledging, "We will water you, we will build you, the Negev, and you will be built."[57] An educational narrative presents well drillers as committed workmen who give up life's comforts in order to perform "a simple and sacred work," displaying an "unwavering belief that at the end they will find water . . . to settle the desolate, arid land."[58]

The new Hebrew lore highlighted the importance of pipes and watering devices to the success of the national goal of making the desert bloom. One of the famous expressions of the water lore of the mid-1950s was the "Sprinkler Hora Dance" (*Hora mamtera*),[59] performed by the popular *NAHAL* ("Pioneering Combat Youth" of the IDF) troupe, affiliated with those who volunteered to settle the frontier. The upbeat song, cheerfully calling on the sprinkler to spin around and disperse its water to the thirsty land, stands in sharp contrast to the monotonous, almost melancholy, desert songs or the heavy, march-like beat of the warrior songs which were typical of the earlier desert lore. The JNF poster of "The Vision of the Negev" (figure 10, chapter 3), similarly, features a water pipe to mark the transition from the early settlement period—illustrated by plowed land with a few temporary tents—to a full-blown settlement with its canonical white buildings, red roofs, and green trees. The pipeline thus extends the earlier emphasis on the introduction of straight lines into the landscape and contributes to the presentation of the Jewish settlement as a colorful, cultivated island surrounded by the desert.

The Negev lore of the 1950s and 1960s reinforced its association with the American West. The Western genre introduced the American frontier with its vast, open spaces, porous borders, and rugged individuals ready to face hardships, themes that appealed to Israeli popular culture.[60] The

Hebrew term *boker*, "cowboy," which the toponym Sde Boker (literally, the cowboy's field) incorporated, made the American West part of the Israeli desert landscape. The widely popular "Cowboys' Song" (*Zemer ha-bokrim*) further reinforced this connection.[61] Its description of riding in the "endless desert" evokes the vistas of the American West but also presents contemporary Israeli riders as the reincarnation of ancient Israelites. The dynamic male figures connect with the desert, represented by the feminine Hebrew term *arava,* thus evoking the sexual allusion of the special bond between them that reinforces the promise of future renewal.

Popular songs of the period also associated the town of Eilat, as well as other new desert settlements, such as kibbutz Yotvata near Eilat[62] and Ein Gedi near the Dead Sea, with a journey into the desert and a sense of adventure or evoked the desert mystique. The song "Ein Gedi" highlighted the contrast between the stillness of the desert land, the soaring heat, and the Dead Sea with the promise of life and change that the young kibbutz represents.[63]

The ideological emphasis on the settlement suggested that the conquest of the desert would transform it from a counter-place into a cultivated Jewish place, yet the reality of the Negev produced a less dichotomized situation, in which the liminal frontier represented elements of both the settlement and the desert. The interweaving of the place and the counter-place were perhaps most prominently illustrated in the case of Eilat, the small settlement at Israel's southern tip.

Eilat became a small frontier town that was isolated and remote, separated from the rest of the country by the Negev desert. In 1950, the opening of a direct flight by an Israeli airline from the center to Eilat made this southernmost Israeli town more easily accessible, but also underscored its remoteness. Following the Sinai campaign of 1956 and the opening of the passage through the Red Sea to its port, and the introduction of a new road across the desert via Mitzpe Ramon in 1958, Eilat rapidly developed.

Yet Eilat also represented the free spirit of the desert as a space that defies the constraints of culture, a transitional space for temporary workers, individuals who sought refuge from society, and beatniks who brought with them the Western youth counterculture of the 1960s. As Maoz Azaryahu notes, Eilat's liminality as a frontier town in the far south established its distinct status in Israeli popular culture. Some articles from the 1950s describe Eilat as "the Israeli brand of the Wild West," praising its wilderness,[64] while other articles address the role of the Wild South as the counter-place, marked by an atmosphere of lawlessness.[65]

New "Dots" on the Map

During the postwar years, Israel also faced the enormous challenge of accommodating the influx of Jewish immigrants, including refugees from Europe and from Middle Eastern countries. Within three and a half years, its population more than doubled, from around 650,000 in 1948 to 1.4 million, aggravating Israel's postwar economic difficulties and leading to the introduction of a strict rationing regime.[66] Faced with a housing crunch, the state placed new immigrants in transit camps (*ma'abarot*) that lacked the necessary foundations to meet the newcomers' basic health, employment, and educational needs.

In time, the state sought to resolve both its critical need to settle new immigrants and its unmet goals of enhancing the Jewish population in the sparsely inhabited Negev desert and ensuring its borders, in directing new immigrants to the desert. As earlier, security considerations continued to govern the settlement agenda in the southern region. The kibbutzim whose members were ideologically committed to the settlement ethos and better prepared for the desert environment were strategically located near the border with the highly populated Gaza Strip. When the *moshav* movement undertook the major task of absorbing the new immigrants, it established thirty-five *moshavim* in the Negev desert during the 1950s. The army's involvement in the planning process of the new settlements indicated the importance of their strategic locations to enhancing Jewish control over the sparsely inhabited desert land.[67] Special guides from veteran *moshavim* came to help the newcomers, the majority of whom came from the Middle East and northern Africa, had no experience in farming, and did not share Labor's redemptive vision of cultivating the land or becoming "productive" Jewish workers.[68]

The government also experimented with another solution to accommodating the influx of new immigrants, namely settling them in former Arab settlements and constructing new "development towns." In the Negev, it directed new immigrants to Beer Sheva and built eleven new towns, mostly in the western and central Negev. Although the idea was that these new settlements would serve as urban centers for the agricultural settlements around them and support the industrial development of the Negev, their rushed construction was not based on sufficient economic and environmental considerations to support this vision. As a result, the limited economic resources available to the residents of the development towns compounded their encounters with the hardship of life in the desert frontier. The government attempted to develop mining, mineral, and chemical industries that would draw on the natural resources of the desert, as well as other industries that required cheap labor, most visibly the textile industry. But in spite of the government's incentives, some of the industries and factories did not survive for long, and those that continued could not provide enough employment opportunities to sustain the population. The small development towns thus suffered from endemic unemployment, weak educational and community institutions, and high turnover in their population. Those who had the resources or motivation moved away, leaving behind a struggling population that had no choice but to stay.[69]

When new immigrants who had been placed in the transit camps located in the center of the country objected to the plan to settle them on the faraway desert frontier, the government tried a new strategy, transporting newly arrived immigrants directly from the boat to their designated settlement in the Negev in order to minimize the possibilities for them to object to this plan.[70] Most immigrants thus arrived in the desert without prior knowledge of their destination, often misled by those who had organized their transport to the desert and their arrival there timed for the dark of the night. The recurrent themes of the nocturnal journey and the traumatic impact of being dumped in the desert in the middle of the night distinguish these new immigrants' narratives from the prototypical desert settlement stories presented by those who chose to settle in the desert. As folklorist Esther Schely-Newman notes, the nocturnal journey emerged as a metaphor for the immigrants' profound feeling of lack of agency and their lingering sense of victimhood.[71]

In reconstructing this experience in recorded interviews, these settlers describe their initial delight at seeing the coastal cities on their way, their bewilderment at the prolonged trip, and the traumatic encounter with the desert landscape on the following morning. As Ilana Rosen's study of immigrant settlers' narratives indicates, the recurrent use of words such as "lack," "nothing," and "no" in their narratives, even the narratives of those who had agreed to come to the desert, reveals the shock of the emptiness and desolation of the desert that they faced.[72] One immigrant recalls that his family, arriving from Romania in 1951, was told that they would be located "near Tel Aviv." They were taken to Beer Sheva, where they stopped for several hours, "probably because [they] wanted us to reach Yerucham by night so that we wouldn't see the place in daylight."[73] Another immigrant says that they asked to be near Jerusalem and were reassured that their destination was near it. She describes the "thorns and desolation" around their shacks and the fear at night. They were promised electricity within two months, but it did not materialize until two years later.[74] Another immigrant recalls how the truck driver who brought them to the desert at night told her, "don't worry, Miss, wait until tomorrow and you will see the greenery, lawn and trees, many trees," leaving her to discover the bitter truth the following morning.[75] A woman describes her total shock at seeing "only piles of sand rising to the sky, not even one green branch, nothing, nothing, nothing. No bird, no greenery, no car, no road, no house, nothing." She concludes, "There was nothing I could do. I sat near the shack, sat down to cry, cry, cry."[76] An interview with Arie (Lova) Eliav, a Labor leader who was in charge of settling new immigrants in the Negev in the mid-1950s,

FIGURE 15. Ein Husub transit camp for new immigrants in the Negev (1950s?). The Central Zionist Archives (NKH\403288).

affirms these recollections: "There was nothing there. Truly nothing. Thorns and arid land. And they [the new immigrants] did not want to get off [the truck], and for good reason." To get them off, he reveals, the driver would raise the truck on a slant "and they were poured on the ground. The truck would leave, and the people remained on the ground."[77]

The officials' patronizing and instrumental approach to the new immigrants was also evident in the common reference to immigrants by veteran Israelis as human "material" (*homer*) that could be molded by the state to meet its needs.[78] Unlike members of the Negev kibbutzim who had chosen to live on the desert frontier, most of these new immigrants were carrying out the mission of settling the frontier without having had any clear notion of their destination or any choice in the matter. Thus, they became "reluctant pioneers," or "pioneers in practice," who did not share the settlement ideology of Labor Zionism and its goal of "making the desert bloom."[79] The children, however, though affected by the difficulties and the isolation of the settlements in the desert, found it easier to adjust to the new conditions (see figure 15). Similarly, the documentary film *Dimona Twist*, directed by Michal Aviad (2016) and based on interviews with women who came to Dimona as a young age, reveals both positive and critical memories of their experiences growing up in the desert environment.

The difficult situation of the new immigrants who were settled in frontier settlements was exacerbated by the security concerns. The new settlers were confronted with the task of becoming an "organic wall" to defend and protect the state's borders, but As Arie Navon's cartoon (figure 16) suggests, this was a heavy burden, and one that they were ill-prepared to carry.[80] The pervasive fear of infiltrators drove new immigrants to barricade themselves at

FIGURE 16. "Frontier settlements carry the border line," cartoon by Arie Navon (1955). Courtesy of his son, David Navon.

home behind closed windows and doors in their isolated desert settlements. By the mid-1950s, those who had stayed in the *moshavim* demanded that the government equip them with fences, electricity, and military protection.[81] The large population turnover during those years undermined the development of the new settlements. Some were deserted as their members moved away or joined other nearby communities, but other settlements survived these difficult years in spite of the hardships.

The paternalistic and instrumental attitude of government officials and already established Israelis toward the new immigrants was not limited to the Negev, but the extreme conditions in the desert frontier aggravated the impact of those attitudes. In Aharon Megged's 1965 novel *The Living on the Dead*, the protagonist addresses the excessive glorification of the early Zionist pioneers and the settlement ethos and sarcastically notes how the state forced this ethos on the new immigrants: "They send unfortunate Moroccans to the Negev, unwillingly, and put up a sign to welcome them at the *moshav*'s entrance: 'The arid desert shall be glad, and the wilderness shall rejoice.' "[82] One cannot miss the irony of the discrepancy between this utopian biblical verse and the upbeat Hebrew folksong based on it, on the one hand, and the newcomers' own response to their situation, on the other. A kibbutz member who helped new immigrants in the Yeruham transit camp writes about how he tried to appeal to young immigrants to go to the desert by highlighting the analogy with the settlement of the American Wild West.[83] The historian Avi Picard points out that in a 1962 film produced by the Jewish Agency, the narrator, similarly, comments on footage displaying North African settlers' protests against being taken to the development town Dimona: "They do not yet know that they are truly . . . pioneers who will settle the Negev, and would not believe now that in ten years they will be proud of that."[84]

The discrepancies between the official rhetoric and attitude and their implications for those who are the object of their policies is the subject of a song by Kobi Oz, the lead singer and songwriter of the famous Israeli rock band *Teapacks*. Oz, whose family came from Tunisia, was born in 1969 and grew up in the development town Sderot, in the western Negev. The title of the song, "Dusty Slope" (literally also "Raising Dust"), is the name of a fictitious desert town. The song addresses the Israeli officials' arbitrary and instrumental approach to establishing a new settlement in the middle of nowhere in order to add a "dot" on the map ("dot" also means a "settlement" in Hebrew) to get newspaper coverage, and their indifference to the far-reaching implications of their decision for the people whose lives it would shape. The lyrics underscore the sense of banishment of those sent to the desert, where life seems to pass them by, turning their dreams into dust, as they remain forgotten "on the side of the road."[85] Another prominent Israeli poet and author, Shimon Adaf, who was born in 1972 in Sderot to parents who came from Morocco, confesses in a poem, "It has taken me twenty years to love this hole / In the middle of this nonplace."[86] The allusion to the desert settlement as a "nonplace" (*shum makom*) conveys the nondescript character of the settlement, which fails to provide the sense of a home and a place.[87] The film scholar Miri Talmon notes the cultural trope of the black road that cuts across the vast desert landscape and a lonely bus station in Israeli film.[88] The road, which represents dynamic movement, progress, and a sense of purpose, serves as a constant reminder of the life that has remained out of reach for those stuck in the desert.

Uri Zohar's 1965 film *Hole in the Moon* (*Hor ba-levana*) presents a parody of the Zionist vision of making the desert bloom, in which the road trope plays a central role. As a new immigrant arrives in the desert, the camera emphasizes the long road stretching to the open horizon of the desert landscape, with nothing else in sight and no one passing by. The newcomer builds a kiosk on the roadside and waits for customers. The situation becomes more absurd when another person arrives and builds a kiosk across from him, on the other side of the road, leaving them to stare at each other in the middle of the deserted landscape. Avi Nesher's 2004 film *Turn Left at the End of the World* (*Sof ha-olam smola*) features a small and nameless development town, the embodiment of "nonplace," surrounded by the desert. As the film scholar Yaron Shemer notes, the road signs at the bus station indicate that this obscure town is defined by its distance both from the center of the country and from Eilat.[89] The film highlights the insularity and cultural tensions within the small and isolated community of Jewish immigrants from North Africa and India. The immigrants' memories of their life prior to their arrival in Israel, on the one hand, and the life they imagine elsewhere in Israel, on the other hand, further emphasize their sense of being stuck at "the end of the world." Here too, the bus station on the desert road represents the possibility of escape, and the film ends with one of the two young lead characters taking her farewell from her friend, whom she leaves behind in the desert at the side of the road.

A similar sense of isolation and disconnection from the rest of the world pervades *The Band's Visit*, a 2007 film directed by Eran Kolirin, recently turned into a Broadway play. The film revolves around a visiting Egyptian band that is invited to play in the center of the country and instead is mistakenly directed to a development town, ironically named the "House of Hope," in the Negev. The band's walk from the desert road toward the distant development town represents a symbolic inversion of the biblical exodus: the Egyptians are the ones who come to the Promised Land and end up in the desert, and they are the ones who bring a human touch to the isolated residents of this desert town.[90] The film demonstrates the possibility of fostering a human connection between the Israeli Jews and the Egyptian visitors who are likewise stranded in the desert environment and suggests that their brief encounter affects both sides. The camera work highlights the small desert town as a metaphoric island cut off from the larger social and cultural scene in Israel.

In 1962, the government established a new small town, Arad, as a social experiment in creating a new kind of urban environment in the desert region. Unlike the hastily built immigrant towns, Arad was designed to attract middle class residents who were already rooted in Israeli society, and the extensive process of planning its architecture, infrastructure, social fabric, and economic base articulated a more deliberate effort to take the desert environment into account. Its location was determined by the need to introduce more Jewish settlements into the sparsely populated northeastern Negev, yet its proximity to the industrial plants of the Dead Sea presented economic opportunities for its residents. In its early years, Arad succeeded in attracting veteran Israelis and a minority of immigrants; it also attracted artist residents, the most famous among them being the writer Amos Oz. The social experiment was a success during the town's earlier years.[91]

The overall attempt to transform the Negev desert from an external counter-place into an internal frontier and a settled Jewish place had mixed results during the early decades after independence. In spite of some developments, the Negev remained a challenging territory marked by its vastness, scant settlements, and remoteness from the center. The new reality of an internal frontier challenged the dichotomized view of the desert and the settlement, and the marginality of the Negev in the face of new developments introduced further ambiguity into its status as a frontier.

Periphery and Frontier

The 1967 Six-Day War was a watershed in Israeli history in many respects, among them its impact on the role of the desert and the changing status of the Negev as a frontier. The new territories Israel occupied when the war ended, including the Golan Heights, the West Bank, the Sinai Peninsula, and the Gaza Strip, transformed its geopolitical position and weakened the acute sense of danger of the post-1948 years. Israeli military control of the Golan Heights meant that the Syrian forces were now further away from their superior, pre-1967 position above Israeli settlements in the north; the Sinai Peninsula provided a large physical buffer between Israel and Egypt in the south; and the West Bank expanded the narrow "corridor" at Israel's center. For the first time since the establishment of the state, Israelis were able to cross the border of their state, and they flocked to the occupied territories now accessible to them. The lure of border crossing—once requiring illegal expeditions undertaken at great personal risk—was now openly and eagerly pursued.

Political debates over the status of the occupied territories and their future divided Israeli society: proponents of the "Greater Land of Israel" advocated partial or complete annexation of the territories as part of the biblical "Land of Israel" and as critical for ensuring Israel's security, while others advocated the return of land in exchange for Arab recognition of the state of Israel, with the goal of establishing long-lasting peace.[92] Although the conflict around the future of the territories deepened the fissures within Israeli society, there was greater consensus over the strategic value of the Golan Heights and the northern Jordan Valley and the national significance of annexing East Jerusalem. The earliest settlements of the occupied territories were created under Labor governments, with the kibbutz and *moshav* movements resuming their lead role in establishing frontier settlements.[93] But the ideological shift toward defining the occupied Palestinian territories as new Jewish frontiers became more pronounced following the 1973 Yom Kippur War and Labor's subsequent political loss to the rightist Likud party in 1977.

When Israel signed a peace treaty with Egypt in 1979 and returned the Sinai Peninsula to it, this turn of events and departure from its earlier agenda led the Likud government to unilaterally declare Jerusalem "complete and united" as the "capital of Israel" in 1980 and to apply Israeli law and jurisdiction to a significant area of the Golan Heights in 1981.[94] The rekindling of messianic beliefs led to a new emphasis on the

Jewish settlement of the West Bank and Gaza, claiming Israel's historical right to these territories, and resulted in the emergence of a new Zionist movement, *Gush Emunim* (the Block of the Faithful), which promoted this agenda. The previously accepted designation of the "West Bank" (*ha-gada ha-ma'aravit*) was soon eliminated in favor of the biblical terms "Judea and Samaria," and Israeli law was applied to Jews who settled in these areas. Israel's unilateral steps did not receive international recognition, yet they turned the territories into de facto frontiers. This process became the subject of international contention and has fueled the ongoing Israeli-Palestinian conflict, leaving the future of a Palestinian state in limbo. But our immediate focus here is on the implications of these changes for the Negev as an internal frontier.

Although Israeli governments continued to pay official homage to the settlement of the Negev as a national priority, the internal desert frontier could not compete with the ideological appeal and economic incentives that supported the Jewish settlements in the occupied territories. Furthermore, as a result of the relocation of army and air force bases to the Negev following the return of Sinai, most of the Negev's territory was now designated as national parks, nature reserves, military bases, or fire zones, thereby limiting the potential land available for new settlements. And while these developments weakened the perception of the Negev as a frontier and contributed to its decline into a neglected periphery, other geopolitical changes, demographic changes, economic factors, and internal dynamics left the southern desert region oscillating between periphery and frontier.[95] The goal of "making the desert bloom" seemed to lose its appeal within the larger political context, and the development of some existing Jewish settlements in the Negev was arrested, until further waves of immigration added to their population. With the passage of time, the desert region acquired a limited reputation as an alternative space for new kinds of Jewish settlements, and regained some of its earlier appeal as a Jewish frontier.

Perhaps most significant was the development of Beer Sheva, the capital of the southern district, from a population of around 43,000 in 1961 to 110,800 in 1983, spiking to 215,000 in 2017. Beer Sheva became the home of a new university in 1969, renamed the Ben-Gurion University of the Negev after the former prime minister's death in 1973, which gradually developed into one of Israel's four major universities; the university's Soroka Medical Center became the main hospital serving the southern region.[96] With major educational, health, and government institutions, Beer Sheva enjoyed a distinct status within the desert region and became one of the major cities of Israel, and the installation of a rapid train line further connected it to the center.[97]

The older desert towns continued to struggle socially and economically during the 1980s. Compared to other development towns in the Negev, Dimona fared better, as it enjoyed a broader and more stable industrial base.[98] Yet a persistent exodus by families and younger people continued to undermine other towns' growth, and industrial projects failed to sustain their economy. Furthermore, the disparity between urban settlements, which typically have a large population concentrated within a small territory, and rural settlements, which belong to regional councils with disproportionately sizable territories relative to their small population, accentuated the social and economic disadvantages of the residents of the development towns. Similarly, the emergence of satellite suburban communities in the Beer Sheva metropolitan area, with their populations of a notably high socioeconomic level, highlighted the disadvantaged situation of the small towns and the much larger gaps with the nearby Bedouin population.

FIGURE 17. View of the town of Mitzpe Ramon. Photo by author.

The arrival of large waves of immigrants from Ethiopia and from the former Soviet Union (identified as "Russians" in Hebrew) reshaped Israel's demographics in the 1980s and 1990s and stimulated population growth in some of the desert towns. A large proportion of the nearly 55,000 immigrants from Ethiopia was settled in some of the development towns of the southern periphery. As for the Russian immigrants, although the majority of those who arrived in 1989 and those who had more resources chose to settle in the center of the country, the housing crisis of the 1990s led many of the newcomers to move to low-cost apartments that the government built in the development towns.[99] While increasing the population, however, the creation of new enclaves of "Russian neighborhoods" within the largely Mizrahi veteran population also introduced social tensions.[100]

Other developments reveal the ability of some of these marginal desert towns to create distinct cultural niches that contribute to a distinct local identity and bring visitors from the center. Located near the unique Ramon Crater and surrounded by the desert, Mitzpe Ramon, as seen in figure 17, developed its reputation as a tourist destination. Other towns, as Tzfadia and Haim Yacobi point out, have turned their marginalized position on the periphery into an advantage that offers residents creative ways to interweave their diasporic Mizrahi traditions with contemporary Israeli culture and to create alternative forms that make an impact on mainstream Israeli culture.[101] Three development towns, Netivot, Yerucham, and Sderot, provide examples of this trend.

Netivot developed its distinct niche as a religious center as part of the revival of the North African Jewish tradition of pilgrimage to the graves of rabbis (*tsaddikim*) known for their piety, learning, and spiritual powers and the holding of large communal celebrations (*hillulot*) in their honor. The tradition, which had been disrupted by the communities' immigration and Israeli society's pressures on new immigrants to relinquish their diasporic traditions, began to reappear on the Israeli periphery. By the 1980s, their revival began to attract considerable media coverage and scholarly interest.[102] In Netivot, the death of the much-admired Moroccan rabbi Yisrael Abuhatzeira (known as the "Baba Sali") in 1984 brought large crowds of followers in succeeding years to mark the annual anniversary of his death. A new memorial complex was soon erected around his tomb and became the destination of a new religious pilgrimage. This development was supported by the local municipality, and the memorial site was later recognized by the state.[103]

Yerucham provides an example of the process of acculturation to Israeli mnemonic traditions and the interweaving of new and old. The town changed the celebration of its origins from its historical date at the beginning of the Hebrew month of Shevat to Tu Bishvat, the holiday celebrated on the fifteenth of the same month. As I mentioned earlier, the cultural strategy of using a day that is already marked on the calendar as a site for the commemoration of another historical event makes room for the reinterpretation of that historical event.[104] This association links Yerucham with an important holiday in Hebrew culture that embodies the Zionist ethos of "making the desert bloom." The new dating adds a "mnemonic veil,"[105] obscuring the founders' own narratives of ambivalence and resentment at being sent to the desert without prior consent or sufficient support and fitting Yerucham's commemoration of its beginnings to the Zionist redemptive narrative. Similarly, the establishment of a "Founders' Park" (*Park Rishonim*) at the center of the town conforms to the Israeli mnemonic practice and the emphasis on pioneers as representing collective beginnings.

The desert town of Sderot in the western Negev presents yet another example of the creative accommodation of new and old. Sderot established a unique reputation as a cultural hub associated with such famous cultural figures as Shimon Adaf and Kobi Oz, mentioned earlier, as well as being the home of popular musical bands including *Sefatayim*, *Teapacks*, and *Knesiyat Hasechel*. The anthropologist Galit Saadia-Ophir observes that the bands' eclectic style represents the sensibilities of second-generation Mizrahi Israelis in fusing rock and pop music with North African musical traditions, and in their linguistic shifts from their parents' Arabic dialects to other languages, including Hebrew. Drawing on their marginalized experience growing up in immigrant families and on the periphery, they experiment in boundary crossing and interweaving old and new and Eastern and Western elements, while writing lyrics that often have a subversive edge.[106] Sderot's distinct cultural contribution is further enhanced by the establishment of the nearby Sapir College, the opening of the Sderot Cinematheque, and the annual *Darom* (*South*) *Film Festival*, which draw in visitors from other parts of the Negev and the center of the country.[107]

The fluctuating security situation in the western Negev following the beginning of the Second Intifada in 2000 and, more acutely, following Israel's withdrawal from Gaza in 2005 has a direct and deep effect on the residents of this area. In periods of heightened tensions, when rockets are fired from the Gaza Strip and when Israel conducts military operations against Gaza, siren warnings allow for a few seconds only to find refuge in a sheltered space. At such times, the proximity to the border creates an acute sense of being exposed to danger at the frontier and triggers traumatic responses to this situation. Laura Bialis's film *Red in Sderot*, which was initially designed to focus on the town's special bands and musical life, turned into a documentary of everyday disruptions to life in a frontier town under the threat of destruction and death. The film features residents' responses to the situation, ranging from those determined to stay at any cost to those who wish they could leave, and presents vivid expressions of frustration at the government's failure to guarantee their safety. As Tzfadia and Yacobi note, the duality of "periphery" and "frontier" contributes to the complexity of life in the development town. Whereas the low socioeconomic status of the town's population reinforces their sense of living in a neglected periphery, the periods of heightened military tension redefine them as frontierspeople who contribute to the country's defense and to the cultural capital and material benefits that this situation brings with it.[108] The sense of the duality of periphery and frontier that marks their experience is also articulated by other Negev residents.

The New Pioneers

Since the 1980s, the Negev has regained some of its appeal as an open space that offers new venues in which to pursue the settlement agenda and the pioneering ethos of "making the desert bloom," while providing affordable housing and the opportunity to experience a different environment. Furthermore, as opposed to the occupied territories, the desert region represents a legitimate frontier within Israel's pre-1967 borders that enjoys a broad consensus. This new period has thus seen the emergence of new types of Zionist pioneers in the southern region. Some of them arrived with the conscious wish to become a new type of Zionist pioneer, whether in support of existing settlements or by experimenting with new forms of settlement. Others were motivated by the wish to introduce a change into their lives or to move away from the societal pressures and economic cost of the urban center. Significantly, local authorities and national agencies, alarmed that the fast-growing Bedouin population in the Negev posed a demographic and security threat (see chapter 6), mobilized to support a new drive to enhance and diversify the Jewish settlement of the desert. This change thus articulated the revival of the view that the Negev could become a viable frontier.

Some religious Zionist youth groups chose the mission of settling in the Negev and strengthening Israel's struggling development towns, in contrast to the more visible religious Zionist drive to establish new Jewish settlements in the West Bank and Gaza. Members of the Benei Akiba youth movement from Jerusalem arrived in Yerucham in the 1980s within the framework of a combined military and communal service, with the goal of staying there beyond that period. In time, the new residents contributed to the development of the town, and in spite of some reservations by the older immigrant community and periodic tensions, the new residents became a part of the town's social landscape. Other religious Zionist groups and individuals joined Yerucham and other desert towns such as Sderot, Netivot, Arad, and Mitzpe Ramon. Their contribution was most salient in the educational domain, as they established a variety of religious schools (*yeshivot*) that diversified the educational offerings for local students and attracted religious students from other areas of the country.[109] Expanding beyond formal education in Yerucham, they also created a pluralistic learning center, *Ba-Midbar* ("In the Desert"), as a meeting place for Negev residents, as well as a public history project to interview older residents about their lives and the town's past.[110]

A similar drive to strengthen the periphery led young members of kibbutzim and the secular Zionist youth movements to introduce a new model of "urban kibbutz" pioneering, which departed from the earlier emphasis on rural communes. In 1987, Kibbuts Migvan joined the town Sderot. As one of its founders explained her decision,

> I grew up on a rural kibbutz characterized by its closed and homogenous society, which surrounded itself by a physical fence that developed, in time, into a cultural and mental fence. We had no point of contact with the outside world.[111]

The move to urban kibbutzim thus grew out of the desire to repair the historical rupture between the kibbutzim and the development towns as well as to address the crisis that the kibbutz movement was experiencing in the 1980s, by modifying its vision and agenda for social action. In 1994, the urban kibbutz movement established an organization named *Gvanim* that sponsors multiple social and educational projects.[112] In spite of the movement's social vision, however, these newcomers, who come from the Ashkenazi middle class and have a different lifestyle and values, are not always welcomed by the old-timers in town, who resent their ability to reshape their community's economic and social development.[113]

Another grassroots organization promoting pioneering values and social activism, *Ayalim*, was formed by students of the Ben-Gurion University of the Negev in 2002. Its founders had the agenda of creating student villages near existing settlements in the periphery and volunteering for community service in low-income urban neighborhoods in return for a stipend to help with tuition fees. Within three years, the organization had grown to two hundred members, selected from five thousand applicants, and their first new student village, Kfar Adiel, became the model for renewed pioneering. *Ayalim's* website now features its members as "21st-century pioneers" and notes their achievements in constructing various compounds and communities in peripheral spaces around the country.[114]

In 2005, a student-member of this village described to me the impact of participating in this experiment: "It was an amazing experience to see how a new village is built within a month in an entirely desolate desert landscape. I'm proud to say that I live there."[115] He further added that given the deeply rooted view of the desert as desolate and unexciting, their most difficult challenge was to convince other students to join this village: "We first try to bring people to see the desert, to break the myth that the desert is dry and there is nothing there." Later he mentioned that they also attempt to use "teasers" (he used the English word in Hebrew), such as: "When did you last do something for the very first time? Who says that one cannot fulfill one's dreams?" As is often the case, references to the desert environment alternated between "an entirely desolate desert landscape" and "the myth that the desert is dry and there is nothing there" within the same conversation, without my interlocutor being aware of the underlying contradiction between these references. Like other new pioneers in the Negev, his explanation drew on old-school pioneering values, but added an emphasis on the more current individualistic ethos of self-fulfillment.

The sparsely settled Arava desert along the southeastern part of the Negev became home to other experimental settlements. In 1989, a group of young people from Jerusalem who were inspired by the vision of creating a different community in the desert established kibbutz Neot Semadar, in the southern Arava. This small kibbutz community has emphasized the development of organic agriculture, ecological buildings, and the arts, and has become known for its distinct culture.[116] Another experimental settlement is the first residential community in the central part of the Arava desert, named Tsukim, which was established in 2004.[117] Its founders were urbanite professional Israelis who wanted to make a significant midlife change and were attracted to this remote desert area. As a resident of Tsu-kim explains it, he experiences a qualitative difference in his life in his new desert environment:

> One lives differently here. One lives at a slow pace. Everything is slow, the
> air is clean, there is a consensus, there are no Arabs, not even Bedouins.
> This is the place where one can truly turn over a new leaf.[118]

The desert environment he describes represents for him a detachment from the past and from the maladies of the present: the hectic pace of modern life, the polluted air, the argumentative culture, and the Arabs. The "emptiness" of the nonplace thus offers a refuge from the "place" and a symbolic suspension from the flow of time. This approach evokes the desert mystique that fundamentally differs from the negative view of the desert as the counter-place, and will be further explored in chapter 6.

Another new trend that has emerged in the Negev since the early 2000s focuses on the establishment of new residential religious settlements. Unlike religious kibbutzim and the traditionally oriented immigrant *moshavim* that had been established earlier, the new religious settlements draw on a religious population that is better known for its political support of the Right and includes those who come to the Negev from Jewish settlements in "Judea and Samaria," the Hebrew names referring to the West Bank. The first new religious Zionist settlement at the center of the Negev, in Ramat Negev, was Merchav Am, a small residential community that was founded in November of 2001. Its name alludes to the quality of the "open space" (*merhav*) that the desert landscape represents and redefines it as a "national space" (*merhav*). As its website explains, the name also serves as a commemorative toponym for the late Rehavam Ze'evi, the far-right politician and minister of tourism who was assassinated by a Palestinian in Jerusalem at around that time. The website interweaves the old pioneering rhetoric with allusions to religious discourse.

> The foundation of the settlement was another phase in a long and ex-
> hausting process: the struggle for the renewal of the settlement of the
> Negev and for continuity in Zionist activism (for more than thirteen
> years there was no new settlement in the Negev!) . . . On the *Va Yir'a*
> Sabbath, the first four families arrived in the settlement. . . . For the first
> time in two thousand years (probably) we lit the Sabbath candles and
> received the Sabbath on the hilltop in the middle of nowhere, looking
> into the infinite vastness of the Negev.[119]

The introduction of a religious Zionist settlement whose members had grown up in Jewish settlements in the occupied territories and who identify with the Israeli Right provoked strong opposition among veteran kibbutzim members in the region, who identified with secular Labor Zionism. The head of the Ramat Negev Regional Council, Shmuel Rifman, while acknowledging that opposition, insisted that the growth of the Jewish population in Ramat Negev would ultimately depend on the mobilization of religious Zionist youth who were ideologically committed to the Jewish settlement mission and had the experience of living in challenging conditions.[120]

A grassroots organization called *Or* National Missions (*Or*, i.e. light, for short) was founded in 2002 to advance the agenda of creating settlements in the peripheries, and it developed into a major driving force behind new settlement initiatives in the Negev, promoting the model of homogenous religious or secular Jewish communities.[121] While this policy was designed to minimize internal frictions, it further enhanced the religious and ethnonational divisions within the Negev population. *Or*'s publicity associates its agenda with the old Zionist pioneering ideals, prominently displaying Ben-Gurion's famous dictum—"It is in the Negev that the creativity and the pioneer vigor of Israel shall be tested" (see figure 13). But it is also grounded in the contemporary individualistic ethos that it emphasizes, "the pursuit of meaningful life with the most promising opportunities for investment, innovation, and economic growth."[122] *Or* National Missions has received national awards, among them the President's Volunteers Award, for being "new pioneers in the settlement of the country" and for "their contribution to communities in the Negev and the Galilee."[123]

The diversification of the Jewish population, with Haredi (ultra-Orthodox) communities joining development towns, has introduced further changes into the Negev population. Traditionally concentrated in a few large cities, Haredi communities have now moved into new cities, where they form a majority, as well as into towns on the periphery, where they can find affordable housing for their quickly expanding society. The move of Haredi families, notably from the Gur Hasidic community, into Arad provoked tensions in the town, which recently erupted in a violent clash between secular and Haredi residents. The changing trends within Haredi society and the impact of their movement into various urban centers have been widely covered by the media.[124] The government's approval of a new Haredi city, Kasif, to be built in Tel Arad is similarly discussed as designed to meet the housing needs of this rapidly growing Jewish sector and contribute to the government's agenda of increasing the Jewish population on the periphery. Yet opposition to this plan focuses on social, economic, and environmental concerns, including the argument that the addition of a large and less-productive community would aggravate the economic difficulties and social tensions in the Negev.[125]

By 2016, the population of the Negev had increased to 712,000, which represents less than nine percent of Israel's population. Of the Jewish population, which totals 422,000, more than half lives in the Beer Sheva region (with the rest much more geographically spread out), compared to the Arab population, whose 249,800 are concentrated in the Beer Sheva region.

Perhaps the most interesting phenomenon among the new settlement projects is the emergence of the individual farmsteads (*havot bodedim*) as an innovative and attractive kind of settlement. Although the individual farm has been prominent in the global history of other frontiers, it was rare in the history of Israeli society, given the predominant collectivist ethos of Labor Zionism during the pioneering period and the historical reliance on communal settlements in settling the frontier. There were only two individual farms in the 1950s and seven in the 1970s, the most famous of these being the general-turned-politician Ariel Sharon's Sycamore Farm, in the Negev, near Sderot. The individual farm emerged as an attractive settlement model during the 1980s, and by the early 2000s there were 54 farms on the southern periphery and 31 in the Galilee.[126] This model was a good fit with the turn towards a neoliberal economy and the growing individualistic ethos, and combined the benefit of economic incentives with the cultural capital of agricultural settlements in advancing the Jewish national agenda.[127] When the Ramat Negev Regional Council, which administered the rural settlements at the center of the Negev, announced the development of a large project of individual farms along Route 40 (the highway that cuts through its territory from north to south) in the late 1990s, the novelty and scope of this project soon attracted public attention.[128]

This project of establishing individual farms along what was to be called the "Wine Route" was, however, promoted without the required official process and approval. This move followed the pre-state settlement strategy of establishing "facts on the ground" with the assumption that approval would be granted retroactively—or, as one newspaper headline put it, "build today and get approval tomorrow."[129] This strategy had been proven effective during the mandatory period and more recently in promoting Jewish settlements in the occupied territories.[130] At the turn to the twenty-first century, the growing urgency felt by the Ramat Negev Regional Council to restore the viability of the Negev as a Jewish frontier led to its embrace of this strategy. As expected, it received the tacit collaboration of cabinet members and national agencies: the Jewish Agency, the Israel Land Authority, and the Jewish National Fund participated in the process; Israel's water and electrical companies connected the new farms to their infrastructure; and Rifman, the head of the Regional Council, provided the new settlers with guidance and support.[131]

The Wine Route project aroused public attention, including strong opposition from the environmental lobby, which resulted in a series of lawsuits. Thus, the Israel Union for Environmental Defense (known as *Adam, Teva, V'din*) and the Society for the Protection of Nature in Israel (SPNI) filed a lawsuit against individual farms, focusing on their lack of compliance with the legal procedure. The lawsuit presented the argument that by directing resources to the farms, the Ramat Negev Regional Council and other ministries and national agencies involved in the settlement process were violating the approved national priority of strengthening the existing struggling settlements on the periphery. The environmental organizations further warned that the infrastructure designed for multiple farms spread over a large territory would inflict irreversible damage on the desert landscape. The State Comptroller and Ombudsman's report affirmed the lack of compliance with regulations by the government offices and national agencies that supported these farms. The Supreme Court's ruling acknowledged the impropriety of the procedure and required the government to present a legal framework that would support the Wine Route farms project, but allowed the existing farms to remain intact until the legal paperwork was produced.[132]

In 2002, the Sharon government issued a formal resolution highlighting the national significance of individual farmsteads as a means "to realize the government's policy to develop the Negev and the Galilee and to protect state lands."[133] When additional farms were added to the Wine Route project without approval, the SPNI filed a further lawsuit with the court of the southern district. By the end of 2004, the government had submitted an official plan for the Wine Route farms to the court, presenting the framework based on agriculture and tourism for a total of thirty farms.[134] The official name of the project (the Wine Route) foregrounded the agricultural component and evoked an association with wine tourism as well as with the ancient Nabbatean Incense Route. The loose economic basis, combining agricultural production with tourism, nonetheless left room for individual choices for farm owners to establish their farms' distinct character and touristic appeal, as discussed in chapter 7. In May of 2006, the National Council for Planning approved this plan.

The establishment of a new cabinet-level ministry for the development of the Negev and the Galilee further indicated the priority the government gave to the Jewish settlement of these regions. Yet the lack of clarity about the situation of the existing farmsteads led to new tensions when farm owners objected to an open public procedure about the land on which their farms had been built, for fear it might jeopardize their claim to and investment in their farms. Ironically, the State of Israel and the Israel Land Authority now opposed the individual farm owners and the Ramat Negev Regional Council, labeling the owners "trespassers" on state land. The "Individual Farms Forum," representing the owners, in turn sued the government in 2008, refuting this accusation by providing evidence of the extensive support that government ministries and public agencies had provided them. In 2010, further legislation recognized the special circumstances of the existing farms, thereby opening the way for approval of ten individual farms in 2012.[135] The minister of tourism and deputy prime minister, Silvan Shalom, stated that the owners were "the new Zionists who cultivate the virgin land by their own hands" and reiterated the government's support of their venture.[136]

Although references along these lines to the new "Zionist pioneers" are repeated often by others, the settlers did not explicitly use this term, even when their stories revealed a close resemblance to the plot structure of the pre-state narratives discussed in chapter 3.[137] Like the earlier pioneers, the present-day settlers typically framed the settlement process as a continuing struggle in which they encountered multiple obstacles in their effort to create a new place out of the desolation of the desert, highlighting their persistence, optimism, and resourcefulness as the key to their success. In a dramatic contrast to the earlier narratives, however, the new narratives present the conflictual framework as revolving around the government bureaucracy that piled hardships on them. This theme is salient not only in the narratives told by those who settled along the Wine Route but in other settlement narratives as well. Thus, the owners of an ostrich farm in the western Negev describe a year-long process of running back and forth between various government ministries, until they used a personal connection to reach a top government official who supported their application, and the farm was finally approved.[138] An article about an experimental farm that specializes in cultivating cacti describes the approval process as a "long and torturous track that threatens to destroy [the owner's] life project and ruin his family's future." The journalist expresses outrage at the negative role that the government plays in the settlement process that it advocates:

> One would assume that an old-school Zionist who went to the Negev on his own initiative to build a farm that is praised by experts and developed a new, upgraded variety of Sabra cactus . . . would have received any aid possible from the establishment. They should have applauded him, raised him up as a model [and] as an educational figure. Instead, [he suffered] abuse.[139]

The bureaucratic requirements are thus reconstructed as an obstacle analogous to those introduced by external hostile forces in the earlier narratives. In the case of the Wine Route farms, the stories revolve around the adverse impact of the long litigation process, anxiety over the future of the farm, the conflicting messages received from the government and the national agencies at various levels, and the difficulties of living in provisional housing, lacking basic infrastructure, for such a long time.[140] Indeed, the impact of the prolonged transitional phase without a housing permit could also be observed in what Eitan Elgar referred to as the "gray" structures the settlers used for their homes, which had "fluid foundations" to comply with the legal restrictions on permanent structures, but attempted to project the look of a permanent home.[141]

Another important departure is the theme of self-realization and the possibilities inherent in the move to the desert for introducing a change in one's life, for realizing a personal dream, and for personal growth. The centrality of this theme highlights the individualistic framework typical of these narratives and stands out in its contrast to the immigrants' stories from the 1950s and 1960s, which articulate their lack of choice and agency, their fear, and the sense of closed opportunities. An advertisement quotes a farm owner's emphasis on self-realization: "Instead of fantasizing about a house in nature, I got up and moved to a farm in the desert."[142] His website further elaborates on this theme:

> In 1998, Dandan and Lilach came from northern Tel Aviv and arrived at an isolated hill overlooking the vast expanses of the Negev, and fell in love with it. They packed their belongings and moved into a small trailer without water, sewage, or electricity but with huge determination to work and realize a dream.[143]

Another website, for a camel ranch in Eilat, similarly describes the settlement as the fulfillment of a personal dream: "In 1987, an exceptional person decided to move heaven and earth in order to achieve his dream of a camel ranch in the middle of the desert."[144] The media, too, picked up on this theme. The headline of a newspaper story about establishing a cattle farm in the western Negev underscores the same theme: "A Dream Was Fulfilled."[145] A 2005 flyer for the Nahal Boker Farm on the Wine Route further elaborates:

> Since he was a child, Moshe had dreamed of an agricultural farm, and Hilda dreamed of a farm in southern France. They dreamed, and dreamed, and dreamed . . . until one day this dream was realized. They both fell in love with the Negev and have been living there since 1984.

The theme of "realizing a dream" is closely linked with the theme of "a new beginning." A farm owner told me that only in the desert can one truly "begin from the beginning," using the biblical term *bereshit*. Another Negev resident explained that "in the city it is difficult to start something from the very beginning; there is no longer any virgin land."[146] The website of the camel farm introduces its settlement story by borrowing from the book of Genesis: "In the beginning there was chaos," and continues by depicting the settlement process as shaping chaos into "a recognizable shape."[147] The imposition of order on a chaotic landscape and the creation of recognizable forms is particularly striking when it involves cultivating plants that serve as characteristic representations of the desert or the untamed natural landscape. Thus, one can observe the straight rows of planted palm trees in Ein Gedi or the Arava plantations or the large field of cacti planted in straight lines in the Orly Cacti Farm, on the road from Yerucham to Dimona.

The theme of self-realization often appears along with an emphasis on the search for a new idea that will set the farm apart from other tourist sites, the better to attract visitors. Thus, the owners of the ostrich farm mentioned above relate that they had gone to South Africa and learned how to raise ostriches while there, and returned to Israel with smuggled ostrich eggs in order to start their own farm.[148] The website of the alpaca farm near Mitzpe Ramon presents a similar theme:

> We wandered as far as the Andes in South America and there we met the charming alpacas and llamas for the first time. This was love at first sight, and this is how the idea of bringing these animals to Israel and raising them here came about.[149]

A 2004 article about the opening of another antelope farm in the Arava alludes to a sudden revelation by a veteran desert resident, who "woke up one morning and decided to realize his dream: to establish a farm that raises antelopes to sell to zoos all over the world."[150] The discovery of a solution is thus described as a sort of epiphany or a love at first sight that further underscores the distinction of their choice.

Less common is the alternative theme of a chance encounter with the Negev that leads to a spontaneous decision to change the course of one's life and move to the desert. The owners of a successful catering company in Tel Aviv learned about the individual farm initiative in Ramat Negev in the paper and, fascinated by the idea, made an immediate change of plans:

> Zohar and Oren, who were on their way to a vacation abroad, turned around and went straight to the offices of Shmulik Rifman, the head of the Ramat Negev Regional Council. The outcome: a fascinating farm with a variety of animals, horses for riding, and a gourmet restaurant overlooking a primal desert landscape.[151]

An artist couple who had decided to leave the fast track of their former city life and start over in the desert told me that they made the change as a result of a mechanical problem that forced them to stop in the middle of the desert while driving from Eilat back to Tel Aviv. Their unexpected stay in a small desert town made them realize the potential for living a different life, and the change made a profound impact on their philosophical outlook and artistic work. But departing from the shared emphasis on the lure of the desert in various stories of those who had decided to become new settlers, a Negev resident of two decades remarked, in a conversation, on his slow and difficult adjustment to the desert. "It took me a long time to feel that this was my home," he noted, and after a short reflection, added: "The desert is large and the dialogue with it is not simple."

5

The Negev Bedouins

THE RELATIVELY LATE DEVELOPMENT of the Negev as a frontier introduced a new geographical proximity between the southern Bedouins and the Jews, who had had more contact, prior to the 1940s, with the Bedouins of northern Palestine and neighboring areas. The shift in the status of the Negev region from an external frontier, far away from the center of the Jewish population, to an internal frontier produced fundamental changes in the relationship between the Jews and the Negev Bedouins following the establishment of the state. The deeply established association of the Bedouins with the desert inspired the romantic lore of the desert mystique, but it also aligned them with the desert as an inherently hostile and chaotic counter-place within the discourse of the settlement. This association played a central role in shaping the ambiguous place of the Bedouins in the Negev, officially belonging to Israeli national space yet often perceived as belonging to the subversive counter-place. Although the complexity of the issues related to the Bedouins' situation (and that of other Palestinian citizens of Israel) obviously extends beyond the present framework, this chapter focuses on the tensions underlying the Bedouins' settlements in the Negev as shaped by their identification with the desert within the discourse of the settlement.

The Negev Bedouins, who had moved to the Negev from the Arabian Peninsula, preserved their distinct identity and the traditions that identified them as the descendants of the original Arabs. Over time, the multi-tribal Bedouin society in the Negev expanded, transforming its earlier nomadic lifestyle to a seminomadic way of life by the end of the nineteenth century.

The incorporation of lower-class *fellahin*, who had migrated from Egypt and introduced limited cultivation of land, supported this change.[1] Estimates of the size of the Bedouin population in the Negev during the British mandatory period vary because they tended to evade official surveys, but Israeli sources estimated it at around 70,000.[2] Bedouins lived in close proximity to the hastily constructed Jewish outposts and communal settlements of the 1940s, and Jews who settled in the desert were mindful of their minority status in the region and the need to foster good neighborly relations with the Bedouins. To accommodate local customs, the Jewish residents introduced hospitality tents at the entrances of their settlements in which they could welcome Bedouin visitors, and designated one of their members to serve as the *mukhtar* (in Arabic, the head of a village) who handled their contacts with neighboring Bedouins.[3]

The United Nations vote on partition in November of 1947 heightened the tensions between Arabs and Jews in Palestine and led to the escalation of hostilities in the Negev as well. The Bedouins were divided in their responses to the situation: while some prominent sheiks aligned themselves openly with the Arabs, others declared their neutrality in the conflict, and a few sheiks aligned their tribes with the Jews.[4] During the course of the 1948 war, many of the Negev Bedouins from the northern and western Negev left the battle zone for other areas, including Gaza, the Sinai Peninsula, the West Bank, and Jordan. When the Israeli army advanced into the Negev and took control of that region, it expelled some Bedouin tribes whom it considered hostile to Israel but let others, who declared their loyalty to the state, stay. As a result of these events, the Negev Bedouin population was drastically reduced, down to a number estimated at between 11,000 to 12,470 persons.[5]

Exiled at Home

The ambiguity of the postwar situation in the southern desert region had direct implications for the position of the Negev Bedouins. Like other Israeli Arabs, the Bedouins lived as a minority on the margins of Israeli society, and Israel assigned priority to its own security needs in determining its policies toward them. The state saw the Bedouins' presence in the northern Negev and near the border with the Gaza Strip, where there was a large population of refugees, as a security threat, and sought to move them away from those areas. It therefore relocated the majority of the Bedouins of the northern and western Negev to an area named Siyag ("fence" in Arabic) located east of Beer Sheva, which had been inhabited by some other Bedouin tribes.[6] Like other Arab citizens at the time, the Negev Bedouins were placed under military administration, and their movements were confined to the Siyag area.[7] Their relocation and the subsequent restrictions imposed on them had long-term consequences. The move weakened their ties to the land on which they had lived and thereby lowered their status within the Bedouin society. Moreover, the mostly arid land of Siyag offered limited options for cattle-grazing and for dry farming, and the scarce economic resources increased their dependence on the military authorities.

While the state was relocating and restricting most of the Negev Bedouins to that small and less desirable desert area, it also advanced legislation to strengthen its hold over land in the northern and western Negev to promote its settlement agenda and security needs.[8] The state drew on an earlier Ottoman law (which the British Mandate upheld) that classified land that was not officially registered as owned by individuals and that remained uncultivated as *mawat* (i.e. "dead"), and allowed the state to claim it as its own. With the majority of the former Negev Bedouin residents now living outside of Israel and formally declared absentee, and with most of those who remained in Israel relocated and without records of land ownership, the state declared the majority of the Negev state land. Large portions of this land were declared military zones and nature reserves, as I noted in chapter 4 and discuss in greater detail in chapter 6. Yet state land was also distributed to existing agricultural Jewish settlements or designated for the establishment of new settlements.

The state also continued to employ the pre-state strategy of afforestation as a means of promoting the settlement ethos of fighting the desert and ensuring its hold over land in the northern Negev. The Jewish National Fund (JNF) thus began planting the Lahav Forest in the northern Negev in 1952 and the Yatir Forest in 1964; the latter has developed into Israel's largest forest. The JNF website marks the achievement of covering 7,500 acres (30,000 dunams) with planted trees in Yatir as evidence that "we can *combat* desertification and *heal the wounded earth*,"[9] thus employing the war rhetoric of the settlement discourse and associating the desert with illness. Yet planting these forests also served the state's political goal of staking ownership over that land to prevent the Bedouins from resettling there and to create buffer zones to protect Jewish settlements in that area.[10]

As Muslim Arabs, the Bedouins residing in the Negev and in the Galilee are part of the Arab minority in Israel. It took several years of transition before the government issued official identity cards to the Bedouins who had remained in the Negev in 1948, affirming their status as Israeli citizens. Some Bedouins who returned to the Negev after the foundation of the state received permanent resident status, while others lacked any proper documentation. Yet Israel has also recognized the Bedouins as having a distinct ethnic identity that differentiated them from other Muslim Arabs.[11] The implications of this distinction were most clearly evident in the military domain. With few exceptions, Muslim and Christian citizens are exempt from service in the Israel Defense Forces (IDF),[12] which is mandatory for most Israeli Jews, but the IDF actively encouraged the Bedouins to volunteer for military service. The army underscored the special connection between the Bedouins and the desert and their outstanding tracking skills. When it formed the special Bedouin Trackers Unit in 1970, the unit's insignia prominently featured the iconic flying camel,

adding a tiny military jeep underneath it. When the IDF formed the Desert Patrol Battalion in the late 1980s, its insignia no longer showed a camel but transferred the wings to the military jeep and introduced the desert landscape as a visual marker of the unit's special identity (figure 18).[13]

Service in the security forces promises certain privileges and educational and economic opportunities, which may be particularly important for those coming from a disadvantaged background, and can even offer an opportunity to gain Israeli citizenship for those without formal citizenship papers. In spite of their reputation as trackers and soldiers, however, the Bedouins' Arab names and identities put them in a more ambiguous position, which limits the opportunities that military service provides.[14] The case of Abd al-Majid

FIGURE 18. The Desert Patrol Battalion's insignia. Courtesy of the IDF Spokesperson's Unit.

Hajer, a Bedouin career officer who was more widely known in Israel by his adopted Hebrew name, Amos Yarkoni, illuminates this ambiguity. Yarkoni, who was a decorated officer and lost his right arm in action, served as the operational commander of the elite patrol unit *Sayeret Shaked* before he was appointed the unit's official head. The unit's website details his heroic and complicated service, and notes that "only few knew that *Shaked's* commander was a Muslim Arab. Even the unit's own soldiers didn't always know the truth and believed that he was a Jew of Middle Eastern origin."[15] Although the phenomenon of Bedouins who volunteer to serve in the IDF has attracted public attention, their numbers have remained relatively small,[16] and further developments in relation to the state have complicated their attitude toward the IDF, as will be further discussed below.

Towns and "Dispersion"

Following the abolition of military administrative control over Arab citizens in 1966, the Bedouins who had been relocated to Siyag were free to leave that area. This change improved their opportunities to earn a livelihood but also made their precarious situation as a marginalized group and as residents of the desert more visible. Those who returned from their exile in Siyag to other parts of the Negev found that they no longer held a recognized home territory, and the majority of the Bedouin population remained in the heart of the Negev, in the area between Beer Sheva, Arad, and Dimona. With land issues pending, and waiting for a settlement with the state over their land claims, the Bedouins took up residence in provisional, spontaneous settlements lacking any official status. The Israeli government, on its part, advanced the strategy of creating specially designed towns for the Negev Bedouins that would concentrate them in a more limited urban setting, modernize them, and resolve land ownership issues by offering them residence in exchange for relinquishing any land claims.

In the 1970s, the government called upon the Bedouins to submit their land claims, requiring written proofs of ownership. The Bedouins' response to this call was limited, and only a small portion of the claims were settled this way.[17] The legal process revealed a cultural clash in approaches to land ownership. The Israeli Supreme Court reaffirmed the 1950s land laws that had identified most of the uncultivated Negev land as *mawat*, and therefore state land, leaving the onus of proof on individual Bedouins; yet without official documents proving ownership, Israeli law recognizes only partial "holding rights" (*hazaka*).[18] The Bedouins, on the other hand, relied on their traditional customs and historical rights to the land and had been historically averse to state bureaucracy. Instead, they point to evidence of their cultivation of land in the Negev since the second half of the nineteenth century, and to their recent return and "revival" of the land.

The Israeli government began to implement its urbanization plan as early as 1968, when it built the first Bedouin town in the Negev, Tel Sheva, and relocated those who had agreed to the government's terms to the town. Not surprisingly, the new town attracted mostly lower-class Bedouins, who were landless and therefore had the most to gain from such a move, and the resulting association of Tel Sheva with the lower stratum of Bedouin society undermined its appeal to others. The planners' disregard for the Bedouins' familial and tribal structures further compounded the lack of fit between the traditional Bedouin lifestyle and the urban setting. The Bedouins soon regarded this urban experiment as a failure. When a second and much larger Bedouin town, Rahat, was built in the early 1970s, its planners attempted to address those earlier shortcomings, yet with mixed results. Rahat first seemed to be a better alternative to Tel Sheva, but the high unemployment rate, rising crime, and low educational standards soon damaged its reputation, and the Bedouins ultimately regarded it as yet more evidence of the government's failure to meet their needs.[19]

The government pursued its urbanization plan during the 1980s and through the early 1990s, adding five more Bedouin towns—Lakiya, Hura, Kusseifa, Aru'er, and Segev Shalom—to the earlier two. The government's 2005 blueprint for the development of the Negev, widely known as "Negev 2015," identified systemic problems in the Bedouin towns compared to other Jewish settlements in the Negev and to Arab towns in the Galilee.[20] In spite of the government's efforts to draw lessons from its past planning mistakes, the Bedouin towns continued to lack basic infrastructure, such as sewage systems and public transportation.[21] Because there was a limited economic foundation and rampant poverty and unemployment in these towns, residents depended on job opportunities in nearby Jewish settlements. There was also a wide educational gap between the Jewish and Bedouin populations, with the Bedouins at the bottom of the scale of educational achievements.[22] Some of the recognized Bedouin towns and settlements were, however, able to improve their economies through communal collaborations and tourist initiatives (see chapter 7). It is important to note that although the Bedouin population as a whole is located at the lowest end of Israeli society's socioeconomic ladder, a professional Bedouin middle class has emerged as individual Bedouins pursue professional careers in health, social work, academia, law, and the military, and the Negev's institutions of higher education have opened special programs to further support Bedouin students.

While the government insisted on the viability of the towns it had built as the solution to the Bedouins' situation, a significant portion of the Bedouin population refused to settle its land claims and move into these towns. The emphasis in traditional Bedouin society on the value of land as a source of power and prestige, the limited monetary and land compensation that the government offered for moving into the designated towns, the Bedouins' refusal to be settled on land contested by Bedouin claims that had been incorporated into the towns' territory, and the difficulties reported by those who had agreed to move to the Bedouin towns, were all reasons why many Bedouins would not comply with the government's relocation plan. In spite of the difficult conditions in their spontaneous villages and the pressures applied by the government, they preferred to stay in the unrecognized settlements and maintain their traditional way of life.[23]

The Bedouin population in the Negev has grown rapidly, and the sight of small Bedouin settlements scattered across the desert landscape (see figure 19) evokes the gloomy images of the *ma'abarot*, the transit camps for new Jewish immigrants of the early post-independence years. Yet the transit camps were created by the young state of Israel at a time when the state had just emerged from a major war, was faced with large waves of

FIGURE 19. A Bedouin site in Negev. Photo by Moshe Milner; courtesy of the Government Press Office.

immigrants, and was under economic duress. The Bedouins' spontaneous settlements, by contrast, are a grassroots phenomenon undertaken by a population that lived in this region before the establishment of the state and prefers this liminal condition to the state's plan to relocate them to urban settings.

Because of their lack of legal status, the settlements lack the basic infrastructure of roads, running water, a central sewage system, electricity, and public transportation to which legal settlements are entitled. Their residents therefore improvise illegal connections to the nearby infrastructure to get electricity or water, or put up generators for their personal use. The proximity of some of these settlements to environmentally unsafe industrial plants and electric grids poses direct health hazards to their residents (see discussion of the village Wadi al-Na'am in chapter 7).[24] Until 1995, when a Supreme Court ruling required the state to open clinics in eleven unrecognized villages to cater to the population's health needs, there were no health clinics in the unrecognized villages. Kindergartens and schools are often located at considerable distances, creating difficulties in reaching them on foot or requiring travel in overcrowded school buses.[25] Residents are not permitted to build permanent homes or commercial structures, which would require official permits, and therefore resort to illegal structures that are at risk of being demolished by the authorities. The lack of official status for these settlements also means that their residents are officially denied the status of Negev residents and cannot participate in the democratic process of voting in local elections. At the same time, the residents of the unrecognized villages do not pay the municipality taxes, permit fees, and service charges that residents of legal settlements must pay.[26]

At the beginning of the twenty-first century, nearly half of the Bedouin population lived in the spontaneous villages, although estimates have varied,[27] and the multiple spontaneous settlements have become a fixture of the desert landscape. But even though these numerous villages are clearly visible to the naked eye and have local names, they do not appear on the map of the Negev and are not officially considered in regional planning. Bedouins and human rights activists accuse the government of rendering these villages "invisible" and their residents "transparent."[28] Along similar lines, media reports on the unrecognized villages and their residents carry headlines such as "Hamira Is a Nonplace" and "The Transparent People of the Negev,"[29] and a recent film by an Israeli Jewish director, Moshon Salmona, entitled *Invisible* (*Shekufim*), portrays young Bedouins' lives in the unrecognized villages. The symbolic erasure of these sites articulates the association of the Bedouins with the "empty" desert landscape, the uncultivated and unsettled space that is distinct from the inhabited, cultivated, ordered, and named "place."

This attitude is similarly reflected in the popular reference to the Bedouin population of the unrecognized villages as "dispersion," in Hebrew *pezura*.[30] It is possible to interpret the term as depicting the " 'scattered' method of settlement over wide open spaces," as Shmuel Rifman, the head of the Ramat Negev Regional Council, explains it.[31] But *pezura* also implies "diaspora," and had otherwise been used primarily in reference to Jewish communities living outside of Israel.[32] Its application to this Bedouin population in the Negev thus suggests that they are an uprooted community that does not belong to that place. Indeed, the term *pezura* captures the paradox of the Bedouins' situation, living in a precarious state of liminality as if they were exiles, but on the very land that they consider their home. The term also reveals the historical reversal in the association of the desert with exile: once relating to the Jewish experience, it is now projected onto the Bedouins. It similarly underscores the significant transformation of the popular image of the Bedouins, who once served as a model of the native for European Jews and are now presented as an uprooted community (although we should note that, as we shall see in chapter 7, the tourist discourse continues to draw on their older image). It is not surprising, therefore, that Bedouins objected to the use of this term, claiming, as a 2007 newspaper headline notes: "We Are Not *Pezura*."[33] Similarly, a forum promoting Jewish-Arab coexistence, Together in the Negev, bluntly demanded that "the term 'the Bedouin *pezura*' be erased from the establishment's lexicon, since it implies the perception of the Arab-Bedouin citizens as a mob without a consciousness and rights."[34]

The administrative structures of governance that the government created for the Bedouins reinforced the policy of designating Bedouin citizens as a distinct population, governed by a separate administration headed by Jewish officials. Thus, in 1965, the government established an inter-ministerial "Supreme Bedouin Committee," which was then replaced by a special "Office for Bedouin Development" and later transformed into the "Authority for the Advancement of the Bedouins" (1986–2000), which was placed within the Israel Land Authority. In the educational domain, the state formed the "Authority for Bedouin Education" in 1983, which was headed by a Jewish official until 2004, when his disparaging remarks led to lawsuits and his eventual dismissal in 2005.

Residents of the unrecognized villages have received the support and professional help of various human rights activists and national and local nongovernmental organizations that advocate coexistence between Jews and Arabs and provide professional legal and planning support.[35] The villages created their own self-governance body, "The Regional Council for Unrecognized Negev Arab Villages" (RCUV; also known by its Arabic name, Al-Una) in 1997. RCUV claimed that it represented forty-six unrecognized villages, and it received the endorsement of the Israeli Arabs' Supreme Civil Council as the official representation of that population. Two years later, the new organization presented an alternative development plan to the government's urban relocation project, including a map featuring the unrecognized villages with their Arabic names. It demanded that the government provide health and educational services for the residents of the villages and allow them to hold local elections.[36] A later initiative pursued in collaboration with *Sidreh*, a civic organization devoted to empowering Bedouin-Arab women of the Negev, focused on promoting women's rights.[37]

In 2003, in the context of the Second Intifada, the government allocated additional funding to the Bedouin towns it had established and expressed its intention to involve the Bedouins in future development plans. In the following year, as a countermove to the formation of the RCUV as a representative of the residents of the unrecognized villages, the government created its own Abu Basma Regional Council to represent the Bedouin population in several recognized villages and granted official status to the historical village of Drejat (also spelled Darijat).[38] In 2012, the government replaced the Abu Basma Regional Council with a new structure of two new regional councils, Neve Midbar and El Kasum, which were governed by appointed committees and headed by Jews, to represent the recognized Bedouin settlements of the Negev.[39] It is interesting to note that the names selected for these councils specifically relate to the desert landscape and its nature: *Neve Midbar* means oasis in Hebrew, and *El Kasum*, in Arabic, refers to a medicinal desert plant (known in Latin as Achillea fragrantissima).

In the summer of 2007, after the legal framework for the Wine Route farms was finally approved, the Israeli government passed two consecutive resolutions on the same day, respectively addressing the problem of trespassing as related to the Negev Bedouins and the plan to advance single farms in the Negev and the Galilee.[40] Although each of these resolutions related to a different subject, the sequence suggested an implicit connection between the two as well as the differences in the government's approach to settling illegal settlements, depending on whether they were created by Bedouins or Jews; its larger emphasis on the priority of advancing the Jewish settlement of the Negev and the Galilee peripheries was also articulated in the creation of a special ministry to carry out this mission. The approval of the law regarding "the removal of trespassers" was followed by lawsuits against Bedouins living in the unrecognized villages for their illegal use of state land. It also opened up the possibility of more forceful measures to enhance the pressure on the Bedouins to evacuate the villages and accept the state's relocation policy. In contesting the state's claim that they were trespassers, Bedouins raised the counterargument that the state was the trespasser that took control of their land after their forced relocation in the 1950s, which prevented them from farming or using it as grazing land.[41] Scholars and activists supporting the Bedouin claims have also raised the argument that the state should recognize the latter as an "indigenous people" whose legal tradition must be honored.[42] Other scholars dispute this argument, supporting the state's position on its right to that land.[43]

There are obviously major differences between the unrecognized Bedouin villages and the unapproved Jewish farms in terms of the size of the population and the scope of the contested land involved. By 2007, the size of the Bedouin population in the Negev was estimated at 172,169, and the estimate of the population of those living in unrecognized villages ranged from 62,487 to 84,641; their total claims covered about 162,500 acres (650,000 dunams). The Wine Route project, on the other hand, involved thirty farms, and the average territory for each was estimated at around 845 acres (3,380 dunams).[44] These illegal Bedouin and Jewish settlements existed in the same geographical area and both were developed without approval and hence lacked any official status. Yet the Wine Route's farms received retroactive approval through special legislation, whereas the Bedouin villages remained, as Oren Yiftachel describes it, within a "gray space" that was "neither integrated nor eliminated," thereby "forming pseudo-permanent margins."[45] Their continuing liminality sustained, as Elya Milner and Haim Yacobi note, "a constant tension between practices of obliteration that are central to Israeli space production and international norms preventing complete demolition."[46] The Bedouins and those advocating their cause pointed out the disparity between the government's dealings with the Jewish farms and the Bedouin villages, yet attempts to connect the resolution of the two issues were unsuccessful.[47]

At the end of 2007, the government formed a special commission to examine the situation of the Negev Bedouins. The eight-member commission, which included two Bedouin representatives, was headed by the retired Supreme Court justice Eliezer Goldberg. The Goldberg Commission's report, based on a lengthy and extensive study, was issued in December, 2008. It supported the state's basic legal position towards the Negev Bedouins and its relocation plan, but it also advocated a fundamental change in the state's attitude toward the Bedouins as citizen residents of the Negev who have a historical connection to the Negev and taking into account their needs. The commission recommended involving the Bedouins in future planning processes, as well as recognizing some of the existing Bedouin villages in order to limit the scope of the Bedouins' relocation, exploring the possibility of relocating some villages, and recognizing "gray structures" that do not interfere with the state's settlement plans.[48]

The follow-up team, headed by Ehud Prawer, the director of planning in the prime minister's office and a former deputy head of the National Security Council for Domestic Policy, worked out guidelines for the implementation of the Goldberg Report, which it submitted in May of 2011. However, its plan presented harsher measures than the commission had recommended: it called for the relocation of thirty thousand Bedouin residents from the 35 unrecognized villages, offered no recognition of existing Bedouin villages, and significantly limited the compensation for Bedouin land claims.[49] The plan triggered harsh public criticism for its deviation from the spirit of the Goldberg Report, for its failure to involve the Bedouins in its deliberations, and for disadvantaging those whom the state had relocated to the Siyag zone by the limited compensations it recommended. The RCUV responded by submitting an alternative plan for resolving the crisis, which was prepared with the help of professional planners.[50] In light of the critical response, the government appointed Minister Benny Begin to lead further dialogue with the Bedouins and revise the Prawer plan.

The revised Prawer-Begin plan,[51] which was approved by the Ministerial Committee on Legislation in May 2013 and barely passed in the Knesset on the first vote, encountered strong opposition from both the right and the left. Its critics on the right objected to any negotiation with the Bedouins on land rights as an implicit acknowledgment of their historical claim to the Negev and presented aerial photos indicating that some of the unrecognized villages had been built as recently as the 1990s.[52] Those on the left argued that the Prawer-Begin plan amounted to dispossessing the Bedouins of about ninety percent of the land that they claimed, and pointed out the difference in the criteria that were applied to the unrecognized Bedouin villages and the illegal Jewish farms. They criticized the exclusion of Bedouins from the planning process and claimed that a forced relocation of thirty to forty thousand Bedouins would deny them their basic right to determine their way of life.[53] The political and civic opposition to the plan culminated in a "Day of Rage," including pro-Bedouin demonstrations in the Negev as well as in major Arab cities within Israel and in the West Bank and involving Israeli Palestinian and Jewish activists as well as Palestinians outside of Israel. The response also drew the attention of international human rights organizations to the government plan. The government decided to officially shelve the Prawer-Begin plan, yet adopted some of its recommendations, including the harsher enforcement of state law in the Negev, as we shall see below.[54]

According to the Israel Central Bureau of Statistics for 2016, the total Arab population in the southern district counted 250,800 persons (out of the total district population of 1,244,200), most of whom were located in the greater Beer Sheva region, with a minority of around 2,200 located in the Arava; about 100,000 of these persons were residents of the unrecognized villages.[55] A recent study shows that the sense of displacement and loss among Bedouins who were relocated to the urban settings gave rise to the nostalgic longing for the past that is typical of "exile mentality."[56] As researchers of Bedouin society note, Bedouins' detachment from their land and increased exposure to Westernized consumer culture have created a spiritual void that Islam has filled. Like other Muslim populations in and outside of Israel, the Bedouin society of the Negev has experienced a rise in religious fundamentalism and political radicalization. The Negev Bedouins' renewed contacts with Palestinians from Gaza and Mount Hebron led to the fostering of closer economic and familial ties.[57] In recent years, some Bedouin activists and others insist on replacing the Hebrew term "Negev" with the Arabic term "Naqab" in discussing Bedouin identity, in order to highlight the fact that their historical ties to the desert region predate the state of Israel.[58] Thus, while the state has a policy of separating the Bedouins from other Arabs by treating them as a distinct ethnic group, the Negev Bedouins, like other Arab citizens of Israel, emphasize the Palestinian dimension of their identity.[59] Likewise, other Palestinians demonstrate their solidarity with the Negev Bedouins, as could be seen in their Day of Rage demonstrations against the Prawer plan.

Given these changes, it is not surprising that military service has become a more contentious issue within Bedouin society. The negative attitude toward those who volunteer for the military service becomes most visible during periods of mourning over Bedouin soldiers killed in action, when bereaved families might feel shunned by their community.[60] Although Bedouin youth continue to volunteer to serve in the IDF, their numbers have decreased, and fewer choose to pursue a military career.[61] For those who serve in the security forces, the disconnect between the fact that they are risking their lives for the state and the state's harsh measures against their unrecognized villages is particularly offensive.[62] A 2013 film, *Sharqiya*, directed by Ami Livne, focuses on these tensions, telling the story of a Bedouin working as a security guard in Beer Sheva's central bus station who finds out that the shack in which he lives, in an unrecognized village, has been designated for demolition.[63] Similarly, the film *Invisible*, mentioned earlier, revolves around a young Bedouin man who returns to his unrecognized village after completing his military service. The film depicts his growing frustration at his lack of economic opportunities, exacerbated when the police removes the Bedouin hospitality site he has begun to develop, an act that drives him to join a criminal activity that he had outright rejected when first returning to the village.

The "Wild South"

The connection that was made between life on the Israeli frontier and in the American West had its roots, as we have seen, in the pre-state period, and became more popular in the 1950s, yet the meaning of this analogy varied: the liminality of the frontier offered a sense of freedom and called for courage and resourcefulness, but it also carried the negative image of a chaotic, lawless, and dangerous counter-place. That analogy led to the emergence of the Hebrew expression "the Wild South," which was first used to refer to Eilat but later extended to other parts of the southern region.[64]

The reference to the Negev as the equivalent of the American Wild West is made explicit in Udi Nathan's piece entitled "Welcome to the 'Wild West' of Israel." As he explains:

> The Negev is Israel's frontier region, for better or worse. Almost anyone who lives here has to cope, as everyone knows, with situations that no one would have put up with for a moment at the center [of the country]. In this respect, it's a bit like the Wild West. There is plenty of roughness, lots of hardship, and lots of social and environmental crime.

But, the author adds, to balance this grim picture of the frontier, "there are also people who create wonderful things there."[65] In conversation with me, several Jewish Israeli Negev residents alluded, at times half-jokingly and at other times in anger, to their sense that they live in the "Wild South." Most often, such references address the impact of the Bedouins on the lack of security in the open desert zone, but they also, occasionally, refer to the lack of security along the border with Egypt or to gang activity in the metropolitan Beer Sheva area.[66] Coverage of violent crime in the Negev highlights the Bedouins' visible involvement in thefts, drug and weapon smuggling, and human trafficking, as well as in intertribal violence that culminates in honor killings. Fear of thefts and violent encounters has motivated some Jewish settlements and businesses in the desert area to reinforce their security and led others to pay protection fees for fear of retribution.[67] In 2007, the killing of a Bedouin trespasser by an individual farm owner, Shai Dromi, triggered a heated public debate over the rise of crime in the Negev and whether manslaughter was justified for self-defense. New legislation, widely known as the "Dromi Law," eventually led to Shai Dromi's acquittal.[68] Along with the frequent negative reporting on crime, however, media reports also provide sympathetic coverage of the Bedouins, stressing their plight and suggesting that despair and frustration drive them to criminal activities and to growing alienation from the state.[69]

The association of the "Wild South" with the absence of the rule of law focuses attention on the danger that the rapidly growing Bedouin population poses to the Jewish population of the Negev.[70] The openness of the desert landscape exacerbates the issue, since it allows the unrecognized villages to expand without physical constraints. The media has resorted to alarmist rhetoric regarding the demographic threat, such as "Bedouins Take over the Negev."[71] Politicians, too, arouse the fear of demographic explosion. In 2000, for example, Ariel Sharon used this strategy in an article addressing land ownership issues:

> In the Negev we face a most challenging problem: About 900,000 dunams of state land *are not in our hands*, but in the hands of the Bedouin population. . . . The Bedouins are *grabbing* new territories, and are *gnawing away* at the state's land reserves, and no one is doing anything significant about this.[72]

Sharon, a former cabinet member and the leader of the Likud, was issuing a stern public warning: "*We* are losing the Negev, the last land reserve we have." In the same year, Shmuel Rifman published an article in the same publication entitled "Israel without the Negev Is Not a State and For Sure Not a Jewish State."[73] A few years later, Rifman was quoted as emphasizing the importance of encouraging the religious Zionist Jewish population to settle in Ramat Negev in order to protect the land from the spread of the Bedouin population. "One needs to bring a million Jews to the Negev in order not to lose it to the Bedouins," he argued. If kibbutz members failed to understand that, he warned, they would soon find themselves "a negligent minority within a Bedouin majority."[74] Avigdor Lieberman, a cabinet member in charge of land management, similarly asserted the danger associated with the Bedouins: "We must stop their illegal invasion of state land by all means possible; the Bedouins have no regard for *our* laws" (emphasis added). Lieberman defined his mission as addressing "the non-Jewish threat to our lands" and encouraging the establishment of new Jewish settlements. "If we do not do this," he warned, "we will lose the Negev forever."[75]

These public statements articulate the view that Bedouin citizens do not belong to the same civic collectivity as the Israeli Jews but are seen, instead, as an invasive external force that the state must resist in order to ensure its survival.[76] Such references to the threat that Bedouins pose to Israel's sovereignty evoke the earlier pre-state conflictual framework of settlement discourse, in which the desert is constructed as the counter-place that exists outside the Jewish settlement and threatens its survival. The settlement thus embodies the Jewish space, and the Bedouins are essentially linked to the desert, thus constructing an us-against-them situation. The physical dispersion of the Bedouins across the desert landscape also evokes the earlier metaphor of the Jewish settlement as the besieged island. Given the Bedouins' multiple spontaneous villages and fast-growing population, the island metaphor arouses deeply rooted Jewish anxiety about future survival.

The legal reference to the Bedouins as "trespassers" against state law further reinforces the perception of them as a threat to the Jewish population. The Hebrew term for "trespassers," *polshim*, also means "invaders," a term that involves more powerful negative connotations than its English translation conveys. Although the use of this Hebrew term is not unique to the Bedouins' case, its application to the large Bedouin population of the unrecognized villages conveys and reinforces their collective othering, as an external power that invades the national territory from the outside. Thus, although they are citizens of the state of Israel, the application of the term, beyond its narrower legal use, suggests that the Bedouins, as Arabs and as children of the desert, are seen as a hostile element and a threat to law and order for the Jewish population of the Negev and, more broadly, for the state.

Havatzelet Yahel, a legal scholar who formerly represented the state, articulated the view of the Bedouins as lawless citizens who are "a significant minority [that] clearly feels they are not obliged to obey Israeli law." Yahel argues that their violent behavior renders the unrecognized villages "inaccessible to any official representative, including the police," and complains that "it is not rare to see a police car chase in the Negev that stops at the edge of a Bedouin cluster, *as if it were extraterritorial.*" Furthermore, she characterizes "the unplanned and irrational way" in which the Bedouins construct their villages as being disruptive to the sense of order in the desert and undermining the development of the existing Bedouin towns.[77] This description of the danger they pose to the public order and to law enforcement clearly identifies the Bedouins as belonging to the chaotic counter-place that is external to the Jewish settlement, thus echoing the earlier view of the desert as existing outside of the settlement and threatening its survival. Supporters of the Bedouins' cause, by contrast, identify the traditions and social patterns that explain the different structure and logic of the Bedouin settlements.[78]

The perception of the Bedouins as the embodiment of the "Wild South" led the government to resort to heightened law enforcement in an attempt to limit their trespassing activities. As early as 1976, the state created a special law-enforcement unit, nicknamed the Green Patrol (*ha-sayeret ha-yeruka*), to defend state land against illegal use, limiting its operations to Israeli territory within its 1967 borders, thus excluding the illegal Jewish settlements in the territories from its scope.[79] The Green Patrol became known for its harsh punitive measures against the unrecognized Bedouin villages, including home demolitions, destruction of crops, and confiscation of herds. When the media reported that the Green Patrol sprayed Bedouins' fields with toxic chemicals, exposing Bedouins to health hazards, the reports led to a major public outcry.[80] Well-known public figures participated in the protest. In an ironic allusion to the biblical manna that saved the ancient Israelites in the desert, the poet Chaim Gouri referred to "poison from the sky." The writer-artist Amos Kenan played on the famous Zionist slogan "making the desert bloom" to characterize the government's policy as a "desolation of the bloom." Along similar lines, the historian Zeev Tzahor, the president of Sapir College, altered the famous verse "do not uproot that which has been planted" to demand that we "do not spray that which has been seeded."[81] The *Ha'aretz* columnist Gideon Levy bluntly noted the discrepancy between the government's attitude towards Jews and towards Bedouins:

> What does one call an Israeli Jew who settles in the Negev to make it bloom? A Zionist, a pioneer, a person with values. And what does one call a Bedouin Israeli who attempts to make the same desert bloom? An invader, a land robber, a demographic danger.[82]

Israel's Supreme Court eventually ruled against the practice of spraying chemicals over illegally cultivated fields. It did, however, allow the destruction of crops by other mechanical means, such as plowing.[83]

The perception of the Negev as the Wild South, a space embroiled in growing violence both in defiance of the law and in the name of the law, reinforced the historical image of the desert as a chaotic and dangerous counter-place. The volatile situation in the Negev became a major concern during the Second (Al-Aqsa) Intifada, when major Israeli newspapers carried headlines suggesting a sense of looming calamity. The daily Ma'ariv published an article about the Negev under the heading "Here the Next Intifada Will Take Place"; Ha'aretz carried the headline "A Moment before the Intifada in the Negev"; and a Yediot Ahronot headline stated, "It Won't Take Long before Fire Breaks Out and the Negev Burns."[84] In informal conversations with Jewish residents of Ramat Negev, I heard them articulating their concern that "the next intifada will be here," using expressions such as "a ticking time bomb" or "a barrel of explosives" to convey the volatile nature of the situation.[85] The narrator of a 2013 television program focusing on the Bedouins stated, "Almost everyone who lives [in the Negev] talks about a war. . . . In some ways, this is a battlefield."[86] This agreement about the danger of the situation did not, however, imply any consensus on how to resolve it. One veteran Negev resident told me that "the next intifada will be [started] by the Bedouins. The only response to the situation is to build up our defense—to guard, to build a fence, to lock the doors." Another resident offered a different historical take on this issue: "A loyal population has been neglected here for decades just because they are not Jewish. How we relate to them is a disaster, and we will bring a calamity (shoah) upon ourselves if we don't address this topic."

A 2007 Hebrew novel entitled The Happy Man, written by the travel and fiction writer Tsur Shezaf, offers a fictional narrative about a Bedouin uprising that ignites the entire Negev.[87] Constructed as a thriller, the novel begins after the state has succeeded in crushing the revolt, and a Jewish security man sets out to locate its fugitive co-leader. The reader pieces together the back story that the revolt was led by two Bedouins—a neurosurgeon and a high-ranking IDF commander. These leaders, who could have otherwise served as successful models of the Bedouins' upward mobility, were profoundly disillused by the state's coercive measures against their people. They initially planned to perform bloodless acts of violence against symbols of the state in order to attract attention to the Bedouins' plight.[88] Yet the conflict soon escalated into a full-fledged war, lasting two years.

The army's fierce retaliation led to the destruction of the Bedouin villages and the expulsion of their residents across the border to Egypt, leaving the desert a scorched land. The novel presents the agent's successful hunt for the fugitive neuroscientist as a "lose-lose" ending, as both the hunter and the hunted are killed. Shezaf's literary imagination was clearly drawing on current anxieties regarding the radicalization of the Negev, bringing the subversive image of the Wild South to a catastrophic ending. The author creates a deliberate ironical reversal, describing the Bedouin leader, who has lost his left arm in action, as "the Arab Trumpeldor," in an allusion to the famous Russian Jewish hero who was killed during the defense of Tel Hai in 1920. The symbolic reversal also extends to the portrayal of the Bedouins' heroic last stand, in which a few resist many but finally surrender to defeat and exile, themes that are prominent in heroic Israeli reconstructions of the defense of Masada and the Bar Kokhba revolt.[89]

Following the collapse of the Prawer Plan, the state resorted to putting increased pressure on the Bedouin residents of the unrecognized villages to vacate their land and force them to accept its urban solution. In 2012, the government formed the Coordination Directorate of Land Law Enforcement in the Negev and commissioned a combat police unit, called Yoav, to carry out demolition activities in these villages.[90] According to reports, 697 houses and structures were demolished in 2013, a number that rose to 982 in 2015, with more than half of these demolitions carried out by the Bedouins themselves in order to avoid the additional cost of state-performed demolition that would otherwise have been billed to them.[91] The Bedouin village al-Araqib (also al-Araqeeb), near Beer Sheva, settled by members of the al Uqbi tribe, emerged as a symbol of this struggle. The Bedouins maintain that their tribe, having lived on its land since the beginning of the twentieth century, was forced by the state to relocate in the early 1950s, but with the assurance that they would be allowed to return to their land. The Israel Land Authority, however, claims that when 45 families of the tribe returned to that area in 1998, they were invading state land. A repeated cycle of al-Araqib residents building provisional residences and law enforcement demolishing those structures reportedly reached its eightieth round in 2015.[92]

At the same time, new afforestation projects in this area have added a particular twist to the displacement of the Bedouins due to insufficient proof of ownership of the desert land. These new initiatives—the "Ambassadors Forest," honoring foreign diplomats to Israel;[93] the "God-TV Forest," supported by a gift from an evangelical organization by the same name;[94]

and the "Forest of German States"[95]—are thus named for foreign states or foreign organizations while representing the Zionist settlement ethos and its persistent efforts to combat desert. As Eyal Weizman observes, the agrarian imagery of the Zionist settlement discourse of the Negev *"forced the desert gradually to retreat.* This displacement of the desert also involved enforced displacement of its Bedouin inhabitants."[96]

Recently, the treatment of Bedouins by a large detachment of armed police at the unrecognized village of Umm Al-Hiran in the Negev, during which a Bedouin man was killed, was compared with the treatment of Jewish settlers evicted from Amona, an unrecognized Jewish settlement in the West Bank built on private Palestinian land, at around the same time. *The Times of Israel* reported that "watching the Amona evacuation, with its unarmed police and efforts to reach a deal with settlers, residents of the Bedouin village of Umm al-Hiran ask why such consideration wasn't afforded them as well." Quoting residents of the village and their frustration and anger over the state's unwillingness to provide acceptable solutions, the article pointed out: "If one were to argue that the settlers of Amona were more loyal to the state, they need only look at those living in Umm al-Hiran and Atir, another Bedouin village on the chopping block, to discover some of them serve in the Israeli army and many of them vote for Zionist parties."[97] Nahum Barnea, a *Yediot Ahronot* columnist, similarly notes the disparity in the current Israeli government's approach to the Negev Bedouins and to the Jewish settlers, a disparity that is rooted in the desire "to conquer the land" from Arabs on the internal as well as the external frontiers, perpetuating the historical conflictual us-against-them formula.[98]

In 2015, the Ramat Negev Regional Council, which had been behind the establishment of the Wine Route farms and a proponent of the Jewish settlement of the Negev, changed course and announced its intention to recognize four more unrecognized villages on its own. Arguing that "the state failed in its treatment of the Bedouin sector," Shmuel Rifman now noted the urgency of improving their situation in order to ensure the future development of the Negev.[99] Thus, while he supported a limited recognition of Bedouin villages that complied with their own preference to remain in their villages, he justified this course of action in pragmatic terms, relevant to Jewish settlement, and avoided the human rights discourse of historical rights and social justice.

Jews and Arabs thus continue to live in the same desert landscape of the Negev, in close proximity to each other; but the two communities largely live in separate social and cultural milieus, marked by separate governance structures and vast differences in education, income and standards of living, social organization, and cultural norms.[100] And yet there are also marked differences within the various groups of Bedouins who live in different localities in the Negev, and there are numerous meeting points between Arabs and Jews offered by the reality of life in the Negev. In this respect, there may be a significant difference between the rural environment, where boundaries are more visible, and the urban environment. Thus, Beer Sheva presents a range of formal and informal opportunities for Jews and Bedouins to meet and interact, which may include the workplace or large service-oriented organizations such as the Ben-Gurion University of the Negev, the Soroka University Medical Center, and government institutions. As more Bedouins are able to take advantage of opportunities that open to them, the situation of the Negev Bedouins will be fluid and open to further changes.

In their resistance to the government's insistence on urbanization as the only legitimate venue for them to realize their rights, the Bedouins display their growing ability to draw on traditional Bedouin values and norms alongside the Israeli cultural practices and symbols with which they have become more familiar. They draw on their collective memory of their historical ties to the region and demonstrate their steadfast connection to the land, known in Arabic as *sumud*,[101] to justify their resistance to the state's urbanization plan. At the same time, as McKee observes, they also modify their narratives in response to the Israeli settlement ethos. Thus, they highlight their farming and grazing history to fit the Zionist emphasis on agriculture, while playing down their traditional mobility, which might weaken their claim to the land. When organizing insurgent planting and harvesting events, they also invite outsiders to participate in them, thereby displaying those guests' solidarity with them.[102]

The Bedouins' protests may also take other forms that draw on Israeli cultural tools. Thus, an improvised road sign, showing the name of an unrecognized Bedouin village that is not marked on the map or the road, displays the settlement name in Hebrew, Arabic, and English and notes that the settlement was "founded during the Ottoman Empire," thereby highlighting the village's pre-Israeli origins. Another improvised warning sign features the image of a bulldozer about to demolish a house. As a Bedouin interviewee explains, the signs constitute a site of protest as well as a public warning that one is about to enter a demolition zone.[103] Bedouin leaders attempt to mobilize Israeli symbols and rhetoric in other ways, as well, in order to reach out to the Israeli public. Thus, Nuri al-Uqbi, the son of the former sheik of the al Uqbi tribe, staged a public protest against the state's repeated demolitions during the Passover holiday, drawing on the exodus myth of liberation from oppression to support his tribe's struggle to regain access to their ancestral land. His public statement not only pointed out the symbolic inversion of Jews' taking on the role of the oppressors but also underscored the socialization of the Bedouins as Israeli citizens who understand the myths and symbols of Zionist discourse and use them to argue their own case against the state's policies.[104]

The government's official position nonetheless makes the integration of the Bedouins into Israeli society more challenging, and the disparities remain visible. The settlement discourse based on the inherently hostile relationship between the desert and the settlement, and the association of the Bedouins with the former, are thus emplaced in policies, practices, and symbolic forms. Thus, for example, Ofer Dagan notes that a settlement map produced by the Ministry for the Development of the Negev and the Galilee features the Jewish settlements exclusively, without marking nearby Bedouin settlements.[105] This symbolic erasure may be seen as a selective representation designed to attract potential Jewish settlers or visitors to the Negev, but it also reinforces the social segregation of the Bedouins from the Jewish society of the Negev.

The landscape reveals the social construction of the opposition between the symbolic desert and the Jewish settlement. A television segment on the unrecognized Bedouin villages, broadcast on Channel 10 on January 9, 2013, features a Jewish Israeli journalist driving toward an unmarked Bedouin village in the Negev. As she approaches her destination, she observes that the paved road is ending. "Perhaps the most symbolic thing," she declares, "is that precisely where the state stopped paving the road and it ends—is where the Bedouin village begins."[106] Her observation of the sudden shift from the orderly "settlement" domain to the chaotic and unformed "desert" echoes Amos Oz's earlier observation, quoted in the introduction: "The desert begins at the end of my street."

6

Unsettled Landscapes

THE CENTRALITY OF THE SETTLEMENT ETHOS gained further importance in the post-1948 period, in the face of the Israeli population's rapid growth and security needs. Yet in the same period, the roots of a counter-discourse began to emerge, enhancing the love of nature as a core value of Hebrew culture. In time, as the Israeli environmental discourse developed, its proponents began to point out more explicitly the tension between the need to protect the natural environment and the ethos of settlement. The desert, representing both Israel's "open space" and the frontier for potential settlements, reveals the disaccord between these different visions.

Revisiting the "Desolate Land"

As early as 1950, a memorandum from the ministry of the interior cautions that "Having been educated by the values of pioneering and 'the conquering of the desolate land,' our public has been unable to form a sufficient understanding of the need to protect natural assets and primordial or traditional landscapes." In recognition of the priority of the state's immediate needs, the memorandum does allow for a limited settlement development within territory designated for national parks; it recommends, however, that those settlements be based on "traditional agriculture" that blends better with the natural landscape.[1]

A national project to drain Huleh Lake in the northern Jordan Valley, in order to turn the dried wetlands into agricultural land, emerged as a turning point in the history of Israeli environmentalism. The state and the media hailed the draining of Huleh Lake and its wetlands, a project that was completed in 1958, as a major technological achievement that fulfilled the Zionist settlement ethos of taming a wild and unproductive area for future cultivation. In a few years, however, it became apparent that the implementation of this idea had brought on an ecological disaster, and that the drained lake and wetlands had little or no agricultural value. To counteract the damage that the project had inflicted on the Huleh ecosystem, the process was partly reversed by reflooding a portion of the wetlands and turning it into a nature reserve.[2]

The mobilization to form an opposition to the plan to drain Huleh Lake led to the establishment of the Society for Protection of Nature in Israel (SPNI) in 1954. Although the SPNI failed to stop the project from proceeding, the organization's membership grew quickly and it developed into a major advocacy group for landscape and nature protection.[3] The SPNI became an active socializing agent for the love of nature and the country, continuing the earlier tradition of touring the land as an important educational and patriotic activity. Its large network of field schools offered educational seminars and hiking tours to schoolchildren, youth groups, and adult groups throughout the country, and it promoted its preservation agenda through publications and public programs. In 1980, the state of Israel publicly recognized the SPNI's important contribution to Israeli society by awarding it the prestigious Israel Prize.[4]

A key cognitive challenge that the discourse of preservation faced was the ambiguous status of agriculture in Israeli culture. Whereas the English language clearly marks "agri/culture" as being within the cultural domain, the equivalent Hebrew term offers no similar association. Moreover, the redemptive Zionist vision of "toiling the land" hailed the transformative value of agriculture for both the land and its nature, thus obscuring the difference between nature and agriculture. Thus, for example, the protection of agricultural products from insects and wild animals was performed in the name of protecting nature. Indeed, a study of the SPNI's journal *Nature and Land* (*Teva va-aretz*) during the early 1960s points out the same tendency to blur nature and agriculture.[5] By the mid-1960s, however, the SPNI had launched a major public campaign promoting the need to protect wildflowers.[6] Addressing the practice, popular among Israelis, of picking wildflowers or transplanting them into private gardens, the campaign warned against the threat of extinction of wildflowers in their natural habitat. The successful campaign transformed the public attitude towards wildflowers and raised awareness about the distinction between wild nature and cultivated landscapes.

The growing awareness of the need to protect and preserve nature led the Israeli Knesset to pass laws in 1963 establishing two distinct national administrations: the National Park Authority (NPA), designed to focus on historical and sacred sites as well as protected areas that allow for some limited development; and the Nature Reservation Authority (NRA), which oversees territories designated for stricter nature preservation.[7] The government divided the responsibilities for carrying out different aspects of this legislation among various ministries, but placed the key office charged with leading this mission within the ministry of agriculture. This designation further reinforced the blurring of nature and agriculture in Israeli culture.

The discourse of preservation underscores the oppositional relationship between settlement and the symbolic desert, in itself it shares with the settlement discourse, but it offers a radically different interpretation of that relationship. Whereas the discourse of settlement emphasizes the need to protect the settlement from the vicious and aggressive nature of the counter-place, the discourse of nature preservation redefines the settlement drive as the aggressor and as a threat to the unsettled land of the symbolic desert, which must be defended and protected. Indeed, the SPNI's Hebrew name (*ha-hevra la-haganat ha-teva*) articulates this dual goal, since *hagana* implies both "defense" and "protection." Thus, although the English names of the "Society for the *Protection* of Nature in Israel" and the "Israel *Defense* Forces" (*tsva ha-hagana le-Israel*) suggest two different concepts, their original names share the same term, *hagana*. A newspaper report on the campaign to protect the dunes blends the two meanings, referring ironically to the activists' readiness to fight "to the last grain of sand,"[8] as a modification of the patriotic fight "to the last drop of blood."

While the promotion of the love of nature in itself was a familiar value in Hebrew culture, the positioning of the natural environment in opposition to the priorities of the settlement agenda could easily be interpreted as subversive to Zionist values. The SPNI therefore decided to address this issue, and in 1981 it sponsored a symposium devoted to *The Zionist Dimension of the Protection of Nature*. This public event, in which prominent Israeli figures participated, became a landmark in the environmental turn in Israel. The writer and satirist Amos Kenan stated that "nature can exist without Zionism, but Zionism cannot exist without nature," and he added, dryly: "Zionism's original sin is its attempt to fit the country to Zionist ideology rather than fit Zionism to this country."[9] The renowned writer and Knesset member S. Yizhar (Yizhar Smilansky) spoke of rejecting the negative connotations of the open space as a wasteland that is empty and threatening. In a radical departure from the discourse of the settlement, he praised the natural landscape, the unsettled and uncultivated land, for its inherent qualities, and spoke of the national urgency of mobilizing to protect it before it disappears.[10] A decade later, he reiterated this position:

> Until yesterday we were still standing facing the future, taking a vow to make the desolate land bloom; today we stand facing the present and we are pleading to stop and leave the desolate land alone. One or two more [settlement] drives and we won't have any piece of desolate land left, either to make it blossom or to protect it.[11]

The discourse of preservation further underscores the themes of injury and loss that result from the aggressive assault by the settlement on nature. The preservationists therefore employ the rhetoric of salvage that stresses the need to use the small window of opportunity that exists for averting the threat of extinction. Recognizing the link between man and the land that the Zionist redemptive narratives promoted, it points out the threats of excessive development to the well-being of both. As the cofounder of the SPNI, Azaria Alon, cautions, "we do not wish to find ourselves one day suffocating in the spider webs that we ourselves formed and from which we will not be able to rescue ourselves."[12] S. Yizhar explains his renewed understanding of "desolate land" as "the last dune, the residue of what has been left. Touch it, and it's gone. Desolate land also refers to the last mountain slopes a moment before they are covered by white cubes with red roofs."[13] His words recapture the binary opposition of the settled and the non-settled land that Zionist settlement ideology constructed, but he offers a dramatic reinterpretation of the meaning of that opposition. Yizhar presents the sand, the dunes, the rocks—the icons of the symbolic desert that appear in earlier narratives as a negative presence undermining the settlement process—as valuable natural assets. Thus, while the prototypical settlement narrative highlights the vulnerability of the settlement in its struggle with the hostile forces of the symbolic desert, the new narrative introduces a role reversal, pointing out that it is the forces of the symbolic desert that now require protection from the settlement. Moreover, if in the past those forces were associated with the destruction of the country, brought about by foreign elements, the environmental narrative now presents those forces as the authentic nature of the land under the threat of extinction. In a similar vein, the art historian Gideon Ofrat observes that Israeli artists, too, shifted from representations of the settlement to ecologically minded art.[14]

Nathan Alterman's lyrics for "Morning Song," mentioned earlier (in chapter 3), became a target of criticism for their representation of settlement and construction, along with working the land, as the embodiment of patriotic love for the country:

> We love you, homeland
> With joy, with song, and with labor.
> From the slopes of Lebanon to the Dead Sea
> We will plant and build for you
> We'll make you most beautiful
> We'll dress you up *with a robe of concrete and cement*.[15]

Critics of the discourse of settlement often quote the reference to "a robe of concrete and cement" as evidence of the distorted view of the landscape as an object of transformation through the lens of the settlement ethos.[16] Instead, they apply the concept of "desert" and "wasteland" to the urban environment, condemning its uniformity along the lines of a similar critique in American culture.[17] Alon criticizes the settled areas as representing the desolation of nature, and Yizhar warns that the "onslaught" of construction threatens to cover the land with concrete and asphalt, characterizing the uniform residential landscape as "devoid of identity."[18] Amos Oz, similarly, refers to the "desert of apartment buildings," and the poet Chaim Gouri applies the concept of "desolation" to Tel Aviv.[19] In a similar reversal of the settlement discourse, the environmental discourse has redefined the Jewish National Fund (JNF)'s uniform pine forests, which destroyed indigenous plants, as "pine deserts."[20]

The environmental discourse extends the symbolic reversal to both work tools and construction materials, which the earlier settlement lore glorified. Kenan thus identifies the bulldozer as the symbol of "Zionism's aggression toward the nature and the landscape."[21] The geologist Emanuel Mazor refers to the need to protect open spaces from the plow, the bulldozer, and the concrete mixer, among other instruments of labor and construction. The geographer Yossi Katz's study of the history of nature preservation carries the telling title *To Stop the Bulldozer*.[22] Another iconic representation of technological progress—the straight lines that mark modern buildings, roads, and the planting of trees—was similarly criticized, and it was noted that the straight lines dissect and constrain the open desert space.[23] Thus, the very tools that promoted the settlement agenda and its civilizing mission became the derided instruments that destroy the natural landscape.

In Israel, in line with a global development, the earlier emphasis on the preservation of nature was later broadened into a growing environmental movement. The SPNI, which had focused its earlier efforts on mobilizing public support for the protection of nature, moved on to environmental advocacy and a greater focus on legal activism. The rise of a global interest in environmentalism encouraged the growth and diversification of environmental organizations, research centers, and programs in environmental studies. An important development was the establishment of an umbrella organization, *Adam, Teva, V'Din* (Man, Nature, and Law, known in English as the Israel Union for Environmental Defense), which was designed to spearhead legal action related to environmental issues. According to Alon Tal, who founded *Adam, Teva, V'Din*, the organization represented more than twenty organizations when it started, and that number had risen to eighty by 2000.[24] Major national academic degree-granting programs, such as the Porter School for Environmental Studies at Tel Aviv University, founded in 2000, further expanded the development of the field.[25] The government, as well, progressively restructured its bureaucracy to address the growing public concern, turning the Environmental Protection Service it had established in the mid-1970s into a full-fledged ministry of the environment in 1988, then renaming it the "ministry of environmental protection" in 2006.[26]

The special challenges of the desert region enhanced the sensitivity to its distinct environmental issues. The Ben-Gurion University of the Negev established an academic institute for desert studies in 1974, which was renamed the Blaustein Institute for Desert Research in 1980. The Blaustein Institute has expanded research and development areas to advance technologies in the fields of water sciences, solar energy and ecological studies, biological and agriculture research, and desert architecture,[27] and hosted the United Nations' international conference on deserts and desertification in 2006.[28] The Arava Institute for Environmental Studies at kibbutz Ketura, founded in 1996, focuses on research related to the desert environment, provides training in environmental activism, and advocates for regional collaboration across national borders.[29] Some Negev high schools include enhanced study of the desert environment in their curriculum as well. The most salient example is the environmental orientation of the Sde Boker Campus (Midrasha) High School,[30] and later examples include the Yeshiva

High School in Mitzpe Ramon, which combines religious studies and environmentalism.[31] Local organizations such as *Negev Bar-Kayma* (Sustainable Development for the Negev) focus on environmental concerns specifically related to this southern region.[32] An important dimension of their advocacy addresses the damaging impact of the state's attitude toward the desert as a remote region marked by emptiness and desolation that can therefore be used for elements and institutions unfit for the populated center.

A National Dump

The negative view of the desert advanced within the settlement ethos defined the desert not only as a frontier and a remote periphery but also as the counter-place to which the state could relegate its undesirable, discredited, or destructive elements. As the sociologist Michael Feige notes, "the Negev has become the *actual and metaphoric garbage can of Israel*. All the institutions and social functions that were not wanted in more central areas were dumped in the seemingly endless planes of the far and unseen south."[33] Bilha Givon, of Sustainable Development of the Negev, addresses the major gap between the government's "flowery slogans" and promises to settle the Negev, on the one hand, and "the process of turning the Negev into the garbage can of the state,"[34] on the other. Negev 2015 (the government's 2005 blueprint for the development of the Negev, mentioned earlier) similarly alludes to the garbage can metaphor in its appendix on environmental issues: "The Negev has for many years been the 'garbage can' of the state, and is loaded with scars that undermine the beauty of its primordial landscape."[35] Environmental activists employ the English acronym NIMBY (Not In My Back Yard) in Hebrew, referring to the attitude of those who live at the center of the country toward the Negev as the "garbage can" of the country.[36]

The NIMBY approach is salient in various domains. The desert became the preferred space for prisons built by the state. In 1970, the state built a new prison facility near Beer Sheva, which was then followed by other prisons further south designed for criminal prisoners as well as the growing numbers of Palestinian inmates during the First and Second Intifadas.[37] The relocation of the most dangerous, high-risk inmates to the desert reinforces its perception as the counter-place associated with dangerous forces that threaten the survival of the settlement. A more recent and highly controversial site was the open detention center named Holot (Sands), for asylum seekers from Africa who have illegally crossed the border into Israel's territory, following the Supreme Court's ruling that it was unconstitutional to imprison them. Although Holot was considered "open," in practice, its location at a remote point in the southern Negev, along with the requirement of daily roll call attendance, kept the detainees isolated and limited their ability to move around.[38] The state's treatment of these asylum seekers was the object of harsh criticism and litigation processes, and following the court's order, Holot was closed by the state in March of 2018.[39] The state's policy of transporting detained asylum workers from the southern neighborhoods of Tel Aviv to the southern desert location further contributed to the perception that the desert serves as the "national dump" for those living in the center of the country.

The metaphorical "garbage can" assumed a more literal meaning when the northern Negev became the dumping area for garbage transported from the highly populated center, after the Hiriyah landfill, at the center of the country, became a safety hazard for the nearby Ben-Gurion national airport. Negev residents protested against the decision to direct the garbage to their region, and Beer Sheva's mayor declared that "We've come to show the government that we are not prepared to be the suckers of the state."[40] The new landfill opened in spite of their opposition, and trucks now transport waste from the Tel Aviv metropolitan area to the desert site. To dispel the negative perception, the new landfill was named after a biblical wild plant, *duda'im* (mandragora), and a visitors' center and a park named Ganei Hadas (the Myrtle Gardens), with an artificial pond, birds, and a small zoo, have been added to showcase the landfill's environmentally friendly orientation.[41] The landfill contributes to the revenues of the Benei Shimon municipality in the northern Negev, in whose territory it is located. While its proximity to Beer Sheva (only ten miles northwest of it) affects the city's residents, it does not contribute to the city's economy.

The development of industries dealing with hazardous materials presents another major issue of concern for the environment. The Negev Nuclear Research Center, located southeast of the town of Dimona, was established in the early 1960s and, like other industries dealing with hazardous materials, it provides work for area residents. But the site also places Negev residents at a higher risk for possible radioactive leaks and makes them more vulnerable to rockets directed at this area.[42] Contrasting with the secrecy surrounding the plans to build the nuclear facility at the time, the news regarding the plan to build the largest radio transmitter in the world for the Voice of America, in the Arava desert south of the Dead Sea, made news: the Israeli public, by then more environmentally aware, rallied around the call to reject it. Although Israel had agreed to the plan in the second half of the 1980s, the SPNI launched a major public campaign within the country, with support from environmental activists in the United States, against the plan. The project was ultimately canceled in 1993, making it "one of the more sophisticated environmental campaigns in Israeli history,"[43] in the assessment of the environmental historian Alon Tal.

The use of the desert as a resource for the chemical industry has emerged as another major environmental issue. Some industries were present in the Dead Sea area even before the establishment of the state, but since the 1950s, state-owned and heavily state-subsidized industries have been encouraged to move to the south to enhance employment opportunities and thereby support the national mission of settling the internal frontier. This policy includes industries based on the natural resources of the desert that involve mining the desert soil and processing chemicals.[44] In 1975, several heavy industries dealing with hazardous materials that had been established close to Beer Sheva were relocated farther south, to a new site, the Ramat Hovav Industrial Park. In time, the industrial park became a destination for other industries dealing with hazardous materials as well.[45] As the main national site for multiple industries disposing of large quantities of hazardous chemicals, Ramat Hovav soon became a primary source of pollution for residents living at the center of the Negev region. The media reported complaints about the strong stench that spread great distances and about health issues caused by the pollution. There were reports of increased diagnoses of cancer among Negev residents, most acutely among the Bedouins living in close proximity to Ramat Hovav.[46] Environmental nongovernmental organizations and Negev residents addressed the environmental discrimination underlying the assignment of industries dealing with hazardous materials to the desert, arguing that "Ramat Hovav is an illustration of the fact that the Negev has become the dumping ground for the country's most polluting activities: hazardous, nuclear, chemical, munitions, and solid waste, to name but a few."[47] As we shall see below, the government was forced to remedy the situation only when the concern extended beyond the residents of the Negev periphery.

The return of the Sinai Peninsula, as an outcome of the 1979 peace treaty between Israel and Egypt, led to a fundamental change in the Negev. Israel's need to relocate its airbases and army units from the Sinai to the

Negev desert required a redrawing of the map to include larger military zones. These zones, in conjunction with the areas protected as nature reserves and national parks (and with a considerable overlap with the areas so designated), meant that about 90% of the Negev territory was now marked as off-limits for settlement.[48] This new reality meant that the Negev could no longer be seen as a potential location for large-scale development projects. As Negev 2015, the 2005 blueprint for the Negev's future development, notes,

> The Negev is the only region in the country that still has large territories of primordial land that are essential to nature and man. Even though these spaces produce the illusion of availability of land for development and a sense of space, the dense network of designated land and its multiple uses present major constraints on its potential for future development.[49]

Leading environmental activists nonetheless sounded the alarm over this militarization of the Negev, arguing that it was incompatible with the view of the desert as a site of nature and damaging to its ecosystem. "In the past, a third of [the Negev map] was green, the color of the proposed nature reserves," Yoav Sagi, who headed the SPNI, observed in 1980. "Today it is yellow, the color designating the IDF (Israel Defense Forces) military zones, which have conquered the Negev as if it had been swept by a storm."[50] A decade later, another local environmentalist complained that the army was "stealing" the Negev.[51] Negev residents objected to the impact on their environment of the enhanced army presence. Amos Oz worried that the Negev would turn into a "gigantic parking lot for tanks" and be filled with "piles of trash, preserve cans, and empty ammunition boxes."[52] Others addressed the impact of military restrictions on the experience of hiking in the desert, which had been one of the hallmarks of Israeli youth culture and a cherished activity pursued by the SPNI, youth movements, and nature lovers. The need to coordinate hiking plans with the military appeared antithetical to the free spirit that this tradition represented.[53] In a public forum about the relocation plan, the chief officer of the Armored Corps attempted to diffuse residents' fears and objections by invoking Jewish mythology: "Like the Jewish people, the Armored Corps too was born in the desert," he stated. Even more outlandish was his analogy between nature and tanks, suggesting that "the tank is also part of nature; it is part of the nature of the human need for self-defense in the twentieth century."[54]

The environmental opposition to the IDF's plan focused primarily on the construction of three new airbases in the Negev and their impact on the landscape and the level of noise they would generate. The most contested case was the building of the Nevatim airbase, southeast of Beer Sheva, in Tel Malhata. The plan required the relocation of Bedouins who had been living in that area, to which the Bedouins objected. The situation led to public protests over their relocation and intense negotiations over the appropriate level of compensation by the state. The priority of the state's immediate military needs overruled environmental and human rights concerns. The state relocated the Tel Malhata Bedouins, and the Nevatim airbase was opened in 1983.[55]

The process of militarizing the Negev continued when Prime Minister Ariel Sharon directed the IDF to relocate major army bases from the center of the country to the southern periphery in the early 2000s. The plan was designed to consolidate military bases into large complexes, introduce upgraded technology, and free expensive real estate in the highly populated center of the country. One of its major construction projects, the creation of a complex named the "Training Bases City"—known by its Hebrew acronym BAHAD City—called for over 625 acres (2,500 dunams) to be used for a wide range of facilities including dining halls, sports complexes, shopping centers, and housing for up to ten thousand trainee soldiers, to be located south of the Beer Sheva metropolitan area.[56]

The state mobilized the settlement discourse in support of the BAHAD City plan, highlighting the potential contribution to the Negev's demographic and economic growth, as military families would strengthen the periphery and local residents and companies would benefit from business opportunities. The combination of the settlement agenda with security interests was not new, but their interplay with environmental concerns introduced a new dimension to this process. The environmental organizations advanced stern warnings about the risks that the pollution produced by the Ramat Hovav Industrial Park would pose not only to the environment and to Negev residents' health but also to the health of the soldiers, given the proximity of BAHAD City to the industrial park. The government tried to address these concerns by signing an agreement with Ramat Hovav, but the environmental nongovernmental organizations, dissatisfied with the limited nature of the agreement, insisted on a fully vetted and enforced approval process for BAHAD City. As a result of this process, Ramat Hovav agreed to comply with demands for more comprehensive measures to correct its impact on the environment, the Supreme Court closed the case in summer 2010, and the plan was approved.[57]

In stark contrast to the earlier failure to elicit any strong action against the industrial complex to ensure the health of Negev resident, the success of this campaign was predicated on the convergence of environmental concerns with the new security agenda and its implications for those living at the center or in the north whose children would be serving in the southern desert. Clearly, the environmental lobby's strategy of mobilizing military interests and focusing the public's concerns on the safety of those called to serve the nation helped achieve this environmental success.[58] For its part, the IDF wished to prove its concern for the environment by announcing the green credentials of the new military complex in terms of its energy sources, materials, and the treatment of water and waste.[59]

The vision of BAHAD City drew on the ethos of settling the Negev, arguing that military families and increased business and job opportunities would strengthen the periphery, while new roads and improved transportation would reinforce the connection between the Negev and the center of the country. At an official ceremony to rename BAHAD City after Ariel Sharon in 2015, the defense minister, Moshe Ya'alon, praised the late prime minister's Zionist vision, which "led him to imagine the Negev moving closer to the center and large numbers of soldiers arriving there, transforming the Negev and helping it to flourish and grow."[60] Critics of the plan, however, point out that it benefits the center, first and foremost, by freeing prime real estate, and that BAHAD City will have a negligible economic and social impact on struggling settlements of the periphery: military families are more likely to move to the more affluent residential neighborhoods and towns in and around Beer Sheva than to struggling towns, and local businesses would not necessarily be hired to provide major services to the military complex. The legal disputes over tax revenues from BAHAD City demonstrated the competing needs of the diverse Negev population, which led to a compromise between the Ramat Negev Regional Council and Yerucham but ignored the Bedouins' demand for a share.[61]

These examples illustrate the continuity in the construction of the desert as a peripheral space outside and away from the populated center. The Negev is treated first and foremost as an empty space that can serve as a destination for dangerous or discarded elements and institutions that are rejected at the center but deemed inconsequential to the desert environment. They also reveal that while the Negev is considered a remote periphery in relation to the center, it represents an additional hierarchy of peripheral status within its own space that creates a diversity of needs and interests within the Negev population. For the environmental lobby, however, the negative attitude towards the Negev has made the need to highlight its inherent positive value, as a site of nature and an open space, all the more urgent, reinforcing the commitment to ensure the protection of the desert environment from its uses and abuses in the name of settlement and development.

The Last Open Space

The environmental organizations' early public campaigns often focused on protecting the desert landscape from the damaging industrial uses of its resources, and on the need to preserve its unique sites for future generations. The preservation approach conveys a romantic view of the desert landscape as representing primordial nature. Environmental campaigns and tourist publications often articulate this view in the Hebrew expression "Genesis Land" (*eretz bereshit*), which appears in official Israeli documents such as "Negev 2015," the government's 2005 strategic plan for the Negev.[62] As the poet Yehuda Amichai describes it, the desert is "an open land, without subconscious, without wrapping, without food coloring, pure landscape, net landscape."[63] At the core of the preservation discourse is a role reversal of the settlement ethos, turning the desert into the vulnerable landscape that must be protected from the aggressive zeal of the settlement.

The use of the island metaphor that was central to the settlement discourse further reveals the role reversal in the preservation and environmental discourse. The settlement, once described as besieged by the vast desert forces, has turned into the invasive force that besieges the desert landscape. "The Negev has remained a nearly isolated island in the entire territory," Uzi Paz of the SPNI observes, noting that there is still some chance to preserve its wild nature for education, research, and pleasure.[64] Alon Tal further notes that the desert has become "a matrix of 'island' habitats within an expanding system of highways."[65] Articles using the rhetoric of salvage portray the desert as an "endangered space," representing the last open space, which might disappear under the pressure of further development plans. "The Negev Space: Is the Mission Lost?" asks one article,[66] while another heading asserts the concern in a definitive statement: "The Negev is Getting Lost." The author further warns that "it won't be long before we lose the last open space."[67] This alarm over the looming crisis in the Negev mobilizes the historical role of the desert for Jews: "Our forefathers, one must remember, had wandered in the desert for forty years before they entered the land. It may be worth thinking about future generations so that they too may enjoy this desert space."[68] The concern about future generations raises the fear that if the desert landscape becomes extinct, their only way to know the desert will be through stories and songs.[69]

SPNI activists also point out the cultural changes that characterize the younger generation's attitude toward the desert landscape. Those growing up in this country "do not wish to dress it up in 'a garment of concrete and cement.' This generation wants to leave significant portions of its childhood landscapes natural, and the desert is amongst them."[70] Along similar lines, Feige notes that "'making the desert bloom' has lost some of its enchantment." With a note of self-irony, he confesses his own ambivalence as a Negev resident: "When I watch the deer eating the lawn from my office window and see Mr. Zamir running out to chase them away, I'm not so sure whose side I am on."[71]

The campaigns to preserve the sand dunes illustrate the symbolic reversal in attitude that the environmental discourse introduces to the relationship between the settlement and the desert. The dunes that once spread along the Mediterranean shore have almost entirely disappeared from that highly congested area. The SPNI therefore launched a public campaign to halt a development plan of the city of Ashdod, on the southern shore, in order to preserve the last "great sand dune," a campaign that led to the formation of the "Sand Park."[72] Another campaign mobilized hundreds of local residents and nature lovers to demonstrate against the mining of sand dunes in the southern Arava for industrial use and construction projects. The campaign's logo featured an image of dunes and a succinct message, "The Great Dune: Don't Turn It into Cement."[73] The environmental discourse thus radically transformed the dunes, from one of the derided icons of the hostile desert into a protected natural phenomenon, and from raw material for building into a cherished treasure that must be preserved and exhibited for future generations. A 1983 editorial in the SPNI's publication marvels over the profound ideological change that this campaign represents:

> Who would have believed that one day we would be called to defend the territories of the beach dunes, those hills of sandstone, and the remaining swamps along the coastal plain? We used to see all those as 'desolate land' that had to be conquered and made to disappear from this land.[74]

The environmental agenda has also focused on the protection of the desert landscape from further industrial mining that would destroy its natural formations. Whereas the industries relate to the desert land as a resource to be exploited, the campaigns highlight its value as a national asset. The major campaign to save the five craters at the center of Ramat Negev addressed their distinctiveness as a natural formation, and a proposal to UNESCO raised global interest in their preservation, featuring them as a single landmark named "Crater Land."[75] This campaign gained momentum when the industrial company Rotem introduced a new mining project in the West Hazeva area, which the environmental lobby opposed, warning that it would bring irreversible damage to that area of the crater. The SPNI produced a slide presentation featuring breathtaking views of the craters and issued a dramatic call to rescue the crater, which went viral on social media.[76] The campaign collected 14,000 signatures and in December 2004 it organized "a massive public demonstration during which hundreds of children created an SOS message at the foot of Mount Zin. Some 1,500 teenagers from SPNI orienteering groups, a jeep trip association, the Hazeva field school, local residents, and hundreds of civilians from all over Israel participated in the event."[77] The industry, for its part, organized its workers for a counterdemonstration with the slogan "Rotem Lives with the Environment."

In 2006, the Southern Regional Planning Council turned down the mining project, delivering a victory to the environmental lobby. The prospect of a UNESCO recognition of the craters as a valuable natural site and the possibility of economic benefits from their emergence as an important tourist attraction thus protected the craters from further mining. The Israel National Parks Authority embarked on its largest landscape restoration project ever, to repair the damage already inflicted on the site. A journalist reporting on this restoration made a note of the symbolic reversal involved in this process: "The trucks are doing the opposite of what they did in the past. They are now returning the soil to the open pits in order to make the area look the way it originally did, decades ago."[78] On July 17, 2010, UNESCO recognized Crater Land as a World Heritage Site.

Other campaigns articulate the global shift from a focus on the preservation of nature to stressing the notion of sustainability as a way to strike a balance between the agenda of settlement and development and the protection of nature.[79] The sustainable approach supports limited development to meet economic needs while also taking into account the needs of the environment. Its emphasis on the "conservation of nature" therefore calls for collaboration between regional planners and environmental experts to shape the planning process. Israeli environmental organizations nonetheless face the continuing challenge of the identification of Zionism with the settlement agenda, which is further complicated by the post-1967 controversy over the Jewish settlement agenda in the occupied territories in the name of Zionism. The environmental lobby does not represent a unified political position in this regard. The SPNI's decision to open field schools in the Golan Heights and the West Bank and its use of the biblical concept of "the Land of Israel" in the early post-1967 period were seen as supporting the right's vision and settlement agenda in the occupied territories.[80] Azaria Alon (the cofounder of the SPNI) also cautioned proponents of nature preservation to avoid a total condemnation of the settlement drive, because that attitude could play into the hands of Israel's critics who condemn Zionism more broadly.[81] However, a later change in the SPNI's leadership and a shift towards legal activism has recently aligned the SPNI with left-leaning environmental organizations in confronting various settlement projects in other areas.

As we saw in chapter 4, the environmental lobby's opposition to the illegal construction of the Wine Route's individual farms as well as to other settlement plans led to charges that the SPNI was anti-Zionist. Farm own-ers put up signs drawing on Ben-Gurion's legacy regarding the Negev and positioned the environmental organization as being in opposition to it: "In the Negev the people of Israel will be tested—in spite of the SPNI." Such signs redefined the environmental organization, which had been awarded the Israel Prize for its patriotic contribution, as antipatriotic. As tensions between the agenda of settlement and security and the environmental in-terests intensified, they moved beyond the courtroom to the social arena, splitting residents of Ramat Negev who had shared a similar background in youth movements, hiking groups, and military service over the SPNI's contestation of the individual farms.[82]

It is not surprising, therefore, that some environmental activists wish to emphasize the Zionist dimension of their advocacy, using such concepts as "green Zionism," "environmental Zionism," or "eco-Zionism" to underscore the national significance of their agenda.[83] As the newly appointed SPNI director, Iris Han, recently stated,

> They say that we are not Zionist and that we oppose settlement. They maintain that we oppose the establishment of new settlements and oppose the development of the country. Yet what we say is, 'Wait,

something has changed since the days of the Tower and Stockade.' The pressing problem that we face today is the scarcity of land. In order to continue to live here our challenge is not to conquer another hill but to conserve our resources. In my opinion, this is the essence of the new green Zionism.[84]

The challenges of green Zionism are also manifested in the tensions between the agenda to combat desertification, which is part of a global trend promoted by the United Nations Convention of 1994, and environmental critiques of afforestation or reforestation, as a means to achieve this goal, for their negative impact on the ecosystem.[85] The JNF, the Zionist agency that had historically promoted afforestation and settlement projects and that planted the large Lahav and Yatir forests in the northern Negev, began experimenting with diversifying its forests and developing the "savannization" method, cultivating plants that make a better fit with the arid desert soil.[86] The JNF emphasizes its identity as a green, ecologically oriented organization, although some environmental critics see its projects as leaning toward the settlement agenda and damaging the desert environment.[87]

The scarcity of water has been a major environmental challenge in the region, and the success of the early settlement efforts in the desert was predicated on the transfer of water to the Negev from the Yarkon River and later from the Jordan River and its tributaries. The progress of scientific research and innovative technologies further contributed to the successful development of farming methods that fit the desert environment. Yet the diversion of water from the Jordan River and its tributaries by Israel, Syria, and Jordan has affected the ecosystem of the Jordan Valley and led to the shrinking of the Dead Sea, raising alarm about its future.[88] The appearance of large sinkholes along the western shore of the Dead Sea in the mid-1990s introduced another, yet related, environmental problem. These multiple sinkholes have undermined the development of this area and provoked predictions of a looming ecological catastrophe. Their appearance has brought about the closing off of beach areas, the abandonment of some areas of cultivated land now barred from use, and damage to the main road leading to this area.[89] This development threatens the safety of residents and visitors and undermines the economy of existing settlements along the western shore of the Dead Sea. A newly formed sinkhole that blocked the major desert road along the Dead Sea and created long traffic delays during the busiest tourist season of the Passover holiday, in the spring of

2015, demonstrated the dramatic impact of these sinkholes and the dangers involved. An article dedicated to the history of this desert road contrasted the bold vision that led to its construction with the current threats to its future.[90] At the same time, the luxury hotels built along the southern basin of the Dead Sea are faced with the danger of rising water levels threatening to flood them. This reverse process is a result of the accumulated salt at the bottom of the evaporation ponds in the southern basin, which are used by the industry to extract chemicals.[91]

One of the proposed plans to combat the impact on the ecosystem of the receding water of the Dead Sea is the "Red Sea–Dead Sea Canal" (also called "Red-Dead Conduit"), which seeks to counterbalance it by transferring water from the Red Sea to the Dead Sea. The plan, promoted during the peace negotiations over the 1993 Oslo agreement, calls for a regional collaboration to address the challenges of a shared desert ecosystem and raises new possibilities for an increased water supply to Israel, Jordan, and Palestine. A nongovernmental group called EcoPeace Middle East was founded the following year with the broader goal of advancing sustainable regional development and promoting environmental peace-building in the region. EcoPeace opened offices in Amman, Bethlehem, and Tel Aviv, where it has been working with local groups of researchers, environmentalists, and volunteers.[92]

Yet the Red Sea–Dead Sea Canal plan has been debated from a number of perspectives. Environmental organizations, most prominently EcoPeace Middle East, have raised concerns about the risk of mixing water from different ecosystems and the potential impact of such mixing on the Dead Sea area.[93] Israeli, Jordanian, and Palestinian officials signed a first agreement in December 2013, which was followed by an agreement between Jordan and Israel in February of 2015. According to reports, the later agreement included the construction of a 112-mile-long pipeline to transfer salt water to the Dead Sea and enhance its water level, as well as a desalination plant in Aqaba. In return for its use of the desalinated water, Israel agreed to double its water supply to Jordan from the Sea of Galilee.[94] The agreement was hailed as a step forward in peaceful collaboration that would relieve some of the chronic water shortage in the countries involved and avert the looming environmental disaster in the Dead Sea. Yet given the current political impasse of the peace negotiations between the Israelis and the Palestinians, the objections raised by environmental organizations, and a lawsuit by some Jewish settlements that object to the directing of more water from the Jordan River to Jordan, the future of this project remains unclear. In spite of these hurdles, the efforts to address shared environmental concerns that traverse political boundaries may lead to greater openness for further collaboration. The issue of environmental activism and its relations to the promotion of peace efforts continues to be studied by Jews and Palestinians.[95] Evidence of collaboration at a civic and local level on the margins of the desert, away from the public eye,[96] may offer an alternative to the separatist besieged-island approach (see epilogue).

As the environmental movement started to gain momentum, the desert emerged as a more complex arena in which security, settlement, and environmental agendas played different roles, at times presenting competing claims over the land and at others forming varying unconventional ad hoc alliances to pursue their shared interests. The Negev has largely remained the ground of conflicting approaches and shifting alliances between institutions promoting these approaches. The priority given to the settlement ethos that is deeply rooted in Israeli culture continues to affect the perception of the Negev as a residual spatial category defined by its contrast to the populated center. The cultural construction of the desert as an empty and barren territory has left a legacy of marginalization that contributes to its use as a "national dump," a trend opposed by the environmentalists. In contrast, the environmental perspective cultivates a positive view of the desert as unspoiled nature, a place of refuge from the predicament of modernity, and a critically important open space for the highly congested center. Its advocacy of the desert is thus linked to predictions that Israel might become the most congested country in the West by 2020.[97]

Historically, the interests of security and settlement have been joined in defining the state's agenda in the Negev, and the unsettled situation of the Bedouins in the unrecognized villages has further contributed to the contested approaches to the desert. The defense of the environment from the Jewish settlement drive is thus measured against the competing national agenda of promoting Jewish ownership of the land in the Negev. However, the discussion also reveals the fluidity of the relationship between environmental advocacy groups and government authorities, particularly at the local level, according to the specific issues at stake. The cases of the Wine Route individual farms, BAHAD City, and the Ramat Hovav Industrial Park thus demonstrate the possibility of shifting coalitions within a complex and dynamic situation. While the environmental discourse often gives way to national and security discourse,[98] economic considerations, which more often side with the settlement discourse, may sometimes be mobilized in favor of protecting the desert for the development of tourism. Indeed, this was the case with the successful campaign for the preservation of the Crater Land. Given the constraints on the settlement of the Negev, tourism emerged as an important domain for further development. The following discussion explores the ways in which Israeli desert tourism draws on these various discourses and negotiates the tensions between them in marketing the desert.

7

The Desert and the Tourist Gaze

MORE THAN ANY OTHER DISCOURSE about the desert, tourism illuminates its multifaceted meanings in Israeli culture as a geographical region and a symbolic landscape. This chapter's discussion of the tourist discourse focuses mainly on the publicity and media directed at Israeli tourists, in order to explore the ways in which the process of marketing desert tourism reshapes the various visions of the desert in Israeli culture. Because the tourist industry desires to attract as many visitors as possible, tourism publicity selectively draws on the various visions of the desert and offers a diversity of options. It is not surprising, however, that tourist publications, publicity for specific tourist sites, and media reports often highlight the contrast between the desert and the urban center of the country, reflecting the desert's roles as the nonplace or the counter-place, within different contexts. The qualities that these media attribute to the desert within this oppositional framework may nonetheless vary according to the writers' point of view, the destination in question, and the targeted audience. Tourist-oriented materials attempt to enhance the consumption of the desert by potential visitors by allowing them to imagine their experiences in the desert as a meaningful diversion from their everyday lives, often framing the positive traits of the desert experience as a surprise. This recurrent theme implicitly acknowledges the challenges that the Israeli desert tourism industry faces in defying the negative image of the desert in an attempt to transform it into an attractive destination for recreational and educational experiences.

The very focus on marketing the desert to tourists, both Israeli and foreign, articulates a relatively recent emphasis on its potential for the economy of the desert settlements. During the early decades of the state, the remote and less-accessible Negev region was largely left outside of the tourist circuit. The Negev represented a sparsely settled frontier that served as a buffer zone from Egypt and Jordan and did not appear particularly inviting, with the exception of Eilat, at its southernmost tip, and the Dead Sea area. Foreign visitors were mostly drawn to Jerusalem and the Galilee, richer in history, holy sites, and vegetation and more easily accessible than the Negev, and to the more dynamic and populated center. For Israelis, the desert landscape was associated with military practices and war experiences. As a journalist describes it,

> What does the word 'Negev' remind you of? A tent, food seasoned with dust, dryness, thirst and intense heat, cold nights, searching for shade, a group of soldiers crowded in the shade of a lone tree . . . everything that is not home.[1]

Israel's wars with its Arab neighbors extended beyond the desert frontier, but the 1948 War of Independence, the Sinai Campaign of 1956, the 1967 Six-Day War, and the Yom Kippur War of 1973 reinforced the association of the desert with grueling battles leading to the loss of lives or close brushes with death. Israeli advertisements from the early decades of statehood disclose the close link between images of soldiers and the desert landscape.[2] These associations with military experiences made the desert appear incompatible with the idea of leisure, relaxation, and fun.

The negative perception of the desert as a barren landscape painted in beige and gray, yellow and brown has further undermined its potential as a tourist destination. In the Israeli semiotics of color, these hues are not only considered dull; they represent the failure of the Zionist pioneering ethos and the goal of making the desert bloom. What Hebrew culture celebrated, in contrast, was the settlement, surrounded by green vegetation and adorned with flowering plants. The Israelis' idealized landscape—a forested landscape with a lake or a river running through it—is much closer to the European environment than to their own immediate one, and serves as a nostalgic object of yearning. This message was bluntly articulated at the entrance to an army base in the Negev desert in the 1990s, where a visitor was confronted with painted pictures of "Swiss landscapes, lakes surrounded by mountains and woods, romantic sunsets, rivers, and waterfalls."[3] The juxtaposition of these images with the soldiers' immediate surroundings articulates their desire to escape from the dire conditions of the desert environment and military life to a fantasized landscape of lush green and plentiful water.[4]

The lure of the faraway green landscape that provides an escape from the local environment is a familiar theme in Israeli literature. In the novel *A Distant Land*, the Israeli writer Yitzhak Ben-Ner describes a cab driver who, burdened by the mounting problems in his family's life and exasperated by the glaring sun and stifling heat that turn his car into "a scalding prison of steel," fantasizes about going away to New Zealand as "a kind of refuge." "That's exactly what I'm looking for . . . the distance and . . . its green color," he explains to a passenger.[5] In another novel, a father cuts short his stay in a small American town, characterized by "the fresh, grass-like green" and "cool smell" of flowerbeds, to search for his missing younger son, who has evaded his mandatory army service. Driving through the desert, he is overwhelmed by the onslaught of the scorching heat and blinding light of the sun and the memories of his elder son's death in the desert during the Yom Kippur War. The journey through the desert and the traumatic past it brings up for him undercut the rescue mission on which the father had set out, instead leading him to his own death in the desert.[6]

The discovery of the Sinai desert as a tourist destination following the 1967 Six-Day War opened up a new and exciting alternative for Israelis who were otherwise barred from entering any neighboring Arab countries.[7] The Sinai Peninsula was accessible by ground travel, and its beach tourist sites made it possible to have a vacation on a shoestring budget. This vast region of desert landscape, with its underdeveloped beaches, primeval nature, and Bedouins, which seemed more authentic and romantic to Israelis than the Negev desert, reinforced the positive image of the desert. For those who stayed at the Israeli "field schools" in the Sinai, "the impact of the environment was enormous. . . . The interaction with the desert, the long stay and the enormous dimensions of that space generated a connection with it . . . the energies were boundless."[8] The ambiguous position of the peninsula as an Egyptian territory under Israeli control yet distant from both countries recreated Sinai's liminal status going back to the biblical exodus narrative. The open vistas of secluded nature produced the sense of a carefree environment that held a countercultural appeal, which was particularly attractive to young people.

After the return of Sinai to Egypt following the 1979 peace agreement with Israel, Israelis continued to flock to the Sinai Peninsula in great numbers, creating long lines as they passed through an official border checkpoint over the long holidays.[9] A study of the relationships between the Egyptian hosts and Israeli tourists indicates that both parties regarded it as an "ex-territory detached from the geographical, cultural, and political centers of both nations," reproducing Sinai as "a tourist bubble."[10] The Israeli government issued warnings against crossing the border to Sinai in response to unrest in the region and following the attacks on tourists in 2004 and 2006, yet although their numbers declined, Israelis continued to travel to Sinai's beaches.[11] A study of the media's warnings about the risk of staying at those popular vacation sites highlights their conflicting messages, ranging from emphatically emphasizing the danger to playing it down by reproducing images presenting these sites as "peaceful and inviting leisure-scapes."[12] The viability of Israeli tourism to Sinai declined following the Arab Spring and the resulting instability in Sinai. Nonetheless, the Sinai has remains an object of longing as a "lost paradise" for some, while others still return to the Sinai beaches during peak holiday periods.[13]

Within the Negev, the two major areas that developed as tourist attractions are Eilat, on the Akaba/Eilat Bay at the southern tip of the country, and the southern part of the western shore of the Dead Sea. Reaching Eilat from the center of the country required a journey of several hours through the desert terrain, an exceptionally long trip for Israelis given the small size of their country. As Maoz Azaryahu notes, Eilat (the most remote settlement on the southern frontier after 1949), offered the liminal space of a small, desert-and-beach resort town, at what was seen as "the end of the world."[14] When a new road to Eilat was built in 1958, it made Eilat into an important vacation destination for Israelis.[15] From 1967 to 1982, however, the lure of the Sinai Peninsula as a major desert tourist destination overshadowed Eilat's special appeal. The opening of direct charter flights to Eilat in 1975 made it more easily accessible to foreign visitors, and following the return of Sinai to Egypt, the town went through rapid urban development that turned it into a major desert resort. With beaches known for their coral reefs, the warm winter climate, and a variety of hotels, shopping centers, and sports and entertainment venues, Eilat became a favored destination for Israelis and foreign tourists.[16] Among the nature sites in its vicinity, the Timna Valley National Park and Nature Reserve to the north stands out; the reserve features ancient copper mines and unique geological formations, best known as "Solomon's Pillars."[17] Since the 1994 peace treaty with Jordan, Eilat has also served as a point of departure to the red rocks of Petra, the Nabbatean World Heritage Site across the Israel-Jordan border.

The Dead Sea emerged as another area of relatively early desert tourism. In 1956, an outpost that the NAHAL ("Pioneering Combat Youth") had establ-ished in Ein Gedi, a natural oasis near the Dead Sea, became a kibbutz. The first "field school" of the Society for the Protection of Nature in Israel (SPNI) was established there in 1959. The Ein Gedi Field School offered educational hiking tours of the desert environment for individuals, families, and school and youth groups, and provided simple and affordable accommodations for visitors to this area. In the post-1967 period, the construction of a new road through the Judean desert (passing in part through the West Bank) dramatically enhanced the accessibility of the Dead Sea area. The opening of large hotels on the Dead Sea's western shore, with the expansion of guest accommodations at kibbutz Ein Gedi, turned this part of the desert into a major tourist resort during the 1980s and 1990s. The unique medicinal qualities of the Dead Sea water, the beauty of its landscape, and the warm winter climate attracted visitors from Israel and abroad to this area.[18] The proximity to the ancient site of Masada (see below) added another major attraction in the area, although a visit to the site no longer requires an overnight stay. In recent decades, however, development there has been arrested due to major environmental issues in the Dead Sea area (see chapter 6).

The return of Sinai raised hopes that desert tourism would become a major economic resource and an incentive for the development of other parts of the Negev that had remained outside the tourist circuit. In 1988, a multi-year plan entitled "Negev 7" was approved and led to the formation of a new Negev Tourism Development Administration, signaling the government's greater commitment to this cause. The new administration faced the challenge of attracting investors to Ramat Negev to expand its offering of tourist accommodations and services and thereby enhance its touristic appeal. Various ideas for large-scale projects emerged during the 1980s and 1990s that suggested combining the agendas of settlement and tourism. A major project, known as "The Heart of the Negev," involved a large space of about five thousand acres (twenty thousand dunams) that would feature a casino, hotels and rental apartments, golf courses and stores, a biblical theme park, an artificial lake, and other tourist attractions.[19] The project drew on the Zionist ethos of developing the desert, but was inspired by the American Las Vegas model of a major tourist attraction based on casinos and mega-scale attractions in a desert landscape.

Such plans provoked strong opposition from environmental groups as well as local residents, who regarded these grandiose plans as fundamentally at odds with the character of the desert environment and the culture of existing Negev settlements.[20] Dreams of large-scale tourism to the Negev also suffered a major blow when foreign tourism dropped drastically following the outbreak of the Palestinian Intifada and given the plans to further expand the army bases and military presence in the Negev.[21] The realization that the central Negev could not compete with the lure of desert beach resorts and the opposing pulls of settlement, security, and environmental discourses made it clear that desert tourism had to be reimagined within these constraints. A more pragmatic approach shifted the emphasis to smaller-scale tourism projects and to reshaping Israelis' attitude toward the desert as a viable touristic alternative. "Desert tourism is an economic product," an official involved in the development of Negev tourism noted in a conversation. "It is based on marketing nature and the desert landscape and on creating all kinds of slogans that fine-tune the product called 'desert.'" This approach has led to growing experimentation with a wider range of tourist options that feature different aspects of the desert, to appeal to diverse clienteles, thereby contributing to the plasticity of its representations within the discourse of tourism.

Nature, Adventure, and Leisure Tourism

The discourse of tourism highlighted the positive qualities of the desert as the "nonplace," the uncultivated environment that was defined by its contrast with the inhabited and cultivated "place" but provided an attractive alternative mode to everyday life in the highly populated center. Like the environmental emphasis on the significance of the desert as an open space, adventure tourism underscores the potential of the wild desert terrain for those who are looking for a challenging physical environment.[22] Promoting the slogan "Negev Action," publicity for this kind of tourism features the appeal of the Negev to four-wheel drivers seeking adventure, evoking the associations of the jeep as a military icon representing power, masculinity, mobility, and daring.[23] A newspaper article describing a variety of four-wheel-drive excursions further illuminates these military connotations in its heading, "Travel, Travel to the Desert,"[24] a take-off on the opening line of a popular Israeli desert song, "Go, Go to the Desert." The song lyrics describe a group of soldiers walking in the desert landscape, "a land of salt, wind, and fury," and allude to the theme of a double return: both to the desert land and to their ancient historical roots.[25] However, as discussed below, the advertisements that draw on such military and patriotic associations are often reoriented toward a more individualistic or romantic frameworks in order to enhance their appeal to potential visitors.

Given the military's need for large areas of desert land and the belated realization that four-wheel-drive vehicles cause damage to the desert terrain, stricter rules were applied to limit the use of such vehicles to designated routes. Although four-wheel-drive trails continue to be one of the options that desert tourism promotes, tourist publicity often combines adventure with other kinds of elements. Thus, for example, it advertises excursions that include "challenging driving, geology, water sources, and ancient agriculture"; that combine visits to archeological sites and into nature with social time around the campfire; or that offer the opportunity for the romantic experience of "an enchanting drive" at night under the full moon.[26] The rising popularity of eco-adventure tourism presents bike rides as a more environmentally friendly and more physically challenging alternative. The desert biking experience similarly combines cycling with sightseeing of nature and other points of interest, and cyclists have become part of the desert landscape in the Negev and the Arava.[27]

Like desert tourism in other places, the discourse of Israeli tourism highlights the "primordial landscape" of the desert as a mythical site of unspoiled nature, immune to the impact of time and civilization.[28] While the settlement discourse condemns the desert as antithetical to the Zionist vision and the modernist ideology of progress, the tourism rhetoric underscores its intrinsic value for defying the impact of modernity and providing a refuge from the trappings of modern life. It therefore positions the desert in opposition to city life and emphasizes the opportunities the desert provides for experiences no longer available in the urban environment. A 2004 advertisement sponsored by the Negev Tourism Forum carries this message, in large print: "Stop the city! I want the Negev!"[29] A flyer for a kibbutz's hospitality accommodations in Ramat Negev echoes this approach: "Get away from everything, come to the tranquility of the desert."[30] The owner of a desert site told me that it is "only when you arrive in a place that offers one total freedom, like the desert, that your soul has the space to expand." And another site owner elaborated on this theme: "People think that there is nothing in the desert, but the desert has so much to offer! When I take people on tours I attempt to connect them with the beauty that one can discover in the desert. . . . More than anywhere else, people can experience here the ability to connect."

This emphasis on the positive qualities of the desert is also tied to a deliberate attempt to change the view of the once-stigmatized desert colors and repackage them as "exciting" by virtue of their difference. Desert tourism thus advances the message, "Get out to the Negev to be moved by different colors!" An advertisement carrying this theme further suggests that the Negev's colors may trigger a refreshing movement away from one's habitual aesthetic standards.[31] This theme is also part of the logo of the Hebrew website for Negev tourism ("gonegev.co.il"), which features the motto "take a vacation in different colors," with the words "different colors" displayed in orange.[32]

At the same time, and somewhat incongruently with the above message, Negev tourism publicity also repeatedly features the theme "Green in the Negev" and the unexpected colors of blooming plants in the desert as a way to draw visitors. Similarly, articles in the media feature headlines such as "A Green Weekend: Festival and Surprises in the Negev," or "Seeing Green in the Negev Is Not a Mirage (*fata morgana*)."[33] Another article suggests that going to the Negev to see the color green presents an alternative to going abroad.[34] The SPNI's successful campaign to protect wildflowers (discussed in chapter 6) has reinforced the Israeli practice of making special trips to see flowers blooming in their natural setting. Tourist materials further highlight the element of surprise and delight in discovering blooming flowers in the desert landscape:

> It's an erroneous idea that the desert, the wasteland, does not grow anything. . . . As one travels in the desert, on unpaved roads, waiting to find that place, that hidden corner where the flower and its intense color will suddenly appear, one is filled with anticipation, suspense, and [the] exhilaration [of discovery].[35]

The flowering season of the red anemone (*kalanit*), a beloved wildflower that covers entire fields in the northern Negev in the early spring, has become the occasion for an annual festival with the catchy name *Darom Adom* (the Red South), which highlights the unusual combination of the southern region and the color red. Extensive publicity and media coverage not only bring attention to nature, but also use the opportunity to feature diverse tourist attractions in the area. During the weeks of the Darom Adom festival, Israelis flock to this area to see the flowering fields and visit other sites in their vicinity.[36] Other blooming plants are similarly presented as an occasion to bring visitors to the Negev desert, though they have a more limited appeal.[37] It is interesting to note that similar themes are also associated with private cultivated gardens in the desert landscape, including the allusion to a fantasy or a hallucination.[38] The critical difference is that the tourist publicity focuses on wildflowers in the public space, while the private gardens feature the success of the settlement ethos of cultivating plants as the fulfillment of the goal of making the desert bloom.

UNESCO's recognition of the distinct formations of the Negev craters as a World Heritage Site in 2010 was an important development for local and foreign tourism to the desert. As the folklorist Valdimar Hafstein notes, "to label a practice or a site as heritage is not so much a description, then, as it is an intervention."[39] In this case, the campaign to protect the craters (see chapter 6) raised public awareness of the desert landscape, and led the way for the public recognition of Crater Land as a World Heritage Site. This status had an impact on the nearby desert town Mitzpe Ramon, which expanded its tourist accommodations and services and helped highlight the numerous tourist attractions in the town and its vicinity. A new area in Mitzpe Ramon, overlooking the Ramon crater, which the town developed and named the Desert's Edge (*sefat ha-midbar*, which also means "the language of the desert"), features the positive qualities of the desert landscape.[40]

Nature tourism draws on romantic attitudes toward the desert mystique and environmental discourse and highlights closeness to desert nature as an opportunity to engage with it more fully. The publicity for the new Hotel Beresheet in Mitzpe Ramon underscores its open approach to the environment, advertising "this exceptional desert hotel, which maintains a dialog with the surrounding desert, allowing its essence to penetrate every corner."[41] The "penetration" of the desert into the inhabited space—a theme that the settlement discourse defines as an alarming threat calling for protective measures or even a counterattack—is thus transformed into a positive "embedded"[42] experience for hotel guests.

The new approach to the desert environment has also been articulated in the emergence of the "desert style" that characterizes some of the more ecologically oriented tourist sites. Low-to-the-ground structures, the use of organic materials (such as mud and clay), a preference for the desert color scheme to make the structures' exteriors blend into the desert landscape, and the use of local arts and crafts for decoration are expressions of this trend. At some of the smaller tourist sites, structures are covered with mud in order to produce this style. Interior spaces and yards are often decorated with Bedouin rugs, water jugs, and other clay and brass objects. This "desert style" thus projects a sense of local décor that differs from the "rural style" typical of tourist accommodations in the Galilee.[43] Some of its traits, such as the use of desert colors and organic materials, may have been influenced

FIGURE 20. Lodging at the Echo Farm Tzell Midbar. Photo by the author.

FIGURE 21. The desert site Succah Ba-Midbar. Photo by the author.

by similar global trends in desert tourist destinations (such as Santa Fe, New Mexico or Sedona, Arizona).

Such stylistic preferences are more typical of the smaller desert sites offering simple, ecologically oriented accommodations that contribute to their claim to authenticity and offer of an embedded desert experience. Thus, for example, the English version of the website for Khan Beerotayim (literally, the Two-Well Encampment) in the western Negev highlights the desert style of its accommodations, which are "built of mud and date palms and decorated with carpets and recycled items—all natural. The variety of natural colors, shapes and textures and the peaceful environment produce a charming, soothing sensation and a sense of complete detachment from the hubbub of everyday life. These lodgings blend in harmoniously with their natural surroundings."[44] Another ecologically-oriented site, Tzell Midbar (Desert Shade, figure 20), located across from Mitzpe Ramon, offers huts built from natural materials and ecological tents.[45] Yet another secluded site, Succah Ba-Midbar (Hut in the Desert, figure 21), located not far from Mitzpe Ramon, "nestled in the rocks" and surrounded by the desert landscape, offers hospitality in huts that provide "electricity by solar energy, clay water jugs, comfortable beds, and more."[46]

The distinct qualities of the desert have also drawn artists to the Negev and inspired artistic creativity. The open desert landscape serves as a particularly inviting space for large-scale environmental sculpture, including the Desert Sculpture Park, along the edge of the Ramon Crater,[47] with its "Sounds Park" section: sound-producing works that interact with the desert wind. Some other monumental artworks in the Negev are Dani Karavan's "Negev Brigade Memorial" near Beer Sheva and "Way of Peace" (derekh ha-shalom) in the western Negev, near the border with Egypt,[48] as well as Ezra Orion's "Line of Stones" in Sde Zin, "Rock Boulevard" on the edge of the Ramon Crater, "Human Condition" near Sdom, and "Identity" in Yerucham.[49] The desert towns of Arad and Mitzpe Ramon have developed artists' quarters featuring studios and galleries, and kibbutz Neot Semadar, which had a significant number of artists among its founding members, became known (among other things) for its unique art center and products.[50] Beer Sheva, the largest city of the Negev and the home of Ben-Gurion University of the Negev, is home to an art museum and various galleries that devote attention to desert art and contemporary arts in the desert.[51]

The discourse of tourism addresses the powerful impact of the desert as a liminal space for revelations and transformations that lead to personal growth. The solitude and tranquility of a secluded desert site provides visitors with the opportunity to experience the welcoming facets of the absence associated with the desert to focus inward and to observe the environment. The motto that appears on Tzell Midbar's website—"listen to the silence"—highlights this approach to the desert experience. Succah Ba-Midbar juxtaposes "the city with its growing noise and pressures" with the "space, purity and silence" offered by the desert, allowing visitors to "rebalance their lives." The lack of cell phone or internet reception or any television or radio at the site means that visitors can fully benefit from their unmediated experience of the desert without the distractions of modern technology.

The blending of ecotourism with spirituality is underscored in the publicity for the "eco-spirit-lodge" Zman Midbar (Desert Time), overlooking the Judean desert on the route from Arad to Masada and the Dead Sea. The site offers a variety of desert experiences as well as spiritual activities, such as workshops in yoga and meditation, a weekly peace prayer, and a ritual to welcome the Sabbath.[52] Other sites also offer special workshops, alternative therapies, holistic treatments, and spiritual experiences.[53] While such offerings are part of a broader trend in Israeli culture,[54] their alternative character particularly resonates with the role of the desert as the nonplace associated with transformative experiences.

The growing Israeli trend towards rural tourism in the form of bed and breakfast (B&B) hospitality first developed in the Galilee, the northern periphery, in the 1980s and then spread to the desert periphery.[55] When established agricultural settlements extended their economic base by offering accommodations to tourists, the rural base was already in place as part of the setting of their hospitality venue. Yet in new sites that develop with the plan to combine tourism and agriculture from the outset, this relationship has at times become more ambiguous, giving rise to "post-rural tourism"[56] that shapes the rural character of the host settlement to fit tourists' expectations. As we saw in chapter 4, the Wine Route individual farms project was designed to pursue the joint agenda of agriculture and tourism to ensure a stronger economic base. As a result, each farm had to find the particular niche that would mark it as different from other desert settlements in order to attract potential visitors. The individual farms thus present a diversity of choices such as growing vineyards, herbs, or other specialty plants; raising sheep, goats, camels, horses, or other animals; and drawing on these activities to define their tourist profile. Visits to the farms may thus include riding, feeding, eating, tasting, baking, and the purchase of local produce, among other desert experiences.[57]

In searching for their special marketing niche, some sites focus on camels, as the animal most identified with the desert experience; others have looked for more exotic choices, such as ostriches, antelopes, or alpacas. The importation of animals that are not indigenous to the region highlights the association of the desert with a wild terrain and a different nature that lies outside the boundaries of the familiar settled place. The publicity for these farms therefore underscores their unique character and the opportunity to encounter the unknown. Thus, for example, the website of the Alpaca Farm highlights its distinction: "Today we raise a herd of llamas and alpacas, horses, donkeys, angora sheep and many more animals. The whole process of the wool production takes place in the farm—the raising of the animals, the shearing and the spinning of the wool—and that makes the farm one of its kind in the world!"[58]

While desert tourism often underscores the themes of simplicity and closeness to nature, in contrast to the materialistic and hedonistic urban lifestyle, it also faces the challenge that the perception of the desert as an austere environment could deter those interested in leisure tourism. In an effort to lure the latter, the new approach to Negev tourism redefines the desert as a welcoming and relaxing environment that offers visitors the advantages of being in nature and, at the same time, of experiencing an indulgent vacation.[59] The establishment of a few upscale hotels and lodgings in the heart of the Negev has opened up the possibility of enjoying the unique desert environment while staying in chic accommodations equipped with modern amenities. Thus, the publicity for the Ramon Inn in Mitzpe Ramon offers visitors "a combination of activities and adventures amid the breathtaking desert scenery, in pleasant and comfortable weather conditions year round—with a host of indulgent treats."[60] The new, upscale Hotel Beresheet, mentioned above, offers a wide range of accommodations with breathtaking views of the Ramon Crater and the desert landscape, a spa, a large outdoor swimming pool, and private villas with indoor pools.[61]

Along these lines, the publicity for the desert spa Neve Midbar (Desert Oasis) at the center of the Negev presents it as "a romantic, pleasurable corner between the sky and the desert, where we'll provide you with indulging and relaxing personal treatment." Following the description of its thermal mineral pools and various treatments, the publicity alludes to the transformational impact of its unique experience: "Here, in the desert spa, we'll rinse away the pressures of everyday life, and you'll enjoy the purifying effects of an experience the likes of which you have never had."[62] A more recent version of the spa's website further highlights these themes:

> Alone or together, we all need a moment of respite. Breathing interval. Time to rest, to breathe, to stop the race of our daily lives. . . . In the desert spa you will find a green garden in the heart of the desert, a dry sauna, a massage pool, sun beds, a luxurious tea corner and especially the quiet, calm and peaceful [place] that will recharge you long after the visit.[63]

Another facet of desert tourism that caters to urban middle-class visitors is the special gourmet experience it offers. This growing trend in Israeli tourism is not specific to this region, but its association with the desert is a novelty, as an article on "desert gourmet" suggests.[64] Desert tourism's emphasis on wines and cheeses produced locally by various individual farms and a wide array of culinary offerings of organic and gourmet food indicates the effort to repackage Negev tourism for the urban tourist's taste. Touring companies similarly attempt to indulge tour participants with a gourmet meal set in a remote natural site, at times as a surprise awaiting the unsuspecting tourists.[65] While the diversity of culinary offerings and their level has clearly been improved, a study on marketing the desert indicates that so far these gourmet offerings have failed to produce a distinctive culinary trend that is associated with this region.[66]

Another, related, phenomenon that is part of the attempt to make desert tourism attractive to urban tourists involves surprise cultural performances in nature. I experienced this surprise on an organized tour for Israeli visitors from Tel Aviv, which I joined in the spring of 2005. At some point during the tour, as we got off the bus and started walking in the desert landscape, we were surprised by the sounds of music, floating up as if from nowhere. Only when we climbed down to reach a spring hidden away below did we discover the musicians, whose performance we continued to enjoy in this natural setting. As with the gourmet meals, the incongruity of the cultural performances with the rugged nature and uninhabited space enhance the element of surprise and defy the tourists' expectations.

Clearly, the upscale trend in desert tourism is part of a global trend of post-rural tourism. The influence of European tourism on Israelis can be easily detected in the conventional reference to "B&B hospitality" in

Hebrew as *zimmerim*, a Hebraized plural form of *Zimmer*, the German word for "room."[67] Much like the importation of foreign animals as tourist attractions, the use of foreign terms and phrases in conjunction with the tourist experience suggests the need to upgrade the experience of going to the periphery—and even more so, to the desert—by comparing it with going abroad. The analogy made between the Negev's agricultural tourism sites and those of Tuscany (in conversations about Negev tourism, in a newspaper article, and in the title of a recent MA thesis, " 'Tuscany Is Here' "[68]) evokes similar associations. While this analogy is generally designed to highlight the improvements in Negev tourism, some Negev residents cynically dismiss it as a pretentious attempt to "Provençalize" or "Tuscanize" the Negev, criticizing it as undermining the Negev's distinct local character.

A rather different tourism focus involves inviting visitors to come to major festivals held in the Negev desert. Here, the desert is secondary to the event in question, providing the setting rather than the focus for participants. Several annual festivals take place in different parts of the Negev, offering a diversity of musical performances (from rock and popular music to opera, jazz, and classical music) and other cultural programs that draw large numbers of visitors and local residents for the duration of the specific event.[69] This trend is expanding, as new large annual festivals are added that attract thousands of visitors to the Negev, including the Indie-Negev musical festival of rock and indie music, held in Mitzpe Gevulot in the western Negev, and the more recent Midburn Festival, modeled after the Burning Man event held annually in Nevada's Black Rock Desert.[70] The publicity for the former suggests that it transforms the usually quiet desert into a lively environment, thereby "making the silence bloom."[71] Like the unexpected flowers that bloom in the desert, these public events receive attention because they are the exceptions in the desert, whereas at the center they might have been lost among the multitude of cultural offerings there. Traveling to the desert to attend a festival, and the freedom that is associated with the open space, produce the experience of a symbolic shifting in time and place for the duration of these events. For some of the Negev residents, however, the Midburn Festival, drawing thousands of visitors to their area, can turn into an unwelcome development. According to a recent news report, "Hundreds of residents call for relocating the overcrowded festival due to environmental damage and noise", but the head of Ramat Negev points out the far-reaching importance of the event, which "brands this place as a center of desert tourism in Israel."[72]

As the discussion of the discourse of tourism shows, marketing the desert means interweaving various themes and images that may appear incompatible. Tourism underscores the beauty of the unspoiled, primordial nature of the desert but hails the creation of farms and the raising of various domesticated animals; it highlights simplicity and spiritual growth along with luxurious accommodations, gourmet meals, and large-scale cultural events. While some desert tourism offerings highlight the nature/culture, desert/settlement opposition, leisure tourism offers a competing version of the desert that defies these dichotomies and presents a more fluid and complex reality. This multifaceted character of the desert becomes apparent in an advertisement for a desert lodging that promises potential customers that it provides an "urban-desert experience."[73]

Archeology and Ancient Heritage

The link between the desert and antiquity, which was cultivated in pre-state Hebrew culture and is embedded in Israeli national memory, presents the desert as a mythical space that connects the present with the past and allows contemporary Israelis and foreign tourists to bond with the ancient Jewish and Christian pasts. Desert tours include visits to archeological parks and heritage sites that have become a core component of the Israel experience. Masada, an archeological park on top of a mountain overlooking the Dead Sea, is the most famous archeological site in the southern region. The story of Masada is based on the writings of the ancient Jewish historian Josephus, in which he describes the fate of close to one thousand Jewish men, women, and children who found refuge in this remote yet well-supplied fortress during the Jewish revolt against Rome. Following the Roman conquest of Jerusalem and the destruction of the Second Temple in 70 CE, Roman forces proceeded to Masada and besieged it. The Jewish refugees held out for a long time, but when their leader realized that they would no longer be able to prevent the Romans from entering the fortress, he persuaded the men to kill their families and then themselves in order to die free.[74]

Though Josephus's story of Masada did not play an active role in Jewish memory for many centuries of life in exile, the dramatic event he recounted became better known after his work was translated into Hebrew, and grew in significance among activist Zionist circles in Europe and Palestine in the first half of the twentieth century.[75] Masada soon became the destination for a new youth pilgrimage that made hiking through the desert, climbing to the top of the isolated mountain (see figure 29, in the epilogue), and reading aloud from Josephus's text into the performance of a patriotic ritual. Following the extensive excavation of the site in the mid-1960s and the establishment of a large archeological park there, it became a required stop for Israeli and foreign tourists.[76]

Fame also brought more attention to the problematic aspects of the Masada story, yet in spite of the ensuing polemics about its interpretation and its relative decline as a heroic model, the archeological site has retained its position as a major tourist destination. In 2001, UNESCO recognized Masada as a World Heritage Site. As the UNESCO website explains,

> Masada is a rugged natural fortress, of majestic beauty, in the Judean Desert overlooking the Dead Sea. It is a symbol of the ancient kingdom of Israel, its violent destruction and the last stand of Jewish patriots in the face of the Roman army, in 73 A.D. . . . Masada is a poignant symbol of the continuing human struggle between oppression and liberty.[77]

From 1995 to 2000, to accommodate the crowds of foreign tourists that were anticipated following this international recognition, the archeological site at Masada went through another round of renovations, building a visitors' center and the Yigael Yadin Masada Museum to house the findings from the site, previously displayed at the Israel Museum in Jerusalem.[78]

The transformation of Masada from a grassroots pilgrimage tradition into a tourist destination has introduced ironic historical twists: although several Orthodox scholars objected on religious grounds to the glorification of the ancient suicide as a heroic act, the state of Israel and, more recently, the ultra-Orthodox Chabad movement have been actively engaged in promoting tourism and religious ceremonies at Masada.[79] Other critics see the foreign elements associated with Masada, such as the cable car to the top and the opening of a McDonald's restaurant at the site, as an "attack on our values and national culture" and an indication that the "forces of global capitalism are taking the fight to the heart of the Zionist narrative."[80]

The Qumran National Park is another important ancient site on the main road leading from Jerusalem to the Dead Sea. The discovery of the Dead Sea Scrolls led to growing interest and additional excavations in this area, throwing further light on the life of the Qumran commune.[81] Members of this commune had found refuge in this remote desert location during the time of the Second Temple in order to pursue a life of seclusion, purity, and spirituality according to their beliefs. In spite of a scholarly debate about the identification of the Qumran group with the ancient sect of the Essenes, who were important to Christian church history, Qumran has become a major stop for Christian tourists.[82] Similarly, desert tourism also includes visits to the Karkom Mountain area in the Negev, which has been identified as the biblical Mount Sinai, even though this identification has been contested.[83]

Another important aspect of heritage tourism is the focus on the ancient Nabbatean Incense Route, which UNESCO recognized among its World Cultural Heritage sites in 2005. According to the UNESCO website,

> The four Nabatean towns of Haluza, Mamshit, Avdat and Shivta, along with associated fortresses and agricultural landscapes in the Negev Desert, are spread along routes linking them to the Mediterranean end of the incense and spice route. Together they reflect the hugely profitable trade in frankincense and myrrh from south Arabia to the Mediterranean, which flourished from the 3rd century BC until the 2nd century AD. With the vestiges of their sophisticated irrigation systems, urban constructions, forts and caravanserai, they bear witness to the way in which the harsh desert was settled for trade and agriculture.[84]

Archeological research and excavations of the Nabbatean sites long preceded this recognition, and Israeli archeologists and scientists had focused on the excavation and reconstruction of Mamshit, Avdat, and Shivta since the late 1950s. In 1966, these sites were recognized as national parks, and in 1973, archeological excavation was extended to Haluza.[85] Some of the Nabbatean sites along the Incense Route, like Avdat and Mamshit, are easily accessible to visitors to the Negev, while the others have largely remained off the tourist track.[86] In Shivta, an individual farm located near the entrance of the archeological park combines hospitality services with recapturing the ancient Nabbatean agricultural practices in the desert landscape. The proximity of the contemporary farm to the archeological ruins serves to guard the site as well as embody the connection between the ancient desert dwellers and their Zionist followers.

Israelis are fascinated by the archeological evidence of the Nabbate-ans' settlements and their methods of water collection and cultivation in the desert environment, and have adopted them as the forerunners of the Zionist settlers, who share the goal of making the desert bloom. A brochure issued by the ministry of tourism and the Negev Development Authority highlights the special Nabbatean heritage, and another site advertises "the legendary Incense Route" and notes that "many travelers set out to follow them in exploring the desert and try to experience the lifestyle of the masters of the desert."[87] Desert tourism presents a mythical framework that collapses the biblical and Nabbatean pasts into the Bedouin present for the benefit of the tourist, thereby drawing on the Bedouins to serve as the "surrogate descendants" of both the ancient Hebrews and the Nabbateans.[88] An advertisement for the Mamshit National Park foregrounds a nearby "Nabbatean Market," with a picture of visitors riding camels in the desert landscape, which are typical representations of the Bedouin experience, as discussed below.[89]

More broadly, beyond the archeological sites, desert tourism draws on the mythical qualities of the landscape as creating a link with the biblical past. References to the primordial character of the desert landscape are popular in both environmental and tourism discourses, as the frequently repeated Hebrew expression *nof bereshit*, "Genesis landscape," suggests. The evocative double meaning of Genesis alludes to "origins" but is also an allusion to the Hebrew name of the first book of the Hebrew Bible. The phrase was featured prominently in the campaign to save the Crater Land from mining (see chapter 6) and in promoting other products related to the desert. In addition to the aforementioned Hotel Beresheet, the owners of the Nahal Boker farm on the Wine Route named the first wine they produced "Genesis" (*Bereshit*) and a later harvest "In the Desert" (*ba-midbar*, also the Hebrew name of the biblical book of Numbers). The use of the biblical term *succah* in the hospitality site Succah Ba-Midbar (Hut in the Desert) and the naming of its guest huts after biblical figures similarly links contemporary visitors with the biblical past.[90] Works of art displayed in the desert landscape, such as the outdoor sculpture of the biblical Ruth at kibbutz Ketura and the burning bush image projected by the synagogue at BAHAD City, further enhance the link to the biblical past.[91] Perhaps most remarkable is the recent success in reviving an ancient palm seed that was discovered in the Masada excavations of the mid-1960s, and its eventual planting on the grounds of Ketura. The revived plant embodies the Zionist paradigm of revival and demonstrates the role of the desert landscape in preserving the seed and in allowing such direct continuity with the ancient past.[92]

The idea of restoring biblical wildlife in the desert landscape led to the creation of a wildlife park, Hai-Bar, near kibbutz Yotvata in the southern Arava. The Hai-Bar Park raises extinct or threatened indigenous species in a monitored and protected environment and then reintroduces them into the desert ecosystem. In 1977, Hai-Bar opened its safari attraction to visitors and its success has been reported by the media.[93] The contemporary animals in the park, such as wild donkeys and ostriches, represent their biblical ancestors, and in so doing affirm the mnemonic role of the desert landscape as a symbolic bridge to the biblical past.[94]

The familiarity of this mnemonic role of the desert can lead to casual or humorous references to the projected continuity between antiquity and present. Thus, a newspaper article about Negev tourism during the long Sukkoth holiday encourages Israelis to go to the desert by comparing their experience to that of their biblical ancestors:

> The Israelites spent forty years in huts in the desert before they reached the Promised Land. Three days are sufficient to discover the remnants of life in the desert and the hidden wonders of nature, from Beer Sheva to Eilat.[95]

During a "Ben-Gurion Walk" in the desert, I witnessed a casual intergenerational transmission of this mythical connection when I overheard a young Israeli man responding to his tired son's complaint about walking. "You think this is difficult?" the father replied. "Just imagine what it was for the Israelites to walk in the desert for forty years!" His response was meant as a good-humored rebuke to his child, but it also reinforced the symbolic link between the desert and the ancient past, and at the same time transformed the memorial walk honoring the late Israeli prime minister into a modern reenactment of the biblical exodus.

Bedouin Hospitality

Heritage tourism in the desert often includes the presentation of "Bedouin hospitality" as a core component. The Bedouin practice of welcoming visitors in a large hospitality tent or an open structure, sitting on the rug-covered ground on pillows or mattresses, and serving tea to their guests is a common feature of desert tourism (figure 22). Bedouin hospitality may include the performance of a traditional coffee grinding and preparation by a Bedouin dressed in traditional garb; at some Jewish desert tourist sites, the Jewish host or tour guide delivers the explanations while the Bedouin performs. Although the performance of Bedouin hospitality is designed to enhance the tourists' "desert experience," the hosts adjust the Bedouins' practices to visitors' needs. When visitors stay for dinner, some desert sites extend the Bedouin heritage to the meal, referring to it by the traditional Arabic term *hafla* (feast). The food is served on large trays placed on the rugs

FIGURE 22. "Bedouin hospitality" for tourists. Photo by the author.

FIGURE 23. A Bedouin worker sweeping the ground of a desert tourist site. Photo by the author.

in front of the guests, or on low tables to make it more comfortable for the Western visitor. Yet it is not unusual to see, on the menu of Israeli desert tourist sites, the oxymoronic label *kosher Bedouin hafla* (kosher Bedouin feast), indicating that the meal conforms to Jewish dietary laws. Similarly, an overnight stay in an authentic Bedouin tent, which is presented as part of a traditional desert experience, may include a safely installed heater to warm up the tent on cold desert nights.[96] Perhaps the least expected practice I witnessed was a Bedouin worker sweeping the desert ground for the benefit of visitors (figure 23).

The marketing of certain features of Bedouin culture as part of the desert experience echoes the practices of "indigenous tourism" associated with colonial traditions and reinforces the Orientalist view of Bedouins as exotic desert natives, whose identity has remained monolithic and unchanging.[97] While levels of traditionalism vary among Israeli Bedouins, the performers of Bedouin hospitality at tourist sites are typically dressed in full traditional garb in order to provide the staged authenticity that conforms to viewers' expectations.[98] Yet although this Bedouin hospitality is performed in the desert, it is often disconnected from its cultural setting. As Steven Dinero argues, the touristic commodification of Bedouin hospitality denies the very spirit of their tradition, which emphasizes the importance of welcoming guests without charge.[99] And while other Bedouin workers at the very same sites are dressed in casual, everyday clothes that do not distinguish them from other Israelis, the performing Bedouins are turned into "signs of themselves" as part of the transformation and commodification of "Bedouin hospitality" for tourist consumption.[100]

The Museum of Bedouin Culture, which opened under the auspices of the Joe Alon Center for Regional Studies in Lahav in 1985, focuses on the tradition and culture of the Bedouins of Sinai and the Negev. The initiative to establish the museum was Jewish, as is its management, but Bedouins are now represented on the board and the museum guides are Bedouin. The guides lead tours of the ethnographic exhibit in Hebrew and Arabic and discuss their past traditions, and they perform "Bedouin hospitality" in a tent in the museum's yard.[101] The museum's focus is clearly on Bedouins' past traditions; it does not address the profound changes that they have undergone in recent decades and it dissociates them from the Palestinian dimension of their identity.

The layered connection to the past within the discourse of tourism relates to contemporary Bedouins as iconic representations of the mythical

Bedouin who, in turn, represents the ancient Hebrew. The tourist discourse often takes these symbolic links for granted. This is evident, for example, in a guide's reference to Abraham the Patriarch as "the first Bedouin,"[102] or in a video that alludes to Abraham the Patriarch as visiting a market that was probably similar to the Bedouin market of Beer Sheva.[103] The website for *Desert Ashram* displays an ironic distance in suggesting to visitors that "you can get in touch with *your inner Bedouin* and sleep in an authentic woolen tent."[104] Traces of the earlier use of the Bedouin as a trope for the native in the pre-state and early state years may be seen in the custom of some Jewish desert tour guides of wearing a white *kaffiyeh* as part of their professional outfit. While the practice might be explained by the need to protect their heads from the blazing desert sun, a Western hat would clearly accomplish this task as well. The choice of a *kaffiyeh* displays the guides' strong affinity with the desert culture, while the selection of a white one represents a safer choice than the red or black checkered kaffiyehs that have become political Palestinian and Arab symbols. The white *kaffiyeh* also projects simplicity and purity and evokes the image of the ancient Hebrews, who are often imagined as dressed in white gowns and white head covers, thus connecting these guides to both the ancient Hebrews and the Bedouins.[105]

Like the Bedouin, the camel emerged as a multilayered feature in Israeli tourism. Closely associated with the desert and with Bedouin culture, the camel became the logo of some Jewish Negev organizations that wished to underscore their local roots.[106] But the camel has also become an iconic representation of the biblical past and an important feature of Israeli tourism more broadly. Israeli postcards thus include camels as part of their touristic representation, and camel figurines and stuffed animals are among the souvenirs commonly displayed in Israeli tourist shops. Camel rides have become a salient feature of the "Israel experience," as demonstrated in the publicity for the Birthright Israel trips for Jewish youth demonstrates[107] and as seen as well in various desert sites that offer camel rides as an important component of their tourist attractions.[108] Bedouin workers are commonly employed to take care of the camels, help visitors mount them and dismount from them, and guide the camels during the rides (see figure 24). On longer camel-riding excursions through the desert, desert guides share their personal stories and often bring the tourists to a Bedouin site, thus allowing for a direct encounter with Bedouin culture in its own setting.[109]

Camels are not a common feature of the Israeli landscape, and riding a camel may be as rare for an urban Israeli Jew as it is for a foreign tour-

FIGURE 24. Tourists taking a camel ride in the Negev desert. Photo by the author.

ist.[110] An Israeli journalist unceremoniously sums up her experience riding a camel for the first time, complaining that "it is quite boring to sit on a camel and not particularly comfortable." She nonetheless proceeds to convey the cultural trope of being transmitted to the ancient past: "I imagine those ancient caravans, the three patriarchs and the four matriarchs and myself in an embroidered dress and a veil." This brief romantic note quickly fades away again, though, as she concludes: "I enjoy the quiet and the view, but a half hour on a camel is enough for me."[111] Such short camel rides provide little more than a photo opportunity for tourists, not unlike elephant rides in India. By contrast, camel rides that last several days, like cycling tours or the earlier hiking tradition of the Hebrew youth, often combine a kind of nature and heritage tourism that is specific to the desert environment.

The romantic image of Bedouin culture within Israeli desert tourism is often presented as if it were in a bubble detached from the reality on the ground. It thus obscures the otherwise largely negative Israeli Jewish view of the Bedouins as a poor, less educated, crime-ridden community, and one that the state and some Jewish residents of the Negev see as a threat to their safety and security. It is not surprising, therefore, that professional and activist Bedouins respond with indignation to the proliferation of Bedouin heritage practices in desert sites, regarding them as a cooptation of their traditions and the employment of Bedouins for this purpose as a form of exploitation:

> We are the authentic face of the Bedouin community. We are troubled that Bedouin life and tradition are mostly disseminated by museums and people who are not part of this tradition and whose main goal is economic profit. *We are not a museum but an authentic tribe*, interested in opening its gates to different populations in the country so that those who come to visit it receive an authentic experience."[112]

Jewish activists and nongovernmental organizations as well as specialists in desert tourism have advocated the development of Bedouin tourism as an avenue for their economic advancement. Although the ministry of tourism and other government agencies have articulated their approval of this idea,[113] the development of Bedouin-sponsored tourism has been relatively recent. Yet the Hebrew websites sponsored by government agencies do not always make clear the distinction between "Bedouin tourism" or "Bedouin experiences" provided by Jewish-owned sites and those provided by Bedouin-owned sites.[114]

A Bedouin-owned site that was recognized early on, Sefinat Ha-Midbar (Desert Ship), was a rare example of a Bedouin farm that was included on the Ramat Negev Wine Route map. The site, which draws on the nickname "desert ship" for a camel, offers tent and room accommodations, Bedouin meals, camel rides, and other kinds of desert excursions that are typical of Israeli desert sites.[115] Other early initiatives featuring women's crafts in the Bedouin town of Lakiya combined the empowerment of women with tourism and the marketing of their products. Two nonprofit organizations that developed as grassroots initiatives—"Desert Embroidery" and "Sidreh-Lakiya Negev Weaving"[116]—encourage women to produce traditional crafts in their own homes while providing them with a support system and an organizational base to display and to market their products. The success of these initiatives, which were designed to improve women's income, education, and social position, came from their accommodation of traditional communal norms that allowed women to work at home. The women's crafts have met with international success and have brought tourists to Lakiya,[117] which has spurred other Bedouin tourist initiatives in the area. A website entitled "Bedouin Experience" features

Bedouin guides and Bedouin-owned sites in the Negev that provide "true Bedouin hospitality" and "authentic Bedouin tourist attractions."[118] The publicity for a new annual Bedouin festival, "Desert Charm," presented it as the first of its kind, inviting visitors "to experience a thousand-year-old tradition" during the week-long Jewish holiday of Sukkoth, when Israeli families are free to travel.[119] Bedouin tourism thus mobilizes the rhetoric and practices of the Israeli tourist discourse and highlights the concepts of authenticity, antiquity, and uniqueness that Jewish tourist sites emphasize to lure Israeli visitors.[120]

The village of Drejat represents another unique tourist attraction and a successful communal organization that supports it. Drejat presents the distinct cultural heritage of Arab farmers who had become farmers (*fellahin*) from the southern Hebron area who later moved to the Negev near the Arad valley, where they preserved their tradition of living in caves. As an unrecognized village, Drejat remained without basic infrastructure even after its residents had left the caves. In time, the village residents organized to improve their situation, including the introduction of alternative solar energy. Derjat was among several unrecognized villages that were selected to receive official governmental recognition, and it has become a tourist attraction. Its publicity highlights the theme of its residents' distinct ancient heritage, but also associates it with the biblical past:

> In the landscape of the serene desert frontier, at the foot of Mount Amasa, and on the edge of the Arad Valley, the picturesque village of Drejat can be found. Theirs is a captivating story of human perseverance. It is a tale of the lives of a wonderful people, who have preserved their heritage and ancient civilization to this day. . . . The settlement was founded next to a famous biblical path on which Abraham, Isaac, and Jacob traveled from Beit El and Hebron south to Beer Sheba, the Negev, and on to Egypt as is related in the book of Genesis.[121]

These and other Bedouin-based initiatives demonstrate the Bedouins' agency in developing their own tourist sites that introduce a more authentic portrayal of their cultural heritage in various domains. Combining agriculture and tourism following the model of the Wine Route individual farms, the "Desert Daughter's Farm" (Havat Ha-Midbar), located near the Bedouin town of Tel Sheva, introduces "the first line of Bedouin cosmetics in the world," based on a centuries-old family tradition and new technologies. The farm offers tours, products, and a variety of workshops related to medicinal plants, health foods, and Bedouin traditions.[122] Another recently approved project, the Wadi Attir farm near the town of Hura, is designed to develop a model for sustainable desert agriculture, "combining traditional agricultural skills with cutting-edge technology." The farm develops agricultural projects with special emphasis on saving water and energy and will establish a visitor's center with space for exhibition and educational programs, a restaurant, and a shop for local crafts and the farm's agricultural products.[123]

Bedouin tourism also includes organized visits to Bedouin towns and unrecognized villages, tours that are usually more educationally oriented and focus on social issues. Israeli Jewish visitors and, to a lesser degree, foreign tourists meet local Bedouin leaders, educators, social workers, and activists to learn about the special challenges that the Bedouin population faces in that particular locality as well as in other locales. The presentations and the exchanges with the visitors are inevitably constrained by the nature of the tourist encounter, the site, and the identity of the visitors involved.

Desert tourism thus presents a complex picture in relation to the Bedouins. It colonizes and commodifies their tradition of hospitality in some venues, but it also opens up the possibility for greater agency by the Bedouins to develop their own tourist initiatives. These initiatives are, however, still constrained by the need to appeal to Jewish visitors and accommodate their expectations, while selectively sharing the Bedouins' perspective on their traditions and current lives in the Negev. Given the vast economic, social, cultural, and political differences between the Jewish and Bedouin settlements that exist in close geographical proximity to each other, tours often separate visits to Bedouin towns and unrecognized villages from visits to Jewish settlements. Although the camel may serve as a unifying icon of the desert (illustrated, for example, by a postcard in the shape of a camel head with the inscription "Hi from Israel"), the habitual emphasis on distinguishing between ethnic categories may be projected onto the camels as well. On entering a tourist shop at the Ben-Gurion airport, my daughter pointed out to me a display of two groups of stuffed camels placed next to each other. The camels were identical, but one group was adorned with an ethnic marker identifying them as "Jewish camels," while the other group was identified as "Bedouin camels." The display thus made it clear how deeply entrenched in Israeli culture the ethnic divisions are, so much so that even the souvenirs designed for tourists have to be marked and grouped accordingly.

Zionist and Religious Highlights

Along with the emphasis on the desert as an open space and a site of primordial nature, Negev tourism also highlights the Zionist settlement ethos and the special place of the desert in the fulfillment of that ethos. This settlement-focused tourism resorts to the settlement discourse that defines the desert as the counter-place. Visits to Jewish desert settlements pay symbolic homage to the historical challenges that Yishuv society and the state of Israel have confronted in transforming the desolate wasteland into marked and inhabited places. Desert tours that focus on Negev settlements are first and foremost geared to internal tourists and may not have a strong appeal for foreign tourists on a brief visit to Israel. More typically, they are part of Israeli educational tours designed for Israeli students and Jewish youth groups from abroad, as well as for families, senior groups, and foreign tourists who have a greater interest in Zionism and the history of Israeli society.

Perhaps the single most important historical Zionist site in the Negev is the home of the late David Ben-Gurion, the famous Zionist leader who led the Jewish struggle for a state, proclaimed Israel's independence in 1948, and served as the country's first prime minister. A visit to his home in kibbutz Sde Boker provides an educational opportunity to discuss Ben-Gurion's historical role in promoting the settlement of the Negev and his personal commitment to pioneering values. The simple residence where he spent his last years is widely referred to in Hebrew as "Ben-Gurion's hut (*tsrif*)," providing concrete evidence of the modest, almost austere, lifestyle that Ben-Gurion and his generation of leaders pursued, in sharp contrast to the luxurious lifestyle of contemporary Israeli leaders and the allegations of corruption that have been leveled at them. Nearby, a visitors' center offers a historical exhibition about Ben-Gurion and educational programs.[124] Famous sayings by Ben-Gurion are engraved in this area, highlighting his vision of the settlement of the Negev (see figure 13). The tombs of David and Paula Ben-Gurion constitute another national memorial site, a few miles away at the edge of Ben-Gurion University's Sde Boker campus, offering a breathtaking view of the Zin canyon and the Avdat highlands. Their gravesite is the setting for an annual state-sponsored memorial marking Ben-Gurion's death, and as Michael Feige and David Ohana observe, this has "'forced' the Israeli leadership to follow a ritualistic pilgrimage path leading from Jerusalem to Sde Boker" during the ceremony, as an homage to Ben-Gurion's legacy.[125] An annual "Ben-Gurion Walk" in Sde Boker is another commemorative ritual, during which participants symbolically reenact Ben-Gurion's deep connection to the desert in honor of his practice of a daily walk in the rugged landscape. In 2014, the Ben-Gurion Walk was held on November 29, the date of the United Nations' historic 1947 vote on the partition of Palestine into Jewish and Arab states (Resolution 181), thus enhancing its patriotic meaning as a memorial ritual.[126]

Following a broader trend in Israeli culture, many individual localities have established historical museums or preserved historical sites that display key points in their history and include ethnographic exhibits, storytelling by veteran members, and workshops for children. These historical sites and settlement museums have become tourist destinations that largely attract Israeli visitors and organized educational tours.[127] In the Negev, these destinations focus on the early settlement and defense history and the immigrant villages and development towns, and also include more recent residential communities. Among the historical destinations is Ruhama, the earliest Jewish settlement in the Negev (it was established before World War I), which has set up a small historical area called "the Founders' Site" (*atar rishonim*) that displays its old structures. Kibbutz Revivim, first established as an outpost in 1943, has created a historical museum that includes a reconstruction of its historical defense in the 1948 war (figure 25).[128]

FIGURE 25. Reconstruction of Mitzpe Revivim's 1948 defensive structures. Mitzpe Revivim Museum. Photo by author.

Another historical settlement, kibbutz Yad Mordechai (named after Mordechai Anielewitcz, one of the leaders of the Warsaw Ghetto), interweaves the memory of the Holocaust with the 1948 war. In 1963, the kibbutz (which already had a tradition of commemorating the Holocaust every year) established a historical museum. The museum's motto, "from the Holocaust to revival," underscores the historical links between the Warsaw Ghetto revolt, the Holocaust, and the kibbutz's pioneering past and historical role in the defense of the Negev in 1948.[129] This multi-layered commemorative framework is also manifested in the decision to place Nathan Rapport's large statue of Mordechai Anielewitcz in front of the historic water tower, which has become a monument to the 1948 war.[130]

Zionist educational tours of the Negev that revolve around the settlement ethos include visits to one of the development towns or small rural immigrant communities to learn about their history and transformations over time, as well as visits to recent residential communities or individual farms. A visit to a development town often provides the opportunity to meet with residents—and may in some cases include a home visit and/or a homemade meal—and to hear firsthand from them about their family history and experiences, recent demographic and economic developments in their town, and the challenges they continue to face. Visits to individual farms and new residential communities highlight the continuing resonance of the settlement ethos but also display the experimentation that is taking place in new forms of settlement. The tourist discourse thus mobilizes the settlement narrative to enhance the tourists' experiences. Farm owners share with visitors their settlement experiences, and those who live in the center of the country often express their puzzlement over their hosts' choice to settle in the desert and raise families "in the middle of nowhere."[131] A farm owner whose immigrant parents had to live in a transit camp (*ma'abara*) in the post-1948 period told me that when his mother first visited his new site, it reminded her of the *ma'abara*. Undoubtedly, the "otherness" of living in an isolated site in the desert by choice triggers visitors' interest, and at the same time invariably turns them into active participants in the process, supporting the farm as consumers.

Visits to the Negev settlements may have a political subtext, based on the comparison of the Negev's status as a frontier to the contested Jewish settlements in the post-1967 territories. This subtext, however, does not represent a uniform ideological position. For those who oppose the Jewish settlements in the "occupied territories," touring the Negev settlements affirms their belief in the strength of the old Zionist pioneering values and the importance of focusing on this frontier. For proponents of the Jewish settlement of "Judea and Samaria," touring the Negev affirms their belief in the common agenda and shared ideological foundations of the Jewish settlement drive in all areas where Jews seek to establish greater presence, whether in the concrete or the symbolic desert. The more recent move of Orthodox settlers to the Negev and the rise in the Haredi (ultra-Orthodox) population in desert towns may further obscure the differences between these two geographical areas that serve as frontiers.

Desert tourism that focuses on the Zionist settlement achievements typically features Israel's scientific contributions and technological innovations that support the settlement agenda and make Israel highly visible in the global struggle against desertification. Israel developed irrigation methods to fit the arid landscape and hot climate, and it holds the world record in the agricultural reuse of treated wastewater.[132] Educational tours to the Negev may therefore include stops at university research centers, agricultural stations, and experimental greenhouses, learning about Israel's various methods of manufacturing water to support desert agriculture.[133] The Jewish National Fund advertises the large public parks in various locations of the Negev region that feature greenery and water, such as the Golda Meir Park near Revivim, with its small lake; the Yerucham park and lake; and Sapir Park in central Arava on the way to Eilat, which features a lake, palm trees, a lawn, and a sculpture garden.[134]

Religious tourism presents a distinct kind of tourism, revolving around pilgrimages to holy grave sites, that attracts Israeli Jews as well as Jewish tourists from abroad. This pilgrimage tourism developed first on the Galilee periphery, where it emerged in recent decades around the graves of famous rabbis, and later expanded to the Negev (see chapter 4). The most prominent destination for religious pilgrimages in the Negev is the grave of the "Baba Sali," Rabbi Yisrael Abuhatzeira, in the town of Netivot. The late Moroccan rabbi's popularity among North African Jews, along with his family's initiatives, has led to the creation of an elaborate memorial site around his grave. The Baba Sali memorial complex has thus become a magnet for heritage and religious tourism to Netivot, bringing in an estimated six hundred thousand annual visitors, culminating in the annual festivity (*hilluah*) in commemoration of the Baba Sali's death, with an estimated hundred thousand participants.[135]

The growing Orthodox and Haredi population in the Negev development towns and the founding of various religious academies (*yeshivot*) at the high school and post–high school levels have further contributed to the attraction of religious visitors to the Negev region. Furthermore, the practice of hiking in the desert has become more popular among *yeshiva* students, who combine the study of Jewish texts related to the desert with the kind of opportunity for spiritual experiences that has appealed to mystically oriented individuals and groups throughout the ages. The various forms of religious tourism in the desert benefit from the greater availability of kosher food and vital religious establishments in a region that was once largely associated with secular Israeli culture. Israeli hotels usually observe Jewish dietary laws, to accommodate observant Jews from Israel and abroad, and religious visitors may find affordable and intimate accommodations on religious kibbutzim or *moshavim* and in the development towns.[136]

Desert tourism markets its main product, the desert, as a distinct geographical space and as a symbolic landscape by selectively presenting it through multiple perspectives. Offering multiple visions of the same landscape is a familiar strategy in tourism in general, a deliberate attempt to maximize the potential number of visitors, who may have diverse interests and be attracted to different tours.[137] Desert tours thus often mix and match elements from various tourist categories in order to attract visitors to the Negev, without necessarily reflecting on the tensions between the different visions of the desert that underlie each of these strands of tourism. The commodification of the desert within the discourse of tourism thus reveals the multiple interpretations of the desert: it is a site of raw nature, a mythical pathway to the ancient past, a fluid and dangerous frontier, a safe place of refuge, a confining periphery, and a site of spiritual inspiration and growth. In offering this broad range of interpretations of the desert, tourism traditionally underscores the desert's *difference* from the populated urban center, yet this trend may be modified to a degree by the competing trend towards minimizing that very difference and presenting a more nuanced picture that might attract more urban Israelis to the desert and make it appear more accessible.

In spite of all these efforts and developments, the Israeli desert appears to lag significantly behind in the vacation preferences expressed by Israelis. An article reporting a recent survey notes that 33% of those surveyed preferred the Galilee, 28% chose Eilat, and only 3% noted the desert as a desired destination for vacation. The article points out that in Israelis' consciousness, "vacation" is still associated with water and green surroundings. "The Negev has remained a periphery. . . . It requires the visitor to invest more effort, to adjust a bit. And in spite of the detailed maps, the attractions are more limited and farther away."[138]

At times, the inconsistencies of the multiple meanings of the desert may be jarring. I experienced this in the most visceral way while driving to visit the archeological site at Shivta in the western Negev and the family-owned guesthouse nearby. Driving along the narrow and little-traveled road, I spotted soldiers training at a distance and saw warning signs of live fire along the way, and began to worry that I might have inadvertently taken a wrong turn onto a military base. When I finally arrived at my destination, I was struck by the contrast between the serenity and calm of this remote place, surrounded by the vast expanse of the desert landscape, and the active military training zone through which I had to travel to arrive there. An Israeli colleague told me that when her daughter got married, the young couple traveled to a romantic and secluded spot in the desert for their honeymoon, only to be startled the next morning by the sound of nearby live fire. The clash between the competing visions of the desert as a military zone and as a site of natural beauty thus shattered the promise of tranquility, beauty, and spirituality that had led them there.

The marketing of the desert also reveals the complex negotiations between the relative geographical proximity of the desert to the center and the larger mental distance that separates them. Tourist materials attempt to emphasize the qualitative difference between the desert landscape and the crowded center while still suggesting that the desert is relatively close and easily accessible.[139] Various advertising materials thus inform potential visitors that the Negev "is only a two-hour drive from Jerusalem and Tel Aviv"[140] or assure them that a visit to the northern Dead Sea area is "only 25 minutes away from Jerusalem." Yet a journalist describing the drive from the center to the western Negev points out the much greater imaginative distance that separates the two:

> The trip from the center [of the country] to Nitzana [in the western Negev] lasts less than three hours; it does not take a long time. But when one travels on route 211 . . . westward, toward Nitzana, the experience is that of landing in the most out-of-the-way, isolated place.[141]

The journalist further explains that "distances appear enormous and the sense of great emptiness and loneliness—a rare experience in most places in Israel—becomes very concrete." Another young Israeli, who lived for a couple of years in the Negev and then moved to the Galilee, explains: "In the desert one feels less secure. The open vistas, the lack of malls, the lack of distant lights, there are no things here that provide one with a sense of security."[142] For those who may feel the mental distance as a deterrent, an advertisement for the cosmetics line *Ahava*, from the Dead Sea Laboratories, offers a way out: "You don't have to travel to the Dead Sea in order to enjoy the luxury of Israeli Spas! *Ahava* brings the comfort of the renowned spas to your home."

Epilogue

Memory, Space, and Contested Visions

In its metaphorical journey through the desert, this study attempts to explore some of the more familiar and lesser-known paths of the desert landscape and the ambiguities that underlie the desert–settlement relations as constructed in Israeli culture. This study investigates the cultural construction of the desert as a symbolic landscape and geographical region from a broad historical framework, as it emerged in the Zionist Hebrew culture of Ottoman and Mandatory Palestine and has developed in Israeli culture. It begins with an examination of the symbolic desert as a category constructed in opposition to the the inhabited Jewish place, i.e. the "settlement"; it then shifts to the analysis of competing visions of the geographical desert as shaped and transformed through various discourses and practices. The discussion illustrates the tension and contradictions between these visions that are at times ignored and at others become the subjects of heated debates and legal disputes.

The interweaving of space and memory in the development of the desert as a symbolic landscape serves as the point of departure for this study and is explored at various junctures throughout this work. The desert emerges as a complex and fluid symbolic landscape, alternating between its functions as the *nonplace* and the *counter-place* within different contexts. As the former, it was conceived as the biblical space for transitions and revelations and as a site of national birth. As the discussion of the desert mystique reveals, it reconnected the new Jewish society in Palestine to its ancient biblical roots and contributed to the formation of a new Hebrew identity and lore. The open vistas of the desert highlighted its role as a site of nature, the nonplace that is defined in contrast to culture and offers the opportunity to find refuge from society and experience profound transitions. In later decades, the growing awareness of nature preservation and the environmental discourse introduced a symbolic reversal of the desert–settlement opposition, highlighting the positive value of protecting the desert as the nonplace.

Yet memory and space have also given rise to the competing vision of the desert as the counter-place, as a result of Jewish exile from the homeland. Projecting the Jewish decline narrative, associated with exile, onto the country's landscape led to the environmental imagery of destruction and desolation. The desolate desert represented a symbolic category that was loosely applied to a variety of terrains that challenged the Jewish settlement. The negative perception of the "symbolic desert" was thus defined from the perspective of the settlement and emphasized their conflictual relationship. The desert, the counter-place, served as the potential frontier for the settlement, and the "conquest of the desert" represented the process by which it was to be reshaped into a Jewish place.

Although historical studies and other descriptions from the period (including those by Jews) contest the characterization of the Palestinian landscape as a "desolate desert," this view is deeply entrenched in Jewish settlement discourse and in popular Israeli memory. Jewish memory and the modernist and colonial discourses supported the desert/settlement, nature/ culture dichotomies, and Jews highlighted the civilizing mission of the settlement in bringing European culture, social order, and advanced technology to the Middle East. The use of "oasis" or "island" as spatial metaphors for the Hebrew settlement underscored both its distinctness from and its isolation within the desert environment.

The establishment of the state of Israel in 1948 presented a major shift from the symbolic to the geographical desert, with the Negev region now included in Israel's territory and serving as Israel's largest internal frontier. The opposition between settlement and desert, once seen as external to the Jewish space, now had to be addressed within Israel's sovereign territory. The discourse of settlement and security presented the national priority as "making the desert bloom," yet this study reveals the complicated realities that challenged the settlement agenda. The decline of the old-school pioneering ethos led the state to direct new immigrants to small, newly established rural and urban frontier settlements in the Negev while relocating the Bedouins to the heart of the desert and placing them under military administration there until 1966. Later, the government directed the Negev

Bedouins to new towns it established, yet a significant part of the Bedouin population continues to live in the "gray zone" of unrecognized villages, refusing to change their lifestyle or settle their land claims with the state. After 1967, the Jewish settlement drive in the occupied territories turned them into alternative frontiers, further weakening the position of the Negev as a viable frontier.

Competing visions of the sparsely inhabited desert region have since come to reshape its landscape. The settlement agenda has given rise to new initiatives, revealing a more individualistic and entrepreneurial approach to the desert. As a rural tourist site, the individual farm has emerged as a new element in the desert landscape, advancing the agendas of both settlement and tourism. The environmentalist advocacy of nature preservation and sustainable development, conversely, represent the push to restrain and contain the settlement drive. State security needs further added to the demand for desert land, including military and air bases and large fire zones. With its territory largely designated as national parks, nature reserves, and military zones, and given the demographic, social, and economic challenges that face many of its small settlements, the Negev has shifted between its competing definitions as a challenging frontier and a neglected periphery.

The gaps and inconsistencies in the construction of the desert as a symbolic landscape may be most evident in the discourse of tourism, which provides wide-ranging alternatives for visiting the desert. Tourism markets the Israeli desert by describing its primordial landscape as untouched by culture, while at the same time highlighting archeological sites that provide evidence of earlier civilizations and offering tours of desert settlements. Adventure and nature tourism emphasize the challenging terrain and the simplicity of life in the desert, while other publicity materials promote luxury hospitality including spas, gourmet food, and other amenities. The performance of "Bedouin hospitality" in a tent or a shed is a common feature of Israeli tourist desert sites, but one may also visit unrecognized Bedouin villages or Bedouin towns and learn about the Bedouins' current lives as Israeli citizens. This multiplicity of tourist visions offers different experiences of the desert, but they can also be interwoven within the course of one visit, without necessarily dwelling on the tensions and contradictions they represent.

The multiple interpretations of the desert and the various developments on the ground reveal that the desert–settlement relationship is more complex and fluid than the opposition that has been constructed between them implies. Yet this opposition is still a strongly entrenched construct in the Israeli mind. An intricate interweaving of historical memories and spatial metaphors shapes Israeli Jews' understanding of their roots in the land and their relationship to the Middle East. As the following discussion suggests, the choice of certain spatial metaphors as templates that shape the perception of Israel's place in the Middle East, and the practices that those perceptions generate, have a direct bearing on the dynamics of the Israeli-Palestinian conflict.

The Oasis, the Island, and the Wall

The use of "oasis" and "island" as spatial metaphors for the Jewish settlement during the first decades of the twentieth century was meant to underscore the difference between the cultivated Jewish settlement and its environment. The two metaphors establish structurally equivalent territories, given that both the oasis and the island are surrounded by a vast expanse of nature, implying an analogy between the desert and the sea. But the two metaphors also differ in a significant way. The oasis preserves a continuity with the desert that surrounds it, manifested lexically in the Hebrew term for "oasis," which incorporates the word "desert" (i.e. *neve midbar*). The island, which is more sharply distinguished from its surroundings, projects greater "insularity," a derivative noun that characterizes its isolation. It is therefore quite telling that as the conflict with the Arabs intensified, Hebrew narratives revealed an increasing tendency to use the island metaphor. The "tower-and-stockade" model of settlement that became prevalent in the late 1930s articulated and reinforced the image of an island that must defend itself from its surroundings.

In 1948, the besieged-island metaphor was applied to the newly estab-lished state of Israel in the face of the combined Arab attack that followed Israel's declaration of independence. The post-1948 political reality rein-forced this metaphor, with Lebanon, Syria, Jordan, and Egypt surrounding Israel from the north, the east, and the south, and the Mediterranean to its west. The island metaphor may have had less overt connotations: as a ter-ritory that is separated from the continent, the island appears as an entity that is symbolically unattached to its surroundings, suggesting that Israel can be seen as floating between its geographical location in the East and its cultural orientation towards the West.

A 1950 cartoon by Arie Navon articulates the sense of besiegement by depicting the young state of Israel as a baby in its crib, surrounded by a pack of wild wolves ready to devour it (figure 26). The baby, who is wearing the iconic woolen hat of the Palmach fighters in the 1948 war, is firing its gun at the frightening-looking wolves, demonstrating an unyielding readiness to fight them to the bitter end. The incongruity of a baby wearing a fighter's hat and making this kind of heroic gesture produces the humor; but the cartoon also evokes powerful anxiety over the survival of the new state in the postwar years, with Israel surrounded by hostile countries intent on its destruction. The flimsy structure of the crib—standing on wheels and with very wide spaces between its slats—conveys the new country's lack of security and stability and suggests that it is not firmly grounded in place. This image stands in sharp contrast to a 1948 poster, produced for Israel's

FIGURE 26. "Israel in the crib," cartoon by Arie Navon (1950). Courtesy of his son, David Navon.

FIGURE 27. Israel National Bonds poster (1948). Design by Gabriel and Maxim Shamir.

national bonds, that features Israel as a solid fortress protected by thick walls (figure 27). Conceived as a fund-raising tool, this idealized image of the new state projects the desired power, durability, and security that were clearly missing in the reality of 1948.

A 1955 election poster for Mapai, the leading Labor party, depicts Israel's insularity as a discrete territory separated and elevated from its immediate surroundings (figure 28). The poster features an illuminated map of Israel, surrounded on three sides by a dark background that represents the symbolic desert and by a bright blue background representing the Mediterranean to its west. An oversized image of an Arab fighter pointing a gun at

FIGURE 28. Election poster for the Mapai party with the inscription "GROWTH vs. Siege" (1955). Courtesy of Moshe Sharett Israel Labor Party Archives, Berl Katznelson Foundation, and "Time Travel," Ephemera Collection at The National Library of Israel.

Israel embodies the threat associated with the desert domain. By contrast, the airplanes and boats depicted in motion display the Mediterranean as an open gateway to Europe. The inscription, "GROWTH vs. siege!" leaves no doubt about the implied contrast between the technological progress associated with the West and the foreboding menace of the East. At the same time, however, the Arab threat "to drive the Jews into the sea" (which has been attributed to various Arab leaders) revealed the potential danger in the openness of the sea, given this spatial configuration.[1]

The isolation of the mountain of Masada, surrounded by the desert (figure 29), along with the growing importance of Masada as a major Israeli national myth (see chapter 7), reinforced the image of the country as a besieged island. Retelling the story of the besieged Jews on the isolated mountain, surrounded by the vast desert and the Roman soldiers, and their choice to die free rather than live in servitude, is a way to articulate Israeli anxiety about Jewish survival. Standing on top of the isolated mountain, surrounded by the desert, visitors can experience the sense of isolation and besiegement that drove ancient Jews to their deaths. As I have written elsewhere, the heroic legacy of Masada was supported by the determination to avoid its recurrence.

FIGURE 29. View of the Masada Mountain. Photo by Yaacov Saar (1980); courtesy of the Government Press Office.

Yitzhak Lamdan's famous verse, "Masada shall never fall again," was rein-
terpreted as a patriotic pledge and used as a rallying call to soldiers. But
this poetic verse also reveals the persistent fears that Israel might become
a second Masada, similar to the "Never Again" slogan referring to the
recurrence of the Holocaust.[2]

The post-1948 reality of a Jewish state with a significant Arab population introduced a new relationship between the Jewish majority and
the Arab minority, which was concentrated on the Negev and the Galilee
peripheries. While Israelis continued to experience their country as a
Jewish island surrounded by the metaphorical "sea of Arabs," the new
power relations within Israel created a symbolic reversal of the pre-state
situation, turning Arab spaces into symbolic islands within the broader
Jewish national space. Gil Eyal points out that the discursive construction of the "Arab village" portrayed it as a traditional island surrounded
by modernity, and Daniel Monterescu notes the common reference to
Ajami, an Arab neighborhood in Jaffa, as "the ghetto" after the 1948 war.[3]
The state's intention to transform Israeli Arab settlements into symbolic
islands is manifested in the goal of "Judaizing the Galilee and the Negev"
and the preferred policy of containment of the Bedouin population in
the Negev. Eyal Weizman and Fazal Sheikh describe the space of the
displaced families of Al-Araqib as "a landlocked 'island' surrounded by
Jewish agricultural settlements, Jewish National Fund forests, a highway,
a railway, and a major waste facility."[4]

The swift victory of the 1967 war and Israel's military conquest of
the Sinai Peninsula, the Gaza Strip, the West Bank, and the Golan Heights
weakened the country's self-image as a besieged island and brought about
a new confidence. Israel's policy of maintaining fuzzy borders with the occupied territories opened up the possibility for Israelis of traveling across
previously sealed borders. The new feeling of openness that Israelis now
experienced stood in sharp contrast to their acute sense of besiegement
prior to the 1967 war. The new situation rekindled the earlier fascination
with the desert as a mythical space that connected modern Jews with their
biblical past. Israelis found the vast expanses of the Sinai desert and its sea-
side resorts more fitting to their romantic image of the desert as refuge and
the opportunity to reconnect with the biblical story of the exodus and the
mythical Mount Sinai. In the early post-1967 period, the encounters with
Palestinian Arabs in the West Bank, with the Druze in the Golan Heights,
and particularly with the Bedouins in the Sinai desert rekindled Jews' interest

in their cultures. Yet this renewed interest was clearly shaped by a radically different power relation and took place in the context of the new reality of military occupation and economic dependence.

The occupied territories represent diverse landscapes and populations that do not (with the exception of the Judean Desert and the large Sinai Peninsula) fall into the geographical category of desert. Nor did the Jewish settlers refer to them as a desert. Yet the application of the pre-state settlement practices to the occupied territories made it clear that the Jewish settlers and the proponents of "Greater Israel" treated them as if they were a "symbolic desert" that could serve as a new frontier. Drawing on the pre-state strategy of establishing facts on the ground, Jewish settlers moved into the occupied territories, settled and renamed the space, and (re)claimed it as part of the biblical land of Israel, with the tacit or explicit support and military protection of the Israeli governments. Israel returned the Sinai Peninsula following its 1979 peace agreement with Egypt, but the government solidified its hold on the other territories. In unilateral moves, it declared a unified Jerusalem as its capital in 1980 and asserted Israeli jurisdiction over a large portion of the strategically important and sparsely populated Golan Heights in 1981. By reinforcing the web of legal, social, economic, and political ties between the Jewish settlements of "Judea and Samaria" on the West Bank and Israel proper, it has transformed its territory from a "gray frontier" to a de facto Israeli periphery, with recent renewed calls from the Right for official annexation.[5]

For a short period, from 1993 to 1995, a new approach, advanced by the Labor government under the leadership of Yitzhak Rabin and Shimon Peres, led to the Oslo Accord with the Palestinians and a peace treaty with the Hashemite Kingdom of Jordan. The peace negotiations, which involved dismantling the besieged-island template, were based on a readiness to make territorial concessions. Inspired by the vision of a "new Middle East," they also promoted the active participation of Israel in regional collaboration. The Oslo spirit generated multiple forums and initiatives revolving around shared environmental and economic interests as well as artistic and cultural cooperation across national boundaries, but it also provoked vocal opposition on both sides. The ensuing Palestinian violence against civilians within Israel and a vehement protest led by the Israeli Right culminated in the assassination of Prime Minister Yitzhak Rabin by a Jew in 1995, derailing the peace process. The vision of Israel as part of a broader and more open environment has faded as Israel has increasingly re-embraced the besieged-island template.

In spite of peace treaties between Israel and both Egypt and Jordan, the reality of a "cold peace" and the breakout of the Second (Al-Aqsa) Intifada in 2000 enhanced the Israeli public's distrust of the peace process and brought the Right back to power. The mounting toll in civilian lives within Israel during the Second Intifada spurred a large civic movement, "Fence for Life" (later relabeled "Security Fence for Israel"), to prevent Palestinians from the West Bank from entering Israel illegally.[6] Although the government and the Jewish settlers in the West Bank originally objected to a barrier that might be perceived as marking a future border between Israel and the West Bank,[7] the escalating public pressure led Ariel Sharon's government to change its position. In 2003, Israel began to build the security barrier, thereby limiting passage to official crossing points and to those with official permits. In spite of Palestinian protests, internal political opposition, legal suits, and international pressures, the construction of a security barrier from the Jordan Valley in the north to the Dead Sea area proceeded.

The security barrier varies from a high concrete wall monitored by watchtowers to barbed fences supported by sophisticated surveillance devices. Its route deviates in various places from the 1967 border with the West

FIGURE 30. Graffiti on the road to Bethlehem in the West Bank. Photo by Marc Venezia (CC BY-SA 3.0).

Bank territory, at times separating the Palestinians from their own fields, a situation that Israel claimed was made necessary by its security needs. The security barrier has helped reduce illegal entry into Israel by Palestinians, but has not entirely prevented them from finding ways to get into the country.[8] The security wall, which Palestinians renamed the "Apartheid Wall" and compared to the Berlin Wall,[9] emerged as an icon of Israeli occupation and a site of protest and resistance (see figure 30). Palestinian, Jewish, and international activists participated in the Anti-Wall Movement, spearheading public protests that condemned its construction and its impact on the Palestinians. The most famous of the popular resistance artworks on the wall are by the guerrilla graffiti artist Banksy, whose paintings of imagined windows and scenery defy and subvert the enclosure imposed by the wall (see figure 31).[10]

While Israel sees the measures as critical for protecting itself from illegal entry and potential terrorist attacks by Palestinians, the wall, along with roadblocks and locked gates, elevated highways and underground tunnels, represents an "architecture of occupation" that dissects and transforms the already divided Palestinian territories, establishing a "geography of immobility and trespass."[11]

FIGURE 31. Banksy graffiti at the Israeli West Bank Barrier in Bethlehem. Photo by Markus Ortner (CC BY-SA 2.5).

At the same time, Israelis continue to see the country as a besieged island surrounded by Arabs, and the current government applies the same imagery to the situation of new Jewish outposts in the West Bank.[12] Thus, both Israelis and Palestinians continue to experience themselves as living in besieged islands, and their competing narratives of insularity and victimhood feed into the ongoing conflict and the current state of impasse.

In recent decades, Israel has gradually introduced barriers along its borders, surrounding itself with fences and walls and turning the metaphorical island into reality. This is a change from its earlier preference for fuzzy borders or the maintenance of a "good fence" with Lebanon from 1976 to 2000.[13] Thus, Israel first upgraded the fence along the border with Gaza, and then began the construction of an additional barrier designed to prevent entry to its territory through underground tunnels.[14] It has constructed a 152-mile-long separation fence along the border with Egypt to prevent entry by terrorists and African refuge seekers,[15] erected a high-security fence in the north to protect itself from possible impact by the civil war in Syria,[16] and introduced a security fence on the border with Jordan, near Ramon Airport, to ensure air accessibility to Eilat.[17] An Israeli newspaper headline described the country as "Surrounded by Walls," and another article noted that the addition of a wall along the border with Jordan would leave "Israel surrounded by a ring of steel and concrete."[18]

Thus, eight decades after Jabotinsky's metaphorical allusion to the "iron wall" as a deterrent to the Arabs, barriers and walls have become part of the physical landscape and political reality in Israel. Israeli Hebrew has enriched its vocabulary for separation and security structures,[19] yet the choice of a term also implies a strategic decision. In the late 1930s, Jews referred to wire fences and wooden barriers as a "wall" (*homa*), a term that evokes the image of a solid, thick defense wall.[20] Going in the opposite direction, the Israeli government refers to the barrier it has built to its east as a "separation fence" (*gader hafrada*), even though some of its sections are made up of high concrete walls. The government's choice of words, suggesting that it has constructed a less durable structure, is designed to minimize the intrusive presence of the wall and its political implications. Israel may be a more radical case of a country surrounding itself with protective fences and walls, but recently some European countries have chosen a similar strategy to prevent illegal immigrant flow, and U.S. President Donald Trump, citing Israel as a model, has championed the construction of a high wall along the border with Mexico to prevent illegal crossing into the United States, although the launching of the project has faced budgetary and other constraints.[21]

The walled island evokes the image of the Jewish ghetto, which represents regressive periods of exclusion and persecution in Jewish exilic history. Jewish emancipation implied Jews breaking out of the walls of the ghetto, and the Jewish Enlightenment (*Haskalah*) and the Zionist movement strongly rejected the "ghetto mentality."[22] From this perspective, Israel's embrace of the oasis/island/ghetto template signals a turning away from the earlier Zionist vision that sought to liberate Jews from the constraints of exile and its culture. Instead, Israeli critics argue, Israel has returned to the discredited exilic mentality and recreated itself as a "fortified ghetto."[23]

The barriers that separate Israel from its neighbors have become such a common view that their absence merits a special note. Driving on Highway 40, which ends in the Arava desert near the border with Jordan, the journalist Gideon Levy describes the unfolding view:

> On the other side of the road, beyond [kibbutz] Ketura's date groves, a yellow sign stuck haphazardly into the ground enjoins people to stop: Border Ahead. There's no fence here, and the dwellings of the Jordanian-Bedouin village of Rahma are within a walking distance—stretch out an arm and touch them. There was a time when good-neighborly relations existed between Ketura and Rahma, including medical assistance. No longer.

Noting that an old barbed-wire fence had been covered by wandering dunes, and the seeming continuity between the adjacent fields of Ketura and Rahma, Levy imagines the unrealized possibilities of that open desert space:

> If Highway 40 were extended by another kilometer or two to the East, it would intersect with the Jordan Valley Highway in Jordan, which runs south to Saudi Arabia and up toward Iraq [as if in a wild, remote Mediterranean fantasy].[24]

This short reverie is cut off, and faced with the current reality, he concludes his essay with the parting words: "Journey's end."

Multiple layers of insularity have been introduced into contemporary Israeli life, in both the public and the private space. These insulated spaces vary in size and scale, yet their pervasive presence normalizes the sense of besiegement and reinforces Israelis' existential anxiety. These spaces range from communal shelters to the "sealed rooms" that exist within individual residential units as protection from possible chemical or biological attacks. Similarly commonplace are guarded entrances to public institutions, malls, and restaurants in the urban space and high fences with electrical gates that surround rural and residential communities. In the United States, such security measures are more typically associated with "gated communities," and have recently been introduced in select public and governmental institutions. Yet in Israel, having to pass through fences, guarded entrances, and security checks upon entering a supermarket, a university, or a shopping mall has become a way of life and is accepted as routine.

A recent cartoon by Eran Wolkowski (figure 32) illuminates the distinct features of the island as a cultural trope. The cartoon refers to Tel Aviv, depicting its highly congested space as surrounded by a high wall and embedded within the open vistas of sand. In this case, the cartoon draws on the popular perception of Tel Aviv's residents as living in a "bubble" of their own, sitting happily in a vast, overcrowded café and oblivious to the wall and desert around them. The contrast between the walled-in space and the sand around it may well provide a visual template for contemporary Israel, surrounded by a desert. While the wall surrounding it protects and insulates those within, it also prevents them from seeing the outside world. Along similar lines, the security barrier not only protects Israelis from

FIGURE 32. Cartoon by Eran Wolkowski published in *Ha'aretz*, March 22, 2015. Copyright © "HA'ARETZ" daily newspaper LTD.

illegal "penetration" into their national space, it also distances and conceals the Palestinians who live on the other side of the wall and their reality, and encourages an isolationist approach.

The walled "island" thus reinforces a popular Israeli view emphasizing Israel's distinctness from other Middle Eastern countries and perpetuating early-twentieth-century views of the Jewish "settlement" as the cultivated, technologically advanced place that stands in contrast to the wild, chaotic, and dangerous symbolic desert surrounding it. Ehud Barak, the former Israel Defense Forces chief of staff and Labor prime minister, reiterated this view when alluding to Israel in the Middle East as "a villa in the jungle."[25] This expression not only articulates old-school European colonialist ideas, it also distances Israel by using geographical metaphors that are foreign to the region. In a later interview, Barak acknowledged the incongruity of his geographical metaphors and offered an alternative analogy: "Twenty years ago, when I was in [military] uniform, I said that Israel is a villa in the jungle. So perhaps it is not a villa in a jungle, but *an oasis in the desert*."[26]

Following the "Arab Spring" of 2011 and the growing instability in the Middle East that came in its wake, Israeli political leaders underscored Israel's distinction as a Middle Eastern democracy (ignoring the Palestinians of the occupied territories) and repeated the reference to it as a "villa in the jungle" or an "island of stability."[27] Some Israeli critics strongly objected to these statements, noting their Orientalist perspective, their dismissiveness, and their selective representation of both Israel and the region.[28] A *Ha'aretz* editorial entitled "Unwarranted Arrogance" criticized the view, promoted by Israeli leaders, that Israel is "an island of progress within a sea of cultural and technological backwardness":

> Many Israelis regard New York, Paris, and London as their cultural reference point, and show no interest in the peoples and countries around them. Arabic studies are marginal in the curriculum for Jewish students in Israel and are often used in preparation for service in the intelligence or security forces rather than as a bridge to gaining greater familiarity with Arabs and their culture in Israel and beyond.[29]

The oasis/island template is the articulation of Israel's embrace of an isolationist, security-based approach, and the use of these metaphors has in turn furthered the country's growing sense of insularity and the view of the world beyond its walls as a symbolic desert. The move away from a more hopeful, linear Zionist narrative and the return to the cyclical view of a history of persecution and death suggests another facet of insularity and contributes to the dominance of the besieged-island metaphor.[30] Israel appears to have lost the ability to envision itself as a part of the Middle East and has replaced peace negotiations with unilateral moves that a collaborative process could have turned into steps toward peace. Yet as this metaphorical journey into the desert reveals, Israeli culture has also continued to cultivate alternative visions of the desert-settlement relation that may present other options. Israel has made peace with two of its Arab neighbors, Egypt and Jordan, a peace that has been held up as preventing further wars with two of the country's fiercest former enemies. Similarly, a move toward the resolution of the conflict with the Palestinians is likely to open up a more hopeful view of the future for Israel and Palestine and the possibility of coexistence between them.

Glossary

Note: All glossary terms are in Hebrew unless otherwise indicated. When possible, the transliteration follows the standard forms included in Merriam-Webster's dictionary.

abbaya (Arabic)—cloak

Aliyah (pl. Aliyot)—literally, ascent; Jewish immigration to Palestine (prior to 1948) and later to Israel; reference to waves of Jewish immigration prior to 1948: *First Aliyah* (1882–1903), *Second Aliyah* (1904–14); *Third Aliyah* (1919–23); *Fourth Aliyah* (1924–28); *Fifth Aliyah* (1929–39)

Ashkenazi (pl. Ashkenazim)—Jews of European origin or ancestry, whose tradition of religious practice differs from that of Sephardi Jews (Sephardim)

boker—shepherd, cowboy

dunam—a unit of land area from the Ottoman period, still used in Israel. One dunam equals a thousand square meters, or about a quarter of an acre.

fallâh (pl. *fellahin*)(Arabic)—peasants or farmers (in Hebrew *fallah*, pl. *fallahim*)

fedayeen (Arabic)—literally, those ready to sacrifice themselves; used to refer to Arab guerrillas operating against Israel in the 1950s, referred to in Hebrew as "infiltrators," *mistanenim*

galabiya (Arabic)—a long gown

ge'ula—redemption

Green Line—the armistice borders of the state of Israel from 1949 to the 1967 war

Hagana—Defense, a civilian Jewish defense organization established in 1920 and operating until May 1948, when the Israel Defense Forces was formed

halutz (f. *halutzah*, pl. *halutzim*)—pioneer; a member of the Second or Third Aliyah who engaged in agricultural and construction work

Ha-Shomer—The Guard, a small Jewish defense organization established in 1909, predecessor of the *Hagana* organization

Haskalah—Jewish enlightenment

havot bodedim—individual farmsteads

hillulah (pl. *hillulot*)—-celebration, often refers to a celebration honoring a late *tsaddik*

homa u-migdal—Tower and Stockade, a reference to the distinctive structures of Jewish settlements established from 1936 to 1939

IDF—Israel Defense Forces

igal (Arabic)—a black cord used to hold the *kaffiyeh* in place on the head

ikar (pl. *ikarim*)—peasant or farmer

JNF—The Jewish National Fund

kaffiyeh (also *kûfîya*)(Arabic)—traditional Middle Eastern headdress (in Hebrew *kafîya*)

kibbush—conquest, control, mastery

Knesset—The Israeli parliament

kibbutz (pl. kibbutzim)—an egalitarian farming community established by socialist Zionist pioneers

ma'abara (pl. *ma'abrot*)—transit camp for new immigrants in the 1950s and early 1960s

midbar—desert

midbar-shemama—a desolate desert

mistanenim—infiltrators; the term was applied to the *fedayeen* in the 1950s and then extended to others who enter Israel illegally

mitzpe (pl. *mitzpim*)—an observation outpost, or outpost built as the basis for a future settlement

mizrah—east; also the sign put on an eastern wall (in the West) to designate the direction of Jerusalem

Mizrahi (pl. Mizrahim)—literally, "Easterner"; collective reference to Israeli Jews from Middle Eastern and North African countries

moledet—homeland

moshav (pl. *moshavim*)—cooperative agricultural settlement *moshava* (pl. *moshavot*)—Jewish agricultural colony based on individual ownership

mukhtar (Arabic)—the head of a village

NAHAL—acronym for "Pioneering Combat Youth" in the IDF who combine combat training with settlement work

nekudot kibbush—literally, conquest points; reference to new core Jewish settlements

pezura—literally, dispersion; also diaspora; "Bedouin *pezura*" refers to residents of the unrecognized Bedouin villages in the Negev

Palmach—acronym for "Strike Forces," a *Hagana*-affiliated unit for young members, established in 1941 and disbanded in 1948; its members fought in the IDF in the 1948 war

pe'ulot tagmul—reprisal operations by the IDF during the 1950s

RCUV—The Regional Council for Unrecognized Negev Arab Villages

Sephardi (pl. Sephardim)—Jews whose ancestry goes back to Spain in the Middle Ages; extended to refer collectively to Jews whose religious practice differs from that of *Ashkenazi* Jews

shemama—a desolate land, a wasteland

SPNI—The Society for the Protection of Nature in Israel

tallit—Jewish prayer shawl

tsaddik (pl. *tsaddikim*)—a rabbi or a righteous person known for piety, learning, and spiritual power

WZO—World Zionist Organization

yediat ha-aretz—literally, knowledge of the land; reference to the knowledge of the geography and history of the Land of Israel

yishuv—settlement

Yishuv—the Jewish society of Palestine; mostly referencing the late Ottoman and mandatory periods (1880s–1948)

Notes

Note: References to Hebrew sources appear in English translation, using the publisher's English titles when provided. When further clarification is needed, the Hebrew title, in transliteration, is added in brackets. Each chapter provides the full reference of a source the first time it is mentioned.

Introduction

1. Amos Oz in *Ma'ariv*, December 2, 1994, reprinted in Amos Oz, *All Our Hopes: Essays on the Israeli Condition* (Jerusalem: Keter, 1998), 251 [Hebrew].

2. Henri Lefebvre, *The Production of Space* [1974] (Oxford: Blackwell, 1991).

3. On the cultural construction of landscapes, see Donald W. Meinig, *The Interpretation of Ordinary Landscapes* (New York: Oxford University Press, 1979), 2–3; Denise Cosgrove, *Social Formation and Symbolic Landscape* (Totowa, NJ: Barnes & Noble, 1985), 13, 17–18; for the concept of "expressive space," see E. V. Waters, *Placeways: A Theory of the Human Environment* (Chapel Hill: University of North Carolina Press, 1988), 215. See also Neil Evernden, *The Social Construction of Nature* (Baltimore: Johns Hopkins University Press, 1992).

4. Lefebvre, *The Production of Space*, 11–27.

5. Beginning in the nineteenth century, several projects focusing on alternative, if limited, territories for Jewish settlement were pursued, in locations including Grand Island in New York, Angola in eastern Africa, Kenya and Madagascar in western Africa, Tasmania in Australia, and Surinam in South America. In 1903, in response to the so-called Uganda crisis, the Sixth Zionist Congress rejected the idea of alternative territories and affirmed its commitment to the Land of Israel. In 1905, those who did not accept this approach split from the Zionist Congress and established the Jewish Territorialist Organization. See Shmuel Almog, "People and Land in Modern Jewish Nationalism," in Jehuda Reinharz and Anita Shapira, eds., *Essential Papers on Zionism* (New York: New York University Press, 1996), 50–54; Adam Rovner, *In the Shadow of Zion: Promised Lands before Israel* (New York: NYU Press, 2014); Gur Alroey, *Zionism without Zion: The Jewish Territorial Organization and Its Conflict with the Zionist Organization* (Detroit: Wayne State University Press, 2016).

6. For the evolution of the term *midbar*, see Yehuda Gur (Grasovsky), *The Hebrew Dictionary* (Tel Aviv: Dvir, 1955), 478 [Hebrew]; Avraham Even-Shoshan, *The New Dictionary* [*Ha-milon he-hadash*] (Jerusalem: Kiryat Sefer, 1988), II, 630 [Hebrew]; and Nogah Hareuveni's extensive discussion in *Desert and Shepherd in Our Biblical Heritage* (Lod: Neot

Kedumim Press, 1991), 26–36 (English edition). See also the extensive discussion of *midbar* in Shemaryahu Talmon, "The 'Desert Motif' in the Bible and Qumran Literature," in Alexander Altman, ed., *Biblical Motifs: Origins and Transformations* (Cambridge, MA: Harvard University Press, 1966), 39–44.

7.   Other biblical terms for "desert," such as *tsiya* and *yeshimon*, represent a higher literary register in modern Hebrew. The biblical scholar Shemaryahu Talmon similarly argues for the translation of the biblical *midbar* as "desert," as being more accurate than "wilderness." See Talmon, "The 'Desert Motif,'" 39.

8.   For the evolution of the term *yishuv* and related terms, see also Ron Kuzar, "The Innovations of *yishev, yishuv*, and *moshava* in early modern Hebrew," in Yehouda Shenhav, ed., *Zionism and the Empires* (Jerusalem: Van Leer & Hakibbutz Hameuchad, 2015), 37, 45–46 [Hebrew]. See also Even-Shoshan, *The New Dictionary*, II, 512; Gur, *The Hebrew Dictionary*, 379. The medieval concept of a "communal ban" similarly draws on *yishuv* (*herem ha-yishuv*). The phrase "member of the *yishuv*" (*adam min ha-yishuv*) refers to a Jew and, by extension, to a cultured person. See Gur, *The Hebrew Dictionary*, 379; Even-Shoshan, *The New Dictionary*, II, 512. For the Zionist settlers' distinction of their society as the "new Yishuv" as compared to the older community of Palestinian Jews, see also note 11.

9.   Various other terms related to the settlement process and the particular forms of settlement developed from the same linguistic root. See Kuzar, "The Innovations of *yishev, yishuv*, and *moshava*."

10.   On the significance of the unmarked as privileged, see Eviatar Zerubavel, *Taken for Granted: The Remarkable Power of the Unremarkable* (Princeton: Princeton University Press, 2018).

11.   This historiographic concept is further underscored by the reference to pre-Zionist Jewish society in Palestine as the "old Yishuv." For a historical reevaluation of the contrast between the "new" and the "old" Yishuv, see Yehoshua Kaniel, *In Transition: The Jews of Eretz Israel in the Nineteenth Century* (Jerusalem: Yad Ben-Zvi Press, 2000), 21–34 [Hebrew]; Israel Bartal, "Old Yishuv and New Yishuv—Image and Reality," *Exile in the Homeland: Essays* (Jerusalem: Mossad Bialik, 1994), 74–89 [Hebrew].

12.   Mikhail Bakhtin, *The Dialogic Imagination* (Austin: University of Texas Press, 1981), 84. Bakhtin refers to the chronotope in literary texts, but the concept may apply more broadly to cultural memory.

13.   See also Zali Gurevitch and Gideon Aran, "On *Makom* [*Al ha-makom*]: Israeli Anthropology," *Alpayim* 4 (1991): 9–44 [Hebrew]; for a shorter English version, see Gurevitch and Aran, "The Land of Israel: Myth and Phenomenon," in Jonathan Frankel, ed., *Reshaping the Past: Jewish History and the Historians. Studies in Contemporary Jewry* vol. 10 (New York: Oxford University Press, 1994), 195–210. See also chapter 1, note 5.

14.   Yael Zerubavel, *Recovered Roots: Collective Memory and the Making of Israeli National Tradition* (Chicago: University of Chicago Press, 1995), 13–36. On the concept of "decline narrative," see Eviatar Zerubavel, *Time Maps: Collective Memory and the Social Shape of the Past* (Chicago: University of Chicago Press, 2003), 16–18.

15. Gur indicates that one of the meanings of *midbar* is *shemama*. See *shemama* in Gur, *The Hebrew Dictionary*, 1043; Even-Shoshan, *The New Dictionary*, IV, 1386. The origin of *midbar-shemama* is biblical (Joel 2:3); it is used to highlight the desolate character of the land in contrast to the fertile image of the Garden of Eden. Gur (*The Hebrew Dictionary*, 379) gives "desolate desert" as an antonym for *yishuv*.

16. See also Yael Zerubavel, "The Desert and the Settlement as Symbolic Landscapes in Modern Israeli Culture," in Julia Brauch, Anna Lipphardt, and Alexandra Nocke, eds., *Jewish Topographies: Visions of Space, Traditions of Place* (London: Ashgate Press, 2008), 201–22. Karen Grumberg uses Foucault's term *heterotopia* to underscore the oppositional relations between the settlement and the desert: Karen Grumberg, *Place and Ideology in Contemporary Hebrew Literature* (Syracuse: University of Syracuse Press, 2011), 30–32. I prefer to use the concepts "place," "nonplace," and "counter-place" to highlight their interconnections.

17. Edward Said, *Orientalism* (New York: Vintage Books, 1979).

18. Prior to the 1940s, the geographical deserts—namely, the Judean and Negev deserts—remained largely outside the scope of the Jewish settlement agenda. On the changing status of the Negev as a Jewish frontier, see chapter 4.

19. On modern European influences on the Zionist settlement of Palestine, see Derek J. Penslar, *Zionism and Technocracy: The Engineering of Jewish Settlement in Palestine, 1870–1918* (Bloomington: Indiana University Press, 1991); Hezi Amiur, *Mixed Farm and Smallholding in Zionist Settlement Thought* (Jerusalem: Zalman Shazar Center for Jewish History, 2016) [Hebrew].

Chapter 1

1. See introduction, note 12.

2. Zali Gurevitch and Gideon Aran, "On Makom [*Al ha-makom*]: Israeli Anthropology," *Alpayim* 4 (1991): 9–44 [Hebrew]; for a shorter English version, see Gurevitch and Aran, "The Land of Israel: Myth and Phenomenon," in Jonathan Frankel, ed., *Reshaping the Past: Jewish History and the Historians. Studies in Contemporary Jewry* vol. 10 (New York: Oxford University Press, 1994), 195–210.

3. Yosef Hayim Yerushalmi, *Zakhor: Jewish History and Jewish Memory* (Seattle: University of Washington Press, 1982), 8–12.

4. Arnold van Gennep, *The Rites of Passage*, [1908] (Chicago: University of Chicago Press, 1960); see also Victor Turner, *The Ritual Process*, [1969] (New York: Penguin Books, 1974).

5. Gurevitch and Aran ("On *Makom*," 15) offer a different typology of exile as "the other place" and the desert as "the non-place."

6. For the story of the exodus as a paradigmatic text, see Michael Walzer, *Exodus and Revolution* (New York: Basic Books, 1985); David Ben-Gurion, *Biblical Studies* [*Iyunim ba-tanach*] (Tel Aviv: Am Oved, 1969), 209–14, 243–52 [Hebrew]; Sarah Yafet, "Aspects of Identity Formation in the Second Temple Period: The Exodus Tradition and the Perception of the Chosen," in Dror Kerem, ed., *Diversity of Views in Jewish Culture* [*Migvan de'ot ve-hashkafot be-tarbut yisrael*] 2 (1992): 49 [Hebrew]; Adriane Leveen, *Memory and Tradition in the Book of Numbers* (New York: Cambridge University Press, 2008). On the early understanding of

the exodus as the "first aliyah" in Zionist historiography, see Hizky Shoham, "From 'Great History' to 'Small History': The Genesis of the Zionist Periodization of the Numbered Aliyot," *Israel Studies* 18, 1 (2013): 31–55.

7. Aviva Halamish, *The Exodus Affair: Holocaust Survivors and the Struggle for Palestine* (Syracuse: Syracuse University Press, 1998).

8. Shalom Seri, *By Way of the Desert* [*Derekh ha-midbar*]: *The Wondrous Journey to the Land of Dreams* (Tel Aviv: E'ele Be-Tamar, 1991) [Hebrew].

9. See Yael Zerubavel, *Recovered Roots: Collective Memory and the Making of Israeli National Tradition* (Chicago: University of Chicago Press, 1995), 13–33. This view was largely based on Jews' history in Europe. See also Arnold M. Eisen, *Galut: Modern Jewish Reflection on Homelessness and Homecoming* (Bloomington: Indiana University Press, 1986), 91–116.

10. Likewise, the lyrics of a famous Hanukkah song written in the 1930s by Aharon Ze'ev, "We Carry Torches" [*Anu nos'im lapidim*], defy the traditional Jewish interpretation of Hanukkah: "No miracle has occurred to us / We found no flask of oil." Instead, the song highlights the self-reliance of the Hebrew youth, thus assigning greater significance to human agency than to divine intervention. See also Charles Liebman and Eliezer Don-Yehiya, *Civil Religion in Israel* (Berkeley: University of California Press, 1983), 28–55.

11. Habib explains his focus on Yemenite Jews in an interview with Nirit Aderman, "Why Was the First Entirely Israeli Film Censored?" *Ha'aretz*, March 29, 2010, http://www .mouse.co.il/CM.articles_item,1050,209,47624,.aspx, accessed May 25, 2011 [Hebrew]. Yemenite Jews used the exodus myth as a paradigm for their 1950s aliyah from Yemen to Israel in an airlift operation nicknamed "Magic Carpet," yet considered their reception in Israel as the most difficult part of their journey. Yaron Tsur, "The Fall from the Magic Carpet," in *Ha'aretz*, March 29, 2010, 7 [Hebrew]; Esther Meir-Glitzenstein, "Operation Magic Carpet: Constructing the Myth of the Magical Immigration of Yemenite Jews to Israel," *Israel Studies* 16, 3 (2011): 149–73.

12. Nathan Gross and Yaacov Gross, *The Hebrew Film: The History of the Silent Film and Cinema in Israel* (Jerusalem: self-published, 1991), 208 [Hebrew]. The film features the well-known Yemenite singer Shoshana Damari, in the starring role. Moshe Vilensky, who composed the score, adapted Middle Eastern music for mainstream Israeli and Western audiences, as was commonly done at the time. See also Moshe Zimerman, *Hole in the Camera: Gazes of Israeli Cinema* (Tel Aviv: Resling, 2003), 173–81 [Hebrew]. For the representation of Mizrahi Jews in Israeli films, see Ella Shohat, *Israeli Cinema: East/West and the Politics of Representation* (Austin: University of Texas Press, 1989), 115–78; Yaron Shemer, *Identity, Place, and Subversion in Contemporary Mizrahi Cinema in Israel* (Ann Arbor: University of Michigan Press, 2013), 18–48.

13. Rachel Weissbrod, "Exodus as a Zionist Melodrama," *Israel Studies* 4 (Spring 1999): 129–52; N. M. Silver, *Our Exodus: Leon Uris and the Americanization of Israel's Founding Story* (Detroit: Wayne State University Press, 2010). Although the Preminger film is American-made, its Zionist framework contributed to its success in Israel. By contrast, the writer Moshe Shamir criticized the film as "a cartoonish portrayal" and "a falsely sentimental-exotic view of us by diaspora Jewry": Moshe Shamir, "The Exodus from Egypt Still Continues" [1960], reprinted in *The Green Place: Without Zionism It Won't Do* (Tel Aviv: Dvir, 1991), 15 [Hebrew].

14. Ada Aharoni, *The Second Exodus: A Historical Novel* (Bryn Mawr, PA: Dorrance, 1983), ix. Shlomo Hillel, in his book on Iraqi Jews' immigration to Israel, makes a similar allusion to the exodus: Hillel, *A Path in the Desert [Derekh be-midbar]* (Jerusalem: World Zionist Congress, 1971) [Hebrew].

15. Aharoni, *The Second Exodus*, 125

16. Following a visit to Palestine in 1912, Chaim Tchernowitz ["Rav Tsair"] referred to his contemporaries as "the desert generation" when comparing them to the younger generation he had encountered there: Chaim Tchernowitz, "Impressions from the Land of Israel," *Ha-Olam* 11 (July 2, 1912): 3–5 [Hebrew]. See also Anita Shapira, "The Image of the New Jew in Yishuv Society," in Israel Gutman, ed., *Fundamental Transformations in the Jewish People Following the Holocaust* (Jerusalem: Yad Vashem, 1996), 411 [Hebrew]. In a later twist, the term was critically applied even to those raised in Palestine. See Natan Shaham, *The Desert Generation* (Tel Aviv: Sifriyat Hapoalim, 1991), 8–9 [Hebrew]; Meron Benvenisti, *Conflicts and Contradictions* (New York: Villard Books, 1986), xii.

17. Uriel Simon, "The Status of the Bible in Israeli Society," in Elchanan Reiner et al., eds., *Yeriot* (Jerusalem: Orna Hess, 1999), 20 [Hebrew]; Benvenisti, *Conflicts and Contradictions*, 60; Shlomo Y. Schwartz [Shva], *New People in the High Mountains* (Tel Aviv: Hakibbutz Hameuchad, 1953), 15, 17, 22 [Hebrew]; Eliezer Schweid, *Homeland and a Land of Promise [Moledet ve-eretz ye'uda]* (Tel Aviv: Am Oved, 1979), 220–23 [Hebrew]. An American colleague who had immigrated to Israel in the 1960s as a young man told me that his Hebrew teacher similarly referred to her adult immigrant students as a "desert generation."

18. Hayim Nahman Bialik, *Metei Midbar* [1902], reprinted in his *Poems [Shirim]* (Tel Aviv: Dvir, 1966), 340–49 [Hebrew]. Bialik was inspired by the talmudic legend of Rabbah b. Bar Hana (Babylonian Talmud, Bava Batra, 73).

19. Esther Nathan, *The Road to the Dead of the Desert* (Tel Aviv: Hakibbutz Hameuchad, 1993) [Hebrew]. Nathan studies the various interpretations of Bialik's poem and the Jewish, Russian, and European sources that may have inspired it. See also Leveen, *Memory and Tradition in the Book of Numbers*, 4–5, 140–41.

20. Mircea Eliade, *The Sacred and the Profane: The Nature of Religion* (New York: Harcourt, Brace & World, 1959).

21. Edmond Jabès, *The Book of Questions* [1963], translated from French by Rosmarie Waldrop (Middletown, CT: Wesleyan University Press, 1976). See also the interview with Edmond Jabès in Sarit Shapira, *Routes of Wandering: Nomadism, Journeys and Transitions in Contemporary Israeli Art* (Jerusalem: The Israel Museum, 1991) [bilingual English/Hebrew edition].

22. Gurevitch and Aran, "The Land of Israel," 196.

23. Yoram Kaniuk, *The Last Jew* (Tel Aviv: Hakibbutz Hameuchad and Sifriyat Hapoalim, 1981), 109–10 [Hebrew].

24. Walzer, *Exodus and Revolution*; Edward Said's critical discussion of the link between the exodus myth and Zionism as a rebuttal of Walzer's thesis can be found in "Michael Walzer's Exodus and Revolution: A Canaanite Reading," in Edward W. Said and Christopher Hitchens, eds., *Blaming the Victims: Spurious Scholarship and the Palestinian Question*

(New York: Verso, 1988), 161–78; see also the analysis of this dialogue in Jonathan Boyarin, "Reading Exodus into History," *New Literary History* 23 (1992): 523–54 (esp. 528–33).

25.　Yaacov Shavit, "The Physical Characteristics of the Land of Israel in Jewish Literature of the Nineteenth and Twentieth Centuries: A Modern Version of the 'Theory of Climatology,'" in Aviezer Ravitsky, ed., *The Land of Israel in Modern Jewish Thought* (Jerusalem: Yad Ben-Zvi, 1998), 391–412 [Hebrew].

26.　See Amnon Raz-Krakotzkin, "*Galut* within Sovereignty: A Critique of 'the Negation of Exile' in Israeli Culture," *Teoria Uvikoret* 4 (Fall 1993): 23–55 [Hebrew]; David Biale, *Power and Powerlessness in Jewish History* (New York: Schocken Books, 1986), 3–144.

27.　For the analogy of the desert with destruction, see Isaiah 64:9–10; Isaiah 34:10–14 presents a more elaborate description of the desolated land, plagued by desert animals and demonic representations; by contrast, his redemption prophecy (Isaiah 35) addresses the abundance of water that transforms the desert. Shemaryahu Talmon argues against what he sees as the exaggerated focus on the desert theme in biblical scholarship, which he links to the discovery of the Dead Sea Scrolls. Although he discusses the "temporal connotation" of the desert in relation to the exodus, Talmon stresses the Bible's negative perception of the desert, which is associated with punishment and transition: Shemaryahu Talmon, "The 'Desert Motif' in the Bible and Qumran Literature," in Alexander Altman, ed., *Biblical Motifs: Origins and Transformations* (Cambridge, MA: Harvard University Press, 1966), 31–37, 48.

28.　Yehoshua Amir, "The Desert in the Bible," *Mahanaim* 118 (1968): 64–71 [Hebrew].

29.　Leviticus 16:21–22; Talmon, "The 'Desert Motif' in the Bible," 43–44. Some rabbinical tales (such as those by Rabbah b. Bar Hana, see note 18) similarly describe the desert as a large and dangerous territory with gigantic animals and supernatural occurrences: Menachem Hacohen, "The Desert in Rabbinical Literature," *Mahanaim* 118 (1968): 72–76 [Hebrew].

30.　See the discussion of these terms in the introduction. See also Yoram Bar-Gal, *An Agent of Zionist Propaganda: The Jewish National Fund 1924–19* (Haifa: Haifa University Press & Zmora Bitan, 1999), 161–62 [Hebrew]. Note the observation that the poet Avraham Shlonsky, in his poem "Facing the Desert" [*Mul ha-yeshimon*], projected history onto nature: Yochai Oppenheimer, *The Right to Say No: Political Poetry in Israel* (Jerusalem: Magnes Press, 2003), 50–53 [Hebrew].

31.　Ze'ev Yavetz, "Travel in the Land" [*Shut ba-aretz*], [1891], reprinted in Yaffa Berlovitz, ed., *Wandering in the Land: Travels by Members of the First Aliyah* [*E'ebra na ba-aretz: Mas'ot anshei ha-aliya ha-rishona*] (Tel Aviv: Defense Ministry Press, 1992), 115 [Hebrew].

32.　Yehudit Harari, "Among the Vineyards" [1947], in Berlovitz, *Wandering in the Land*, 288 (emphasis added).

33.　Nechama Pohachevsky, "From Rishon Le-Zion to Marge Ayun," [1908], in Berlovitz, *Wandering in the Land*, 314–15.

34.　Gordon in fact criticizes the settlers' unappreciative attitude toward nature. See Aaron David Gordon, "Man and Nature," in Samuel Hugo Bergman and Eliezer Shocha, eds., *Gordon's Writings*, (Tel-Aviv: Zionist Library, 1957), II: 158 [Hebrew]. I would like to thank Yuval Jobani for bringing this text to my attention.

35.   Yehoshua Barzilai, "In the Gates of Jerusalem" [1890], in Berlovitz, *Wandering in the Land*, 82. See also the description of Jewish travelers' sadness at witnessing the "desolated land" in Moshe Smilansky, "In the Footsteps of the Daughters of Ruhaniya" [1894], in Berlovitz, *Wandering in the Land*, 187. The encounter with the present conditions was particularly painful around sites of major historical significance in the ancient past. See, for example, the reaction of Ze'ev Yavetz and his company when they observed the desolation around Bnei Brak and the Maccabees' tombs in Modiin. Yavetz, "Travel in the Land," 113.

36.   *The Conquest of the Mountain* (Jerusalem: Jewish National Fund, 1955/6), 41 [Hebrew].

37.   Shlomo Kodesh, *The Founders' Legend [Agadat ha-rishonim]: The War against the Desolation* (Jerusalem: The Jewish National Fund, 1971/2), 2 [Hebrew, (emphasis added)].

38.   See also Shavit, "Physical Characteristics," 404–5.

39.   The diary of Hayim Hissin, entry of March 14, 1882, quoted in Shulamit Laskov, *History of Hibbat Zion and the Settlement of the Land of Israel* (Tel Aviv: Hakkibutz Hameuchad, 1982), I: 426. I would like to thank Alan Dowty for referring me to this quote.

40.   David Ben-Gurion and Yitzhak Ben-Zvi, *The Land of Israel in the Past and at Present* [Yiddish, 1918]; an abridged Hebrew translation (Jerusalem: Yad Ben-Zvi, 1979), 162 and 208–10 [Hebrew].

41.   Ben-Gurion and Ben-Zvi, *The Land of Israel*, 155.

42.   Diana K. Davis, "Imperialism, Orientalism, and the Environment in the Middle East," in Diana K. Davis and Edmund Burke III, eds., *Environmental Imaginaries of the Middle East and North Africa* (Athens: Ohio University Press, 2011), 1; for a definition of the "environmental imaginary," see p. 3.

43.   Yoram Bar-Gal, *Modelet and Geography in Hundred Years of Zionist Education* (Tel Aviv: Am Oved, 1993), 139 [Hebrew].

44.   Nahum Gavrieli, ed., *Knowledge of the Homeland: A Textbook* (Tel Aviv: Omanut, 1934), I: 138, 150 [Hebrew].

45.   Yitzhak Ben-Zvi, in *The Conquest of the Desert: Catalog for an International Exhibition and Fair [Kibbush ha-shemama]* (Jerusalem, [no press], 1953), English-language section, 7.

46.   David Ben-Gurion, "The Conquest of the Land," in *The Conquest of the Mountain*, 6–7.

47.   A. D. Gordon, *The Nation and Our Labor* (Jerusalem: Jewish Agency, 1952), 244 [Hebrew].

48.   Harari, "Among the Vineyards," 291.

49.   Yitzhak Ben-Zvi, "With *Ha-Shomer*," *Ha-Shomer Anthology [Kovetz Ha-Shomer]* [1937] (Tel Aviv: Labor Archive, 1947), 74 [Hebrew].

50.   Ben-Gurion and Ben-Zvi, *The Land of Israel*, 228.

51.   Efraim Talmi, "A Town Is Built in Arad," in Natan Persky, ed., *New Reader for the Sixth Grade [Mikra'ot yisrael hadashot]* (Ramat Gan: Masada, 1977), 70 [Hebrew].

52.   Yehudit E-N [Endelman] in 1930, quoted in Boaz Neumann, *Land and Desire in Early Zionism* (Waltham, MA: Brandeis University Press, 2011), 89–90. Note that nakedness is also associated with the sense of shame.

53. The metaphor of slumber is implied in the title of Yaacov Ben-Dov's film, commissioned by the Jewish National Fund: "The Land of Israel Awakening" (1923). David Meletz describes the mountains deep in slumber in 1925, quoted in Moti Zeira, *We Are Torn* [*Keru'im anu*]: *Rural Collective Settlement and Jewish Culture in Eretz Israel during the 1920s* (Jerusalem: Yad Ben-Zvi, 2002), 52–53 [Hebrew]; see also *The Conquest of the Mountain*, 37; Moshe Unger, "The Water Festival," in *Holidays* [*Mo'adim le-simha*]: *Tales and Plays for the Annual Cycle of Holidays* (Tel Aviv: Shlomo, no year), 63 [Hebrew].

54. The metaphor of death appears in M. Meirovitch, "The First Handful of Seeds," in Nahum Gavrieli and Baruch Avivi, eds., *The Child's Reader* [*Mikra la-yeled*] *for the Fourth Grade* (Tel Aviv: Yavneh, 1955), 117 [Hebrew]; Avraham Shlonsky refers to the land as a "wild corpse" in his poem "Here" [*heneh*], in Avraham Shlonsky, *Ba-Galgal* (Tel Aviv: Davar, 1926/7), 35 [Hebrew].

55. Eliyahu Guttmacher, an early advocate of 19th-century Jewish settlement in Palestine preceding the Hibbat Zion movement, quoted in Yom-Tov Levinsky, ed., *The Book of Holidays* [*Sefer ha-mo'adim*] (Tel Aviv: Dvir, 1956), VIII: 330 [Hebrew]; Kodesh, *The Founders' Legend*, 2. Although this rhetoric was largely in decline in Israeli culture by the late 1960s, the building of a new town, Arad, in 1962 is described in an educational textbook of the mid-1970s as "awakening the desert from its sleep." See Talmi, "A Town Is Built."

56. *The Conquest of the Desert*, 3 (emphasis added); the translation of the Hebrew text is mine since the official English translation provides a softer version, replacing "malignancy" with "curse" and eliminating the reference to the highly negative term "abomination" (*shikutz*).

57. Diana Muir, "A Land without a People for a People without a Land," *Middle Eastern Quarterly* (Spring 2008): 55–62; http://www.meforum.org/1877/a-land-without-a-people-for-a-people-without, accessed April 20, 2015. Muir quotes earlier uses of this phrase by the influential clergyman Alexander Keith in 1844 and by Lord Shaftesbury in 1853. See also David Engel, *Zionism* (Harlow: Pearson Longman, 2009), 68–69.

58. Muir, "A Land without a People." The Swiss traveler Félix Bovet also expressed the view that the Land of Israel was destined for the Jews because the Arabs living in it were transients, and the desert wind that had brought them there would carry them elsewhere without leaving a trace: Félix Bovet, *Egypt, Palestine, and Phoenicia: A Visit to Sacred Lands* (New York: Dutton, 1883), quoted in Michael Ish-Shalom, *Christian Travels in the Holy Land* (Tel Aviv: Am Oved and Dvir, 1965), 714–15 [Hebrew].

59. Rashid Khalidi, *Palestinian Identity: The Construction of Modern National Conciousness* (New York: Columbia University Press, 1997). Khalidi argues against the Jewish claim that Palestinian identity only developed in response to Jewish nationalism.

60. Yehoshua Ben-Aryeh quotes the figure of around two thousand Christian pilgrims during the nineteenth century: Ben-Aryeh, *The Rediscovery of the Holy Land in the Nineteenth Century* (Jerusalem: Carta & The Israel Exploration Society, 1970), 15–16 [Hebrew]; see also Ish-Shalom, *Christian Travels in the Holy Land*. For the discussion of various representations of the Holy Land produced for those unable to travel, see Burke O. Long, *Imagining the Holy Land: Maps, Models, and Fantasy Travels* (Bloomington: Indiana University Press, 2003).

61. Mark Twain's satirical accounts of this journey, first published in newspapers in the USA, were reprinted in Mark Twain, *The Innocents Abroad, or the New Pilgrims' Progress* [1869] (reprinted New York: Harper & Brothers, 1903).

62. Twain, *Innocents Abroad*, II: 233–40.

63. Twain, *Innocents Abroad*, II: 391.

64. Cited in Neil Asher Silberman, *Digging for God and Country: Exploration, Archeology, and the Secret Struggle for the Holy Land, 1799–1917* [1982] (New York: Doubleday, 1990), 41–42 (see also 46–47, 61–62).

65. John Cunningham Geikie, *The Holy Land and the Bible* (London: Cassell and Co., 1887); quoted in Ish-Shalom, *Christian Travels in the Holy Land*, 795–96.

66. For an extensive discussion of the mutual perceptions of and contacts between Arabs and Jews prior to World War I, see Michelle U. Campos, *Ottoman Brothers: Muslims, Christians, and Jews in Early Twentieth-Century Palestine* (Stanford: Stanford University Press, 2011); see also Jonathan Gribetz, *Defining Neighbors: Religion, Race, and the Early Zionist-Arab Encounter* (Princeton: Princeton University Press, 2014); Mohamed Yosef Su'aed, "The Relationship between the Bedouins and the Jewish Yishuv in the Late Ottoman Period," *Notes on the Topic of the Bedouins: A Series in Memory of Itzhaki Netzer* 25 (Feb. 1994), reprinted in http://www .snunit.k12.il/beduin/arti/2554.html , accessed December 30, 2017 [Hebrew]. For the mandatory period, see Abigail Jacobson and Moshe Naor, *Oriental Neighbors: Middle Eastern Jews and Arabs in Mandatory Palestine* (Waltham, MA: Brandeis University Press, 2016).

67. See "Rabbi Rahamim Oplatka's Journey from Jerusalem to Miron," in Avraham Ya'ari, ed., *Tours of the Land of Israel: From the Middle Ages to the Zionist Return to the Land* (Tel Aviv: Modan, 1996), 623–40 [Hebrew].

68. See, for example, Suleiman Mani, "Travel to Gaza" [1885], Berlovitz, *Wandering in the Land*, 50–53; Yavetz, "Travel in the Land," 108; and Ahad Ha'am, "Truth from the Land of Israel (First Essay)" [1891], reprinted in *Ahad Ha'am: Collected Works* (Tel Aviv: Dvir, 1947), 23 [Hebrew].

69. Zalman David Levontin, "To Our Ancestral Land" [*Le-eretz avoteinu*] [1885], in Berlovitz, *Wandering in the Land*, 27–47.

70. Ben-Gurion and Ben-Zvi, *The Land of Israel*, 151–60, 210–11.

71. Ahad Ha'am, "Truth from the Land of Israel," 23.

72. Yitzhak Epstein, "A Hidden Question" [*She'ela ne'elama*], *Ha-Shiloah* 17 (July–Dec. 1907): 193–206 [Hebrew]. For an extensive study of Zionist Jewish attitudes towards the Arabs up to 1948, see Yosef Gorny, *Zionism and the Arabs, 1882–1948: A Study of Ideology* (Oxford: Oxford University Press, 1987).

73. Moshe Smilansky, "In the Homeland. Our Deeds Advance Us, Our Deeds Distance Us," *Ha-Olam*, January 29, 1914, quoted in Yaacov Haroi, "Jewish Arab Relations in the First Aliyah's Colonies," in Mordechai Eliav, ed., *The First Aliyah Book* (Jerusalem: Yad Ben-Zvi, 1981), I: 266 [Hebrew].

74. Bar-Gal, *Moledet and Geography*, 176–81.

75. The Hebrew concept of *aliyah la-regel* denotes pilgrimage. The Jewish immigrants who performed *aliyah* to the Land of Israel were distinguished as *olim*, in contrast to all others who are referred to as "immigrants."

76. Akiba Etinger, *Jewish Farmers in the Diaspora* (Merchavia: Hakibbutz Ha'artzi, 1942) [Hebrew]; Derek J. Penslar, *Zionism and Technocracy: The Engineering of Jewish Settlement in Palestine, 1870–1918* (Bloomington: Indiana University Press, 1991); Jonathan L. Dekel-Chen, *Farming the Red Land: Jewish Agricultural Colonization and Local Soviet Power, 1924–1941* (New Haven, CT: Yale University Press, 2005); Hezi Amiur, *Mixed Farm and Smallholding in Zionist Settlement Thought* (Jerusalem: Zalman Shazar Center for Jewish History, 2016), 19–29 [Hebrew].

77. Shmuel Almog, "Redemption in Zionist Rhetoric," in Ruth Kark, ed., *The Redemption of the Land of Israel: Ideology and Practice* (Jerusalem: Yad Ben-Zvi, 1990), 13–32 [Hebrew]; Aviezer Ravitzky, ed., *The Land of Israel in Modern Jewish Thought* (Jerusalem: Yad Ben-Zvi, 1998) [Hebrew]; Yehoshua Ben-Arieh, "The Debate on the Proposal to Purchase Land in Palestine in the 1870s: An Episode or Prophecy?" in Kark, *The Redemption of the Land of Israel,* 64–79.

78. Ron Kuzar notes that *moshavot* is an older term in Hebrew and that the singular *moshava* was created from it in the modern period, becoming the preferred term to replace the Hebraized foreign term *kolonia.* The new Hebrew term also helped dissociate these new Jewish settlements from the mark of colonialism: Ron Kuzar, "The Innovations of '*Yishev,*' '*Yishuv,*' and '*Moshava*' in Early Modern Hebrew," in Yehouda Shenhav, ed., *Zionism and the Empires* (Jerusalem: Van Leer & Hakibbutz Hameuchad, 2015), 27–58 [Hebrew].

79. Yehoshua Kaniel, *In Transition: The Jews of Eretz Israel in the Nineteenth Century* (Jerusalem: Yad Ben-Zvi, 2000), 199, 204–19 [Hebrew]; Israel Bartal, *Exile in the Homeland: Essays* (Jerusalem: Mosad Bialik, 1994), 164–66 [Hebrew].

80. Almog, "Redemption in Zionist Rhetoric," 15.

81. Bar-Gal, *An Agent of Zionist Propaganda*; see also Batia Donner, *To Live with the Dream* (Tel Aviv: Tel Aviv Museum of Art & Dvir, 1989), 18–27 [Hebrew].

82. Ephraim Moses Lilien, "From Ghetto to Zion" (Von Ghetto nach Zion), 1901. See also the discussion in Gideon Ofrat, "Twilight / In between the Suns" [*Bein ha-shemashot*], found in his text archive, http://gideonofrat.wordpress.com/, accessed April 29, 2018 [Hebrew]; Alec Mishori, *Lo and Behold* [*Shuru, habitu, u-re'u*]: *Zionist Icons and Visual Symbols in Israeli Culture* (Tel Aviv: Am Oved, 2000), 40–41 [Hebrew]; Rachel Arbel, ed., *Blue and White in Color: Zionist Visual Imagery, 1897–1947* (Tel Aviv: Diaspora Museum and Am Oved, 1996), 16–17 [Hebrew].

83. Anita Shapira, *Israel: A History* (Waltham, MA: Brandeis University Press, 2012), 42–53, 103–5; S. Ilan Troen, *Imagining Zion: Dreams, Designs, and Realities in a Century of Jewish Settlement* (New Haven: Yale University Press, 2003), 15–41; Shmuel Almog, "The Second Aliyah: Self-Image and Modern Interpretation," in Israel Bartal, ed., *The Second Aliyah: Studies* (Jerusalem: Yad Ben-Zvi, 1997), 38–59 [Hebrew]; Baruch Ben-Avram and Henry Near, *Studies in the Third Aliyah (1919–1924): Image and Reality* (Jerusalem: Yad Ben-Zvi, 1995) [Hebrew]. On the development of the mixed farm model, see also Amiur, *Mixed Farm and Smallholding,* 247–31.

84. Gur Alroey estimates that the *halutzim,* the Socialist Zionist pioneers, constituted only 16% of the Second Aliyah: Gur Alroey, *Immigrants* [*Immigrantim*]: *Jewish Immigration to Palestine in the Early Twentieth Century* (Jerusalem: Yad Ben-Zvi, 2004), 20–34 [Hebrew]; see also Neumann, *Land and Desire,* 3–7.

85. Tali Tadmor-Shimoni, *National Education and the Formation of the State in Israel* [*Shi'ur moledet*] (Sde Boker: Ben-Gurion Research Institute and Ben-Gurion University Press, 2010), 93–98 [Hebrew].

86. Avraham Shapira points out the religious influence on A. D. Gordon's ideas: Avraham Shapira, *The Kabbalistic and Hasidic Sources of A. D. Gordon's Thought* (Tel Aviv: Am Oved, 1996), 254–55, 284–88 [Hebrew]; Schweid, *Homeland and a Land of Promise*, 170–85.

87. Gordon, "Man and Nature," 158.

88. For a more extensive discussion of the two poems, see my article, Yael Zerubavel, "Rachel and the Female Voice: Labor, Gender, and the Zionist Pioneer Vision," in William Cutter and David C. Jacobson, eds., *History and Literature: New Readings of Jewish Texts in Honor of Arnold J. Band* (Providence: Brown Judaic Studies, 2002), 303–17.

89. Avraham Shlonsky, "Toil" [*Amal*] [1927], reprinted with English translation in T. Carmi, editor and translator, *The Penguin Book of Hebrew Verse* (New York: Penguin, 1991), 534.

90. Shlonsky draws on the Bible to emphasize the theme of the preferred son, invoking Joseph, who receives a special robe of many colors from his father, Jacob (Genesis 37:3); Isaac, who is led by his father, Abraham, at dawn to be sacrificed on Mount Moriah (Genesis 22:2–3); and Ephraim, who is noted as a beloved son (Jeremiah 31:20).

91. Female poets, though marginalized in the literary scene of the Jewish society of Palestine, shared the same ideological and cultural roots as their male counterparts. Their different style of writing and approach to the land has received greater critical attention in recent decades. See Michael Gluzman, "The Exclusion of Women from Hebrew Literary History," *Prooftexts* 11 (1991): 59–78; Hamutal Bar-Yosef, "In the Trap of Equations: Woman=Nature, Man=Culture, and Esther Raab's Poem 'Holy Grandmothers of Jerusalem,'" in Yael Azmon, ed., *A View into the Lives of Women in Jewish Societies* (Jerusalem: The Zalman Shazar Center for Jewish History, 1995), 337–47; Eric Zakim, *To Build and Be Built: Landscape, Literature and the Construction of Zionist Identity* (Philadelphia: University of Pennsylvania Press, 2006), 20–21.

92. Rachel [Bluwstein], "To My Country" [*El artzi*] [1926], English translation by Robert Freund, in Galit Hasan Rokem and Tamar S. Hess, eds., *The Defiant Muse: Hebrew Feminist Poems from Antiquity to Present* (New York: The Feminist Press, 1999), 85.

93. Yehuda Hershkovitch, "The Trip as an Educational Tool," *La-Madrich* 5 (1943): 3–32 [Hebrew]; Shaul Katz, "The Israeli Teacher-Guide: The Emergence and Perpetuation of a Role," *Annals of Tourism Research*, 12 (1985): 49–72; Orit Ben-David, "*Tiyul* (Hike) as an Act of Consecration of Space," in Eyal Ben-Ari and Yoram Bilu, eds., *Grasping Land: Space and Place in Contemporary Israeli Discourse and Experience* (Albany: SUNY Press, 1997), 129–45. On the symbolism of trees, see the discussion in chapter 3.

94. To say that her feet created a path, Rachel uses the expression *kavshu raglai*, which implies the path that her feet both "paved" and "conquered." Her choice of the verb "to conquer" suggests the *halutzah*'s participation in the pioneering discourse discussed in chapter 3, but also the different practices she uses in this context. For further analysis of Rachel's poetry, see Zakim, *To Build and Be Built*, 131–38.

95. N. Karpivner, "The Four Springs," in Z. Ariel, M. Blich, and N. Persky, eds., *Israel's Reader* [*Mikra'ot yisrael*] *for the Fourth Grade* (Jerusalem: Masada, 1958), 163–64 [Hebrew].

96. Fania Bergstein, "The Soil of Galilee" [*Rigvei ha-galil*], in *Red Beads* (Tel Aviv: Ha-Kibbutz Hameuchad, 1955), 164–70 [Hebrew]. The story connects Trumpeldor, whose heroism represents self-sacrifice, with this act of self-sacrifice committed by the soil. See Zerubavel, *Recovered Roots*, 84–95.

97. Rachel returns to the theme of pioneering as an act of creation in her short essay "Sacrifice?" [*Korbanot?*] [1929], reprinted in Mordechai Naor, ed., *The Second Aliya, 1903–1914* (Jerusalem: Yad Ben-Zvi, 1984), 75 [Hebrew]. See also David Ben-Gurion, "In Judea and the Galilee," in *Ha-Shomer Anthology*, 326. The title of Eliezer Smoli's novel, *Anshei bereshit* [1933] (reprinted Tel Aviv: Am Oved, 1973) is translated as *Frontiersmen of Israel*, yet the Hebrew title literally means "The Men of Genesis," evoking the biblical narrative of creation.

98. *The Conquest of the Desert*, English section, 11.

99. Nathan Alterman, "To Create the Land," in *The Conquest of the Mountain*, 34.

100. Anita Shapira, "The Religious Motifs of the Labor Movement," in Shmuel Almog, Jehuda Reinharz, and Anita Shapira, eds., *Zionism and Religion* (Hanover, NH: Brandeis University Press, 1998), 251–72.

101. M. Meirovitch, "The First Handful of Seeds"; S. Reichenstein, "The First Day of Sowing," in Nahum Gavrieli and Baruch Avivi, eds., *My New Book, for the Fifth Grade* (Tel Aviv: Yavne, 1950), 189–92 [Hebrew].

102. Yehuda Raab, *The First Furrow* [*Ha-telem ha-rishon*]: *Memoir, 1862–1930* (Jerusalem: The Zionist Library, 1956), 63–64 [Hebrew]; Kaniel, *In Transition*, 236–37. See also Shaul Katz, "The First Furrow: Ideology, Settlement and Agriculture in Petach Tikva during Its First Ten Years", *Katedra* 23 (April 1982): 57–122 [Hebrew]. Even if Yehuda Raab embellished his description somewhat in his retrospective narrative, his daughter, the poet Esther Raab, also alluded to her father as the one "who plows the furrow in spite of the desert" in her poem "To My Father," published in *Ha'aretz* in January, 1929 (quoted in Ehud Ben-Ezer, *Days of Gall and Honey* [*Yamim shel la'ana u-devash*]: *The Biography of the Poetess Esther Raab* (Tel Aviv: Am Oved, 1998), 38 [Hebrew]). The plowing of the first furrow had clearly been established as part of the Raab family's memories by then.

103. A. Swirsky, "My First Time Plowing," in the newsletter of the Tahkemoni School in Jerusalem, 8, 3 (1928), 1–2 [Hebrew]; found in the Aviezer Yellin Archive for Jewish Education, Tel Aviv University.

104. Tehiya Lieberson, *Autobiography* [*Pirkei hayim*] (Tel Aviv: The Center for Culture and Education, 1970), 12 [Hebrew], quoted in Neumann, *Land and Desire*, 46; Haim Watzman's translation.

105. Yaacov Patt, quoting a letter he wrote to his parents on March 21, 1914, in Patt, "The Conquest of Land at Kalandia (Atarot)," reprinted in *A Man's Path: A Memorial Book for Yaacov Patt* [*Darko shel adam: Kovetz le-zichro shel Yaacov Patt*] (Herzliya: The Committee for the Commemoration of Yaacov Patt, 1958), 9–10 [Hebrew]. The same quotation was also selected as the motto for this memorial book.

106. Rachel Yanait Ben-Zvi, "From *Ha-Shomer* Days," in *Ha-Shomer Anthology*, 534.

Chapter 2

1. Edward W. Said, *Orientalism* (New York: Vintage Books Edition, 1979); James Thompson, *The East Imagined, Experienced, Remembered: Orientalist 19th Century Paintings* (Dublin: National Gallery of Ireland, 1988). On the imagery of the Holy Land and its visual images, see Burke O. Long, *Imagining the Holy Land: Maps, Models, and Fantasy Travels* (Bloomington: Indiana University Press, 2003), and *The Orientalists: Postcards of the Holy Land, 1880–1935*, an exhibit catalog (Tel Aviv: Eretz Israel Museum, 2008) [Hebrew].

2. On this pervasive trend among writers of the *Haskalah* and Zionist Jews in Europe, see Israel Bartal, "To Forget and Remember: The Land of Israel in the Eastern European *Haskalah* Movement," in Aviezer Ravitsky, ed., *The Land of Israel in Modern Jewish Thought* (Jerusalem: Yad Ben-Zvi, 1998), 413–23 [Hebrew]. See also Eliezer Schweid, *Homeland and a Land of Promise* (Tel Aviv: Am Oved, 1979), 39, 44–46 [Hebrew]; Avner Holtzman, *Loves of Zion: Studies in Modern Hebrew Literature* [*Ahavot tsiyon*] (Jerusalem: Carmel, 2006), 188–89, 207 [Hebrew]; Aviva Mahalo, *Between Two Horizons: The Fiction of the Third Aliyah between the Diaspora and Eretz Israel* [*Bein shenei nofim*] (Jerusalem: Reuven Mass, 1991), 3–5, 19–24 [Hebrew].

3. Yaron Peleg, *Orientalism and the Hebrew Imagination* (Ithaca: Cornell University Press, 2005), 22–74; Yigal Zalmona, "To the East," in Yigal Zalmona and Tamar Manor-Friedman, eds., *To the East: Orientalism in the Arts in Israel* (Jerusalem: The Israel Museum, 1998), 49–52 [Hebrew]; Ariel Hirschfeld, "To the East: On the Perception of the East in Israeli Culture," in Zalmona and Manor-Friedman, *To the East*, 11–31; Tamar Manor-Friedman, "Our Present as the Days of Yore," in Zalmona and Manor-Friedman, *To the East*, 96–99.

4. The Hebrew term *mizrah* implies "east," but it may also serve as an acronym for the formulaic phrase "from this side the spirit of life" (*mi-tsad ze ru'ah hayim*). See Yossi Nahmias, "The Infected Gaze," *Studio* 95 (July–Aug. 1998): 33 [Hebrew]; see also Gideon Ofrat, "Twilight / In between the Suns" [*Bein ha-shemashot*], found in his text archive, http://gideonofrat.wordpress.com/, accessed April 29, 2018 [Hebrew].

5. Yehuda Halevi, "My Heart Is in the East" [*Libi ba-mizrah*], in T. Carmi, trans. and ed., *The Penguin Book of Hebrew Verse* (Harmondsworth, Middlesex: Penguin Books, 1981), 347.

6. Hayim Nahman Bialik, "To the Bird" [*El ha-tsipor*] [1891], reprinted in Bialik, *Poems* (Tel Aviv: Dvir, 1966), 9–11 [Hebrew].

7. On the strategies of archaizing and contemporizing, see Yael Zerubavel, "Back to the Bible: Hiking in the Land as a Mnemonic Practice in Contemporary Israeli Tourist Discourse," in Meir Hazan and Uri Cohen, eds., *History and Memory: Essays in Honor of Anita Shapira* (Jerusalem: Zalman Shazar Center for Jewish History, 2012), II: 497–522 [Hebrew]. See also Johannes Fabian, *Time and the Other: How Anthropology Makes Its Object* (New York: Columbia University Press, 1983), 25–35, 71–87.

8. For Said's East/West dichotomy see his *Orientalism*, 31–73, 226–54.

9. Priya Satia, "A Rebellion of Technology: Development, Policing, and the British Arabian Imaginary," in Diana K. Davis and Edmund Burke III, eds., *Environmental Imaginaries of the Middle East and North Africa* (Athens: Ohio University Press, 2011), 23–59, quote from p. 24.

10.   Arieh Bruce Saposnik, *Becoming Hebrew: The Creation of a Jewish National Culture in Ottoman Palestine* (Oxford: Oxford University Press, 2008), 149–58.

11.   Ofrat, "Twilight / In between the Suns."

12.   Anthony D. Smith, *The Ethnic Origins of Nations* (New York: Basil Blackwell, 1986), 174–208.

13.   Oz Almog, *The Sabra: The Creation of the New Jew* (Berkeley: University of California Press, 2000); Yael Zerubavel, "The Mythological Sabra and Jewish Past: Trauma, Memory, and Contested Identities," *Israel Studies* 7, 2 (Summer 2002): 115–44. For further discussion on gendered images, see chapter 3.

14.   Yael Zerubavel, *Recovered Roots: Collective Memory and the Making of Israeli National Tradition* (Chicago: University of Chicago Press, 1995), 96–113; Yael Zerubavel, "Antiquity and the Renewal Paradigm: Strategies of Representation and Mnemonic Practices in Israeli culture," in Doron Mendels, ed., *On Memory: An Interdisciplinary Approach* (Bern: Peter Lang, 2007), 331–48.

15.   See Yehoshua Kaniel, *In Transition: The Jews of Eretz Israel in the Nineteenth Century* (Jerusalem: Yad Ben-Zvi, 2000), 319–63, 368–75 [Hebrew]; Saposnik, *Becoming Hebrew*, 169–80; Michelle U. Campos, *Ottoman Brothers: Muslims, Christians, and Jews in Early Twentieth-Century* Palestine (Stanford: Stanford University Press, 2011), 197–211; Jonathan M. Gribetz, *Defining Neighbors: Religion, Race, and the Early Zionist-Arab Encounter* (Princeton: Princeton University Press, 2014), 93–130; Abigail Jacobson and Moshe Naor, *Oriental Neighbors: Middle Eastern Jews and Arabs in Mandatory Palestine* (Waltham, MA: Brandeis University Press, 2016).

16.   Yemenite Jews arrived in small groups at the end of the nineteenth century and the beginning of the twentieth century. Nitza Druyan, *Without a Magic Carpet: Yemenite Settlement in Eretz Israel, 1882–1914* (Jerusalem: Yad Ben-Zvi, 1981) [Hebrew], 19, 57, 134–48; Kaniel, *In Transition*, 375–89; Yehuda Nini, *Yemen and Zion: The Jews of Yemen, 1800–1914* (Jerusalem: The Zionist Library, 1982), 237–87 [Hebrew].

17.   Dalia Manor, "Orientalism and Jewish National Art: The Case of Bezalel," in Ivan Davidson Kalmar and Derek Jonathan Penslar, eds., *Orientalism and The Jews* (Waltham, MA: Brandeis University Press, 2005), 150. Saposnik emphasizes the messianic and Orientalist dimensions of Boris Schatz's vision of forging a national style of art (*Becoming Hebrew*, 121–44). On the symbolism of the Yemenite Jews' craft, see Yael Guilat, *Yemeni Jewish Silver Craft in the Israeli 'Melting Pot'* [*Tsorfut be-kur hitukh*] (Sde Boker: The Ben-Gurion Research Institute and Ben-Gurion University Press, 2009), 65–153 [Hebrew].

18.   Batsheva Goldman Ida, ed., *Ze'ev Raban, A Hebrew Symbolist* (Tel Aviv: Tel Aviv Museum of Art & Jerusalem: Yad Ben-Zvi, 2001) [Hebrew]; Yigal Zalmona, ed., *The Art of Abel Pann: From Montparnasse to the Land of the Bible* (Jerusalem: The Israel Museum, 2003) [Hebrew].

19.   Ilana Pardes, *Agnon's Moonstruck Lovers: The Song of Songs in Israeli Culture* (Seattle: University of Washington Press, 2013), 60–65.

20.   Sari Elron, "To Dance in Hebrew: Hebrew-ness in Rina Nikova's and the Yemenite Ensemble's Work," in Henia Rottenberg and Dina Roginsky, eds., *Dance Discourse in Israel* [*Rav koliyut ve-shiah mahol be-yisrael*] (Tel Aviv: Resling, 2009), 176, 182, quote from p. 172 [Hebrew].

21.   Ruth Eshel, "Characters and Trends from the Yemenite Jews' Tradition in Theatrical Dance in Israel," in Naomi Bahat-Ratzon, ed., *Barefooted: Jewish-Yemenite Tradition in Israeli Dance* (Tel Aviv: E'ele Be-Tamar and Inbal Dance Theater, 1999), 93–100 [Hebrew].

22.   Ruth Eshel, *Dancing with the Dream: The Development of Artistic Dance in Israel 1920–1964* (Tel Aviv: Sifriyat Hapoalim & Israel Dance Library, 1991), 24–26 [Hebrew]; Nina S. Spiegel, "Cultural Production in Tel Aviv: Yardena Cohen and the National Dance Competition of 1937," in Judith Brin Ingber, ed., *Seeing Israeli and Jewish Dance* (Detroit: Wayne State University Press, 2011), 74–75.

23.   On Sara Levi-Tanai and the Inbal Dance Theater, see Eshel, *Dancing with the Dream*, 90, 94–100; Judith Brin Ingber, "Shorashim," in *Seeing Israeli and Jewish Dance,* 127–34; Giora Manor, "Inbal's History," in Bahat-Ratzon, *Barefooted*, 133–47.

24.   Quoted in Ingber, "Shorashim," 132.

25.   The etymology of the word "Bedouins" in Arabic suggests their identity as desert dwellers. See the entry for "Bedouins" at the Online Etymology Dictionary, http://www.etymonline.com/index.php?term=Bedouin, accessed May 4, 2017.

26.   See Shemaryahu Talmon, "The 'Desert Motif' in the Bible and Qumran Literature," in Alexander Altman, ed., *Biblical Motifs: Origins and Transformations* (Cambridge, MA: Harvard University Press, 1966), 34–36; Yosef Braslavi, "Relations between Nomads and the Settled Population during the Biblical Period," in Yaacov Eini and Ezra Orion, eds., *The Bedouins: Notes and Essays* (Beer Sheva: Ben-Gurion University Press, 1988), 9–17 [Hebrew]; Saposnik, *Becoming Hebrew*, 161; Ze'ev Meshel, "The Israelites' Journeys in the Desert," *Kardom* 1, 11 (1981/2): 155–60 [Hebrew]; Yuval Yakutieli, "The Negev's Archeology," *Ariel* 151–52 (2002): 79–88 [Hebrew].

27.   David Tidhar, *Encyclopedia of the Founders and Builders of Israel* (Tel Aviv: Sifriyat Rishonim, 1947), II: 953, available online at http://www.tidhar.tourolib.org/tidhar/view/2/953, accessed April 22, 2018 [Hebrew].

28.   On the Orientalist tendency to stereotype, see Said, *Orientalism*, 230–31; Fabian, *Time and the Other*, 71–87. For this tendency in Jewish art, see Manor, "Orientalism and Jewish National Art," 150–55, 159n68; Yigal Zalmona, "To the East," 49–62. See also Ida, *Ze'ev Raban*, 84–87, and Zalmona, *The Art of Abel Pann*.

29.   Dalia Manor, *Art in Zion: The Genesis of Modern National Art in Palestine* (London: Routledge, 2005), 114, 134–62. According to Manor, Reuven Rubin was considered "Palestine's Gauguin" (137). See also Zalmona, "To the East," 56–59.

30.   The Hebraized terms *falah* and *falha* appear in Avraham Even-Shoshan, *The New Dictionary* [*Ha-milon he-hadash*] (Jerusalem: Kiryat Sefer, 1988), III: 1062 [Hebrew]. The term *falha* for grain cultivation has remained popular among kibbutzim. Nahum Karlinsky, *Citrus Blossoms: Jewish Entrepreneurship in Palestine, 1890–1939* (Jerusalem: Magnes Press, 2000), 7 [Hebrew], and Hezi Amiur, *Mixed Farm and Smallholding in Zionist Settlement Thought* (Jerusalem: Zalman Shazar Center for Jewish History, 2016), 28 [Hebrew].

31.   *Ha-Shomer Anthology* [*Kovetz ha-shomer*] (Tel Aviv: Labor Archive, 1937), 49–50 [Hebrew].

32.   On the social construction of "co-descent," see Eviatar Zerubavel, *Ancestors and Relatives: Genealogy, Identity and Community* (New York: Oxford University Press, 2012), 34–48; Eviatar Zerubavel, *Time Maps: Collective Memory and the Social Shape of the Past*

(Chicago: University of Chicago Press, 2003), 63–66. The term "cousins" is used in Hebrew to allude to Arabs, and may be used in a similar fashion by Arabs to refer to Jews.

33. See David Ben-Gurion and Yitzhak Ben-Zvi, *The Land of Israel in the Past and at Present* [*Eretz yisrael be-avar uva-hove*] [Yiddish, 1918] (Jerusalem: Yad Ben-Zvi, 1979), 196–206 [Hebrew]; A. N. Pollack, "The Origins of Palestine's Arabs," *Molad* I (24), 3 (213) (Oct.–Nov. 1967): 297 [Hebrew]; Yaffa Berlovitz, *Inventing a Land, Inventing a People: The Literature of the First Aliyah* [*Le-hamtsi eretz, le-hamtsi am*] (Tel Aviv: Hakibbutz Hameuchad, 1996), 121–40 [Hebrew]. See also Gribetz's discussion of Ben-Zvi's fascination with this theory in Gribetz, *Defining Neighbors*, 123–26.

34. Quoted in Yosef Gorny, *Zionism and the Arabs, 1882–1948: A Study of Ideology* (Oxford: Oxford University Press, 1987), 103.

35. Hemda Ben-Yehuda, "The Farm of Reikhav's Sons" [1903], reprinted in Yaffa Berlovitz, ed., *Stories by Women of the First Aliyah* (Tel Aviv: Tarmil, 1984), 43–77, quote from p. 77, emphasis added [Hebrew]. For further discussion, see Berlovitz, *Inventing a Land*, 34–140, and Nurith Govrin, *Honey from the Rock: Study of the Literature of the Land of Israel* (Tel Aviv: Defense Ministry Press, 1989), 45–50 [Hebrew]. Twenty-six years later, a Second Aliyah writer wrote a novel on a similar theme: Ya'akov Rabinowitz, *The Wandering of Amasai the Guard* [*Nedudei amasi ha-shomer*] (Tel Aviv: Mitzpe, 1929) [Hebrew].

36. Rachel Yanait Ben-Zvi, *We Arrive in the Land* [*Anu olim*] (Tel Aviv: Am Oved, 1960), 54–55, 58 [Hebrew].

37. See Eviatar Zerubavel's concept of "out-pasting" to convey earlier roots in *Time Maps*, 105–9. Hillel Cohen notes that Arab historians do not view the issue of earlier roots in the land as critical, given the history of migrations within the Middle East, in Cohen, *1929, Year Zero of the Jewish-Arab Conflict* (Jerusalem: Keter, 2013), 69 [Hebrew].

38. Gorny, *Zionism and the Arabs*, 129–55; Anita Shapira, *Visions in Conflict* [*Ha-halikha al kav ha-ofek*] (Tel Aviv: Am Oved, 1988), 46–47 [Hebrew]. Some Socialist Zionists also believed that Jewish and Arab workers would form an alliance based on shared class interests.

39. See Zvi Shiloni, "The First Land Acquisition of the Jewish National Fund, 1904–1908," in Ruth Kark, ed., *Redemption of the Land of Eretz Israel: Ideology and Practice* [*Ge'ulat ha-karka be-eretz yisrael*] (Jerusalem: Yad Ben-Zvi, 1990), 118–50; see group photo of the orphans on p. 134 [Hebrew].

40. Meir Wilkansky, "Following Arrival" [*Mi-yemei ha-aliya*], *Ha-Poel Ha-Tsair* 4, 23–24 (September 20, 1911): 18–22, and Itamar Ben-Avi, "What Did the Land of Israel Give Us?" *Hashkafa* 9, 18 (November 19, 1907): 2, quoted in Saposnik, *Becoming Hebrew*, 156, 181. See also Rachel Elboim-Dror, "Here He Comes from Our Midst, the New Hebrew: On the Youth Culture of the First Aliyot" [*Hu holekh u-va mi-kirbeinu*], *Alpayim*, 12 (1996): 104–35 [Hebrew]; and Itamar Even-Zohar, "The Emergence of Native Hebrew Culture in Palestine, 1882–1948," *Studies in Zionism* 4 (Oct. 1984): 167–84.

41. See Ze'ev Yavetz, "Wander in the Land [*Shut ba-aretz*], [1891], reprinted in Yaffa Berlovitz, ed., *Wandering in the Land: Travels by Members of the First Aliyah* [*E'ebra na ba-aretz*] (Tel Aviv: Defense Ministry Press, 1992), 109 [Hebrew]; see also Berlovitz, *Inventing a Land*, 222–23. Raban's illustration for Lag Ba'Omer appears in *Hageinu* [*Our Holidays*]: *A Picture Book*, New York: Miller-Lynn, 1928, n.p. (digital copy at the National

Library of Israel). See also Raban's painting on a ceramic tile in Ida, *Ze'ev Raban*, 41, and a 1925 drawing of a farmer plowing the land for the JNF's calendar in Ida, *Ze'ev Raban*, 100, plate 118.1.

42. Yigal Zalmona, ed., *Boris Schatz: The Father of Israeli Art* (Jerusalem: Israel Museum, 2006) [Hebrew].

43. For an earlier version of this discussion, see Yael Zerubavel, "Memory, the Rebirth of the Native, and the 'Hebrew Bedouin' Identity," *Social Research* 75, 1 (Spring 2008): 315–52.

44. Walid Khalidi, *Before Their Diaspora: A Photographic History of the Palestinians, 1876–1948* (Washington, DC: Institute for Palestinian Studies, 1984).

45. Even-Zohar, "The Emergence of Native Hebrew Culture," 174.

46. Israel Bartal, "Cossack and Bedouin: A World of New, National Imagery" [1998], reprinted in Bartal, *Cossack and Bedouin: Land and People in Jewish Nationalism* (Tel Aviv: Am Oved, 2007), 68–79 [Hebrew].

47. Israel Bartal, "Michael Halperin," in Zeev Tzahor, ed., *The Second Aliyah: Biographies* (Jerusalem: Yad Ben-Zvi, 1997), 143–45 [Hebrew]; Yirmiyahu Halperin, *My Father, Michael Halperin* (Tel Aviv: Hadar, 1964) [Hebrew]; Jacob Goldstein, *The Shepherd Group: The Idea of the Conquest of Shepherding during the Second Aliyah and Its Realization, 1907–1917* [*Havurat ha-roim*] (Tel Aviv: Defense Ministry Press, 1993), 14–15, 18, 21 [Hebrew]. For the story of a female *Ha-Shomer* member, see Hagar Salamon, "A Woman's Life Story as a Foundation Legend of Local Identity," in Ruth Kark, Margalit Shilo, and Galit Hasan-Rokem, eds., *Jewish Women in Pre-State Israel: Life History, Politics, and Culture* (Waltham, MA: Brandeis University Press, 2008), 141–65.

48. The exhibit of the history of Jewish defense is at the Eliyahu Golumb Hagana Museum in Tel Aviv. A 2007 commemorative stamp includes two canonical photos of *Ha-Shomer* members, one of which features them riding horses, dressed in hybrid clothing styles, while the other presents a studio portrait of two leading *Ha-Shomer* members dressed in European clothing and a third sporting a *kaffiyeh*. These photos appeared in *Ha-Shomer Anthology* [*Kovetz Ha-Shomer*], 59, 211.

49. Ted Swedenburg, *Memories of Revolt: The 1936–1939 Rebellion and the Palestinian National Past* (Minneapolis: University of Minnesota Press, 1995), 32–35.

50. A 1992 publicity brochure of the *Hagana* Museum featured a photo of its display of a young female *Palmach* member wearing a *kaffiyeh*. Uri, the archetypical *Palmachnik*, is featured wearing a white *kaffiyeh* around his neck in the film *He Walked through the Fields* (Yosef Milo, 1967), based on Moshe Shamir's novel *He Walked through the Fields* [*Hu halakh ba-sadot*] [1947] (Tel Aviv: Am Oved, 1972) [Hebrew].

51. A member of *Ha-Shomer* notes that he joined the group only after he had learned how to ride a horse and speak some Arabic. See Tsalel, "Memoir" [*Zichronot*], in *Ha-Shomer Anthology*, 195. For Jews' public display of horsemanship, see Halperin, *My Father, Michael Halperin*, 199; Zalman Asushkin, "From Hadera to Hamra," in *Ha-Shomer Anthology*, 179; Mendel Portugali, "A Bundle of Letters," in *Ha-Shomer Anthology*, 34; Saposnik, *Becoming Hebrew*, 185–86.

52. Herzl's diary entry [1898], reprinted in Avraham Ya'ari, ed., *Tours of the Land of Israel: From the Middle Ages to the Zionist Return to the Land* (Tel Aviv: Modan, 1996), 740

[Hebrew]; see also Anita Shapira, *Land and Power: The Zionist Resort to Force, 1881–1948* (Stanford: Stanford University Press, 1999), 61.

53. Halperin, *My Father, Michael Halperin*, 127.

54. Celina Mashiah, *Childhood and Nationalism: Imagined Childhood in Hebrew Children's Literature, 1790–1948* (Tel Aviv: Cherikover, 2000), 205 [Hebrew]. Mashiah notes that Gutman created this picture in 1948 to attract young Hebrew readers to a new edition of Hayim Nahman Bialik's poetry by relating to their reality (228n18).

55. On a minority call for Jews to learn Arabic in 1913–14, see Campos, *Ottoman Brothers*, 228–31; for a broader discussion of Arabic in Yishuv society, see Liora R. Halperin, *Babel in Zion: Jews, Nationalism, and Language Diversity in Palestine* (New Haven: Yale University Press, 2014), 142–50. Sephardic intellectuals and European scholars had literary and academic knowledge of Arabic. See Gribetz, *Defining Neighbors*, 15–38, 186–203.

56. Moshe Smilansky, "Hawaja Nazar" [1910], reprinted in Moshe Smilansky, *Collected Works* (Tel Aviv: Omanut, 1930), III: 27 [Hebrew].

57. Ya'acov Ya'ary-Poleskin, *Dreamers and Warriors* (Petach Tikva: Gissin, 1922), 23, quoted in Gluzman, *The Zionist Body: Nationalism, Gender and Sexuality in Modern Hebrew Literature* (Tel Aviv: Hakibbutz Hameuchad, 2007), 23–24 [Hebrew]. Bar-Adon describes a Hebrew guard who curses in Arabic in a short story, "Reconciliation Ceremony" [*Sulha*], in Pesach Bar-Adon, *In Desert Tents: With the Bedouins* [1934] (Jerusalem: Kiryat Sefer, 1981), 250–64 [Hebrew].

58. Netiva Ben-Yehuda, *1948—Between Calendars* [*Bein ha-sefirot*] (Jerusalem: Keter, 1981), 175–76 [Hebrew]. On the use of Arabic in the *Palmach's chizbat* tale genre, see Elliott Oring, *Israeli Humor: The Content and Structure of the Chizbat of the Palmah* (Albany: SUNY Press, 1981). Moshe Shamir describes a native Hebrew guard who patrols the fields on his horse and communicates with the Arabs in their own language in Moshe Shamir, *With His Own Hands* [*Bemo yadav*] (Tel Aviv: Am Oved [1951], 1972), 133–35 [Hebrew].

59. See Oz Almog, *The Sabra: The Creation of the New Jew* (Berkeley: University of California Press, 2000), 185, and his discussion of the *Palmach* members' Arabism and hybrid dress, 198–200. Uri, as mentioned earlier, draws on Moshe Shamir's famous protagonist in *He Walked through the Fields*.

60. Field guides often display their knowledge of Arab customs and Arabic expressions as evidence of their familiarity with the environment and its culture. See Orit Ben-David, "*Tiyul* (Hike) as an Act of Consecration of Space," in Eyal Ben-Ari and Yoram Bilu, eds., *Grasping Land: Space and Place in Contemporary Israeli Discourse and Experience* (Albany: SUNY Press, 1997), 132, 136.

61. A new Israeli law, "Israel as nation-state of the Jewish people," was approved by the Knesset in July 2018, recognizing only Hebrew as a national language and granting Arabic a "special status." For the Yishuv period, see Halperin, *Babel in Zion*; Anat Helman, "'Even the Dogs in the Streets Bark in Hebrew': National Ideology and Everyday Culture in Tel-Aviv," *Jewish Quarterly Review* 92, 3–4 (2002): 359–82; Rachel Elboim-Dror, *Hebrew Education in Eretz Israel* (Jerusalem: Yad Ben-Zvi, 1996), II: 328–30, 359–62 [Hebrew].

62. Michal Sadan, *The Hebrew Shepherd: The Transformation of Image and Symbol from Hebrew Enlightenment Literature to the New Hebrew Culture in Israel* (Jerusalem: Yad Ben-Zvi, 2011) [Hebrew]; Tova Cohen, *From Dream to Reality: Descriptions of the Land of Israel in Haskalah Literature* (Ramat Gan: Bar Ilan University Press, 1982) [Hebrew]; Nogah

Hareuveni, *Desert and Shepherd in Our Biblical Heritage* (Neot Kedumim: The Biblical Landscape Reserve in Israel [1991], 2000).

63. Goldstein, *The Shepherd Group*, 20–25; Eliyahu Eilat, "Personal Ties with Transjordan Bedouins during the 1930s," in Yaacov Eini and Ezra Orion, eds., *The Bedouins: Notes and Essays* (Sde Boker: Ben-Gurion University Press, 1988), 424–32 [Hebrew].

64. Bar-Adon, *In Desert Tents*, 14. He also published another book on shepherding: Pesach Bar-Adon [Aziz Effendi], *Among the Herds* (Jerusalem: Ahi'asaf, 1942) [Hebrew].

65. Sadan, *The Hebrew Shepherd*, 35, 44–45.

66. Moshe Zhaludin, "In Smoke and Deprivation" [*Be-ashan uve-mahsor*], *Ha-Shomer Anthology*, 282, 283. See also Sadan, *The Hebrew Shepherd*, 40–44. Perhaps the most famous shepherd group settled in Sheik Abrek in the Galilee in 1926.

67. Yosef Luidor, "Yo'ash," *Ha-Shiloah* 26 (1912), 226–46 [Hebrew]. See also Yigal Schwartz's discussion of Luidor's work and the tension between the nomads and the settlers in Hebrew literature of the period, in Schwartz, *The Zionist Paradox: Hebrew Literature and Israeli Identity* (Waltham. MA: Brandeis University Press, 2014), 97–141.

68. Eliezer Smoli, *The Loyal Shepherd* [1928], reprinted in *The Loyal Shepherd* (Tel Aviv: Am Oved, 1978), 107–12 [Hebrew].

69. The anthology was reissued in 1978 to mark the fiftieth anniversary of the publication of Smoli's story by that title. See Smoli, *The Loyal Shepherd* (1978), 1; cover image by Giora Carmi.

70. Eliezer Smoli, *Frontiersmen of Israel* [*Anshei bereshit*], [1933] (Tel Aviv: Am Oved, 1973), 51 [Hebrew]. English translation by Murray Roston, *Frontiersmen of Israel* (Tel Aviv: Masada, 1964). References are to the English edition unless otherwise noted. See also Schwartz, *The Zionist Paradox*, 132–38.

71. Smoli, *Frontiersmen of Israel*, 38–40.

72. Smoli, *Frontiersmen of Israel*, 78. The daughter's confusion echoes Ze'ev Yavetz's interpretation of the *abbaya* as deriving from the ancient Jewish prayer shawl (*tallit*). Roston's translation replaces the daughter's reference to the prayer shawl with "that funny box on his head," alluding to another Jewish ritual object and thus missing the irony of her use of the Arabic term *abbaya* for the Jewish *tallit*.

73. For a broader discussion on hybrid identity, see Mary C. Waters, *Ethnic Options: Choosing Identities in America* (Berkeley: University of California Press, 1990), 16–51; see also Stuart Hall, "Introduction: Who Needs 'Identity'?" in Stuart Hall and Paul du Gay, eds., *Questions of Cultural Identity* (London: Sage, 1996), 1–17.

74. Gribetz, *Defining Neighbors*, 114.

75. The term "Arab Jews" was also used in the late Ottoman Empire to refer to Middle Eastern or Sephardic Jews. See Gribetz, *Defining Neighbors*, 36–37, 111. On its recent revival as an ideological position by Mizrahi Jews, see Ella Shohat, "Dislocated Identities: Reflections of an Arab-Jew," *Movement Research: Performance Journal* 5 (Fall-Winter, 1992): 8; Yehouda Shenhav, *The Arab Jews: A Postcolonial Reading of Nationalism, Religion and Ethnicity* (Stanford: Stanford University Press, 2006); Yehouda Shenhav and Hannan Hever, "'Arab Jews' after Structuralism: Zionist Discourse and the (De)formation of an Ethnic Identity," *Social Identities* 18, 1 (January 2012): 101–18.

76. On the core ("unmarked") and qualifying ("marked") components of identity, see Linda Waugh, "Marked and Unmarked: A Choice between Unequals in Semiotic Structure," *Semiotica* 38, 3–4 (1982): 299–318. On the symbolic role of the hyphen, see Rachelle Germana, "Hyphenation and Its Discontents: Hyphenators, Hyphen Haters, and the Cultural Politics of Ambiguity," PhD dissertation, Rutgers University, 2012; and Berel Lang, "Hyphenated-Jews and the Anxiety of Identity," *Jewish Social Studies* 12, 1 (Fall 2005): 1–15.

77. The Young Hebrews advocated a unified society of indigenous groups underneath an overarching "Hebrew" identity. See Yaacov Shavit, *From Hebrew to Canaanite* (Jerusalem: Domino Press, 1984) [Hebrew].

78. Yavetz, "Wander in the Land," 120–21; Berlovitz, *Inventing a Land*, 181–82.

79. According to his son, Michael Halperin, who lived among the Bedouins, could not be told apart from them. Halperin, *My Father, Michael Halperin*, 127, 144; Asushkin, "From Hadera to Hamra," 186; Ben-Zvi, "With *Ha-Shomer*," in *Ha-Shomer Anthology*, 70; Meir Spector, "Guarding the Galilee and Judea," in *Ha-Shomer Anthology*, 227; Alexander Zeid, "A Chapter in Life" [*Perek hayim*], in *Ha-Shomer Anthology*, 85–93. See also Yaacov Zerubavel, *Life* [*Alei hayim*] (Tel Aviv: Y. L. Perez, 1960), 356 [Hebrew].

80. Gershon Fleisher, "In the Pasture," *Ha-Shomer Anthology*, 277–78; Arye Abramson, "On Comrades' Blood: With the Herds" [*Al dmei re'im*], in *Ha-Shomer Anthology*, 268; Eilat, "Personal Ties with Transjordan Bedouins," 428.

81. Uri Cohen, "The Zionist Animal: A Study in Zionist Figures," *Jerusalem Studies in Hebrew Literature* 19 (2003): 167–217 [Hebrew].

82. Alexander Penn wrote the poem "Carry Us to the Desert" in the late 1920s. For the song lyrics based on his poem, see "Zemereshet," a website of Hebrew songs, https:// www.zemereshet.co.il/song.asp?id=629, accessed August 24, 2012 [Hebrew]. See also Hagit Halperin, *The Star Fall: Alexander Penn, His Life and Work until 1940* [*Shalekhet kokhavim*] (Tel Aviv: Papirus, 1989), 194–95 [Hebrew].

83. For the lyrics of the song "A Caravan in the Desert," see "Zemereshet," http://www .zemereshet.co.il/song.asp?id=115, accessed August 24, 2012 [Hebrew]; and Gil Aldema and Natan Shahar, eds., *The Song Book for the Student* (Tel Aviv: Nasimov Library, 1995), 190–91 [Hebrew].

84. See also Hirschfeld, "To the East," 15. It should be noted that Fichman's original text describes the caravan's route "from sea to sea," thus conveying a clear destination and sense of purpose that are missing in Zehavi's more popular adaptation.

85. Sara Levi-Tanai, "From Street Urchin to International Acclaim: A Personal Testimony," in *Seeing Israeli and Jewish Dance*, 25–42; the text is based on Levi-Tanai's notes for a curtain speech, December 1977.

86. Mordechai Naor and Batia Karmiel, *The Flying Camel: Eighty-Five Years of Exhibits and Fairs in Tel Aviv* (Tel Aviv: Eretz Israel Museum, 2011)[Hebrew].

87. On the shearing festival, see Sadan, *The Hebrew Shepherd*, 42, 113–16. On the work of Matityahu Shelem and Lea Bergstein, see Yoram Goren, *The Fields Were Adorned by Dance: On Lea Bergstein and Her Contribution to Israeli Holidays and Dance* (Ramat Yohanan: The Kibbutz Press, 1983), 34–36 [Hebrew]; Eshel, *Dancing with the Dream* 88–89; Ingber, "Shorashim," 141–45.

88. Quoted in Ingber, "Shorashim," 122.

89.   On the Yemenite step, see Ingber, "Shorashim," 121; see also Dan Ronen, "Components of Yemenite Jews' Dance Tradition in Israeli Folkdances," in Bahat-Ratzon, *Barefooted*, 63–81.

90.   See, for example, Ingber, "Shorashim," 111, 136, 146; Levi-Tanai, "From Street Urchin to International Acclaim," 33, 36, 40. In contrast to the Orientalist tradition of picturing women dressed in gowns and carrying a pitcher, an ironic image from the 1970s portrays water pouring out of a large plastic bottle. See Muki Tsur, ed., *Next Year: Greeting Cards from the Kibbutz* (Yad Ya'ari, Ben-Gurion Research Institute, and Yad Tabenkin, 2001), 86 [Hebrew].

91.   For the lyrics of "To the Water Spring," written by Yaacov David Kamzon in the late 1920s, see "Zemereshet," http://zemer.co.il/song.asp?id=356, accessed September 29, 2012 [Hebrew].

92.   On symbolic journeys across time and space, see Yael Zerubavel, "Transhistorical Encounters in the Land of Israel: National Memory, Symbolic Bridges, and the Literary Imagination," *Jewish Social Studies* 11, 3 (Spring/Summer 2005): 115–40.

93.   For the lyrics of Emanuel Zamir's "A Well in the Field" (1947), see "Zemereshet," http://www.zemer.co.il/biography.asp?artists_id=276&id=31, accessed August 21, 2012 [Hebrew].

94.   For further information about these songs and their lyrics, see "Zemereshet," http://www.zemereshet.co.il/song.asp?id=348, and http://www.zemereshet.co.il/song .asp?id=1612&artist=1215, accessed August 21, 2012 [Hebrew]. For the dances, see Ingber, "Shorashim," 107–10, 166n19; Nina S. Spiegel, *Embodying Hebrew Culture: Aesthetics, Athletics, and Dance in the Jewish Community of Mandate Palestine* (Detroit: Wayne State University, 2013), 139.

95.   For images of children as shepherds, see Tsur, *Next Year*, 48, 50, 88, 108, 114, 160, 176, 230. See also Nadav Mann, "New Year from '*Beitmuna*'" [*shana tova mi-beitmuna*], *Ynet*, Sept. 7, 2007, at http://www.ynet.co.il/articles/0,7340,L-3446462,00.html, accessed March 5, 2014 [Hebrew].

96.   See Levi-Tanai, "From Street Urchin to International Acclaim." Dov Nir, "The Perception of the Desert in New Hebrew Literature," *Lashon Ve-Ivrit* 6 (1990): 17 [Hebrew]) notes the gap between the reality and the romantic perception of the desert in Yitzhak Shenhar's story "Like Grapes in the Desert," in *Time Will Tell* [*Yamim yedaberu*] (Jerusalem: Schocken, 1945) 103–16 [Hebrew]). Sadan (*The Hebrew Shepherd*, 50) makes a similar observation, noting that raising herds became economically unviable and that therefore most kibbutzim did away with their herds.

97.   On the nostalgic canon of songs identified as "the songs of the Land of Israel," see Motti Regev and Edwin Seroussi, *Popular Music and National Culture in Israel* (Berkeley: University of California Press, 2004), 49–70. Folk dancing, which draws, among other sources, from the dances created during the pre-state and early state periods, is a lively leisure activity enjoyed in many localities.

98.   Quoted in Schweid, *Homeland and a Land of Promise*, 151–54.

99.   Ben-Zvi, "With *Ha-Shomer*," 74; see also Meir Vilensky, "To the Galilee" [1909], quoted in Avner Holzman, "A Country Loaded by Vision and Wine," in Mordechai Naor, ed., *The Jezreel Valley: 1900–1967* (Jerusalem: Yad Ben-Zvi, 1993), 206–7 [Hebrew].

100. *The Conquest of the Mountain* (Jerusalem: Jewish National Fund, 1955/6), 35 and 47 [Hebrew].

101. As discussed in chapter 1, Gordon was also critical of the settlers' attitude toward the landscape and its nature. Shapira notes that Gordon's relationship to the landscape remained complex and mediated by its association with the Bible. Avraham Shapira, *The Kabbalistic and Hasidic Sources of A. D. Gordon's Thought* (Tel Aviv: Am Oved, 1996), 253–54 [Hebrew]; see also Schweid, *Homeland and a Land of Promise*, 155–56.

102. Avraham Shlonsky, "We All," in Z. Ariel, M. Blich, and N. Perskey, eds., *Israel's Reader [Mikra'ot yisrael] for the Fourth Grade*, 7th ed. (Jerusalem: Masada, 1958), 160 [Hebrew]; Yitzhak Lamdan, *Masada* [1927] (Tel Aviv: Dvir, 1972), 56 [Hebrew].

103. For the meaning of *pere* as a wild donkey, see Jeremiah 2:24. The Hebrew Bible applies the term to Ishmael as a wild man (literally, "a wild donkey of a man") in Genesis 16:12; see also Even-Shoshan, *The New Dictionary* III: 1088.

104. Moshe Smilansky, "Bataiha," *Travel in the Country [Mashot ba-aretz]*, in Smilansky, *Collected Works* (Tel Aviv: Dvir, 1953), VI: 112–19 [Hebrew].

105. Yosef Weitz, *To the Galilee* (Jerusalem: Jewish National Fund, 1937), 3 [Hebrew].

106. Yitzhak Ben-Zvi, *Memoir and Notes [Zikhronot u-reshumot]* (Jerusalem: Yad Ben-Zvi, 1966), 151 [Hebrew].

107. Hemda Ben-Yehuda, "Everyone under His Own Vine and Fig Tree" [1944], reprinted in Berlovitz, *Wandering in the Land*, 165.

108. Ben-Zvi, "With *Ha-Shomer*," 71.

109. Quoted in Anat Helman, *Young Tel Aviv: A Tale of Two Cities* (Waltham, MA: Brandeis University Press, 2010), 84.

110. Zvi Zameret, "Gordon and Brenner," in Mordechai Naor, ed., *The Second Aliyah, 1903–1914* (Jerusalem: Yad Ben-Zvi, 1984), 89 [Hebrew].

111. Yosef Aharonowitz, "Conventional Truths," *Hedim* 11–12 (1923): 30–31, quoted in Anat Helman, *Urban Culture in 1920s and 1930s Tel Aviv [Orr ha-yam hikifu'ha]* (Haifa: Haifa University Press, 2007), 180 [Hebrew].

112. Roderick Nash, *Wilderness and the American Mind*, 3rd edition (New Haven: Yale University Press, 1982), 29–30.

113. Yosef Klausner, "Concern" [*Hashash*], *Ha-Shiloah* 17 (July–December 1907): 574–76 [Hebrew]; quoted in Gorny, *Zionism and the Arabs*, 49.

114. Ya'acov Rabinowitz, "On Education in the Land of Israel," *Ha-Poel Ha-Tsair* 6 (8), November 15, 1912 and "Notes" [*Reshimot*], *Ha-Poel Ha-Tsair*, 7 (38), July 17, 1914, 8–9 [Hebrew], quoted in Saposnik, *Becoming Hebrew*, 159.

115. Ze'ev Jabotinsky, "The East," quoted in Gorny, *Zionism and the Arabs*, 160.

116. Ahad Ha'am, "Truth from the Land of Israel (First Essay)" [1891], reprinted in *Ahad Ha'am: Collected Works* (Tel Aviv: Dvir, 1947), 24 [Hebrew].

117. Yitzhak Epstein, "A Hidden Question" [*She'ela ne'elama*], *Ha-Shiloah* 17 (July–Dec. 1907): 193–206 [Hebrew]. For a broader discussion of Epstein and others who supported "the integrationist-altruistic orientation," see Gorny, *Zionism and the Arabs*, 42–49.

118. Quoted by Gorny, *Zionism and the Arabs*, 119.

119. *Encylopaedia Judaica* (Jerusalem: Keter, 1974), 4: 632–33; Gorny, *Zionism and*

the Arabs, 118–28, 189–201; see also Shalom Ratzabi, *Between Zionism and Judaism: The Radical Circle in Brit Shalom, 1925–33* (Leiden: Brill, 2002).

120. See also two collections of articles on this topic: Ivan Davidson Kalmar and Derek J. Penslar, eds., *Orientalism and the Jews* (Waltham, MA: Brandeis University Press, 2005); and Ethan B. Katz, Lisa Moses Leff, and Maud S. Mandel, eds., *Colonialism and the Jews* (Bloomington: Indiana University Press, 2017). See also Saposnik, *Becoming Hebrew*, 145–68; Daniel Boyarin, "The Colonial Costume Party: Zionism, Gender and Imitation," *Teoria Uvikoret* 11 (1997): 123–44 [Hebrew]; and Aziza Khazzoom, *Shifting Ethnic Boundaries and Inequality in Israel, or: How the Polish Peddler Became a German Intellectual* (Stanford: Stanford University Press, 2008).

121. Julie Kalman, *Orientalizing the Jew: Religion, Culture, and Imperialism in Nineteenth-Century France* (Bloomington: Indiana University Press, 2017), 122.

122. The reception of the Yemenite Jews by the Jewish society of Palestine has been the subject of a critical reassessment. See Druyan, *Without a Magic Carpet*; Helman, *Urban Culture*, 179–83; Yehuda Nini, *The Yemenites of Kinnert: The Story of Their Settlement and Displacement, 1912–1930* (Tel Aviv: Am Oved, 1996) [Hebrew].

123. Much has been written on the complex identification of Middle Eastern Jews in the pre-state and early state periods. See Sammy Smooha, *Israel: Pluralism and Conflict* (Berkeley: University of California Press, 1978); Shenhav, *The Arab Jews*, 49–76, 136–42; Khazzoom, *Shifting Ethnic Boundaries*.

124. Elron, "To Dance in Hebrew," 175, 181.

125. Jehoash Hirshberg, *Music in the Jewish Communities of Palestine, 1880–1948* (Oxford: Clarendon, 1995), 187–98.

126. According to Spiegel ("Cultural Production in Tel Aviv," 76), Yardena Cohen overcame her musicians' objection to wearing tunics by arguing that by doing so they would emulate the appearance of ancient musicians.

127. Dean MacCannell, *The Tourist: A New Theory of the Leisure Class* (New York: Schocken, 1976), 91–107.

128. Yosef Hayim Brenner, quoted in Hirschfeld, "To the East," 18; on Brenner's negative view of the Arabs, see also Shapira, *Land and Power*, 77–82.

129. Moshe Beilinson, "Rebelling against Reality," *Davar*, Spring 1929, reprinted in Naor, *The Second Aliyah*, 71–73 [Hebrew].

130. See Jonathan Frankel, "The 'Yizkor' Book of 1911: A Note on National Myths in the Second Aliya," in *Religion, Ideology and Nationalism in Europe and America: Essays Presented in Honor of Yehoshua Arieli* (Jerusalem: Historical Society of Israel, 1986), 370–72; Jacob Goldstein, *From Fighters to Soldiers: How the Israeli Defense Forces Began* (Portland: Sussex Academic Press, 1998), 101–4; Shapira, *Land and Power*, 71–73.

131. Israel Shohat, "*Ha-Shomer*" [The Guard], *Ha-Shomer Anthology*, 578; Spector, "Guarding the Galilee and Judea," *Ha-Shomer Anthology*, 11–12. Tsalel ("Memoir," *Ha-Shomer Anthology*, 191–213) recalls how what he had heard from the Bedouins later helped save his life. See also Goldstein, *The Shepherd Group*, 11–12; Saposnik, *Becoming Hebrew*, 183–84.

132. See Saposnik, *Becoming Hebrew*, 184. Gil Eyal discusses various hybrid Jewish-Arab identities in Gil Eyal, *The Disenchantment of the Orient: Expertise in Arab Affairs and the Israeli State* (Stanford: Stanford University Press, 2006).

133. Ruth Dayan claimed that Maskit "never pretended to create a national garment; but an Israeli garment . . . made of local materials, local knowledge and skills of the local people, and the local conditions of life." See Batia Donner, *Maskit: A Local Fabric* (Tel Aviv: Eretz Israel Museum, 2003), English section, 7–8.

134. Finy Leitersdorf joined Maskit soon after its establishment and was its lead fashion designer. She designed her first desert coat in 1955 and continued to design different versions of that coat in the following decades. See Donner, *Maskit*, 18, 82–83; and the catalog of an exhibit in Leitersdorf's honor, *Finy Leitersdorf: An Israeli Fashion Designer* (Tel Aviv: Tel Aviv Museum), 1983 [Hebrew].

135. Hadas Sho'ef, "Ben-Yosef and the Dress of Many Colors," *Xnet*, fashion section, May 13, 2011, http://xnet.ynet.co.il/fashion/articles/0,14539,L-3082528,00.html, accessed June 21, 2016 [Hebrew]; Itai Ya'acov, "Farewell from Rosie Ben-Yosef," *Nrg*, fashion section, May 30, 2008, http://www.nrg.co.il/online/55/ART1/738/763.html, accessed June 21, 2016 [Hebrew]. Ben-Yosef's Rikma company and Maskit faced economic challenges due to changes in the textile industry. Rikma was sold in the 1980s and Maskit was first sold to private investors, then closed in 1994. See Donner, *Maskit*, 60.

136. See Ya'ara Kedar's photo review, "Ten Phases in the *Kaffiyeh* Fashion," in *Nrg*, October 29, 2011, http://www.nrg.co.il/online/55/ART2/299/208.html, accessed June 23, 2016 [Hebrew]; "The *Tallit* Which Is Entirely *Kaffiyeh*: 'Threeasfour' for Peace in the Middle East," *Nrg*, September 19, 2011, http://www.nrg.co.il/online/55/ART2/287/917.html, accessed June 23, 2016 [Hebrew]. The *galabiya* designed by Dorit (Dodo) Bar Or and her company, *Pas Pour Toi*, were displayed during Israeli Fashion Week in 2013. See Re'ut Inbar, *"My Heart Is in the East: You Must Have a Galabiya in the Closet,"* Fashion Forward, July 17, 2013, http://fashionforward.mako.co.il/trend/alert/57313, accessed June 23, 2016 [Hebrew]. See Bar Or's *kaffiyeh* dresses at http://www.dodobaror.com/, accessed June 23, 2016.

137. See Shachar Atwan, "Vacation in the Shop Window," *Ha'aretz*, fashion section, June 20, 2012, http://www.haaretz.co.il/gallery/fashion/collection-review/1.1735582, accessed June 23, 2016 [Hebrew]; Shachar Atwan, *"Maskit*: The Mythical Label Returns for a Second Round," *Ha'aretz*, November 15, 2013, http://www.haaretz.co.il/gallery/fashion/.premium-1.2163443, accessed June 23, 2016 [Hebrew]; Neri Avidan Sela, "Ruth Dayan and Sharon Tal in *Maskit*'s Studio: 'Manhattan's Women Wear the Desert Coats,'" *Xnet*, October 18, 2015, accessed June 23, 2016 [Hebrew].

138. The article *"Al Quds Elarabiay* Accuses: An Israeli Designer Judaized the *Kaffiyeh*," dated December 3, 2006, was found on the website of the Jerusalem Center for Public Affairs, http://www.jcpa.org/JCPA/, accessed September 24, 2007.

139. Significantly, these article headings are formulated as questions. See Liron Ohana, "What's Arab?" in *Saloona*, a women's website, http://saloona.co.il/blog/%D7%9E%D7%94%D7%A2%D7%A8%D7%91%D7%99/, October 30, 2015, accessed May 9, 2018 [Hebrew]; Itai Ya'acov, "Is the *Kaffiyeh* Ours? The Loaded Middle Eastern Item Returns to Israeli Fashion," *Xnet*, June 25, 2015, http://xnet.ynet.co.il/fashion/articles/0,14539,L-3109756,00.html [Hebrew]; and Revital Madar, "Mizrahi, Ashkenazi and Palestinian Wear *Galabiya*: Who Has the Right to Wear It?" *Ha'aretz*, June 5, 2015, http://www.haaretz.co.il/gallery/black-flag/.premium-1.2651120, accessed June 25, 2016 [Hebrew].

140. Ohana, "What's Arab?"

141. See interviews with designers and fashion experts in the articles cited above. Unlike other designers, Jennifer Kim expresses the view that the *kaffiyeh* is an icon of defiance with which she personally, as a transgender person, identifies. The Israeli Palestinian designer Naim Qasim objects to the description of these trends as a "local" style, which he considers to be a strategy to avoid attributing it to Arab culture. Ya'acov, "Is the *Kaffiyeh* Ours?"

142. Madar, "Mizrahi, Ashkenazi and Palestinian Wear *Galabiya*."

143. Zalmona, "To the East," 85. See for example Tsibi Geva's 1992 painting entitled "*kaffiyeh*," which he dedicated to the memory of Asim abu-Shaqra, an Israeli Palestinian artist who died of cancer in 1990 at the age of 29 (Zalmona and Manor-Friedman, "To the East," 169), and the discussion of Geva's *kaffiyeh*-inspired work in Bouarrouj, "The Way of the *Kaffiyeh*."

144. For the work of the designers Adi Gil, Ange Donhauser, and Gabi Asfour, see "First Impressions: Threeasfour," in *The Fashion Informer*, September 29, 2011, http://the-fashioninformer.typepad.com/informer/2011/09/first-impressions-threeasfour-.html, accessed June 25, 2016.

145. Fadi Eadat, "Not Only the Hummus: The *Kaffiyeh* Too Has Become Jewish," *Ha'aretz*, January 11, 2007, http://news.walla.co.il/item/1039036, accessed June 21, 2016 [Hebrew]; Ruth Eglash, "Heads Up! It's the New 'Israeli *Keffiyeh*,'" *Jerusalem Post*, January 29, 2010, http://www.jpost.com/Israel/Heads-up-Its-the-new-Israeli-keffiyeh, accessed June 23, 2016. A "Jewish *Kafiya/kufiya*" was offered for sale on eBay on October 13, 2007, and an advertisement claiming to be "introducing the First Ever Israeli Kaffiyeh!" was posted at http://shemspeed.com/introducing-the-first-ever-israeli-kaffiyeh/, on March 17, 2011, accessed June 25, 2016. See also Bouarrouj, "The Way of the *Kaffiyeh*."

146. See the special report by "The Committee to Empower the Heritage of Sephardic and Mizrahi Jews in the Education System," headed by the Israeli poet Erez Biton and submitted to the minister of education on June 29, 2016, http://edu.gov.il/owlHeb/Tichon/RefurmotHinoch/programs/Documents/bc.pdf [Hebrew]; see also Yarden Skop, "Education Panel Calls for Mandatory Study of Mizrahi Culture in Israeli Schools, Trips to Morocco," *Ha'aretz*, July 7, 2016 http://www.haaretz.com/israel-news/1.729574.

Chapter 3

1. Yigal Zalmona, "To the East," in Yigal Zalmona and Tamar Manor-Friedman, eds., *To the East: Orientalism in the Arts in Israel* [*Kadima: Ha-mizrah be-omanut yisrael*] (Jerusalem: The Israel Museum, 1998), 64 [Hebrew].

2. The Hebrew title of Judah Leman's film was "To New Life" [*Le-hayim hadashim*], but it was marketed abroad as *The Land of Promise* (in French, *Terre Promise*). See also Hillel Tryester, "'The Land of Promise' (1935): A Case Study in Zionist Film Propaganda," *Historical Journal of Film, Radio and Television* 15, 2 (1995): 187–217; Ruth Oren, "The Construction of Place: Propaganda and Utopian Space in Zionist Photography, 1898–1948," in *Devarim Aherim* 2 (1997): 13–31 [Hebrew].

3. Diana K. Davis, "Restoring Roman Nature: French Identity and North African Environmental History," in Diana K. Davis and Edmund Burke III, eds., *Environmental*

Imaginaries of the Middle East and North Africa (Athens: Ohio University Press, 2011), 60–86; Priya Satia, "A Rebellion of Technology: Development, Policing, and the British Arabian Imaginary," in Davis and Burke, *Environmental Imaginaries*, 23–59. Satia points out the dual images of the Iraqi landscape as, on the one hand, the Fertile Crescent and the cradle of civilization, but, on the other, "the archetypical wasteland, a barren desert of glaring sun and bleak horizons" (23). See also Timothy Mitchell, *Rule of Experts: Egypt, Techo-Politics, and Modernity* (Berkeley: University of California Press, 2002).

4.   Derek J. Penslar, "Is Zionism a Colonial Movement?" in Ethan B. Katz, Lisa Moses Leff, and Maud S. Mandel, eds., *Colonialism and the Jews* (Bloomington: Indiana University Press, 2017), 291, 275–300 passim. I largely agree with Penslar's main arguments about the impact of Western colonialist discourse and practices during the pre-state period as well as the critical differences in ideology, political status, and power relations as compared to classical modes of European colonialism in the pre-1948 period.

5.   See Yosef Gorny, *Zionism and the Arabs, 1882–1948: A Study of Ideology* (Oxford: Oxford University Press, 1987), 30–33; Derek J. Penslar, *Zionism and Technocracy: The Engineering of Jewish Settlement in Palestine, 1870–1918* (Bloomington: Indiana University Press, 1991), 42, 47–52; and Yigal Schwartz, *The Zionist Paradox: Hebrew Literature and Israeli Identity* (Waltham, MA: Brandeis University Press, 2014), 49–96.

6.   David Ben-Gurion and Yitzhak Ben-Zvi, *The Land of Israel in the Past and at Present* [*Eretz yisrael be-avar uva-hove*] [Yiddish, 1918] (Jerusalem: Yad Ben-Zvi, 1979), 151, 158 [Hebrew].

7.   Leah Temper, "Creating Facts on the Ground: Agriculture in Israel and Palestine (1882–2000)," *Historia Agraria* 48, 1 (2009): 75–110 (79 in particular); Shaul Katz, "The First Furrow: Ideology, Settlement and Agriculture in Petach Tikva during Its First Ten Years", *Katedra* 23 (April 1982): 57–122 [Hebrew]; Nahum Karlinsky, *Citrus Blossoms: Jewish Entrepreneurship in Palestine, 1890–1939* (Jerusalem: Magnes Press, 2000), 116 [Hebrew]; Penslar, *Zionism and Technocracy*, 123.

8.   Beshara Doumani, *Rediscovering Palestine: Merchants and Peasants in Jabal Nablus, 1700–1900* (Berkeley: University of California Press, 1995), 95–181.

9.   The area planted in citrus groves increased from around 1,650 acres (6,600 dunams) in 1895 to around 7,555 acres (30,000 dumans) in 1915. See James Reilly, "The Peasantry of Late Ottoman Palestine," *Journal of Palestine Studies* 10, 4 (1981): 85; Rashid Khalidi, *Palestinian Identity: The Construction of Modern National Consciousness* (New York: Columbia University Press, 1997), 97. Nahum Karlinsky provides a similar figure for the total area of citrus cultivation in 1920 (the war years had undermined further expansion): Karlinsky, *Citrus Blossoms*, 16–17. Hezi Amiur notes that at the beginning of the twentieth century, Jewish grain cultivation did not differ significantly from that of the Arab farmers: Amiur, *Mixed Farm and Smallholding in Zionist Settlement Thought* (Jerusalem: Zalman Shazar Center for Jewish History, 2016), 28 [Hebrew].

10.   Reilly, "The Peasantry of Late Ottoman Palestine"; Karlinsky, *Citrus Blossoms*, 10.

11.   See Alexander Scholch, "The Economic Development of Palestine, 1856–1882," *Journal of Palestine Studies* 10, 3 (1981): 35–58; Marwan R. Buheiry, "The Agricultural Exports of Southern Palestine, 1885–1914," *Journal of Palestine Studies* 10, 4 (1981): 61–81.

12.   William Gray Dossett, "New Growth in Ancestral Lands: Agricultural Development in Palestine, 1880–1948," PhD diss., University of Pennsylvania, 2016, 42–43, 88–89. See also Alan George, "'Making the Desert Bloom': A Myth Examined," *Journal of Palestine Studies* 8, 2 (1979): 88–100; Karlinsky, *Citrus Blossoms*, 10, 17; for Karlinsky's figures on the areas of the citrus groves cultivated by Jews and Arabs, see 65 and 103, respectively.

13.   See Abraham Granott, *A Land System in Palestine: History and Structure* (London: Eyre and Spottiswoode, 1952). Kenneth Stein notes that the total land area registered to Jewish ownership by the end of the British Mandate amounted to about 348,250 acres (1,393,531 dunams), though by May 15, 1948, it may have reached 500,000 acres (2 million dunams): Kenneth W. Stein, *The Land Question in Palestine, 1917–1939* (Chapel Hill: University of North Carolina Press, 1984), 226, 227n5.

14.   Khalidi, *Palestinian Identity*, 90–117. Khalidi argues that although they received some compensation, the displaced Arab peasants did not consider it adequate and objected to the loss of their homes and livelihoods as a result of the purchase of the land by Jews.

15.   Khalidi, *Palestinian Identity*, 100. Note that in contrast to Khalidi's positive assessment of the First Aliyah's employment of Arabs from the Palestinians' perspective, Anita Shapira emphasizes the Socialist Zionist workers' perspective in objecting to the *moshavot's* "quasi-colonial" character: Anita Shapira, *Israel: A History* (Waltham: Brandeis University Press, 2012), 47–52. See also Penslar, "Is Zionism a Colonial Movement?" 279.

16.   Hizky Shoham, "'Buy Local' or 'Buy Jewish'? Separatist Consumption in Interwar Palestine," *International Journal of Middle East Studies* 45, 3 (2013): 469–89.

17.   See Gershon Shafir, *Land, Labor and Origins of the Israeli Palestinian Conflict, 1882–1914* [updated version] (Berkeley: University of California Press, 1996).

18.   Karlinsky, *Citrus Blossoms*, 258–65.

19.   William Gray Dossett presents a critique of the broader Zionist claim that the Jewish settlement was responsible for agricultural growth in Palestine beyond its impact on citrus fruits: Dossett, "New Growth in Ancestral Lands, 42–43, 88–89. See also Alan George's earlier article, "'Making the Desert Bloom': A Myth Examined," 88–100.

20.   Gur Alroey, *An Unpromising Land: Jewish Migration to Palestine in the Early Twentieth Century* (Stanford: Stanford University Press, 2014), 116–17, 179.

21.   See Shapira, *Israel*, 112. Yaacov Shavit notes that Tel Aviv's population made up 39% of the entire Jewish population of Palestine by 1939: Yaacov Shavit, "Telling the Story of a Hebrew City," in Maoz Azaryahu and S. Ilan Troen, eds., *Tel Aviv: The First Century* (Bloomington: Indiana University Press, 2012), 9.

22.   Karlinksy, *Citrus Blossoms*, 6–7. Karlinsky also notes that in 1936, 77% of the Jews who were engaged in agriculture (76,000 out of 98,000) lived in settlements on privately owned land; Amiur's study, *Mixed Farm*, focuses on the private farms.

23.   Yoram Bar-Gal, *An Agent of Zionist Propaganda: The Jewish National Fund 1924–47* (Haifa: Haifa University Press and Zmora Bitan, 1999) [Hebrew]; Ruth Oren, "The Construction of Place"; Dalia Manor, *Art in Zion: The Genesis of Modern National Art in Palestine* (London: Routledge, 2005), 94–97; Maoz Azaryahu, "The Water Towers in the

Zionist Commemorative Landscape: Negba, Yad Mordechai, and Be'erot Yitzhak," *Katedra* 79 (1996): 160–73 [Hebrew].

24. The song, *Shuru, habitu u-re'u*, was written and composed by Zalman Chen in the mid-1930s. For the lyrics, see "Zemereshet," a website of Hebrew songs, at http://www.zemereshet.co.il/song.asp?id=134, accessed January 9, 2017 [Hebrew].

25. Yehudah Grazovsky, "Hiking in the Mountains" [1937/8], reprinted in A. Gondelman and Y. Gefen, eds., *From Dan to Beer Sheva: A Reader for the Study of the Homeland [Moledet] for the Fourth and Fifth Grades* (Tel Aviv: Am Oved, 1945), 16–17 [Hebrew].

26. Yosef Weitz, "Herzliya," in Gondelman and Gefen, *From Dan to Beer Sheva*, 106; A. Braverman, "The Hefer Valley," in Gondelman and Gefen, *From Dan to Beer Sheva*, 107–8.

27. Michael Deshe, "Our Negev," reprinted in Natan Persky, ed., *Israel's Reader [Mikra'ot yisrael] for the Sixth Grade* (Ramat-Gan: Masada, 1977), 59 [Hebrew].

28. S. Yizhar, *On the Edge of the Negev [Be-fa'atei negev]*, [1945] (Tel Aviv: Hakibbutz Hameuchad, 1978), 134–35 [Hebrew].

29. Eliezer Smoli, *Frontiersmen of Israel [Anshei bereshit]* [1933] (Tel Aviv: Am Oved, 1973) [Hebrew]; English translation by Murray Roston, *Frontiersmen of Israel* (Tel Aviv: Masada, 1964), 17 (emphasis added). References are to the English translation unless otherwise noted. It is interesting to compare Smoli's reference to the Garden of Eden with a similar allusion to the Jewish colony Rosh Pina in Nechama Pohachevsky, "From Rishon Le-Zion to Marge Ayun" [1908], reprinted in Yaffa Berlovitz, ed., *Wandering in the Land: Travels by Members of the First Aliyah [E'ebra na ba-aretz]* (Tel Aviv: Defense Ministry Press, 1992), 307 [Hebrew].

30. Smoli, *Frontiersmen of Israel*, 20 (emphasis added).

31. The Hebrew expression used in the original text is *midbar-shemama*: Smoli, *Frontiersmen of Israel [Anshei bereshit]*, 184.

32. See George L. Mosse, *Fallen Soldiers: Reshaping the Memory of the World Wars* (New York: Oxford University Press, 1990), 107–25. For a more extensive discussion of these themes, see Yael Zerubavel, "The Forest as a National Icon: Literature, Politics, and the Archeology of Memory," *Israel Studies* 1, 1 (Spring 1996): 60–99.

33. Herzl's cypress (mistakenly identified earlier as a cedar) became a pilgrimage site and inspired artistic works, and although the original tree was chopped down during World War I, iconic "Herzl's cypresses" have been planted to represent its continuity. See Itzik Shweiki, "The Cypress Rejoiced over You, The Cedars of Lebanon," in *Et-Mol* 233 (2014): 12–14, https://www.ybz.org.il/_Uploads/dbsArticles/etmol233_12_14.pdf, accessed January 20, 2017 [Hebrew]. See also Alec Mishori, *Lo and Behold: Zionist Icons and Visual Symbols in Israeli Culture [Shuru, habitu, u-re'u]* (Tel Aviv: Am Oved, 2000), 256–60 [Hebrew].

34. Doron Bar, "To Where Shall We Turn on *Yom Ha-Shoah?* The 'Martyrs' Forest' and Doubts about the Memorialization of the Holocaust," *Katedra* 140 (2011): 103–30 [Hebrew]. The memorial function of trees as embodying the dead was spelled out to schoolchildren, reminding them that "you are not planting trees but people"; see Nahum Vermel and Baruch Ben-Yehuda, eds., *Youth's Parties on Sabbath and Holiday Eves, for Schools and Youth Movements* (Jerusalem: Masada, 1957), 140 [Hebrew].

35. See photos reproduced in Zerubavel, "The Forest as a National Icon," 61, 63.

36. See Avraham Granott, "Jewish Afforestation Policy in Palestine," *In the Building*

Field [Bi-sedot ha-binyan] (Jerusalem: Mosad Bialik, 1951), 162–78 [Hebrew]; Zerubavel, "The Forest as a National Icon"; Nili Liphschitz and Gideon Biger, "Afforestation Policy of the Zionist Movement in Eretz Israel, 1895–1948," *Katedra* 80 (1996): 88–108 [Hebrew]; Nili Liphschitz and Gideon Biger, "Afforestation Policy of the British Mandatory Authority in Palestine," *Ofakim Be-Geographia* 40–41 (1994): 5–16 [Hebrew].

37. Liphschitz and Biger, "Afforestation Policy"; see also Davis, "Restoring Roman Nature," 70–74; Jeannie Sowers, "Remapping the Nation, Critique of the State: Environmental Narratives and Desert Land Reclamation in Egypt," in Davis and Burke, *Environmental Imaginaries*, 159; Shaul E. Cohen, *The Politics of Planting: Jewish-Palestinian Competition for Control of Land in the Jerusalem Periphery* (Chicago: University of Chicago Press, 1993).

38. Shoshana Sitton, *National Education: The Educational Plan of the Teachers' Council for the Jewish National Fund, 1925–53 [Hinukh be-ru'ah ha-moledet]* (Tel Aviv: Tel Aviv University Press, 1998) [Hebrew]; Bar-Gal, *An Agent of Zionist Propaganda*, 173–212.

39. Similarly, a shift in the Israeli commemoration of the Bar Kokhba revolt from the fast day of Tish'a Be-Av to the festive holiday of Lag Ba-Omer transformed the meaning of the holiday and the memory of the revolt. See Yael Zerubavel, *Recovered Roots: Collective Memory and the Making of Israeli National Tradition* (Chicago: University of Chicago Press, 1995), 48–59, 96–113.

40. Moti Zeira, *We are Torn: Rural Collective Settlement and Jewish Culture in Eretz Israel during the 1920s [Keru'im anu]* (Jerusalem: Yad Ben-Zvi, 2002), 228–32 [Hebrew]; Hizki Shoham, *Israel Celebrates: Jewish Holidays and Civic Culture in Israel* (Leiden: Brill, 2017), 64–116. Planting trees as a Tu Bishvat ritual has persisted in Israeli culture, and ceremonies are held in local communities and schools; Jewish politicians are often photographed planting a tree during this festival.

41. On the analogy between trees and children, see Tsili Doleve-Gandelman, "The Symbolic Inscription of Zionist Ideology in the Space of Eretz Yisrael: Why the Native Israeli Is Called Tsabar," in Harvey E. Goldberg, ed., *Judaism Viewed from Within and from Without* (Albany: SUNY, 1987), 260, 265–77. This theme is central to the popular Tu Bishvat story by Levin Kipnis, "The Almond Tree's Birthday," *Gilyonot* 1 (1930): 25–27 [Hebrew]. The practice of naming children after trees and flowers articulates this symbolic link. See also Mishori, *Lo and Behold*, 261–77.

42. Davis and Burke, *Environmental Imaginaries*; Mitchell, *Rule of Experts*; Michael Adas, *Machines as the Measure of Men: Science, Technology, and Ideologies of Western Dominance* (Ithaca: Cornell University Press, 1989). On the cult of "Man the Machine" in revolutionary Russia, see Richard Stites, *Revolutionary Dream: Utopian Vision and Experimental Life in the Russian Revolution* (New York: Oxford University Press, 1989), 145–64.

43. For an extensive discussion of experts in the work of the Palestine Land Development Company and its training farms, see Penslar, *Zionism and Technocracy*, 97–127. On the role of experts and technology, see also Karlinsky, *Citrus Blossoms*, 142–97; Amiur, *Mixed Farm*, 73–144; Shaul Katz, "On the Technological History of Palestine in the Late Ottoman Period: Three Case Studies," in Israel Bartal, ed., *The Second Aliyah: Studies* (Jerusalem: Yad Ben-Zvi, 1997), 189–212 [Hebrew]. See also the unique case of Hannah Meisel, who received her PhD in France in 1909 and established the Young Women's Farm in Kinneret in 1911.

44.   Ziva Galili, "Zionism in the Early Soviet State: Between Legality and Persecution," in Zvi Gitelman and Yaacov Ro'i, eds., *Revolution, Repression, and Revival: The Soviet Jewish Experience* (New York: Rowman & Littlefield Publishers, 2007), 37–67. For the influence of Soviet education on Hebrew culture and especially on the kibbutz movement, see Rena Peled, *The "New Man" of the Zionist Revolution: Ha-Shomer Ha-Tsa'ir and Its European Roots* (Tel Aviv: Am Oved, 2002), 189–93, 200–16 [Hebrew]. See also the catalog exhibit curated by Batia Donner, *Propaganda and Vision—Soviet-Israeli Art 1930–1955* (Jerusalem: Israel Museum, 1997) [Hebrew].

45.   For the song *Shuru, habitu u-re'u*, see note 24.

46.   Eric Zakim, *To Build and Be Built: Landscape, Literature and the Construction of Zionist Identity* (Philadelphia: University of Pennsylvania Press, 2006), 151–80; Hadas Yaron, *Zionist Arabesques: Modern Landscapes, Non-Modern Texts* (Boston: Academic Press, 2010), 54–56; Tali Tadmor-Shimoni, *National Education and Formation of State in Israel* [*Shi'ur moledet*] (Ben-Gurion Research Institute and Ben-Gurion University Press, 2010), 215–21 [Hebrew]. See also Derek J. Penslar, "Zionism, Colonialism, and Postcolonialism," in Anita Shapira and Derek J. Penslar, eds., *Israeli Historical Revisionism from Left to Right* (London: Frank Cass, 2003), 92.

47.   Nathan Alterman, "The Road Song" [1934], reprinted in Yoram Tehar-Lev and Mordechai Naor, eds., *The Stories Behind the Songs* [*Shiru, habitu u-re'u*] (Tel Aviv: Defense Ministry Press, 1992), 20 [Hebrew]; melody by Daniel Sambursky. The song was featured in the 1935 Judah Leman film *The Land of Promise* (see note 2).

48.   Lea Goldberg, "The Port Song" [1936], reprinted in Tehar-Lev and Naor, *The Stories Behind the Songs*, 32–33.

49.   Like "The Road Song," Nathan Alterman's "Morning Song" (also known by its first verse, *Be-harim kevar ha-shemesh melahetet*), with a melody by Daniel Sambursky, was featured in Leman's film *The Land of Promise*. For further discussion, see also Zakim, *To Build and Be Built*, 169–75.

50.   Motti Regev and Edwin Seroussi, *Popular Music and National Culture in Israel* (Berkeley: University of California Press, 2004), 49–70.

51.   Yael Raviv, *Falafel Nation: Cuisine and the Making of National Identity in Israel* (Lincoln, Nebraska: University of Nebraska Press, 2015), 52–59, quote on p. 55; Shoham, "'Buy Local' or 'Buy Jewish'?"

52.   Yoram Bar-Gal, *Moledet and Geography in a Hundred Years of Zionist Education* (Tel Aviv: Am Oved, 1993) [Hebrew]; Ruth Firer, *The Agents of Zionist Education* (Tel Aviv: Sifriyat Hapoalim, 1985), 152–63 [Hebrew]; Yuval Dror, *National Education through Mutually Supportive Devices: The Zionist Story* [*Kelim sheluvim ba-hinukh ha-leumi*] (Jerusalem: Magnes Press, 2008), 51–62 [Hebrew]; Tadmor-Shimoni, *National Education and Formation of State*, 84–108.

53.   Bar-Gal, *Moledet and Geography*, 49–98; Dror, *National Education*, 63–76; Tadmor-Shimoni, *National Education and Formation of State*, 63–108.

54.   Michel de Certeau refers to the use of the synecdoche as a common spatial practice in Michel de Certeau, *The Practice of Everyday Life*, trans. Steven Rendall (Berkeley: University of California Press, 1984), 101.

55. Maoz Azaryahu, *Tel Aviv—The Real City: A Historical Mythography* (Sde Boker: Ben-Gurion Research Institute and Ben-Gurion University Press, 2005), 37, 55–64 [Hebrew]. See also Sharon Rotbard, *White City, Black City* (Tel Aviv: Bavel, 2005) [Hebrew].

56. Yitzhak Ben-Zvi, in *The Conquest of the Desert: Catalog for an International Exhibition and Fair [Kibush ha-shemama]* (Jerusalem [no press], 1953), bilingual English/Hebrew edition; quote from English section, p. 7 (emphasis added).

57. Quoted in Bar-Gal, *Moledet and Geography*, 129.

58. Rachel Yanait Ben-Zvi, "From Ha-Shomer Days," in *Ha-Shomer Anthology [Kovetz Ha-Shomer]* [1937] (Tel Aviv: Labor Archive, 1947), 562 [Hebrew].

59. Dvora Baron, "Chronicles," in Y. Aricha, ed., *Tel Aviv: A Historical and Literary Anthology* (Tel Aviv, 1959), 55; and Uri Kesari, "There Are Still Jackals in Tel Aviv," *Do'ar Ha-Yom* (December 5, 1934), 3; quoted in Azaryahu, *Tel Aviv—The Real City*, 59 and 60 respectively.

60. Azaryahu, *Tel Aviv—The Real City*, 60.

61. Azaryahu, *Tel Aviv—The Real City*; Yaacov Shavit notes that Tel Aviv remained dependent on Jaffa for many years, in Yaacov Shavit, "Telling the Story of a Hebrew City," in Azaryahu and Troen, *Tel Aviv: The First Century*, 3–12. For studies of the history of Tel Aviv and its evolving relations with Jaffa, see Rotbard, *White City, Black City*, 78–128; Mark Levine, *Overthrowing Geography: Jaffa, Tel Aviv, and the Struggle for Palestine*, 1880–1948 (Berkeley: University of California Press, 2005), 126–32; and Hizky Shoham, "Tel Aviv's Foundation Myth: A Constructive Perspective," in Azaryahu and Troen, *Tel Aviv: The First Century*, 34–59. On Tel Aviv's Hebrew culture, see Anat Helman, *Young Tel Aviv: A Tale of Two Cities* (Waltham: Brandeis University Press, 2010); and Barbara E. Mann, *A Place in History: Modernism, Tel Aviv, and the Creation of Jewish Urban Space* (Stanford: Stanford University Press, 2006).

62. Rotbard, *White City, Black City*, 83–84; Shoham, "Tel Aviv's Foundation Myth," 35.

63. See Eviatar Zerubavel's discussion of relevance and irrelevance in *Hidden in Plain Sight: The Social Structure of Irrelevance* (Oxford: Oxford University Press, 2015), 49–93 (for "tunnel vision," see p. 75).

64. Israel Bartal makes this observation based on his study of Zionist anthologies published in the 1920s through the 1960s in Bartal, "The Ingathering of Traditions: Zionism's Anthology Projects," *Prooftext* 17 (1997): 82–83. Amos Ron similarly observes the remarkable absence of Arabs in settlement museums, with the exception of references to Jewish casualties, in Ron, "Representational and Symbolic Landscapes of the Early Zionist Rural Settlement in the Kinneret (Sea of Galilee) Valley," PhD diss. (Jerusalem: The Hebrew University, 2002), 195, 212–17 [Hebrew].

65. Yechiel Halperin, in a letter about the writing of a monograph on Merhavia, the first Jewish settlement in the Jezreel Valley, in the Central Zionist Archives, KKLS 2/2487; quoted in Yoram Bar-Gal, "Landscape Representations of the Land of Israel in the Jewish National Fund's Propaganda during the Yishuv period," *Motar* 11 (2003–4): 25 [Hebrew].

66. See Ellah Shohat, *Israeli Cinema: East/West and the Politics of Representation* (Austin: University of Texas Press, 1989), 27–38; Ariel L. Feldstein, *Pioneer, Toil, Camera: Cinema in the Service of the Zionist Ideology, 1917–39* (Tel Aviv: Am Oved, 2009), 109–10, 134, 152

[Hebrew]; Manor, *Art in Zion*, 123–25; Graciela Trajtenberg, *Between Nationalism and Art: The Construction of the Israeli Field of Art during the Yishuv Period and the State's Years* (Jerusalem: Magnes Press, 2005), 211–13 [Hebrew].

67. Ruth Oren, "The Construction of Place"; Tryester, "'The Land of Promise.'" However, Tryester also quotes a different view, from a memorandum by Elias M. Epstein of the JNF, suggesting that there was no harm in showing the Arab presence in the country (190).

68. Theodor Herzl, *Old New Land* [Altneuland] (New York: Block Publishing Company & Herzl Press, 1960), 47 (emphasis added).

69. Ahad Ha'am, "All in All" [*Sach ha-kol*], *Ha-Shelah* 26, 3 (Spring 1912), may be found in the digitized archive of classics of Hebrew literature, "Ben-Yehuda Project," http://benye huda.org/ginzberg/Gnz_127.html, accessed January 20, 2017 [Hebrew] (emphasis added).

70. Moshe Tzusmer, *Geography* (Frankfurt: Omanut, 1918) [Hebrew], quoted in Yoram Bar-Gal, "From 'European Oasis' to Downtown New York: The Image of Tel Aviv in School Textbooks," in Azaryahu and Troen, *Tel Aviv: The First Century*, 63.

71. Aharon Ever Hadani, quoted in Yossi Ben-Artzi, "The Development of the First-Aliyah Colonies and the Establishment of New Colonies in the Second Aliyah Period," in Bartal, *The Second Aliyah: Studies*, 168.

72. Quoted in Yaron, *Zionist Arabesques*, 89; Avraham Negev, "The First Years in the Negev," *Ariel* 152–53 (2002): 205–6 [Hebrew].

73. On the analogy between the sea and the desert as contrasting with the settlement, see my discussion of the term *yishuv* in the introduction. See also Harold Fisch, *Remembered Future: A Study in Literary Mythology* (Bloomington: Indiana University Press, 1984), 132; and Abraham Melamed, *On a Desert Island: A History of a Motif in Jewish Thought* (Tel Aviv: Resling, 2012), 33 [Hebrew].

74. For further discussion of the symbolic meaning of the island, see Melamed, *On a Desert Island*, 10–12, 22–23.

75. Moshe Smilansky in his *Memoirs* [1935], quoted in Yaffa Berlovitz, ed., *Inventing a Land, Inventing a People: The Literature of the First Aliyah* (Tel Aviv: Hakibbutz Hameuchad, 1996), 280n22 [Hebrew].

76. Smoli, *Frontiersmen of Israel*, 60. The European Jewish settlers are also described as people who had reached an isolated island in the sea in Yehuda Ya'ari, "As Light Shines" [*Ka-or yahel*, 1936], reprinted in *Yehuda Ya'ari's Stories* (Jerusalem: The Association of Hebrew Writers, 1969), I: 215 [Hebrew]. For a different interpretation of Defoe's work at the time, see Schwartz's discussion (*The Zionist Paradox*, 104–6) of Yosef Louidor's 1921 review of Defoe's book.

77. Amos Oz, "Before His Time," trans. Gavriel Moss, in Robert Alter, ed., *Modern Hebrew Literature* (West Orange: Behrman Books, 1975), 348.

78. Smoli, *Frontiersmen of Israel* [*Anshei bereshit*], 13; note that the English edition (11) refers to foxes.

79. Hamutal Bar-Yosef, "The Jackals," *Ma'ariv*, May 5, 2002, 27 [Hebrew]. Nahum Gutman's illustration for Lea Goldberg's lullaby, written for the children of kibbutz Afikim in 1936, depicts a lighted home in which children and sheep cuddle together, engulfed by the darkness outside. See Michal Sadan, *The Hebrew Shepherd: Transformation of Image and*

Symbol from Hebrew Enlightenment Literature to the New Hebrew Culture in Israel (Jerusalem: Yad Ben-Zvi, 2011), 124 [Hebrew].

80.   Roderick Nash, *Wilderness and the American Mind*, 3rd ed. (New Haven: Yale University Press, 1982), 35.

81.   Shaul Katz notes that the early settlers of Petach Tikvah followed the model of building the houses on the outskirts of the settlement and keeping the public area protected within it: Shaul Katz, "The First Furrow: Ideology, Settlement and Agriculture in Petach Tikvah during Its First Ten Years", *Katedra* 23 (April 1982): 85 [Hebrew]. Tel Hai, the small outpost in the northern Galilee that was surrounded by a wall, was among the exceptions at the time.

82.   S. Ilan Troen, *Imagining Zion: Dreams, Designs, and Realities in a Century of Jewish Settlement* (New Haven: Yale University Press, 2003), 64.

83.   Quoted in Gorny, *Zionism and the Arabs*, 166. See his discussion of Jabotinsky's views, 164–74.

84.   Ian Lustick and Avi Shlaim argue that over time, Jabotinsky's approach in "On the Iron Wall" gained influence, yet his Revisionist Zionist followers misunderstood his metaphoric reference to "the iron wall." Ian Lustick, "To Build and to Be Built By: Israel and the Hidden Logic of the Iron Wall," *Israel Studies* 1, 1 (Spring 1996): 196–223; Avi Shlaim, *The Iron Wall: Israel and the Arab World*, 2nd ed. (New York: W. W. Norton, 2014), 13–17. In a school play, a *halutz* character conveys a similar view of the ethos of settlement and defense: "I will revive the desolate land / For the sake of the homeland / I will erect a wall in my own hands / A wall of cement and steel." Mila Ohel, "The Maccabees' Spinning Top [*sevivon*]," in *Hanukkah Plays for Children* (Jerusalem: Jewish National Fund, 1955), 14 [Hebrew]

85.   See Troen's chapter "The Village as Military Outpost" in Troen, *Imagining Zion*, 62–82, and his quotation of Moshe Sharett, the head of the political department of the Jewish Agency at the time: "From the political point of view, I know of no more pressing tasks, no more effective weapon, than founding settlements in [border] areas, and thereby creating facts" (69).

86.   Elchanan Orren, "The Security-Settlement Assault of 1936–1939," in Mordechai Naor, ed., *The Tower-and-Stockade Period, 1936–39* (Jerusalem: Yad Ben-Zvi, 1987), 13–34 [Hebrew]; Troen, *Imagining Zion*, 69–73; Ruth Kark, *Pioneering Jewish Settlement in the Negev 1880–1948* [1974] (Jerusalem: Ariel, 2002), 124 [Hebrew]. For a full list of the settlements built between 1936 and 1939, see Naor, *The Tower-and-Stockade Period*, 205–26; see also Tamar Katriel and Aliza Shenhar, "Tower and Stockade: Dialogic Narration in Israeli Settlement Ethos," *Quarterly Journal of Speech* 76, 4 (1990): 359–380.

87.   On the worker-warrior of the Palmach, see Uri Ben-Eliezer, *The Emergence of Israeli Militarism 1936–1956* [*Derekh ha-kavenet*] (Tel Aviv: Dvir, 1995), 86–94 [Hebrew].

88.   *NAHAL* is an acronym for *No'ar Halutzi Lohem*, i.e. "Pioneering Combat Youth," and it combines military service with a settlement mission. Established by a 1949 law regarding military service, *NAHAL* contributed to the frontier settlement mission and received the 1984 Israel Prize for outstanding contributions to Israeli society. See Dvorah Hacohen, "Israel Defense Forces and the Absorption of Immigrants," in Mordechai Naor, ed., *Immigrants and Transit Camps, 1948–52* [*Olim u-ma'abarot*] (Jerusalem: Yad Ben-Zvi, 1987), 120–21

[Hebrew]; and Stuart A. Cohen, *Israel and Its Army: From Cohesion to Confusion* (London: Routledge, 2008), 32, 95.

89. The tents appear similar to those used by the *halutzim* and may connect the almost barren hill with the early transitional period, still close to the representation of the symbolic desert.

90. J. B. Jackson, "The Order of a Landscape," in Donald W. Meinig, ed., *The Interpretation of Ordinary Landscapes* (New York: Oxford University Press, 1979), 158–60. See also Neil Evernden, *The Social Construction of Nature* (Baltimore: Johns Hopkins University Press, 1992), 66.

91. Ze'ev Yavetz, "Wander in the Land [*Shut ba-aretz*]," [1891], reprinted in Berlovitz, *Wandering in the Land*, 117; see also Zalman David Levontin, "To Our Ancestral Land" [*Le-eretz avoteinu*] [1885], reprinted in Berlovitz, *Wandering in the Land*, 30–31.

92. A. G. Herschberg [1901], quoted in Ben-Artzi, "The Development of the First-Aliyah Colonies," 165.

93. Helman, *Young Tel Aviv*, 24–25. On the cultural significance of straight lines, see Dvora Eilon-Sireni, "In the Negev," in Nahum Gavrieli and Baruch Avivi, eds., *My New Reader for the Fifth Grade* (Tel Aviv: Yavneh, 1950), 41 [Hebrew]; Michael Chyutin, "The Biblical, the Jewish, the Hebrew, the Secular, the Canaanite, and the Converted," in *The Look of a Place: Four Approaches to Landscape Architecture in Israel* [*Mar'eh makom*] (Tel Aviv: Shreiber Art Gallery, Tel Aviv University, 1996), 27 [Hebrew]. See also the emphasis on planting tree saplings in straight lines in Shlomo Y. Schwartz [Shva], *New People in High Mountains* (Tel Aviv: Hakibbutz Hameuchad, 1953), 63, 97, 118 [Hebrew].

94. Aharon Ever Hadani, *The Arava Project* (*Mif'al ba-arava*) (Tel Aviv: Mitzpe, 1931), I:55, 87 [Hebrew].

95. Yaron, *Zionist Arabesques*, 29–31.

96. Michael Gluzman, *The Zionist Body: Nationalism, Gender and Sexuality in Modern Hebrew Literature* (Tel Aviv: Hakibbutz Hameuchad, 2007), 11–29 [Hebrew]; Meira Weiss, *The Chosen Body: The Politics of the Body in Israeli Society* (Stanford: Stanford University Press, 2002), 3–5, 18–21; Peled, *The "New Man" of the Zionist Revolution*, 117, 143.

97. Deborah S. Bernstein, ed., *Pioneers and Homemakers: Jewish Women in Pre-State Israel* (Albany: SUNY Press, 1992); Yossi Ben-Artzi, "Between Farmer and Laborer: Women in Early Jewish Settlements in Palestine, 1882–1914," in Yael Azmon, ed., *A View into the Lives of Women in Jewish Societies* (Jerusalem: Zalman Shazar Center for Jewish History, 1995), 309–24 [Hebrew].

98. For the influence of Soviet ideology on Hebrew culture and especially on the kibbutz movement, see Peled, *The "New Man" of the Zionist Revolution*, 189–93, 200–216; Batia Donner, *Propaganda and Vision—Soviet-Israeli Art*.

99. "The Network Song" [*Shir ha-reshet*] by Mordechai Zeira (1934) was a popular song. See "Zemereshet," http://www.zemereshet.co.il/song.asp?id=326, accessed August 6, 2014. On the broad implications of introducing a Jewish electric company, see Ronen Shamir, *Current Flow: The Electrification of Palestine* (Stanford: Stanford University Press, 2013).

100. Ever Hadani, *The Arava Project*.

101. The novel highlights the cultural significance attributed to materials. The engineer's strength is compared to cement, and the workers assert that "we are strong only when we become the nation of rock, iron, and cement" (Ever Hadani, *The Arava Project*, II: 13). For the pervasive use of war rhetoric against the desert in this work, see, for example, I: 38–42, II: 9, 49.

102. Shaked notes that the value of *The Arava Project* lies more in its documentation efforts than in its literary achievements: Gershon Shaked, "Build: Essays on the Settlement Novel between the Two World Wars," *Moznaim* 52, 5–6 (1981): 340–49 [Hebrew].

103. Aharon Megged, "The Abyss on the Way to Sodom," in Natan Persky, ed., *New Israel's Reader for the Sixth Grade* [*Mikra'ot yisrael hadashot*] (Ramat Gan: Masada, 1977), 53–57.

104. Gideon Ofrat points out the linguistic and cultural connections between the Hebrew terms *adama*, *adam*, and *dam* in his book by the same title, *Earth, Man, Blood: The Myth of the Pioneer and the Ritual of the Earth in Eretz-Israel Settlement Drama* (Tel Aviv: Gome/Tcherikover Press, 1980) [Hebrew]. See also Zakim, *To Build and Be Built*, 78–79.

105. Neumann, *Land and Desire*, 81–86. See also the discussion of the sexual connotations of the commemorative theme of red poppies growing out of the soil suffused with the dead hero's blood in Zerubavel, *Recovered Roots*, 90; and Schwartz, *The Zionist Paradox*, 116–24.

106. From Esther Raab's poem "To Father" (1929), quoted in Ehud Ben-Ezer, *Days of Gall and Honey: The Biography of the Poetess Ester Raab* [*Yemei la'ana u-devash*] (Tel Aviv: Am Oved, 1998), 38 [Hebrew] (emphasis added).

107. Mordechai Hadash, "Wandering and Doubts," in Yehuda Erez, ed., *The Third Aliyah Book* (Tel Aviv: Am Oved, 1964), II:802 [Hebrew] (emphasis added).

108. Quoted in Yaron, *Zionist Arabesques*, 86.

109. Moshe Smilansky, *In the Judean Vineyards* (Tel Aviv: Masada, 1954), 83, quoted in Berlovitz, *Inventing a Land*, 169; *The Conquest of the Mountain* (Jerusalem: Jewish National Fund, 1955/6), 53 [Hebrew].

110. See also Zali Gurevitch and Gideon Aram, "On *Makom*" [*Al ha-makom*], *Alpayim* 4 (1991): 9–44 [Hebrew].

111. Uri Cohen, "The Zionist Animal," *Jerusalem Studies in Hebrew Literature* 19 (2003): 192–93 [Hebrew]. A natural site in western Negev, *Hamukei Nitzana*, similarly alludes to the curves of the female body.

112. Ever Hadani, *The Arava Project*, I: 64 and II: 54. *Arava* refers to the desert territory stretching from the Dead Sea to Israel's southernmost city, Eilat.

113. Avraham Shlonsky, "Facing the Desert" [*Mul ha-yeshimon*] [1929], *Collected Poems* (Tel Aviv: Sifriyat Hapoalim, 1965), I: 311–17 [Hebrew].

114. In "Facing the Desert," Shlonsky similarly describes the jackals as observing the construction work from a distance. In Smoli's *Frontiersmen of Israel*, the Bedouins stand aside and watch Hermoni as he begins plowing the land, and Dan Miron notes that in Pesach Ginzburg's poem "The City of Sand" (1925), the Bedouins are surprised to discover a new city that has emerged out of the sand after a major storm, and escape to the desert: Dan Miron, *Founding Mothers, Stepsisters* (Tel Aviv: Hakibbutz Hameuchad, 1991), 189–90 [Hebrew].

115. The term *kibbush* was associated with overcoming a desire (*kibbush ha-yetzer*) or a negative emotion such as anger (*kibbush ha-ka'as*) and later became more closely associated with conquest by military force. See Avraham Even-Shoshan, *The New Dictionary* [*Ha-milon he-hadash*] (Jerusalem: Kiryat Sefer, 1988), II: 520 [Hebrew].

116. On the conquest of the mountain, see note 109; on the exhibit about the conquest of the desert, see note 56. See also David Benvenisti, *Teaching about the Conquest of the Mountain* (Jerusalem: Jewish National Fund, 1959) [Hebrew]; and see references to the conquest of the sea in David Ben-Gurion, "Going Down to the Sea" [1937], reprinted in Eran Kaplan and Derek J. Penslar, eds., *The Origins of Israel, 1882–1948: A Documentary History* (Madison: University of Wisconsin Press, 2011), 110–14; and Goldberg, "The Port Song." For the conquest of swamps, see Nahum Gavrieli, *Knowledge of the Homeland: A Textbook* (Tel Aviv: Omanut, 1934), 28 [Hebrew], and Bar-Gal, *Moledet and Geography*, 147–48.

117. *Ha-Shomer Anthology*, 51–55, 93–116, 284–86; Jacov Goldstein, *The Shepherd Group: The Idea of the Conquest of Shepherding during the Second Aliyah and Its Realization, 1907–1917* [*Havurat ha-ro'im*] (Tel Aviv: Defense Ministry Press, 1993) [Hebrew]. See also Shafir, *Land, Labor and Origins of the Israeli-Palestinian Conflict*, 45–90. For a discussion of the "conquest of Hebrew," see Yitzhak Avineri, *The Conquest of Hebrew in Our Generation* (Tel Aviv: Sifriyat Hapoalim, 1946) [Hebrew]; Arieh Bruce Saposnik, *Becoming Hebrew: The Creation of a Jewish National Culture in Ottoman Palestine* (Oxford: Oxford University Press, 2008), 213–36. On the conquest of the Hebrew press, see Jonathan M. Gribetz, *Defining Neighbors: Religion, Race, and the Early Zionist-Arab Encounter* (Princeton: Princeton University Press, 2014), 186–91.

118. Anita Shapira, *Land and Power: The Zionist Resort to Force, 1881–1948* [1992] (Stanford: Stanford University Press, 1999).

119. Chanina Porat, *From Wasteland to Inhabited Land: Land Purchase and Settlement in the Negev, 1930–1947* (Jerusalem: Yad Ben-Zvi & Ben-Gurion University Press, 1996), 103–9 [Hebrew].

120. Yisrael Betser, "The Shack in the Transjordan," in *Ha-Shomer Anthology*, 131 (emphasis added).

121. For the political controversies around the legacy of Yosef Trumpeldor, see Zerubavel, *Recovered Roots*, 91–95, 148–57. In the song "In the Galilee, in Tel Hai," written by Abba Hushi soon after the incident, Trumpeldor delivers his own message as constructed in the Socialist Zionist circles: "All day long I plowed / And at night I held the gun / Until the very end" (Zerubavel, *Recovered Roots*, 155).

122. Nash, *Wilderness and the American Mind*, 24–25.

123. Shmuel Dayan, "Here We'll Settle," in Z. Ariel, M. Blich, and N. Persky, eds., *Israel's Reader* [*Mikra'ot yisrael*] *for the Fourth Grade* (Jerusalem: Masada, 1958), 161–63 [Hebrew].

124. Yehudit Harari, "Among the Vineyards" [*Bein ha-keramim*] (Tel Aviv: Dvir, 1947), reprinted in Berlovitz, *Wandering in the Land*, 294–95.

125. Moshe Smilansky, "Batayha," reprinted in N. Gavrieli and Baruch Avivi, eds., *My New Book for the Fifth Grade* (Tel Aviv: Yavneh, 1950), 21 [Hebrew].

126. Shlomo Kodesh, *The Founders' Legend* [*Agadat ha-rishonim*]: *The War against the Desolation* (Jerusalem: The Jewish National Fund, 1971/2), 2 [Hebrew].

127.   Sandra M. Sufian, *Healing the Land and the Nation: Malaria and the Zionist Project in Palestine, 1920–1947* (Chicago: University of Chicago Press, 2007).

128.   S. Shaked, *This is My Homeland* (Tel Aviv: Yesod, 1962), 78, quoted in Bar-Gal, *Moledet and Geography*, 145.

129.   Zakim, *To Build and Be Built*, 54–90; quote on p. 83.

130.   For further discussion of these films, see Feldstein, *Pioneer, Toil, Camera*, 108–27, 133–38, 150–56.

131.   The song lyrics are based on a biblical verse (Isaiah 12:3) and the melody was composed by Emanuel [Pogatchov] Amiran. A dance created for this song was performed at the Dalia Dance Festival of 1944. See "Zemereshet," http://www.zemereshet.co.il/song.asp?id=348, accessed January 16, 2013 [Hebrew]; see also Judith Brin Ingber, "Shorashim," in Judith Brin Ingber, ed., *Seeing Israeli and Jewish Dance* (Detroit: Wayne State University Press, 2011), 110.

132.   Arye Yechieli, who was one of the founders of kibbutz Revivim, wrote the lyrics of the song "You, the Land" (*At adama*) and the melody is based on a Bedouin song. See "Zemereshet," http://zemer.co.il/song.asp?id=239, accessed August 21, 2012 [Hebrew]; Yosef Goldenberg, "The Hebrew Folksong: The Representation of the Desert in Israeli Folk Music," in Tuvia Friling, Gideon Katz, and Michael Wolpe, eds., *Music in Israel, Iyumin Bitkumat Israel*, Thematic Series 8 (2014), 286–87 [Hebrew].

133.   The lyrics of "Dunam Here and Dunam There," by Yehoshua Freedman, are overtly didactic: "I will tell you, girls / And you, boys / How the Land of Israel / Is redeemed. / Dunam here and dunam there / A clod after a clod of soil, / This is how the land is redeemed / From the North to the Negev." The melody was composed by Menashe Ravina. The first known recording of the song was in 1938. See "Zemereshet," http://www.zemer.co.il/song.asp?id=262, accessed August 27, 2013 [Hebrew].

134.   *The Conquest of the Mountain*, 37.

135.   The birth of the "first son" of a settlement was significant for the entire community and conferred a special status on the newborn. Uri, the canonical literary Sabra of Moshe Shamir's novel, is the first son of his kibbutz: Moshe Shamir, *He Walked through the Fields* [*Hu halakh ba-sadot*] [1947] (Tel Aviv: Am Oved, 1972) [Hebrew].

136.   Smoli, *Frontiersmen of Israel*, 65 (English edition). I have modified Roston's translation in order to more closely reflect the original Hebrew (*Anshei bereshit*, 57).

137.   Alroey, *An Unpromising Land*, 209–32. Alroey notes that between 1905 and 1907, emigration reached about 75% to 80% of those immigrating to the country, and in 1912 to 1914 that proportion dropped to around 51%. Anita Shapira (*Israel*, 112) notes that the emigration rate from Palestine equaled the immigration rate into Palestine during the economic crisis of 1928. The suicide rate was also high during that crisis.

138.   Aharon Ashman's 1942 play *This Land* was performed at the Habima Theater; Yitzhak Ben-Mordechai referred to it as "*Habima*'s first popular hit" in Ben-Mordechai, "Hadera's Sacred Land," *Mishkafayim* 31 (December 1997): 10–13 [Hebrew]; see also Ben-Ami Feingold, "Theater and Struggle: Hadera and 'This Land,'" in *Katedra* 74 (1994): 140–56 [Hebrew].

139. The film *Sabra* (also known as *Halutzim*), directed by Fred Aleksander, was filmed in Palestine and produced in Poland in 1933. See the Internet Movie Database (IMDb), https://www.imdb.com/title/tt0130234/, accessed April 26, 2018; J. Hoberman, "Aleksander Ford," *The YIVO Encyclopedia of Jews in Eastern Europe*, http://www.yivoencyclopedia.org/article.aspx/Ford_Aleksander, accessed April 26, 2018.

140. S. Y. Agnon, *Only Yesterday* [*Temol shilshom*] (Tel Aviv: Shocken, 1945) [Hebrew]; English translation by Barbara Harshav (Princeton: Princeton University Press, 2000), 91–92.

141. See also Feldstein, *Pioneer, Toil, Camera*, 111.

142. Smoli, *Frontiersmen of Israel*, 214 (Hebrew) and 249 (English translation) (emphasis added). I have modified the English translation of the last sentence to reflect more closely the original phrase: "*aleinu le-hat'hil tamid mi-bereshit*" ("we should always begin from the beginning"). Roston's translation—"Everything has to have a beginning"—loses the first person plural and the ambiguity of the original Hebrew, which alludes to the possibility of a cyclical return to the beginning.

143. See my discussion of story boundaries in reference to the commemoration of the battle of Tel Hai in March 1, 1920 and the Bar Kokhba revolt in *Recovered Roots*, 39–47 and 48–56, respectively , and 221–28.

144. Alexander Zeid immigrated to Palestine in 1904 as a seventeen-year-old. He was among the founding members of the *Bar-Giora* and *Ha-Shomer* organizations and among the founders of kibbutz Kfar Giladi in 1916. Zeid left the kibbutz in 1926 to become a JNF ranger and built a farm in Sheikh Abrek. He was killed in 1938, after having survived earlier attacks on his life. A statue depicting Zeid on horseback was placed on top of "Zeid Hill," overlooking the area: Israel Bartal, "Alexander Zeid," in Zeev Tzahor, ed., *The Second Aliyah: Biographies* (Jerusalem: Yad Ben-Zvi, 1997), 168–70 [Hebrew].

145. *Davar*, January 10, 1936, published an article on "Mosad Bialik's literary prizes" [*Ha-perasim shel mosad bialik*], which can be found in the digitized archive of Jewish Press, http://jpress.org.il/, accessed August 2, 2014 [Hebrew].

146. *The Conquest of the Desert: Catalog for an International Exhibition and Fair* (see note 56). See also Ofira Gruweis-Kovalsky and Yossi Katz, " 'The Conquest of the Desert' Exhibit: The First International Exhibition in Jerusalem, 1953," *Israel* 20 (2012): 153–80 [Hebrew].

147. *The Conquest of the Desert*, 16, 90.

148. *The Conquest of the Desert* catalog features greetings from international organizations, among them UNESCO, the Food and Agriculture Organization, the World Health Organization, the International Labor Organization, and the World Meteorological Organization. It also refers to symposia and cultural events organized along with the exhibit.

149. See also Gruweis-Kovalsky and Katz, "The 'Conquest of the Desert' Exhibit," 156–60, 168–70. A cartoon by Dosh in the daily *Ma'ariv* (September 2, 1953, 4) features the character Srulik, Dosh's iconic representation of the young state of Israel, extending the flower-like exhibit logo to Uncle Sam, who turns up his nose in disapproval.

150. Gruweis-Kovalsky and Katz, "The 'Conquest of the Desert' Exhibit," 160, 179–80.

Chapter 4

1.   Ruth Kark, *Pioneering Jewish Settlement in the Negev 1880–1948* [1974] (Jerusalem: Ariel, 2002), 181–83 [Hebrew]; Chanina Porat, *From Wasteland to Inhabited Land: Land Purchase and Settlement in the Negev, 1930–1947* (Jerusalem: Yad Ben-Zvi, 1996), 205–6 [Hebrew].

2.   Shemaryahu Talmon, "The 'Desert Motif' in the Bible and Qumran Literature," in Alexander Altman, ed., *Biblical Motifs: Origins and Transformations* (Cambridge, MA: Harvard University Press, 1966), 39–42.

3.   "Negev," *Encyclopaedia Britannica*, https://www.britannica.com/place/Negev, accessed January 30, 2017; Yoel Dan, "The Negev Lands," *Ariel* 152–53 (June 2002): 51–58 [Hebrew]. On the conflicting definitions of the Negev and the historical construction of its boundaries, see Gideon Biger, "The Negev—Boundaries and Territory," and "The British Mandate and the Negev," in Mordechai Naor, ed., *The Settlement of the Negev, 1900–1960* (Jerusalem: Yad Ben-Zvi, 1985), 11–14 and 49–58 respectively [Hebrew].

4.   On various ideas for settling the Negev from the end of World War I to 1939, see Kark, *Pioneering Jewish Settlement*, 65–91.

5.   The *moshava* Qastina, established in 1888, was renamed Beer Tuvia. See http://www.moshav-beer-tuvia.co.il/cgi-webaxy/item?19 and http://www.moshav-beer-tuvia.co.il/cgi-webaxy/item?20, accessed May 27, 2015 [Hebrew].

6.   Eliyahu Canaani, *Ruhama: The First Jewish Settlement in the Negev* (Jerusalem: Yad Ben-Zvi, 1981) [Hebrew]; Kark, *Pioneering Jewish Settlement*, 44–49, 69–73. Following its evacuation in 1917, Ruhama was resettled in 1943.

7.   Porat, *From Wasteland to Inhabited Land*, 15.

8.   Kenneth W. Stein, *The Land Question in Palestine, 1917–1939* (Chapel Hill: University of North Carolina Press, 1984), 202–11; Porat, *From Wasteland to Inhabited Land*, 50–109.

9.   Porat, *From Wasteland to Inhabited Land*, 50–71, 201–7; Kark, *Pioneering Jewish Settlement*, 57.

10.   Kark, *Pioneering Jewish Settlement*, 107–108, 179; Porat, *From Wasteland to Inhabited Land*, 153–59; Ilan S. Troen, *Imagining Zion: Dreams, Designs, and Realities in a Century of Jewish Settlement* (New Haven: Yale University Press, 2003), 74–76.

11.   Porat, *From Wasteland to Inhabited Land*, 180, 200.

12.   Yosef Weitz in his diary, February 21, 1947, quoted in Kark, *Pioneering Jewish Settlement*, 111.

13.   Porat, *From Wasteland to Inhabited Land*, 157. Members of the Beit Eshel outpost, built in 1943, described their isolation and feeling of estrangement from the desert environment. See Dan Bar-On, *The Rebels against the Desert* [*Mordim ba-yeshimon*]: *Beit Eshel's Story, 1943–1948* (Moshav Yogev Press, 1984), 10, 25 [Hebrew]. Kark (*Pioneering Jewish Settlement*, 124–31) notes that because of the limitations of their first locations, which were determined by defense considerations, several settlements relocated to more viable locations in the post-1948 years.

14.   Porat, *From Wasteland to Inhabited Land*, 159–67.

15.   Jewish territory according to the 1947 partition plan was to include 55% of Man-

datory Palestine and most of the Negev (see Map 1): Porat, *From Wasteland to Inhabited Land*, 177–82; Charles D. Smith, *Palestine and the Arab-Israeli Conflict* (Boston: Bedford/St. Martin, 2001), 192–94, 202; Benny Morris, *1948: The First Arab Israeli War* (New Haven: Yale University Press, 2008), 47–48, 63.

16. See Elchanan Orren, "The Settlements in the Negev Battles during the War of Independence," in Naor, *The Settlement of the Negev*, 107; Israel Central Bureau of Statistics, Statistical Abstract of Israel, 2013, table 2.15, http://www.cbs.gov.il/shnaton67/st02_15x.pdf/.

17. Ben-Gurion's speech at the Zionist Executive meeting in April 1948, quoted in Orren, "The Settlements in the Negev Battles," 105 (emphasis added).

18. The Egyptian forces moved along two tracks, one toward Tel Aviv and the other toward Beer Sheva and Hebron, and were positioned along the Faluja-Hebron axis. Morris, *1948*, 232–44, 277–78, 296, 302.

19. Britain's pressure to take the Negev away from the Jews was further advanced by the United Nations mediator, Count Bernadotte of Sweden, with the support of the United States, which later changed its position and backed Israel's claim to the Negev. See Smith, *Palestine*, 201–3; Orren, "The Settlements in the Negev Battles," 114–16, 120–22.

20. Yoav Gelber, *Independence versus Nakba: Israel, the Palestinians, and the Arab States, 1948* (Or Yehuda: Kinnert, Zmora Bitan & Dvir, 2004), 314–45 [Hebrew]; Morris, *1948*, 320–37, 358–68, 375–84. The Negev Brigade soldiers reached Eilat on the anniversary of the historic defense of Tel Hai and referred to this symbolic connection in the telegram announcing their achievement: Orren, "The Settlements in the Negev Battles," 114–25.

21. For a broader discussion of the centrality of these themes in Israeli collective memory, see Yael Zerubavel, *Recovered Roots: Collective Memory and the Making of Israeli National Tradition* (Chicago: Chicago University Press, 1995), 44, 91, 217, 222–23; Nurith Gertz, *Myths in Israeli Culture: Captives of a Dream* (London: Vallentine Mitchell, 2000), 5–26; Maoz Azaryahu, *State Cults: Celebrating Independence and Commemorating Fallen Soldiers in Israel 1948–56* (Sde Boker: Ben-Gurion Research Center and Ben-Gurion University Press, 1995), 115–21 [Hebrew].

22. Orren, "The Settlements in the Negev Battles," 103–11; Gelber, *Independence versus Nakba*, 235; Benny Morris, *The Birth of the Palestinian Refugee Problem Revisited* (New York: Cambridge University Press, 2004), 81, 208, 270–71, 312. After a fierce attack on Yad Mordechai, kibbutz members evacuated for a short period and then returned. Other examples of long-term impacts of the war include Beit Eshel, which was destroyed in the war (its residents later built a new *moshav* in the north), and Be'erot Yitzhak, which was rebuilt at the center of the country. In other cases, such as Beit Ha'arava and Kalia in the Dead Sea area, and Nitzanim and Kfar Darom in the northern Negev, new settlements carrying their names were established after 1967.

23. Kibbutz Revivim, where *Pillar of Fire* was shot, was one of the early outposts established in 1943: Nathan Gross and Yaacov Gross, *The Hebrew Film: The History of the Silent Film and Cinema in Israel* (Jerusalem: self-published edition, 1991), 242–43 [Hebrew]; Nirit Anderman, "Editing out a frame of history," *Ha'aretz*, March 18, 2011 [Hebrew]. Revivim's experiences also inspired works of fiction by kibbutz members Yonat and Alexander Sened.

24.   See the list of canonical songs for Israel's Memorial Day at the Shironet website for Israeli and global songs, http://shironet.mako.co.il/html/indexes/works/106.html, accessed August 26, 2014 [Hebrew]. On the theme of "the living dead," see Zerubavel, *Recovered Roots*, 91–95; Hannan Hever, *Suddenly the Sight of War: Nationality and Violence in Hebrew Poetry of the 1940s* (Tel Aviv: Hakibbutz Hameuchad, 2001), 50 [Hebrew]. On the presence of the same theme in German memorial culture, see also George L. Mosse, *Fallen Soldiers: Reshaping the Memory of the World Wars* (Oxford: Oxford University Press, 1990), 70–78.

25.   Anita Shapira (*Israel: A History* [Waltham: Brandeis University Press, 2012], 274) refers to around ten thousand infiltrations into Israel per year between 1949 to 1951 and more than three hundred Israelis killed by infiltrators between 1949 and 1956. Dvorah Hacohen notes the impact of the deteriorating situation, which reached seven thousand infiltrations in 1953 alone: Dvora Hacohen, *The Grain and the Millstone: The Settlement of Immigrants in the Negev in the First Decade of the State* [*Ha-gar'in ve'ha-reihayim*] (Tel Aviv: Am Oved, 1970), 119–23, 242, 278–79 [Hebrew]. See also Adriana Kemp, "The Janus Face of the Border: Space and National Consciousness in Israel," in *Teoria Uvikoret* 16 (2000): 18–25 [Hebrew]; Benny Morris, *Israel's Border Wars, 1949–1956: Arab Infiltration, Israeli Retaliation, and the Countdown to the Suez War* (Oxford: Oxford University Press, 1997), 34–35, 108–15.

26.   Benny Morris, *Jews and Arabs in Palestine/Israel, 1936–1956* [*Tikun ta'ut*] (Tel Aviv: Am Oved, 2000), 175–97 [Hebrew]; Uri Ben-Eliezer, *The Emergence of Israeli Militarism 1936–1956* [*Derekh ha-kavenet*] (Tel Aviv: Dvir, 1995), 299–300 [Hebrew].

27.   Amos Oz, "Before His Time" [*Kodem zemano*] [1962], reprinted in *Where the Jackals Howl* [*Artsot ha-tan*] (Tel Aviv: Am Oved, 1986), 82 [Hebrew]; English translation by Gavriel Moses in Robert Alter, ed., *Modern Hebrew Literature* (West Orange: Behrman Books, 1975), 333–50, quotation from p. 348 (modified).

28.   See the praise of the desert photography in Michael Ohad, "Four that Are Five," *Ha'aretz*, September 9, 1967, 20–21, 38 [Hebrew]. This review and those quoted in the following notes were retrieved from the *Scouting Patrol* file at the Film Library of the Tel Aviv Cinematheque in June 2011.

29.   The film shows the courage and resourcefulness of the commando soldiers, but also the risks they take, either when their overconfident and careless behavior leads to the death of one of them or when one of them pities an Arab civilian and thereby endangers the soldiers' lives. The director, Micha Shagrir, expressed his intention to present a more balanced view of the reprisal operations than the idealization and demonization they had received, respectively, in the press. See Nathan Gross, "The Scouts are Coming," *Al Hamishmar*, September 26, 1967 [Hebrew].

30.   The ending clearly demonstrates the theme of the "living dead" in the memorialization of fallen soldiers, which is further articulated in the dead soldier's name, Amichai (literally, "my people lives"). For a critique of this ending as sentimental, see Ohad, "Four that Are Five," and Yosef Srik, "Israeli—In Its Best," *Ha'aretz*, November 17, 1967 [Hebrew].

31.   Azaria Alon, "What Did the Judean Desert Mean to Us?" in Mordechai Naor, ed., *The Dead Sea and the Judean Desert, 1900–1967* (Jerusalem: Yad Ben-Zvi, 1990), 270 [Hebrew].

32.   On pilgrimage to Masada and its patriotic meaning, see Zerubavel, *Recovered Roots*, 119–29.

33. An official memorandum on "Permissions for Trips and Trekking in the Country," written by Eliezer Rieger, March 31, 1954 (ministry of education archive, file 5/22/1234), indicates the importance for school trips at the time of receiving official permission and complying with security requirements. In his story "Before His Time," discussed above, Amos Oz describes a confrontation between a teacher father and his officer son over student security on a field trip to the Negev.

34. For a detailed study of the youth who hiked to Petra and the lore of Petra, see Nessia Shafran, *The Red Rock: Forbidden Travels to Petra* (Jerusalem: Yad Ben-Zvi, 2013) [Hebrew]; for a description of the hike itself, see pp. 73–74.

35. "The Red Rock" (melody by Yohanan Zarai) was censored in 1958, but it later became part of the period song repertoire. See Arie Gilai, "Petra and the Paratroopers," on the Paratroopers website, http://www.202.org.il/Pages/moreshet/petra/petra_main.php, accessed July 20, 2011 [Hebrew], and Shafran, *The Red Rock*, 74–75, 391–95.

36. Meir Har-Zion, *Diary Chapters* [*Pirkei yoman*], ed. Naomi Frankel (Tel Aviv: Levin Epstein, 1969), 79 [Hebrew].

37. Nurit Baretzky, "Rachel Talks about the Red Rock," *Ma'ariv*, Weekend Supplement, July 16, 1971; quoted in Shafran, *The Red Rock*, 110. Her response and, in particular, her reference to the "Green Line," reflect the political subtext regarding the post-1967 polemics about the West Bank.

38. Naomi Frankel, "Introduction" to Har-Zion, *Diary Chapters*, 10.

39. Ehud Ben-Ezer, *The People of Sodom: A Novel* (Tel Aviv: Am Oved, 1968), 62 [Hebrew].

40. Arnold Van Gennep, *The Rites of Passage* [1909] (Chicago: University of Chicago Press, 1960); Victor Turner, *Dramas, Field and Metaphors: Symbolic Action in Human Society* (Ithaca: Cornell University Press, 1974).

41. Interview with Micha Shagrir in Gross, "The Scouts Are Coming"; memorial page for Ram Pargai at the Paratroopers website, http://www.202.org.il/Pages/moreshet/petra/zar .php, accessed May 26, 2011 [Hebrew]; Arie Gilai, "Petra and the Paratroopers."

42. Gross and Gross, *The Hebrew Film*, 243–44, 95; Meir Schnitzer, *Israeli Cinema* (Or Yehuda: Kineret, 1994), 51 [Hebrew].

43. For other negative reviews retrieved from the film's file at the Tel Aviv Cinematheque library (June 2011), see "The Director of Blazing Sands Declares, 'Israel Is a Third-World Country,'" *Yediot Ahronot*, Oct. 10, 1960 [Hebrew]; Ze'ev Rav-Nof, "The Petra Scrolls," *Davar* 1965, n.d. [Hebrew]; "Blazing Sands," in *Omanut Ha-Kolno'a* 21 (Aug. 1960): 14 [Hebrew]; Heda Boshes, "What Was the Fuss About?" *Ha'aretz*, Sept. 30, 1960 [Hebrew].

44. Quoted in Rav-Nof, "The Petra Scrolls"; see also "Blazing Sands"; Nurith Gertz, *Motion Fiction: Israeli Fiction in Film* (Tel Aviv: The Open University, 1993), 18–19 [Hebrew]; Shafran, *The Red Rock*, 396–404. A memorial site in the Arava and a memorial book for five men and women who were killed on the way to Petra in September of 1953 articulate their special place in Israeli memory and conform to memorials for fallen heroes. See *To the Rock: Five Who Went* [*Ad sela: Hamisha she-halkhu*] [1960] (Tel Aviv: Hakibbutz Hameuchad, 2001) [Hebrew]).

45. David Ben-Gurion, in a speech on "The Meaning of the Negev" [*Mashma'ut ha-negev*], January 17, 1955 [Hebrew].

46. David Ben-Gurion, "Southwards" [1956], reprinted in *Readings in the Bible* [*Iyunim ba-tanach*] (Tel Aviv: Am Oved, 1969), 132–44 [Hebrew]. See also Hacohen, *The Grain and the Millstone*, 147–48, 248–57; Daniel Guttwein, "On the Contradiction between the Pioneering Ethos and Socialist Ideology in the Israeli Labor Movement," *Iyunim Bitkumat Israel* 20 (2010): 208–28 [Hebrew].

47. Yechiam Weitz, "To the Fantasy and Back: Why Did Ben-Gurion Decide to Go to Sde Boker?" *Iyunim Bitkumat Israel* 8 (1998): 298–319 [Hebrew]; Zeev Zivan, "The Negev in Ben-Gurion's Vision," *Ariel* 152–53 (2002): 11–18 [Hebrew].

48. Orit Rozin, *The Rise of the Individual in 1950s Israel: A Challenge to Collectivism* (Waltham, MA: Brandeis University Press, 2011).

49. Micha Talmon, "The Agricultural Settlement of the Negev, 1949–59," in Naor, *The Settlement of the Negev*, 146–56. Among the transitory military settlements that evolved into full-fledged kibbutzim are Nahal Oz in the western Negev, Yotvata in the southern Negev, and Ein Gedi near the Dead Sea.

50. The new pipeline increased the amount of water for the Negev from one million to one hundred million cubic meters of water per year. The pumping stations were built underground for security reasons. See Alon Tal, *Pollution in the Promised Land: An Environmental History of Israel* (Berkeley: University of California Press, 2002), 206–7.

51. Samer Alatout, "The Hydro-Imaginaries and the Construction of the Political Geography of the Jordan River," in Diana K. Davis and Edmund Burke III, eds., *Environmental Imaginaries of the Middle East and North Africa* (Athens: Ohio University Press, 2011), 218–45; Tal, *Pollution in the Promised Land*, 209–15.

52. Anat First and Na'ama Sheffi, "Borders and Banknotes: The National Perspective," *Nations and Nationalism* 21, 2 (2015): 330–47; Shaul Cohen, "Environmentalism Deferred: Nationalism and Israeli/Palestinian Imaginaries," in Davis and Burke, *Environmental Imaginaries*, 256.

53. Bar-Gal observes that geography textbooks of the pre-state period made little mention of the Negev and notes the shift in emphasis in the 1950s and 1960s: Yoram Bar-Gal, *Moledet and Geography in a Hundred Years of Zionist Education* (Tel Aviv: Am Oved, 1993), 137–38, 150–51 [Hebrew]. See, for example, Nahum Gavrieli and Baruch Avivi, eds., *My New Book for the Fifth Grade* (Tel Aviv: Yavne, 1950) [Hebrew]; and Z. Ariel, M. Blich and N. Persky, eds., *Israel's Reader for the Fourth Grade* [*Mikra'ot yisrael*] (Jerusalem: Masada, 1958) [Hebrew].

54. Avraham A. Reifenberg, *The War between the Cultivated Land and the Desert* [*Milhemet ha-mizra veha-yeshimon*] (Jerusalem: Mosad Bialik, 1950) [Hebrew]. Berta Hazan, *Man Subdues the Wasteland* [*Ha-adam madbir ha-shemama*] (Merhavia: Sifriyat Hapoalim, 1952) [Hebrew] is a high school textbook. See also Shlomo Kodesh, *The Founders' Legendary Tale* [*Agadat ha-rishonim*]: *The War against the Desert* (Jerusalem: The Jewish National Fund, 1972) [Hebrew].

55. Hazan, *Man Subdues the Wasteland*, 248.

56. The song "The Desert Will Rejoice" [*Yesusum midbar ve-tsiya*], composed by David Zehavi in 1951, articulates the joy of the desert when water fills up its streams. See the Zemereshet website for Hebrew songs, http://www.zemereshet.co.il/song.asp?id=1910, ac-

cessed June 12, 2015 [Hebrew]. Dov Seltzer also composed another song based on Isaiah (41:19) that alludes to the planting of a variety of trees in the desert. See the Israel Broadcast Authority's archive, http://www.iba.org.il/zemerivri/?entity=775080, accessed June 12, 2015 [Hebrew].

57.   Shlonsky wrote the lyrics in the mid-1940s; the melody was composed by Alexander Uriah Boskovitz. The song was performed in 1947. See the Zemereshet website, http://www.zemereshet.co.il/song.asp?id=236, accessed June 12, 2015 [Hebrew].

58.   A.T., "Those Who Search for Water in the Arava Desert," in Nahum Gavrieli and Baruch Avivi, eds., *My New Book, for the Fourth Grade.* Tel Aviv: Yavne, 1955/6, 44–46 [Hebrew].

59.   The lyrics were written by Yechiel Mohar and the melody by Moshe Vilensky in the mid-1950s. See Yosef Goldenberg, "The Hebrew Folksong: The Representation of the Desert in Israeli Folk Music," in Tuvia Friling, Gideon Katz, and Michael Wolpe, eds., *Music in Israel, Iyunim Bitkumat Israel,* Thematic Series 8 (2014): 282 [Hebrew].

60.   On the influence of the American Western on Israeli films, see Gertz, *Motion Fiction,* 70–83; Yigal Schwartz, *The Zionist Paradox: Hebrew Literature and Israeli Identity* (Waltham, MA: Brandeis University Press, 2014), 201, 207–8.

61.   The "Cowboys' Song" [*Zemer ha-bokrim*], lyrics by Yaakov Orland, melody by Mordechai Olari-Nojick. See the Zemereshet website, http://www.zemereshet.co.il/song.asp?id=2341, accessed June 12, 2015 [Hebrew]. Chaya Shacham notes that the popular singer Israel Yitzhaki asked Orland to write a song "in the style of the "Wild West," which he did while sitting in a café in Tel Aviv: Chaya Shoham, "Reality and Ideology in the Songs of the First Decade of Statehood," in Friling, Katz, and Wolpe, *Music in Israel,* 389–91; Goldenberg, "The Hebrew Folksong," 291.

62.   The lyrics of "The Way to Eilat" were written by Yechiel Mohar and the melody by Shlomo Weissfish, at the Shironet website for Israeli and global songs, http://shironet.mako.co.il/artist?type=lyrics&lang=1&prfid=521&wrkid=5341, accessed June 15, 2015 [Hebrew]. "The Yotvata Dance," [*Me'hol yotvata*], lyrics and melody by Emanuel Zamir, was performed in the 1950s; see the Zemereshet website for Hebrew songs, http://www.zemereshet.co.il/song.asp?id=4489 and http://www.zemereshet.co.il/song.asp?id=4444, accessed June 12, 2015 [Hebrew].

63.   "Ein Gedi," lyrics by Eitan Peretz, melody by Dov Aharoni [aka Sh. Dibbon], at the Shironet website, http://shironet.mako.co.il/artist?type=lyrics&lang=1&prfid=332&wrkid=2520, accessed June 12, 2015 [Hebrew].

64.   A. Yanai, "A Letter from Eilat, Land of Wonders," *Herut,* October 17, 1951, 3 [Hebrew]; Yosef Ben-Aharon, "With Agudat Israel's Youth," *She'arim,* July 16, 1956 [Hebrew].

65.   "The Wild South," *Emda,* January 9, 1978, 11 [Hebrew]; "Eilat Is Outraged," *Davar,* December 16, 1960, 11 [Hebrew]; "The Wild South is Extending to the North," *Ha-Boker,* May 12, 1952 [Hebrew].

66.   See Moshe Sikaron, "The Mass Immigration—Its Dimensions, Characteristics and Influences on Israel's Demography," in Mordechai Naor, ed., *Immigrants and Transit Camps, 1948–1952* (Jerusalem: Yad Ben-Zvi, 1986), 31–32, 42 [Hebrew]; Sammy Smooha, *Israel: Pluralism and Conflict* (Berkeley: University of California Press, 1978), 48–65, 281.

67. Ze'ev Drori, *Utopia in Uniform: The Israel Defense Forces' Contributions to Settlement, Aliyah and Education in the Early Days of the State* (Sde Boker: Ben-Gurion Research Center and Ben-Gurion University Press, 2000), 36–64 [Hebrew]; Erez Tzfadia, "Militarism and Space in Israel," *Israeli Sociology* 11, 2 (2010): 337–61 [Hebrew]; Daniel De Malach, "The Kibbutz Movement and the Struggle for Jewish Control of Land: 1967 and Afterward," *Teoria Uvikoret* 45 (Winter 2015): 139–44 [Hebrew].

68. Chanina Porat, "Geographic and Settlement Aspects of the Establishment of New Immigrant Moshavim in the Negev, 1948–52," in Dalia Ofer, ed., *Israel in the Great Wave of Immigration, 1948–53 [Bein olim le-vatikim]* (Jerusalem: Yad Ben-Zvi, 1996), 227–60, quotation and *moshavim* figures on p. 230 [Hebrew]. Troen gives the number of new *moshavim* between 1948 and 1952 as 213, compared to 79 new kibbutzim: Troen, *Imagining Zion*, 216–19; see also Hacohen, *The Grain and the Millstone*, 70–79, 248–68.

69. See Zvi Zameret, Aviva Halamish, and Esther Meir-Glitzenstein, eds., *The Development Towns* (Jerusalem: Yad Ben-Zvi, 2009) [Hebrew]; Elisha Efrat, "Development Towns in Israel," in Zameret, Halamish, and Meir-Glitzenstein, *The Development Towns*, 38–46; Zeev Zivan, "The Beginning of the Development Towns South of Beer Sheva," *Ariel* 152–53 (2002): 137–46 [Hebrew]. See also Erez Tzfadia and Haim Yacobi, *Rethinking Israeli Space: Periphery and Identity* (New York: Routledge, 2011), 8–19.

70. Hacohen, *The Grain and the Millstone*, 237–41; Avi Picard, "Who Among Those Who Go: Populating the Development Towns," in Zameret, Halamish, and Meir-Glitzenstein, *The Development Towns*, 198–202.

71. Esther Schely-Newman, "The Nocturnal Voyage: Encounters between Immigrants and Their New Homes," in Ofer, *Israel in the Great Wave of Immigration*, 294–95. By contrast, some of the stories by the earlier settlers who chose to go to the Negev indicate that they arrived at their destination in daylight (295–98). See also Ilana Rosen, *Pioneers in Practice: An Analysis of Documentary Literature by Veteran Residents of the Israeli South [Halutzim be-fo'al]* (Sde Boker: Ben-Gurion Research Institute, 2016), 86–199 [Hebrew].

72. Rosen, *Pioneers in Practice*, 96, 157.

73. Michael Singolda's oral history, interview by Leah Shakdiel on October 27, 1988, oral history archive, the Yerucham public library, accessed February 2005. My special thanks to Leah Shakdiel for discussing the oral history project with me.

74. Rachel Oriel, a Jewish immigrant from Morocco; interview quoted in Rosen, *Pioneers in Practice*, 160–61.

75. From the oral history with Hanna Azulai, who arrived in Yerucham in 1957, "The Gathering of Exiles in Yerucham," *Pioneers in the Negev—Development Towns*, Hatsav Series, Ministry of Education and Culture, The Southern District (n.d.), 16, at the Yerucham public library.

76. Schely-Newman, "The Nocturnal Voyage," 292. The testimony of a Moroccan Jewish immigrant whose family was brought to the desert in 1954 reiterated a similar response: "We saw only mountains and the desert around us. My mother cried and didn't want to stay there": Simi Krispin's oral history, quoted in "The Gathering of Exiles in Yerucham," 11.

77. Rogel Alper quotes from an interview with Aliav in the early 1980s in Rogel Alper,

"When They Poured out the Moroccans in the Lachish Region," *Ha'aretz*, June 14, 2015, http://www.haaretz.co.il/opinions/.premium-1.2659258 [Hebrew].

78.   Human material is the Hebrew translation of the German *Menschenmaterial*, which articulated the modern state's approach to its citizens. See its early use by Arthur Ruppin, originally published in German: Arthur Ruppin, "Die Auslese des Menschenmaterials für Palaestina," *Der Jude*, 3 (1919): 373–83; and translated into Hebrew in 1936: Arthur Ruppin, "The Choice of Human Material," *Thirty Years of Building in the Land of Israel* (Jerusalem, 1936), 63–74 [Hebrew]. Hanna Yablonka marks its use in reference to Holocaust survivors in Hanna Yablonka, *Survivors of the Holocaust: Israel after the War* (Houndmills: Macmillan Press, 1999), 63, 77.

79.   I am quoting here book titles from Alex Weingrod, *Reluctant Pioneers: Village Development in Israel* (Ithaca: Cornell University Press, 1966) and Ilana Rosen, *Pioneers in Practice*. See also Gershon Shafir and Yoav Peled, *Being Israelis: The Dynamics of Multiple Citizenship* (Cambridge: Cambridge University Press, 2002), 76–77; Adriana Kemp, "The 'Great Migration' or the 'Great Fire': Political Control and Resistance on the Israeli Frontier," in Hannan Hever, Yehouda Shenhv and Pnina Motzafi-Haller, eds., *Mizrahim in Israel: A Critical Observation of Israel's Ethnicity* (Tel Aviv: Hakkibutz Hameuchad, 2002), 39–44 [Hebrew]; Picard, "Who Among Those Who Go," 196–210.

80.   In a speech to the foreign volunteers of the IDF on November 13, 1948, David Ben-Gurion asserted Israel's need to establish settlements along the borders as a defense from outside attacks, emphasizing that it would be best achieved "not through fortification by stone, but by *an organic human wall* that is working and productive"; quoted in Tzfadia, "Militarism and Space in Israel," 342 (emphasis added).

81.   Orit Rozin, "Infiltration and the Making of Israel's Emotional Regime in the State's Early Years," *Middle Eastern Studies* 52, 3 (2016): 448–72; Kemp, "The 'Great Migration,'" 43–48; Hacohen, *The Grain and the Millstone*, 186–204.

82.   Aharon Megged, *The Living on the Dead* [*Ha-hai al ha-met*] (Tel Aviv: Am Oved, 1988), 63 [Hebrew]. The biblical quote is from Isaiah 35:1.

83.   Rosen, *Pioneers in Practice*, 173–74.

84.   Quoted in Avi Picard, *Cut to Measure, Israel's Policies Regarding the Aliyah of North African Jews, 1951-56* [*Olim bi-mesura*] (Sde Boker: Ben-Gurion Research Institute and Ben-Gurion University of the Negev, 2013), 209 [Hebrew], from the film "First Days" (VT DA0755 at the Spielberg film archive of the Hebrew University). Ephraim Kishon's popular satirical film *Sallah* (1964) gives a cartoonish portrayal of new immigrants, kibbutzniks, and Israeli bureaucrats and politicians in the 1950s. For critical views of the portrayal of Mizrahi immigrants in this and other Israeli films, see Ellah Shohat, *Israeli Cinema: East/West and the Politics of Representation* (Austin: University of Texas Press, 1989), 138–55; Yaron Shemer, *Identity, Place, and Subversion in Contemporary Mizrahi Cinema in Israel* (Ann Arbor: University of Michigan Press, 2013), 18–48.

85.   Kobi Oz, "Dusty Slope" [*Ma'ale avak*], 1995 [Hebrew]; for the song lyrics, see the Shironet website at https://shironet.mako.co.il/artist?type=lyrics&lang=1&prfid=429&wrkid=2205; accessed April 29, 2018.

86.   Shimon Adaf, "Sderot," in *Icaros' Monolog* (Gevenim, 1997), reprinted in *Desert*

Anthology (Heksherim Research Center, Ben-Gurion University, May 2001), n.p. [Hebrew/ English].

87. The sense of "lack" of specificity and character underlies Marc Augé's concept of non-place: Augé, *Non-Places: Introduction to an Anthropology of Supermodernity* (London: Verso, 1995).

88. Miri Talmon, "Somewhere in Israel: Representations of Development Towns and the Discourse on the Place in Israeli Film," in Zameret, Halamish, and Meir-Glitzenstein, *The Development Towns*, 420. See also Rosen, *Pioneers in Practice*, 157.

89. Shemer, *Identity, Place, and Subversion*, 110–14.

90. The Egyptians, who have come to perform in the historically important Petach Tikvah, are misunderstood and directed to a fictitious development town ironically named Beit Ha-Tikvah (House of Hope). The reality of this town, whose residents are isolated and stuck in the desert, stands in stark contrast to its uplifting name. For a more elaborate discussion, see Shemer, *Identity, Place, and Subversion*, 114–21.

91. Myron J. Aronoff provides a thick description of the early development and social life of the desert town, in Myron J. Aronoff, *Frontiertown: The Politics of Community Building in Israel* (Manchester: Manchester University Press, 1974). See also Efrat, "Development Towns in Israel," 53–55, 69. Amos Oz draws on life in the desert town in his novel *Don't Call It Night* [1994] (San Diego: Harcourt Brace & Co., 1997).

92. Baruch Kimmerling, "Between Primordial and Civil Definitions of the Collective Identity: Eretz Israel or the State of Israel?" in Erik Cohen, Moshe Lissak, and Uri Almagor, eds., *Comparative Social Dynamics: Essays in Honor of S.N. Eisenstadt* (Boulder: Westview Press, 1983), 262–83; Ian S. Lustick, *Unsettled States, Disputed Lands: Britain and Ireland, France and Algeria, Israel and the West Bank-Gaza* (Ithaca, NY: Cornell University Press, 1993), 354–61; Gershon Shafir, "Changing Nationalism and Israel's 'Open Frontier' on the West Bank," *Theory and Society* 13, 6 (1984): 803–27.

93. Daniel De Malach notes the important role of the kibbutz movement, most particularly Ha-Kibbutz Ha-Meuchad, in developing the new settlements in the Golan Heights, the Jordan Valley, and northern Sinai, as well as the impact of this settlement drive on the movement's development, in De Malach, "The Kibbutz Movement and the Struggle for Jewish Control of Land."

94. The Knesset passed the Jerusalem law on July 30, 1980 (*The Book of Laws* [*Sefer Ha-Hukim*] no. 980, August 5, 1980, 186) and passed an amendment to it on November 27, 2000 (*Book of Laws* no. 5762, 28). See the Knesset site at http://www.knesset.gov.il /laws/special/eng/basic10_eng.htm, accessed April 28, 2017. The Knesset passed the Golan Heights Law with a majority of 63 to 21 votes on December 14, 1981. See the ministry of foreign affairs site at http://www.mfa.gov.il/mfa/foreignpolicy/peace/guide/pages/golan% 20heights%20law.aspx, accessed April 28, 2017.

95. Shlomo Hasson, "From Frontier to Periphery," *Studio* 37 (October 1992): 12–16 [Hebrew]. See also the new compound Hebrew term "*Sefariphery*" (combining the Hebrew terms for frontier, *sefar*, and periphery, *periferia*) to represent the ambiguity of a liminal position that contains elements of both: Oren Yiftachel and Erez Tzfadia,

"*Sefariphery*," in *Block* 6 (2008): 40–46, quoted in Tzfadia, "Militarism and Space in Israel," 340–41.

96.   For Ben-Gurion University's development, see its website, http://in.bgu.ac.il/en/Pages/milestones.aspx, accessed on July 19, 2015. According to the site, the student body of Ben-Gurion University doubled, from 10,000 in the early 1990s to 20,000 in 2009, representing the largest student growth at any Israeli university.

97.   Although Beer Sheva became the fourth biggest city in the country at one point, it was later surpassed by other cities. See Yehuda Grados and Eliyahu Stern, *The Beer Sheva Book* (Jerusalem: Keter, 1979) [Hebrew], and Eitan Cohen, *Beer Sheva: The Fourth City* (Jerusalem: Carmel, 2006) [Hebrew]. The Central Bureau of Statistics identifies Beer Sheva as the eighth largest city in Israel in 2014: http://www.cbs.gov.il/hodaot2015n/11_15_355matzeget.pdf, accessed April 28, 2017 [Hebrew]. In 2017, the city's municipal website gave Beer Sheva's population as 215,000, and the city as servicing about 750,000 persons: http://www.beer-sheva.muni.il/City/OnTheCity/pages/b7–misparim.aspx, accessed April 28, 2017 [Hebrew].

98.   Dimona grew from 5,000 in 1961 to 27,000 in 1983 and to 33,452 in 2016; the population of Netivot rose from 2,900 in 1961 to 8,100 in 1983 and to 32,513 in 2016; Ofakim's population, about 4,800 in 1961, rose to 12,800 in 1983 and to 26,625 in 2016; Sderot was about 3,500 in 1961 and increased to 9,000 in 1983 and to 24,016 in 2016; Yerucham, with a population of only 485 in 1955, grew to a population of 6,200 in 1983 and 9,230 in 2016; Mitzpe Ramon, finally, stayed about the same size, with a population under 5,000 in 1983 and 5,123 in 2016. See Efrat, "Development Towns in Israel," 43–45, 63–69, and, for the 2016 population data, the website of the Israel Central Bureau of Statistics, http://www.cbs.gov.il/reader/cw_usr_view_SHTML?ID=807, accessed May 31, 2018 [Hebrew].

99.   Ethiopian Jews settled in development towns in the desert including Kiryat Gat, Kiryat Malachi, Sderot, Ofakim, Arad, and Dimona: Fred A. Lazin, "The Housing Policies for Ethiopian Immigrants in Israel: Spatial Segregation, Economic Feasibility and Political Accessibility," *Nationalism and Ethnic Politics* 3, 4 (1997): 39–68. Around 18.6% of the 885,000 persons who immigrated to Israel from the former Soviet Union settled in development towns, and their population ranged from ten to forty percent of the population in those towns: Erez Tzfadia, "From Russia With Love? The Large Absorption in the 1990s," in Zameret, Halamish, and Meir-Glitzenstein, *The Development Towns*, 218, 231; see also Efrat, "Development Towns in Israel," 59–60.

100.   According to the public policy scholar Erez Tzfadia, the addition of mostly older people, dependent on government support, further stretched the towns' limited resources and moved struggling development towns even lower on the national socioeconomic scale: Erez Tzfadia, "Between Nation and Place: Localism and Development Towns Confront Russian Immigration," *Studies in the Geography of Israel* 16 (2003): 97–123 [Hebrew]; see also Daniel Ben-Simon, *Dirty Business in the South* [*Iska afela ba-darom*] (Jerusalem: Keter, 2002), 23–26, 29–47 [Hebrew].

101.   Tzfadia and Yacobi, *Rethinking Israeli Space*, 26–32.

102.   On the annual *hillulah* for the Tunisian rabbi Chaim Chouri following his death in 1957 see Alex Weingrod, *The Saint of Beer Sheba* (Albany: SUNY Press, 1990).

103.   Alex Weingrod, "Changing Israeli Landscapes: Buildings and the Uses of the Past," *Cultural Anthropology* 8, 3 (1993): 370–87; Haim Yacobi, "From State-Imposed Urban Planning to Israeli Diasporic Place: The Case of Netivot and the Grave of Baba Sali," in Julia Brauch, Anna Lipphardt, and Alexandra Nocke, eds., *Jewish Topographies: Visions of Space, Traditions of Place* (London and Aldershot: Ashgate Press, 2008), 63–80; Eyal Ben-Ari and Yoram Bilu, "Saints' Sanctuaries in Israeli Development Towns: On a Mechanism of Urban Transformation," in Eyal Ben-Ari and Yoram Bilu, eds., *Grasping Land: Space and Place in Contemporary Israeli Discourse and Experience* (Albany: SUNY Press, 1997), 61–83.

104.   On the significance of Tu Bishvat in Israeli culture, see chapter 3. For the significance of shifting the commemorative date of a historical event to transform its meaning, see Zerubavel, *Recovered Roots*, 48–59, 96–113.

105.   For the concept of the "mnemonic veil" see Yael Zerubavel, "Numerical Commemoration and the Challenges of Collective Remembrance in Israel," *History and Memory* 26, 1 (Spring/Summer 2014): 19.

106.   Galit Saada-Ophir, "Mizrahi Subaltern Counterpoints: Sderot's Alternative Cultural Bands," *Anthropological Quarterly*, 80, 3 (2007): 711–36; Motti Regev and Edwin Seroussi, *Popular Music and National Culture in Israel* (Berkeley: University of California Press, 2004), 226–29.

107.   A new train station that opened in December 2013 in the western Negev improves Sderot's connections both with the northern Negev and with the center of the country. On the history of Sapir College, see the memoir of its founding president and historian, Zeev Tzahor, *We Were the Revival* (Tel Aviv: Hakibbutz Hameuchad, 2015), 172–206 [Hebrew].

108.   See the discussion by Tzfadia and Yacobi (*Rethinking Israeli Space*, 118) of the tension between the competing definitions of frontier and periphery, noting the residents' sense of being "trapped between spatial, economic and social marginality and the desire to be part of the national ethos and collective belonging of the frontier."

109.   J. Schmidt, "Fringe Benefits: Israeli Desert Pioneering in the 21st Century: The Case of Mitzpe Ramon," *Negev, Dead Sea and Arava Studies* 6, 2 (2014): 20–32; Yair Sheleg, "The Settlers in the Heart of Distress," *Ha'aretz*, October 28, 2005 [Hebrew]; Elyashiv Reichner, "The Settlement of Ideological Groups in Development Towns," in Zameret, Halamish, and Meir-Glitzenstein, *The Development Towns*, 245–58; Yair Ettinger, "Haredi Quarter Blending Torah Study with Employment Will Be Founded in Yerucham," *Ha'aretz*, January 13, 2006, 1–2 [Hebrew].

110.   Debbie Goldman-Golan and Leah Shakdiel, "History and Social Change in Yerucham," *Aleh: A Newsletter for Public School History Teachers* (Jerusalem: Ministry of Education, Curriculum Department, 1991) [Hebrew]. Special thanks to Tamar Biton and Debbie Goldman-Golan for sharing information about *Ba-Midbar*.

111.   Quoted in Shahar Raz, "Together but Apart: A Good Life in the Urban Kibbutz," *Nrg*, October 1, 2009, http://www.nrg.co.il/online/55/ART1/948/658.html, accessed July 31, 2015 [Hebrew]. See also Reichner, "The Settlement of Ideological Groups," 248–57.

112.   See *Gvanim*'s website, http://www.gvanim.org.il/, accessed July 31, 2015 [Hebrew]. In 2015, *Gvanim* employed 260 paid staff members and 150 volunteers.

113. Reichner, "The Settlement of Ideological Groups," 255–57; Shai Parnas, "Sderot's Residents Still Find It Difficult to Accept Kibbutz Migvan," *Ynet*, July 1, 2010, http://www.mynet.co.il/articles/0,7340,L-3913534,00.html, accessed July 31, 2015 [Hebrew].

114. See Ayalim's website on "Ashalim (Kfar Adiel)," http://ayalim.org/, accessed on May 9, 2017. The website credits the organization with "twenty-two compounds, which include student villages, alumni compounds, and new communities of families, containing over a thousand people" in peripheral spaces.

115. Conversation with a student and founding member of Kfar Adiel, February 25, 2005.

116. See Neot Semadar's English website, which includes a short video: http://neot-semadar.com/?lang=en, accessed June 2, 2015.

117. Elyashiv Reichner, "What Led a Bourgeois Group to Establish a Settlement in Central Arava?" *Makor Rishon*, January 16, 2004, http://makorrishon.co.il/print/php?ib=1543, accessed September 8, 2005 [Hebrew]; and Dotan Malach, "A Small House on the Prairie: A Wondrous Journey to the Settlement Tsukim," *Nrg*, September 18, 2013, http://www.nrg.co.il/online/54/ART2/507/704.html and http://www.arava.co.il/cgi-webaxy/item?152, accessed March 13, 2015 [Hebrew].

118. Reichner, "What Led a Bourgeois Group?"

119. Marchav Am's website, http://rng.org.il/?page_id=201 [Hebrew], accessed May 16, 2015. Following the religious custom, the dating of the Sabbath is marked by the weekly Torah portion, in this case *Va Yir'a*.

120. Vered Levy-Barzilai, "The New Settlers," *Ha'aretz*, Weekend Supplement, December 20, 2002, 32 [Hebrew]. See also Elisha Efrat, *Man and Environment in Israel* (Tel Aviv: Ramot and Tel Aviv University Press, 2004), 198–99 [Hebrew]. To emphasize their distinction from the settlers of the West Bank, residents of Ramat Negev referred to their own young generation as "farm youth" (*no'ar ha-havot*), in opposition to the nickname of the radical Right youth, i.e., "hilltop youth" (*no'ar ha-geva'ot*), referring to the location they favored for their illegal outposts.

121. See also Zvi Alush, "The Goal: A Hundred Thousand More Families in the Negev and the Galilee," *Yediot Ahronot*, 24 Hours, May 29, 2005 [Hebrew]; Elyashiv Reichner, "A New Phenomenon: Religious Settlers Conquer the Desert," *Nrg*, May 14, 2013, http://www.nrg.co.il/online/1/ART2/469/848.html, accessed February 17, 2015 [Hebrew]; Tzfadia and Yacobi, *Rethinking Israeli Space*, 114–15. According to its website, *Or* National Missions (*Or Mesimot Le'umiyot*) has created eight new settlements and thirty new groups that joined existing settlements in the Negev and the Galilee: http://www.or1.org.il/HTMLs/article.aspx?C2004=15013&BSP=749&BSS53=15013, accessed February 19, 2017 [Hebrew].

122. *Or*'s website, http://ormovement.org/, accessed May 1, 2018.

123. *Or*'s website (http://ormovement.org/our-mission/) lists its awards, among them the Knesset Speaker's Award for Quality of Life (2009) and the Prime Minister's Award for Innovation and Initiatives (2010). The quotation is from the website of the National Council for Volunteering in Israel, http://www.ivolunteer.org.il/Index.asp?ArticleID=430&CategoryID=178&Page=1, accessed Oct. 3, 2011 [Hebrew]. Representing a dis-

senting viewpoint, a young Israeli human rights activist told me that those who oppose *Or*'s ethno-nationalist agenda and its implications for the Negev Bedouins call it "*Or National Schemes*," a feat achieved in Hebrew by changing a single letter in its name (from "*mesimot*" to "*mezimot*").

124. Oded Bar-Meir, "Is Arad Becoming Haredi?" *Kol Ha-Negev*, August 11, 2006, 70–72 [Hebrew]; "The Battle on Arad: Scores of Haredim Burned Tires and Clashed with Secular Residents," *Walla*, September 10, 2017, https://news.walla.co.il /item/3095732 [Hebrew]; Oz Rosenberg, "Not Only Arad: The Next Explosion Is Just a Matter of Time," *Nrg*, September 17, 2017, http://www.maariv.co.il/news/israel /Article-599540 [Hebrew].

125. The plan to build the Haredi city of Kasif includes 16,000 houses for a population of up to 100,000 persons. See Shlomit Tsur, "A New Haredi City in Israel: The Establishment of the City Kasif was approved," *Globes*, January 14, 2015, http:// www.globes.co.il/news/article.aspx?did=1001000786, accessed September 17, 2017 [Hebrew]; on the opposition to this plan, see Ranit Nahum-Halevy, "Arad Leaders Oppose Building New Haredi City Next Door," *Ha'aretz*, October 2, 2009, http:// www.haaretz.com/print-edition/business/arad-leaders-oppose-building-new-haredi-city -next-door-1.6820, accessed February 18, 2015; Zafrir Rinat, "Blooming or Judaizing the Negev Desert," *Ha'aretz*, December 21, 2013, http://www.haaretz.co.il/magazine /tozeret/.premium-1.2194767, accessed February 18, 2015 [Hebrew]. See also Nimrod Bousso, "Gallant Surprises: The City Kasif in the Eastern Negev Will Be Established— Whether Haredi or Not," *TheMarker*, January 2, 2017, http:/www.themarker.com /realestate/1.3193576, accessed March 21, 2017 [Hebrew].

126. See Efrat, *Man and Environment in Israel*, 192–93. Ariel Sharon's sizable "Syca-more Farm" extends over 315 acres (1,258 dunams). The establishment of individual farms during the 1980s attracted some attention, but those appeared to be isolated cases. See for example Zvi Alush, "The Future Is Hidden in the Ostriches' Eggs," *Yediot Ahronot*, Seven-Day Magazine, September 7, 1984 [Hebrew], and "A Camel Oasis in the Desert," *Yediot Ahronot*, *Od Sha'ah* Supplement, March 27, 1989 [Hebrew].

127. Ofer Dagan, "'Tuscany Is Here': Elite Tourism and the Production of the Jewish Ethno-National Space on Family Farms in Southern Israel," MA thesis, Department of Sociology and Anthropology, Ben-Gurion University, 2014, 47, 50 [Hebrew].

128. On the response to the new project along Route 40, see Mittal Yas'ur, "A Small House on the Large Prairie [Arava]," *Tslol*, March–April 1999, 54–59 [Hebrew]; Zvi Alush, "Hot Land," *Yediot Ahronot*, October 15, 1997, Sukkoth Supplement, 38–42 [Hebrew].

129. Zafrir Rinat, "Build Today, Get Approval Tomorrow," *Ha'aretz*, January 15, 1999, B7 [Hebrew].

130. The media discussed the similarities between West Bank settlers and these Negev settlers in their use of the strategy of creating facts on the ground. See Vered Levy-Barzilai, "The New Settlers"; Michal Greenberg and Tzvika Gotlieb, "Thus One Settles in the Desert: Without Approval, but with Government Support," *Ha'aretz*, August 21, 2007, 10 [He-brew]; Liat Natovitz Koshitsky, "The Suffering Drama of the New Negev Pioneers," *Nrg*, July 5, 2014, http://www.nrg.co.il/online/1/ART2/592/307.html, accessed July 17, 2014

[Hebrew]; Reichner, "A New Phenomenon"; *Ha'aretz* editorial, "Ten Unnecessary Settlements," September, 20, 2011 [Hebrew].

131.   Ariel Sharon, the minister of infrastructure at the time and himself a farm owner, supported this settlement model, as did Raphael Eitan, the minister of agriculture. See Eitan Elgar, "The Production of Space in the Individual Settlements of Ramat Negev's Wine Route," MA thesis, Department of Sociology and Anthropology, Ben-Gurion University, 2013, 31–33 [Hebrew]; and Dagan, "'Tuscany Is Here,' 24–26, 33.

132.   Lawsuit 243/99 in December 1999, filed by the Israel Union for Environmental Defense (*Adam, Teva, V'din*) and the Society for the Protection of Nature in Israel. For further information about the legal process, see Ilanit Ben-Dor, "The Experience of Individual Farm Settlers in Ramat-Negev: Between Individualism and Communitarianism," MA thesis, Ben-Gurion University of the Negev, 2004, 96–99, 154–55 [Hebrew]; and Elgar, "The Production of Space," 33–34.

133.   Government resolution no. 2699 of November 8, 2002, addressing the individual farms as a means to advance the state's settlement policy, was followed by a later resolution, no. 2000 of July 15, 2007, creating an interministerial committee to further examine the status of the individual forms as well as the possibility of establishing additional farms. See the website of the office of the prime minister, at http://www.pmo.gov.il/Secretary/GovDecisions/2007/Pages/des2000.aspx, accessed April 30, 2017 [Hebrew].

134.   The Society for the Protection of Nature's position paper, "New Settlement and Individual Settlements," published in May 2003, may be found on the website of the Open Landscape Institute (*Machon Deshe*), at http://www.deshe.org.il/_Uploads/dbsAttachedFiles/new_settlement.pdf [Hebrew]. The official submission of the plan to the southern district was filed as "Regional Policy Plan 14/4 (modification no. 42) for the Wine Route in Ramat Negev." According to Dagan ("'Tuscany Is Here,'" 27), the territory allocation for a farm averaged 845 acres (around 3,380 dunams).

135.   For further information about The Individual Farms Forum's 2008 suit (no. 3076/08) and the Knesset's legislation to resolve the issue entitled "The Authority for the Development of the Negev, amendment no. 4" (approved by the Knesset on July 12, 2010), see also Elgar, "The Production of Space," 35–36, 70.

136.   Shimon Cohen, "Minister Shalom Approved Ten Individual Farms in the Negev," *Arutz 7*, September 12, 2012, http://www.inn.co.il/News/News.aspx/244062, accessed August 31, 2015 [Hebrew]. In 2014, the number of Wine Route farms reached twenty-four, out of a total of fifty individual farms in the Negev. See also Zafrir Rinat, "The State Adopts Again the Individual Farms; Environmental Organizations Oppose," *Ha'aretz*, February 19, 2014, http://www.haaretz.co.il/news/science/.premium-1.2248130, accessed February 17, 2015 [Hebrew].

137.   In one case, a farm owner jokingly referred to himself as a member of the "Second Aliyah" to note that he belonged to the second round of farms that were established in the Wine Route project.

138.   Alush, "The Future Is Hidden in the Ostriches' Eggs"; Cobi Ben-Simhon, "Stake, Someone?" *Ha'aretz*, Weekend Supplement, December 16, 2009, 48–51 [Hebrew].

139. Amira Segev, "Until the Last Sabra," *Ha'aretz*, Weekend Supplement, June 15, 2001, 61–66 [Hebrew]; see also Ben-Dor, "The Experience of Individual Farm Settlers," 82–84; Rinat, "Blooming or Judaizing the Negev Desert."

140. These themes recurred in farm owners' stories during my visits in 2005 and are also noted in Ben-Dor, "The Experience of Individual Farm Settlers," 44–49, 52–53, 110–12 and in Dagan, "'Tuscany Is Here.'" See also Tal Zagraba, "From a Novelist to a Farmer: Tsur Shezaf Makes the Desert Bloom," *Ynet*, April 29, 2014, http://xnet.ynet.co.il/win /articles/0,14717,L-3105519,00.html, accessed January 30, 2015 [Hebrew].

141. Elgar, "The Production of Space," 25, 43–45, 58–59.

142. An advertisement in *Ha'aretz*, the Weekend Supplement, December 14, 2007, 21 [Hebrew]. The man featured in the ad and identified as Dandan Bolotin lives with his family on a farm in the northern Negev, according to his own website: http://dandanbolotin.co.il, accessed July 31, 2015 [Hebrew].

143. Quotation from the website of Dandan Bolotin, http://www.dandanbolotin.co.il /page-w-featured-image-sidebar/, accessed July 31, 2015. The website no longer exists, but these themes also appear in an article about this farm, in Nili Melnitsky, "For Months They Looked for a Place to Build the Farm They Dreamed About," *DeMarker*, April 14, 2017, accessed on May 1, 2018 [Hebrew].

144. The quotation is from an earlier version of the website for the Camel Ranch, which was found at http://www.camel-ranch.co.il/eng/main.html, accessed May 11, 2005, but is no longer active. A more recent version of the website features the theme of a dream but in a more restrained manner: "About 30 years ago, we dreamt about a return to nature, seeking adventure and creativity. Slowly but surely we realized our dream, and now we have over ten thousand visitors a year from all over the world." http://www.camel-ranch.co.il/en /our-story/, accessed May 6, 2017.

145. Marion, "A Dream Was Fulfilled: A Cattle Farm in the Negev," *Ha-Sade* 61, 5 (1981): 822 [Hebrew].

146. Along similar lines, Dagan ("'Tuscany Is Here,'" 41) quotes a farm owner emphasizing the importance of experiencing a totally new beginning.

147. Retrieved from an earlier version of the Camel Ranch's website at http://www .camel-ranch.co.il/eng/main.html, accessed May 11, 2005. The current version of the site refers to the farm as "an oasis" in the desert landscape: https://www.camel-ranch.co.il/about -us/ [Hebrew], accessed Oct. 2, 2017.

148. Alush, "The Future is Hidden in the Ostriches' Eggs"; Ben-Simhon, "Stake, Someone?"

149. Website for the Alpaca Farm, http://www.alpaca.co.il [Hebrew], accessed May 11, 2005.

150. Zvi Alush, "Africa in the Arava," *Yediot Ahronot, Maslul* Magazine, October 25, 2004 [Hebrew].

151. Zvi Alush, "Horses, Goats, and a Wine Glass," *Yediot Ahronot, Maslul* Magazine, March 8, 2001 [Hebrew].

Chapter 5

1. Avinoam Meir, "Territoriality among the Negev Bedouin in Transition from Nomadism to Sedentarism," in P. C. Salzman and U. Fabietti, eds., *Tribal and Peasant Pastoralism: The Dialectics of Cohesion and Fragmentation* (Pavia: Ibis, 1996), 187–207; Yosef Ben-David, *Feud in the Negev: Bedouins, Jews, and the Land Dispute* (Ra'anana: The Institute for Israeli Arab Studies, 1996), 17–29 [Hebrew]; David Grossman, "The *Fellah* and the Bedouin on the Desert Margins: Their Relationship and Strategy of Existence," in David Grossman and Avinoam Meir, eds., *The Arabs in Israel: Geographical Dynamics* (Ramat Gan: Bar-Ilan University Press, 2004), 33–34 [Hebrew]; Tuvia Ashkenazi, *The Bedouins in the Land of Israel* [1956], (Jerusalem: Ariel, 2000), 33–34 [Hebrew].

2. Yosef Ben-David, "The Bedouins in the Negev," in Mordechai Naor, ed., *The Settlement of the Negev: 1900–1960* (Jerusalem: Yad Ben-Zvi, 1985), 94 [Hebrew]; Chanina Porat, "Development Policy and the Question of the Bedouins in the Negev during the Early Years of the State, 1948–1953," *Iyunim Bitkumat Israel* 7 (1997): 398 [Hebrew]; Benny Morris, *The Birth of the Palestinian Refugee Problem, 1947–1949* (Cambridge: Cambridge University Press, 1987), 18.

3. Ze'ev Zivan, "The Relations between the Jewish Society and the Bedouins: The Contact Front and Its Influence on the Shaping of the Frontier in the 1950s," in *Notes on the Topic of the Bedouins: Series in Memory of Itzhaki Netzer* 23 (February 1992): 49; Ben-David, *Feud in the Negev*, 44–45; Porat, "Development Policy," 393 .

4. While the relationships with the Bedouins farther south were strained, the Jewish settlers in the northern Negev cultivated relatively good relations with nearby Bedouins and distributed flyers promising protection for those who collaborated with the Jews: Zivan, "Jewish Society and the Bedouins"; Porat, "Development Policy."

5. Oren Yiftachel indicates that the remaining Negev Bedouin population was around 11,000: Oren Yiftachel, *Ethnocracy: Land and Identity Politics in Israel/Palestine* (Philadelphia: University of Pennsylvania Press, 2006), 197. The report of the public commission on the settlement of the Negev Bedouins, headed by the former chief justice, Eliezer Goldberg (henceforth the "Goldberg Report"), made public on December 11, 2008, quotes the figure of 12,740 Bedouins in 1951: The website of the prime minister's office, http://www.pmo. gov.il/policyplanning/mimshal/Documents/DochGoldberg.pdf, 9, accessed September 3, 2014 [Hebrew].

6. Some Bedouins considered loyal to Israel were allowed to remain in their locations outside of Siyag. See Cédric Parizot, "Gaza, Beersheba, Dhahriyya: Another Approach to the Negev Bedouins in the Israeli-Palestinian Space," *Bulletin du Centre de recherche français à Jérusalem* 9 (2001): 106.

7. Siyag was limited to about 425 square miles (1,100 square kilometers). Estimates of its relation to the size of the land cultivated by the Bedouins prior to 1948 vary, from ten to twenty percent. Ben-David (*Feud in the Negev*, 49–50) quotes 12.5%; Yiftachel (*Ethnocracy*, 197) quotes 10%; and Porat ("Development Policy," 390–96) quotes 20%.

8. Legislation that enabled the state to assume control over land included the Absentee Property Law of 1950, the State Possession Law of 1951, and the Land Acquisition Law of 1953. On its impact in the Negev, see Porat, "Development Policy," 389–92, 429–31, 437;

Ben-David, *Feud in the Negev*, 50–53; Yiftachel, *Ethnocracy*, 138–39, 197–200; Shlomo Swirski, "Transparent Citizens: Israeli Government Policy toward the Negev Bedouins," *Hagar* 8, 2 (2008): 27–28.

9. See the JNF's websites on the Lahav Forest, at http://www.kkl-jnf.org/tourism-and -recreation/forests-and-parks/lahav-forest.aspx, and on the Yatir Forest, at http://www.kkl -jnf.org/tourism-and-recreation/forests-and-parks/yatir-forest.aspx, accessed May 9, 2017.

10. Eyal Weizman and Fazal Sheikh, *The Conflict Shoreline* (Göttingen: Steidl, 2015), 30–31.

11. Parizot ("Gaza, Beersheba, Dhahriyya," 104) notes that the southern and northern Israeli Bedouins had historically belonged to different societies, with little contact between them. The Bedouins who identified as Arab in the 1950s have now adopted "Bedouin" as their ethnic identity.

12. The exceptions to this rule are the Israeli Druze and Circassians, which the state of Israel recognizes as distinct ethnic groups; their military service is mandatory.

13. See also the IDF's websites for these units, at http://www.yehida.co.il/index .php?option=com_content&view=article&id=114&Itemid=91 and http://www.yehida.co.il /index.php?option=com_content&view=article&id=117&Itemid=88, accessed September 8, 2014 [Hebrew]. See also Zvi Alush, "IDF Salutes the Bedouin Trackers in a Moving Ceremony in the South of the Country," *Yediot Ahronot, Koteret*, May 22, 1981, 4 [Hebrew]; and "We Are Part of the State: We'll Remain with It in Fire and Water," *Yediot Ahronot*, 24 Hours, July 31, 1997, 16–17 [Hebrew].

14. Rhoda Kanaaneh notes that until 1978, Bedouins who served in the IDF were officially considered to be "civilians who work in the military": Rhoda Kanaaneh, *Surrounded: Palestinian Soldiers in the Israeli Military* (Stanford: Stanford University Press, 2008), 15–16, 27–30, 52–53; see also Rhoda Kanaaneh, "Boys or Men? Duped or "Made"? Palestinian Soldiers in the Israeli Military," *American Ethnologist* 32, 2 (2005): 260–75; Shlomo Swirski and Yael Hasson, "Transparent Citizens: The Government's Policy toward the Bedouins in the Negev," *Information about Equality* (publication of Adva Center) 14 (September 2005): 3–46 [Hebrew].

15. See *Shaked*'s website, http://www.shaked.org.il/%D7%94%D7%9E%D7%95% D7%A8%D7%A9%D7%AA, accessed Feb. 5, 2008 [Hebrew]. It is difficult to know how prevalent the practice of taking on Hebrew names has been among Arabs who serve in the IDF. For another example, see Yigal Mosco, "A Bedouin Officer Named Guy," *Yediot Ahronot*, 24 Hours, July 12, 1998, 14–15 [Hebrew].

16. The number of Bedouin recruits is estimated at around five to ten percent of the draft-age Bedouin population and makes up less than one percent of the IDF's overall draftees. These numbers include both Bedouins from the Galilee and Negev Bedouins. See Hanne Eggen Røislien, "Religion and Military Conscription: The Case of the Israel Defense Forces (IDF)," *Armed Forces & Society* 39, 2 (2013): 218.

17. The figures relating to the claims vary. The 2008 report by the Goldberg Committee on the Settlement of the Bedouins' Land Disputes quotes the number of claims submitted as 3,220, covering 194,214 acres (776,856 dunams); of the claims submitted, 380 claims (12%) were settled, covering 51,417 acres (205,670 dunams). See the

Goldberg Report, 13. A 2013 report on the settlement of the Bedouins, written by Shiri Spector Ben-Ari and submitted to the Knesset Center for Research and Information on November 5, 2013, quotes this number as 147,250 acres (589,000 dunams). See www. knesset.gov.il/mmm/data/pdf/m03292.pdf, 2, 7, accessed May 1, 2018 [Hebrew]. An earlier article by the district attorney of the south district, Havatselet Yahel, notes 2,700 claims submitted, covering more than 162,500 acres (650,000 dunams), which is about 3% of the total state land in the Negev: Havatselet Yahel, "Land Disputes between the Negev Bedouin and Israel," *Israel Studies* 11, 2 (2006): 12. The difference may arise from the government-initiated resettlement of the Tel Malhata Bedouins for the construction of the Nevatim airbase, discussed in chapter 6.

18.   On the clashing legal approaches, see Ronen Shamir, "Suspended in Space: Bedouins and the Israeli Law," in Daniel Gutwein and Menachem Mautner, eds., *Law and History* (Jerusalem: Zalman Shazar Center for Jewish History, 1999), 473–96 [Hebrew]; Yahel, "Land Disputes," 1–22; Ahmad Amara, "The Negev Land Question: Between Denial and Recognition," *Journal of Palestine Studies* 42, 4 (2013): 36–37.

19.   Yosef Ben-David was commissioned by the ministry of housing to study Tel Sheva in order to learn from those early mistakes. See the resulting study: Yosef Ben-David, *The Urbanization of the Nomadic Bedouin Population of the Negev, 1967–1992* (Jerusalem: The Jerusalem Institute for Israel Studies), 1993 [Hebrew]. See also Avinoam Meir, "Demographic Processes among the Urbanized Negev Bedouins," in Grossman and Meir, *Arab Society in Israel,* 77–95.

20.   "Negev 2015," the 2005 blueprint for the development of the Negev, was available on the website of the prime minister's office, http://www.pmo.gov.il/PMO/Archive/Decisions/2005/11/des4415.htm, accessed June 20, 2006 [Hebrew]. See also Yosef Ben-David, "Accommodation within a Crisis: Social Aspects of the Bedouin Urbanization in the Negev," in Grossman and Meir, *Arab Society in Israel,* 48–76 [Hebrew]; Gideon M. Kressel, "Towns for the Bedouins? A Question for Applied Anthropology," in *The Negev: A Decade of Production* (Lahav: Joe Alon Center, 2003), 92–98 [Hebrew]; Yiftachel, *Ethnocracy,* 200–3; Swirski and Hasson, "Transparent Citizens," 15–19.

21.   In 2009, public transportation connecting Rahat and other recognized Bedouin settlements to Beer Sheva and to each other improved residents' mobility, in particular the mobility of women. See report on "Public transportation for the Arab population: A Snapshot," written by Dr. Yaniv Ronen and submitted on June 25, 2014 to the Knesset's Research and Information Center, at http://www.knesset.gov.il/mmm/data/pdf/m03412. pdf, 4–6, accessed August 24, 2014 [Hebrew].

22.   See "Data on the Education System in the Bedouin Sector", a report of the Knesset Research and Information Center, written by Asaf Wininger, submitted on July 8, 2013, http://www.knesset.gov.il/mmm/data/pdf/m03280.pdf, accessed August 24, 2014 [Hebrew]; Ismael Abu-Saad, "Bedouin Arabs in Israel between the Hammer and the Anvil: Education as a Foundation for Survival and Development," in Duane Champagne and Ismail Abu-Saad, eds., *Future of Indigenous Peoples: Strategies for Survival and Development* (Los Angeles: UCLA American Indian Studies Center, 2003), 103–20; Suleiman Abu-Bader and Daniel Gottlieb, "Education, Employment and Poverty among Bedouin Arabs in Southern Israel," *Hagar* 8,

2 (2008): 121–36; Suleiman Abu-Bader and Yehuda Gardos, eds., *The Statistical Data Book on Bedouins in the Negev*, no. 3 (Ben-Gurion University of the Negev: 2010) [Hebrew]; Norma Tarrow, "Human Rights and Education: The Case of the Negev Bedouins," *Hagar* 8, 2 (2008): 148–50; Sarab Abu-Rabia-Queder, "Between Tradition and Modernization: Understanding the Problem of Female Bedouin Dropouts," *British Journal of Sociology of Education* 27, 1 (2006): 3–17.

23. Emily McKee, *Dwelling in Conflict: Negev Landscapes and the Boundaries of Belonging* (Stanford: Stanford University Press, 2016), 50–68.

24. Wadi al-Na'am is located near Ramat Hovav Industrial Park and Ramat Negev's regional electricity plant and became widely known for its residents' acute health problems. See Michal Greenberg, "Remove the Population within Five Kilometers from Ramat Hovav," *Ha'aretz*, June 4, 2008 [Hebrew]; Yaacov Sitruk-Dahan, "A Dramatic Rise in the Number of Cancer Victims," *Sheva* 1861, September 25, 2011, 28 [Hebrew]; McKee, *Dwelling in Conflict*, 57–61. For further discussion of Ramat Hovav's adverse environmental impact, see chapter 6.

25. See also Yiftachel, *Ethnocracy*, 202–5; Swirski and Hasson, "Transparent Citizens"; Abu-Bader and Gottlieb, "Education, Employment and Poverty"; Abu-Bader and Gardos, *The Statistical Data Book on Bedouins*.

26. Yahel, "Land Disputes," 5–8; Zvi Alush, "Innovation in Bedouin Illegal Construction in the Negev: Villas, Gas Stations, and Supermarkets," *Yediot Ahronot*, July 21, 2000, 5 [Hebrew].

27. Ben-David's 2004 study ("Accommodation within a Crisis," 58) estimates that around 55% of the Bedouin population lived in the unrecognized villages at the time. Later reports by Swirski and Hasson ("Transparent Citizens") and Yiftachel (*Ethnocracy*, 197, 200) indicate that more than half of the Bedouin population now lives in the seven recognized towns; Yahel ("Land Disputes," 3–4) quotes the figure as 62%. See also the Goldberg Report (23–25) on the contested land contained within the territory of the Bedouin towns.

28. Shamir, "Suspended in Space," 478–79; Swirski and Hasson, "Transparent Citizens"; see also the later English version in Swirski, "Transparent Citizens." In November 2006, a symposium entitled "Not on the Map" was held at the Tel Aviv Cinematheque. The same title was used for a 2008 Human Rights Watch report on the unrecognized Bedouin villages: http://www.hrw.org/he/reports/2010/02/12–0, accessed October 16, 2004 [Hebrew].

29. Sarit Fox, "Hamira Is a Nonplace," *Maariv*, Weekend Supplement, October 23, 1992, 18 [Hebrew]; Meron Rappoport, "The Transparent People of the Negev," *Yediot Ahronot*, 24 Hours, August 3, 2003, 12–13 [Hebrew].

30. The term *pezura* (the "Bedouin dispersion") was used in local Negev discourse in the early 2000s, and references to it appear in those years in works by scholars studying the Negev. See, for example, Avinoam Meir, "From Planning Advocacy to Independent Planning: The Negev Bedouin on the Path to Democratization in Planning," Negev Center for Regional Development, Ben-Gurion University, Working Paper no. 22, Jan 2003 [Hebrew]; Kresse, "Towns for the Bedouins?" 92; *Negev Bar-Kaima* newsletter 4 (January 2004). In

time it became more widely used in the media and has appeared in official documents (see, for example, the Goldberg Report, 25.

31. Shmuel Rifman, "Israel without the Negev is Not a State and for Sure Not a Jewish State," *Karka* 57 (2000): 50 [Hebrew].

32. Hebrew dictionaries indicate that the term *pezura* relates primarily to the Jewish diaspora. See Yehuda Gur, *Hebrew Dictionary* (Tel Aviv: Dvir, 1952), 792 [Hebrew]; Avraham Even-Shoshan, *The New Dictionary* (Jerusalem: Kiryat Sefer, 1988), III: 1046 [Hebrew]; Reuven Alcalay, *The Complete Hebrew-English Dictionary* (Ramat-Gan: Massada, n.d), p. 2019 [Hebrew].

33. Ron Paz, "We are Not Dispersion [*pezura*]," *Globes*, December 23, 2007, http://www.globes.co.il/news/article.aspx?did=1000289492, accessed October 7, 2011 [Hebrew].

34. "Together in the Negev" [*Be-Yahad Ba-Negev*] website, http://www.coexnet.org.il/site/common/index.php?where=organization/home_page.php&id=201, accessed October 18, 2011 [Hebrew].

35. An early advocate for the Bedouins, the scholar and author Dr. Clinton Bailey (*Bedouin Poetry: From Sinai and the Negev* [Saqi Books, 2002]) was awarded the Emil Grunzweig Award for human rights for his pro-Bedouin activism in 1994. The civic organizations referred to include *Adalah*, the Legal Center for Arab Minority Rights in Israel, established in 1996, that provides legal assistance to the Negev Bedouins; the Negev Coexistence Forum for Civil Equality (known for short in Hebrew as *Forum Du-Kiyum*), formed by Arabs and Jews in 1997; *Bimkom*, Planners for Planning Rights, an Israeli nonprofit organization established in 1999 and active in alternative planning and related legislation; and Forum Together for the Negev, an umbrella organization of thirty-two communal and public organizations, formed in 2003 to promote Jewish-Arab coexistence and raise public awareness of the Negev Bedouins' situation.

36. Meir, "From Planning Advocacy to Independent Planning"; Avinoam Meir, "Bedouin, the Israeli State and Insurgent Planning: Globalization, Localization or Glocalization?" *Cities* 22, 3 (2005): 201–15; Anat Cygielman and Ruth Sinai, "The Light at the End of the Town; *Ha'aretz* Report on the Unrecognized Villages," *Ha'aretz*, March 28, 2005 [Hebrew]. The RCUV was later challenged internally by competing groups, yet it appears to have emerged as the leading representative forum and to be recognized by outside organizations.

37. See "Blueprint for the Recognition of Unrecognized Villages in the Negev" (abbreviated edition), published in 2012 by the RCUV and *Bimkom* in collaboration with Sidreh (Bedouin-Arab Women of the Negev), http://bimkom.org/wp-content/uploads/bedouins_Mars2012_final_screen.pdf, accessed August 16, 2014 [Hebrew].

38. Nir Hasson, "After Half a Century of Struggle, Negev Village Finally Earns Official Recognition," *Ha'aretz*, August 6, 2004, http://www.haaretz.com/after-half-a-century-of-struggle-negev-village-finally-earns-official-recognition-1.130799, accessed May 5, 2017. See also Swirski and Hasson, "Transparent Citizens," 27–30; Yiftachel, *Ethnocracy*, 207–8. See further discussion of Drejat in chapter 7.

39. According to Israel's Central Bureau of Statistics, in 2014 the Regional Council of El Kasum was in charge of a population of 8,500, while that of Neve Midbar was in

charge of a population estimated at around 7,100. See, respectively, http://www.cbs.gov.il
/publications16/local_authorities14_1642/pdf/946_0069.pdf, accessed April 30, 2017 [He-
brew]; http://www.cbs.gov.il/publications16/local_authorities14_1642/pdf/1102_0068.pdf,
accessed April 30, 2017 [Hebrew].

40. For the government's decision no. 1999 on "removal of trespassers," July 15, 2007,
see the website of the prime minister's office, http://www.pmo.gov.il/Secretary/GovDe-
cisions/2007/Pages/des1999.aspx [Hebrew]. On the resolution regarding the individual
farms, see Zafrir Rinat, "The Government Decided to Advance the Establishment of Individual Farms in the Negev and the Galilee," *Ha'aretz*, July 15, 2007, http://news.walla.co.il/
item/1137313, accessed August 26, 2014 [Hebrew].

41. Ismael Abu-Saad, "The Bedouin's Complaint: 'How Can We Be Defined as Invaders If We and Our Ancestors Have Lived in the Negev for Thousands of Years?'" *Karka* 57
(2003): 31–34 [Hebrew]; Oren Yiftachel and Ortal Tsabar, "Whose Land Is This—the Bedouins' or the State's?" *Yediot Ahronot*, August 5, 2010 [Hebrew]; Nir Hasson, "The Bedouins
Presented a Sale Deed, the Supreme Court Ruled in Favor of the State," *Ha'aretz*, August
5, 2010 [Hebrew]; Zafrir Rinat, "The Bedouins Protested in Tel Aviv: Israel Invaded Our
Land," *Ha'aretz*, September 20, 2011 [Hebrew].

42. O. Yiftachel, S. Kedar, and A. Amara, "Rethinking the Dead Negev Doctrine:
Property Rights in Bedouin Regions," *Mishpat U-Mimshal* 14, 1 (2012): 7–147 [Hebrew];
Abu-Saad, "Bedouin Arabs in Israel," 103–20; Clinton Baily, *Bedouin Law from Sinai and
the Negev: Justice without Government* (New Haven: Yale University Press, 2009); Batia
Roded and Erez Tzfadia, "Recognition of Indigenous People's Land Rights: The Bedouins in
Comparison," *Ha-Merchav Ha-Tsiburi* 7 (2012): 66–99 [Hebrew]; Mansour Nasasra, "The
Ongoing Judaisation of the Naqab and the Struggle for Recognising the Indigenous Rights
of the Arab Bedouin People," *Settler Colonial Studies* 2, 1 (2012): 81–107.

43. See Seth J. Frantzman, Havatzelet Yahel, and Ruth Kark, "Contested Indigeneity:
The Development of an Indigenous Discourse on the Bedouin of the Negev, Israel," *Israel
Studies* 17, 1 (Spring 2012): 78–104.

44. The Goldberg Report, 26; Ofer Dagan, "'Tuscany Is Here': Elite Tourism and
the Production of the Jewish Ethno-National Space on Family Farms in Southern Israel,"
MA thesis, Department of Sociology and Anthropology, Ben-Gurion University, 2014,
27 [Hebrew].

45. Yiftachel further describes the "gray space" as being "between the 'lightness' of
legality/approval/safety and the 'darkness' of eviction/destruction/death," in Oren Yiftachel, "Critical Theory and 'Gray Space': Mobilization of the Colonized," *City* 13, 2–3
(2009): 243.

46. Elya L. Milner and Haim Yacobi, "Spaces of Sovereignty: A Tale of an Unrecognized
Palestinian Village in Israel," *Planning Theory* (April 2017): 1–17, http://journals.sagepub
.com/doi/abs/10.1177/1473095217700687.

47. *Adalah*, *Bimkom*, and the Negev Coexistence Forum for Civil Equality, "Opposition
to the Regional Policy Plan, 14/4 (Modification no. 42): Individual Farms and the Wine Route
in Ramat Negev." For further information see the website of *Adalah*, at http://www.adalah
.org/uploads/oldfiles/features/naqab/metropolin-beersabe-0.pdf [Hebrew], and the website of

Bimkom, at http://bimkom.org/wp-content/uploads/BeerShebaMetro.pdf [Hebrew]. Taleb El-Sana, a United Arab List member of the Knesset, objected to approving the individual farms before settling the situation of the Bedouins' villages during the deliberations of the Knesset's economy committee on July 28, 2009. See the Knesset website at http://webcache .googleusercontent.com/search?q=cache:g8YUSr7MHuAJ:www.knesset.gov.il/protocols /data/rtf/kalkala/2009–07–28–01.rtf+&cd=6&hl=en&ct=clnk&gl=il, 11 [Hebrew]. See also McKee, *Dwelling in Conflict,* 74–81.

48. The Goldberg Report, 26–28; on the status of the population in the unrecognized villages and for its recommendations, 29–40. See also the website of the Association for Civil Rights in Israel (ACRI), http://www.acri.org.il/he/12108, updated May 31, 2011, accessed August 22, 2014 [Hebrew]; Ahmad Amara, "The Goldberg Committee: Legal and Extra-Legal Means of Solving the Naqab Bedouin Case," *Hagar* 8, 2 (2008): 227–43.

49. "The Prawer Report," officially entitled "The Recommendations of the Team for the Implementation of the Goldberg Report for the Resolution of the Bedouin Settlement in the Negev," was submitted on May 31, 2011. See the website of the prime minister's office at http://www.pmo.gov.il/policyplanning/hevra/Documents/goldberg1012. pdf, accessed October 16, 2014 [Hebrew]. The report limited the claims that would be considered to those that had been submitted and approved between 1971 and 1979 and offered limited compensation to those Bedouins who currently lived on the land of which they claimed ownership, and only monetary compensation to those who did not reside on the land to which they had claims. The plan called for a progressive reduction of compensation over the passage of time in order to increase the pressure on the Bedouins to accept its terms.

50. "Blueprint for the Recognition of Unrecognized Villages in the Negev."

51. Zeev Binyamin Begin's revised plan was submitted to the government on January 23, 2013: see the website of the prime minister's office, http://www.pmo.gov.il/MEDIACENTER /Pages/begin.aspx, accessed October 17, 2014 [Hebrew].

52. An active promoter of these claims and legal action was the nongovernmental organization Regavim, The National Land Protection Trust, established in 2006 "to ensure responsible, legal and accountable use of Israel's national lands and the return of the rule of law to all areas and aspects of the land and its preservation." See the website of Regavim at http://regavim.org/about-regavim/ and http://regavim.org/response-to-the-resignation-of -former-minister-benny-begin/, December 12, 2013, accessed July 20, 2018.

53. See the "Response to The Begin-Prawer Plan" in the 2013 archive of *Bimkom,* December 2013, http://bimkom.org/2013/ [Hebrew]; see also "Demolition and Eviction of Bedouin Citizens of Israel in the Naqab (Negev)—The Prawer Plan," *Adalah,* http:// adalah.org/eng/?mod=articles&ID=1589, and Zafrir Rinat and Jonathan Lis, "A Guide for the Perplexed: Israel's Bedouin Resettlement Bill," *Ha'aretz,* June 25, 2013, https:// www.haaretz.com/.premium-bedouin-resettlement-a-primer-1.5241351, accessed October 17, 2014.

54. Jonathan Lis, "Israeli Cabinet Likely to Scrap Controversial Bedouin Relocation Plan," *Ha'aretz,* December 9, 2013, http://www.haaretz.com/news/national/1.562625,

accessed September 3, 2014. See also Mahmoud Zwahre and Eurig Scandratt, "Community Development as Resistance and Resilience: An Interview with Mahmoud Zwahre," *Concept* 5, 2 (2014): 33.

55.   Israel Central Bureau of Statistics of 2016 population data, http://www.cbs.gov.il /shnaton68/st02_17.pdf, accessed December 27, 2017 [Hebrew/English]. For the unrecognized villages, see report by *Bimkom*, from August 2014, http://www.acri.org.il/he/wp-content /uploads/2016/03/unrecognized-villages0814.pdf, accessed April 30, 2017 [Hebrew].

56.   Safa Abu-Rabia, "Between Memory and Resistance, an Identity Shaped by Space: The Case of the Naqab Arab Bedouins," *Hagar* 8, 2 (2008): 93–119. See also McKee's discussion of how the Bedouins' reconstruction of their past is also shaped by Israeli mnemonic culture, in McKee, *Dwelling in Conflict*, 39–49.

57.   Arnon Ben-Israel and Avinoam Meir, "Renaming Space and Reshaping Identities: The Case of the Bedouin Town of Hura in Israel," *Hagar* 8, 2 (2008): 84; see also Ben-David, "Accommodation within a Crisis," 62–66; Parizot, "Gaza, Beersheba, Dhahriyya."

58.   It is interesting to note that while Yiftachel criticizes references to the "Negev Bedouins" as "a forced division of the Naqab Bedouins from other parts of their own society," he acknowledges that the community itself uses both the Arabic and Hebrew terms: Oren Yiftachel, "Epilogue: Studying al-Naqab/Negev Bedouins—Toward a Colonial Paradigm?" *Hagar* 8, 2 (2008), 173.

59.   On the transformation of the Bedouin identity, see Yiftachel, "Epilogue"; Parizot, "Gaza, Beersheba, Dhahriyya," 104–5; Longina Jakubowska, "Resisting 'Ethnicity': The Israeli State and Bedouin Identity," *The Paths to Domination, Resistance, and Terror* 85 (1992): 85–105; Ben-Israel and Meir, "Renaming Space and Reshaping Identities"; Yossi Yonah, Ismael Abu-Saad, and Avi Kaplan, "De-Arabization of the Bedouin: A Study of an Inevitable Failure," *Interchange* 35, 4 (2004): 387–406.

60.   When five soldiers from the Desert Patrol Battalion encountered their death in Rafah, for example, the absence of visitors in their families' mourning tents indicated their social isolation. See Dan Rabinowitz, "Rights before Service," *Ha'aretz* op-ed page, December 22, 2004. Some families refuse the publication of the full names of fallen soldiers: Yehoshua Breiner, "And after That One Wonders Why There Are No Bedouins in the Army," *Walla*, Feb. 1, 2009, http://news.walla.co.il/item/1427301, accessed August 4, 2014 [Hebrew]. Residents of the Bedouin town Rahat responded negatively to having visitors park there for a military display on Independence Day in 2011. See Ilana Curiel, "Rahat Township against Israel Defense Forces," *Ynet*, May 9, 2011, http://www.ynet.co.il /articles/0,7340,L-4066480,00.html, accessed May 23, 2011 [Hebrew].

61.   The IDF's data from 2004 indicate that only a thousand Bedouin soldiers were serving in the army, and it indicates the limited use made by these soldiers of the educational opportunities provided to them by the army. See the State Comptroller Report, 2004, II: 129–34, quoted in Swirski and Hasson, "Transparent Citizens," 35. On April 4, 2012 it was noted that about 450 Bedouin recruits (including both Negev and Galilee Bedouins) were being added each year, and that only one out of nine of them remained in the army as a career soldier. Data accessed on the IDF website at http://www.idf.il/1133–15605–he /Dover.aspx, on August 4, 2014 [Hebrew].

62. See, for example, Zvi Alush, "Four Who Fought in Yom Kippur [War] Fight against the Appropriation of their Area," *Yediot Ahronot*, June 26, 1980, 4 [Hebrew]; "Pride and Shame: The Lieutenant Colonel Lives in a Shack," *Yediot Ahronot*, September 18, 2002 [Hebrew]; Hadad Magen, "What is the Price for Military Service for the Bedouin Patrol Soldiers?" *Globes*, July 12, 2012, http://www.globes.co.il/news/article.aspx?did=1000764656, accessed August 4, 2014 [Hebrew].

63. The film *Sharqiya*, by Ami Livne, features Bedouin and Jewish actors; the director is Jewish. The film received the Jerusalem Film Festival Award of 2012, although it reportedly took close to two years before it was screened in Israeli theaters. See Elad Shalev, "An Impressive First Film that Moves beyond Documentation to the Cinematic Lyrical Narrative," at the Israeli Film website, http://www.seret.co.il/critics/moviereviews.asp?id=1421, n.d [Hebrew]; see also Uri Klein, "Sharqiya—A Film Not to Be Missed," *Ha'aretz*, Galeria Section, Nov. 9, 2013 [Hebrew].

64. See "The Wild South Extends North," *Ha-Boker*, May 12, 1952 [Hebrew]; Danny Tzidkoni, "The Police against the Wild South," *Davar*, March 1, 1978, 6 [Hebrew].

65. Udi Nathan, "Welcome to the 'Wild West' of Israel," *Ynet*, Feb. 28, 2007, http://www.ynet.co.il/articles/0,7340,L-3370825,00.html [Hebrew]. See also the reference to Israel as the "Wild East" in Shmuel A. Katz, *The Wild East* (Jerusalem: Keter, 1995) [Hebrew].

66. See, for example, Lea Etgar, "The Wild South," *Yediot Ahronot*, Seven Days, March 21, 1980, 7–9 [Hebrew]; Rami Shani, "The 'Wild South': That's How an Organization Terrorized," *Walla*, November 8, 2012, http://news.walla.co.il/item/2584003, accessed July 23, 2015 [Hebrew]; Ronen Tal, "The 'Wild South,'" *Yediot Ahronot*, Jan. 28, 2008, 4 [Hebrew]; Paz, "We Are Not Dispersion [*pezura*]"; Dagan, "'Tuscany Is Here,'" 47; Tal Zagraba, "From a Novelist to a Farmer: Tsur Shezaf Makes the Desert Bloom," *Ynet*, April 29, 2014, http://xnet.ynet.co.il/win/articles/0,14717,L-3105519,00.html, accessed January 30, 2015 [Hebrew].

67. Nir Hasson, "Suspicion: Four Bedouins Participate in Trading Weapons to the West Bank," *Ha'aretz*, April 14, 2004 [Hebrew]; Ronen Tal, "The Ministry of the Interior's Report: The Bedouins Are Criminals Who Live on Protection Money," *Yediot Ahronot*, May 31, 2000 [Hebrew]; Anat Bershokovski, "Bedouins Are Involved in Most Severe Accidents in the Negev," *Yediot Ahronot*, Dec. 30, 2006 [Hebrew]; Yonat Atlas, "The Wild South: Camels, Unpaved Roads and Red Highways," *Ynet*, Sept. 10, 2008, http://www.ynet.co.il/articles/0,7340,L-3593331,00.html, accessed July 23, 2015 [Hebrew]; Zadok Yehezkeli, "Lost on the Road," *Yediot Ahronot*, Seven Days, Dec. 24, 2004, 38–43, 92 [Hebrew]; Channel 10, "The True Face of the Bedouin Gangs," broadcast Jan. 9, 2013, https://www.youtube.com/watch?v=C2jPGhxe9SM, accessed January 18, 2015 [Hebrew]; Ahmed abu Swiss, "The Wild South—Illegal Weapons Are Traded by the Negev Bedouins," *Walla*, March 24, 2015, http://news.walla.co.il/item/2839785, accessed July 23, 2015 [Hebrew].

68. For the official court ruling by the regional Beer Sheva court, see http://www.perot.org.il/info/ShayDromiVerdict.pdf, accessed February 15, 2017 [Hebrew]. See also Amnon Meranda, "New Law Allows Homeowners to Shoot Burglars," *Ynet*, June 24, 2008, http://www.ynetnews.com/articles/0,7340,L-3559940,00.html; and Ilana Curiel, "Farmer Who killed Burglar Acquitted of Manslaughter," *Ynet*, July 15, 2009, http://www.ynet.co.il/articles/0,7340,L-3746751,00.html, accessed September 8, 2015 [Hebrew].

69. See, for example, the Bedouins interviewed in *Ynet*, "The Negev's Youth Dream: A State for All Its Citizens" [*Ha-hazon ha-rahut shel tze'irei ha-negev: Medinat kol ezraheiha*], produced by *Ynet* on January 26, 2010, https://www.youtube.com/watch?v=HITSC78JMyk, accessed January 18, 2015 [Hebrew].

70. The Goldberg Report (11–12) refers to a 5.5% average annual population growth rate over 50 years, based on the official 2007 population estimate of 172,169. It points out that at this rate, the Bedouin population will double every 13 years, although other sources point out that the rate might slow down. The current high rate is associated with the practice of polygamy among the Bedouins.

71. Ze'ev Wolfson, "Bedouins Take Over the Negev," *Ha-Yarden Magazine* 222 (2007): 3 [Hebrew].

72. Ariel Sharon, "Land as an Economic Tool to Establish Infrastructure and Reduce Social Gaps," *Karka* 50 (2000): 14–15 [Hebrew] (emphasis added).

73. Rifman, "Israel without the Negev Is Not a State," 50.

74. Vered Levy-Barzilai, "The New Settlers," *Ha'aretz*, Weekend Supplement, Dec. 20, 2002, 29–32 [Hebrew].

75. Avigdor Lieberman, in an interview in *Ma'ariv*, April 14 and 15, 2002, quoted in Yiftachel, *Ethnocracy*, 3.

76. See also Dr. Thabet abu-Ras, from Ben-Gurion University, quoted in Ami Ben-David, Uri Binder, and Shimon Afirgan, "Before the Negev Burns," *Ma'ariv*, July 3, 2003, 2–3 [Hebrew]. The journalist Tom Segev wryly comments on the issue of the Bedouins' trespassing, "Yes, they sit on state land. So what? Most Israelis live on state land": Tom Segev, "Tents and Garbage Sites," *Ha'aretz*, Jan. 7, 1994, 8 [Hebrew].

77. Yahel, "Land Disputes," 7–8, 10 (emphasis added).

78. Yiftachel, Kedar, and Amara, "Rethinking the Dead Negev Doctrine," 95–101.

79. The Green Patrol served the Nature Reserves Authority, the Israel Land Authority, the Jewish National Fund, and the ministries of agriculture and defense. The unit's name was later changed to the "Green Police," to avoid the use of a military term. The Bedouins' renaming of the unit as "the Black Patrol" was reported by Ismail Abu Saad in "The Goal of the Urbanization Plan for the Bedouins in the Negev," *Karka* 50 (2000): 159–69 [Hebrew], quoted in Swirski and Hasson, "Transparent Citizens," 17.

80. The Bedouins offered resistance to the actions of the Green Patrol that led to violent clashes: Yehoshua Bitsur, "The Bedouins Are Taking Control of State Land," *Ma'ariv*, July 31, 1980, 2 [Hebrew]; Ronen Tal, "Nature Conservation or Oppression of the Bedouins?" *Yediot Ahronot*, August 9, 1998, 19 [Hebrew]; Tamar Travalsi, "The Land Authority's Inspectors Attacked by Dozens of Bedouins," *Yediot Ahronot*, November 17, 1988, 11 [Hebrew]; Amir Hillel, "The Green Patrol," *Kan* 10 (January 2003): 26–28 [Hebrew]; Ronen Tal, "Twenty-Four Wounded in Negev Riots," *Yediot Ahronot*, Nov. 16, 2005, 19 [Hebrew]. See also Alon Tal, *Pollution in the Promised Land: An Environmental History of Israel* (Berkeley: University of California Press, 2002), 345–52.

81. Chaim Gouri, "Poison from the Sky on the Negev Fields," *Yediot Ahronot*, 24 Hours, Feb. 15, 2004, 3 [Hebrew]; Amos Kenan, "The Desolation of the Bloom" [*hashmamat hafraha*], *Yediot Ahronot*, 24 Hours, April 17, 1980, 3 [Hebrew]; Kenan, "A Green Day in Our Lives,"

Yediot Ahronot, 24 Hours, Nov. 3, 1987 [Hebrew]; Zeev Tzahor, "Do Not Spray That Which Has Been Seeded," *Yediot Ahronot*, Jan. 30, 2002, 7 [Hebrew]. Agi Mishol wrote a poem entitled *Mishpat sade* (literally, "field sentencing," but also implying "court martial"), which was published in *Yediot Ahronot*, March 29, 2002, 27 [Hebrew].

82.   Gideon Levy, "Those Who Carry Out the Vision," *Ha'aretz*, August 10, 2010 [Hebrew].

83.   Uri Binder and Amir Buhbut, "Planes Sprayed the Fields in the Negev," *Ma'ariv*, Feb. 15, 2003 [Hebrew]; Tsahar Rotem, "Thousands of Dunams of Bedouin Agricultural Land Destroyed in the Negev," *Ha'aretz*, April 3, 2003 [Hebrew]. Swirski and Hasson describe the loss of 7,250 acres (29,000 dunams) of crops to chemical spraying between 2002 and 2004. In October, 2004, the Supreme Court ruling prohibited this practice: Swirski and Hasson, "Transparent Citizens," 34; see also Yiftachel, *Ethnocracy*, 202, 205.

84.   Uri Binder, "Here the Next Intifada Will Take Place," *Ma'ariv*, July 15, 2001, 9 [Hebrew]; Yosef Elgazi, "A Minute before the Intifada in the Negev," *Ha'aretz*, July 20, 2001, B7 [Hebrew]; Zvi Alush, "It Won't Take Long before Fire Breaks Out and the Negev Burns," *Yediot Ahronot*, May 10, 2002, 22–23 [Hebrew].

85.   See also Jackie Khouri and Maya Sela, "Amos Oz: The Situation of the Bedouins in the Negev Is a 'Ticking Time Bomb,'" *Ha'aretz*, Aug. 18, 2010.

86.   Channel 10, "The True Face of the Bedouin Gangs."

87.   Tsur Shezaf, *The Happy Man* (Tel Aviv: Am Oved, 2007) [Hebrew]. Shezaf later became the owner of an individual farm in Ramat Negev, and his views may have been modified since then.

88.   This fictive description resonates with a 2009 case in which Bedouins performed deliberate damage to the Nabbatean archeological site of Avdat, as an act of revenge for house demolitions in their unrecognized villages. A police investigator was quoted as saying, "someone declared a war on the State of Israel in the Negev." See Shimon Ifergan, "Two Men Suspected of Damaging the Avdat Site Were Arrested," *Nrg*, Oct. 5, 2009, http://www .nrg.co.il/online/1/ART1/950/258.html, accessed July 5, 2015 [Hebrew]; Ilana Curiel, "Charged with Destruction of Avdat: Bedouins' Revenge on the Nabateans," *Ynet*, Oct. 4, 2009, http://www.ynet.co.il/articles/0,7340,L-3799959,00.html, accessed July 5, 2015 [Hebrew].

89.   On the heroic image of Trumpeldor and on Masada, see Yael Zerubavel, *Recovered Roots: Collective Memory and the Making of Israeli National Tradition* (Chicago: University of Chicago Press, 1995). Shezaf may also have been inspired by the figure of Amos Yarkoni, discussed earlier in this chapter, who likewise lost an arm in action. Another possible inspiration is Avraham Negev, a member of kibbutz Revivim, who had wished to become a neurosurgeon but, after his left arm was cut off in an accident, became an archeologist. See Avrahan Negev, "The First Years in the Negev," *Ariel* 152–53 (2002): 207–8 [Hebrew].

90.   See the archive website of the ministry of public security, http://archive.mops .gov.il/PolicingAndEnforcement/LandLawEnforceNegev/Pages/LandLawDirectorate.aspx, accessed January 22, 2015 [Hebrew]. A Facebook ad, posted August 3, 2013, specifies that the Yoav unit's recruits are expected to have prior combat experience: https://he-il .facebook.com/israel.giyus.police/posts/101518309900985, accessed January 22, 2015 [Hebrew]. See also Ilana Curiel, "How to Evacuate the Bedouins from Home," *Ynet*,

Oct. 25, 2013, http://www.ynetnews.com/articles/0,7340,L-4445428,00.html, accessed September 3, 2014.

91.   These numbers are from the report on house demolitions in the Negev in 2012–2013 by the Negev Coexistence Forum for Civil Equality, http://www.dukium.org/eng/wp-content/uploads/2011/06/HD_Report_E_2014.pdf, accessed September 3, 2014 [Hebrew]. See their June 2016 report, "Enforcing Distress: House Demolition Policy in the Bedouin Community in the Negev," at their website https://www.dukium.org/wp-content/uploads/2016/06/HDR_2016_ENG-1.pdf, accessed May 2, 2018.

92.   The struggle of al-Araqib has received broad national and international media coverage. See Julie Couzinet, "Bedouin Village of al-Araqib Demolished for the 70th Time Despite Court Proceedings," June 16, 2014, http://mondoweiss.net/2014/06/bedouin-demolished-proceedings#sthash.GcHq3QUn.dpuf, accessed September 2, 2015; Yanir Yagne and Jackie Khouri, "1,500 Policemen Secured the Destruction of Scores of Structures of the Bedouins in the Negev," *Ha'aretz*, July 28, 2010 [Hebrew]; Isabel Kershner, "A Test of Wills over a Patch of Desert," The *New York Times*, August 25, 2010, http://www.nytimes.com/2010/08/26/world/middleeast/26israel.html?pagewanted=all&_r=0, accessed September 5, 2014; Jackie Khouri and Shirly Seidler, "Another Evacuation in Al-Araqeeb: Bulldozers Demolish Buildings in the Cemetery," *Ha'aretz*, June 12, 2014 [Hebrew]. See also Yiftachel, Kedar, and Amara, "Rethinking the Dead Negev Doctrine," 8–10, 120–32; Amit M. Schejter and Noam Tirosh, "Social Media New and Old in the Al-'Arakeeb Conflict: A Case Study," *The Information Society* 28 (2012): 304–15; McKee, *Dwelling in Conflict*, 51–52, 65.

93.   Noga Malkin, "The Eleven Times the Authorities Demolished the Village al-Araqib," *Kvish Arba'im* [Route 40, the Cultural Magazine of the South] 114, February 2011, http://www.kvish40.co.il/2011/02/1148, accessed January 19, 2015 [Hebrew]. On the JNF's Ambassadors' Forest and ecological research, see http://www.moag.gov.il/agri/yhidotmisrad/shimur_karka/sers/publication/2011/yaar_hashagririm.htm, accessed October 18, 2014 [Hebrew].

94.   Jonathan Cook, "Bedouin Tribes' Land Fears over God-TV's Tree Planting," *The National*, Dec. 28, 2010, http://www.thenational.ae/news/world/middle-east/bedouin-tribes-land-fears-over-god-tvs-tree-planting, accessed September 3, 2014; Neve Gordon, "Uprooting the Bedouins of Israel," *The Nation*, Dec. 2, 2010, https://www.thenation.com/article/uprooting-bedouins-israel/, accessed September 3, 2014. God-TV's rejection of reports about their compliance with the displacement of Bedouin people as false (which was accessed on its website: http://god.tv/negev, in October 18, 2014) no longer appears there.

95.   See the JNF website announcing the planting of the Socialist Democratic Party of Germany (SPD) Forest on November 30, 2015, http://www.kkl.org.il/new_in_kkl/spd-germany-forest-planting.aspx [Hebrew]; on the opposition to the establishment of the "Forest of German States" on land disputed by the Bedouins, see the English-language position paper of the Negev Coexistence Forum, March 25, 3013, http://www.palaestina-portal.eu/NCF%20Positon%20Paper%20on%20JNF%20Responses%20to%20SPD%20Project_25.3.pdf, accessed April 30, 2017.

96.   Weizman and Sheikh, *The Conflict Shoreline*, 10 (emphasis added).

97.   Avi Issacharoff, "A Tale of Two Evacuated Villages," *The Times of Israel*, Feb. 5, 2017, http://www.timesofisrael.com/a-tale-of-two-evacuated-cities/. See also "Amona vs Umm al-Hiran: A Reality Check—Rabbis for Human Rights," the website of Rabbis for Human Rights, January 18, 2017, http://rhr.org.il/eng/2017/01/amona-v s-umm-al-hiran-reality-check/; Milner and Yacobi, "Spaces of Sovereignty," 13–14; Ben Lynfield, "State Pressures Beduin to Leave Negev Village to Make Way for Jewish Town," *The Jerusalem Post*, January 16, 2017, http://www.jpost.com/Israel-News /State-pressures-Beduin-to-leave-Negev-village-to-make-way-for-Jewish-town-478536.

98.   Nahum Barnea, "Our Forces Did Not Return Peacefully," *Yediot Ahronot*, January 19, 2017, http://www.yediot.co.il/articles/0,7340,L-4909999,00.html [Hebrew].

99.   Shirly Seidler, "Southern Israeli Council Fights Government Plan to Resettle Bedouin Villages," *Ha'aretz*, July 6, 2015, http://www.haaretz.com/news/israel/.premium-1.664573.

100.   At the official level, see David Newman, "Creating Homogenous Space: the Evolution of Israel's Regional Councils," in S. Ilan Troen and Noah Lucas, eds., *Israel: The First Decade of Independence* (Albany: SUNY Press, 1995), 495–522. McKee (*Dwelling in Conflict*, 14, 16), who has studied both Arab and Jewish communities in the Negev, notes the "emplaced group boundaries" that reinforce their social and cultural segregation.

101.   Yiftachel, "Critical Theory and 'Gray Space,'" 249–50; McKee, *Dwelling in Conflict*, 62.

102.   McKee, *Dwelling in Conflict*, 49, 61–65.

103.   *Ynet*, "The Negev's Youth Dream."

104.   The police removed Nuri al-Uqbi from the contested land and the Israel Land Authority spokeswoman referred to him as a "serial invader." See Yosef Elgazi, "The War on the New House," *Ha'aretz*, July 2, 2003, http://www.haaretz.co.il/misc/1.893060, accessed April 28, 2017 [Hebrew]; Aviva Lori, "Deep in the Soil," *Ha'aretz*, Weekend Supplement, June 23, 2006, 50 [Hebrew]. Oren Yiftachel ("The Horror Show in Al-'Arakeeb," *Ha'aretz*, August 2, 2010, http://www.haaretz.co.il/opinions/1.1214845, accessed September 3, 2014 [Hebrew]) evokes the analogy with the Jewish commemoration of the destruction of the Temple on Tish'a Be-Av. See also Weizman and Sheikh, *The Conflict Shoreline*, 46–50.

105.   Dagan, "'Tuscany Is Here,'" 74–75.

106.   Channel 10, "The True Face of the Bedouin Gangs."

Chapter 6

1.   Yossi Katz, *To Stop the Bulldozer: Establishing Institutions for the Preservation of the Nature and Historical Heritage of Israel* (Ramat Gan: Bar Ilan University Press, 2004), 13–21 and appendix 1, 129–58 [Hebrew].

2.   Alon Tal, *Pollution in the Promised Land: An Environmental History of Israel* (Berkeley: University of California Press, 2002), 114–18.

3.   Tal, *Pollution in the Promised Land*; Offer Regev, *Four Decades of Blossoming: The Society for the Protection of Nature, 1953–93* (Tel Aviv: SPNI, 1993) [Hebrew]. See also Yael Moriah and Sigal Bar-Nir, "The Conquest of the Desert and the Protection of Nature as Two Aspects of Israeli Culture," in *View of the Place: Four Approaches to Landscaping in Israel*

[*Mar'eh makom*] (Tel Aviv: Genia Schreiber University Art Gallery, Tel Aviv University, 1996), 18–21 [Hebrew].

4.   Orit Ben-David, "*Tiyul* (Hike) as an Act of Consecration of Space," in Eyal Ben-Ari and Yoram Bilu, eds., *Grasping Land: Space and Place in Contemporary Israeli Discourse and Experience* (Albany: SUNY Press, 1997), 129–45. See also the SPNI website, http://www .teva.org.il/english/, accessed March 8, 2017. Tal (*Pollution in the Promised Land*, 114–18) notes that the organization had more than 600 employees in 1999.

5.   Daniella Arieli, "The Cultural Construction of Nature: The Case of the Society for the Protection of Nature," *Megamot* 38, 2 (1997): 189–206 [Hebrew]. See also Emanuel Mazor, "Open Spaces and Sustainable Development," Symposium on Geology and Sustainable Development in the Third Millennium: The Case of the Negev, *Ecology and Environment* 3, 4 (1996): 261 [Hebrew]; Avner De-Shalit, "From the Political to the Objective: The Dialectics of Zionism and Environmentalism," *Environmental Politics* 4 (Spring 1995): 70–87.

6.   Tal, *Pollution in the Promised Land*, 172–74.

7.   Katz, *To Stop the Bulldozer*, 122–23. The proposed "Law of National Parks and Nature Reserves," *Knesset Chronicles* [*Divrei yemei ha-knesset*], December 3, 1962, 331–32 [Hebrew] and the modified law that was approved appear in Appendices 7 & 8 respectively, 192–207.

8.   Amir Zohar, "To the Last Grain of Sand," *Ha'aretz*, Weekend Supplement, Aug. 20, 2008, 48–50 [Hebrew].

9.   Amos Kenan, "To Understand the Land," in Bennie Gvirtzman, ed., *The Zionist Dimension of Nature Preservation: A Discussion at the Council of the Society for the Protection of Nature in Israel* (Tel Aviv: SPNI and the Ministry of Education, 1981), 20, 23 [Hebrew].

10.   S. Yizhar, "To Hear the Roots Grow," in Gvirtzman, *The Zionist Dimension*, 11. See also Amos Oz, "On the Love of the Country," in Gvirtzman, *The Zionist Dimension*, 16; de-Shalit, "From the Political to the Objective."

11.   S. Yizhar, "Not to Make the Desolate Land Bloom," *Eretz Va-Teva* (Jan.–Feb. 1995): 6 [Hebrew].

12.   Azaria Alon, "Nature Protection vs. Zionism?" in Gvirtzman, *The Zionist Dimension of Nature Preservation*, 28; Yoav Sagi, "The Preservation of the Negev Landscape: A Grim Assessment," *Teva Va-Aretz* 22 (1980): 222–23 [Hebrew].

13.   Yizhar, "Not to Make the Desolate Land Bloom."

14.   Gideon Ofrat, "From Personification of Nature to Punishing Nature," *Studio* 33 (1992): 8–10 [Hebrew]

15.   Nathan Alterman's lyrics for "Morning Song" [*Shir boker*], melody by Daniel Sambursky. See the Zemereshet website for Hebrew songs, http://www.zemereshet.co.il/song.asp?id=156, accessed March 22, 2015 [Hebrew] (emphasis added). The song was featured, as mentioned earlier, in Judah Leman's 1935 film *The Land of Promise* [*Le-hayim Hadashim*].

16.   The literary critic Dan Miron interprets Alterman's poem as a parody of Avraham Shlonsky's celebratory representation of construction: Dan Miron, *Founding Mothers, Stepsisters* (Tel Aviv: Hakibbutz Hameuchad, 1991), 215 [Hebrew]. Alterman's verse is nonetheless often quoted as representing the excess of the settlement ethos; see Midreshet, the educational website of the Israeli Batei Midrash Network, at http://midreshet.org.il/PageView .aspx?id=1228&back=http%3A//midreshet.org.il/ResourcesView.aspx%3Fid%3D10473, ac-

cessed March 22, 2015 [Hebrew]. Alterman also wrote about the city as a "jungle of concrete and electricity and iron," in "The Camels' Vision," *Ha'aretz*, Nov. 16, 1932, reprinted in *The Small Tel Aviv* [*Tel Aviv ha-ketana*] (Tel Aviv: Hakkibutz Hameuchad, 1979), 9–25 [Hebrew].

17.   Along similar lines, Roderick Nash (*Wilderness and the American Mind* [New Haven: Yale University Press, 3rd edition, 1982, 3]) points out book titles that apply the term "wilderness" to the urban setting, such as *The City Wilderness* by Robert A. Woods (1898) and *The Neon Wilderness* by Nelson Algren (1960).

18.   Alon, "Nature Protection vs. Zionism?" 26; Yizhar, "Not to Make the Desolate Land Bloom," 6.

19.   Oz, "On the Love of the Country," 15; Chaim Gouri, "From Chaim Gouri's Words," in Gvirtzman, *The Zionist Dimension of Nature Preservation*, 32. Similar views are articulated by others in Hadas Yaron, *Zionist Arabesques: Modern Landscapes, Non-Modern Texts* (Boston: Academic Press, 2010), 105–6. The reference to the uniformity of the settled landscape is reminiscent of Malvina Reynolds's lyrics, alluding to "little boxes on the hillside . . . little boxes all the same," in her 1962 song (made famous by Pete Seeger when he sang it the following year).

20.   Tal, *Pollution in the Promised Land*, 69, 94–95.

21.   Kenan, "To Understand the Land."

22.   Mazor, "Open Spaces and Sustainable Development," 261; Katz, *To Stop the Bulldozer*.

23.   Amir Idelman, "The Negev Space: Is the Mission Lost?" *Teva Va-Adam* 27, 3 (1985): 2–3.

24.   Tal, *Pollution in the Promised Land*, 375–76, 386–87, 401. Among other environmental organizations, the Open Landscape Institute (*Machon Deshe*) and the Heschel Sustainability Center were founded in the 1990s.

25.   The website of the Porter School for Environmental Studies of Tel Aviv University, https://en-environment.tau.ac.il/, accessed March 17, 2015.

26.   The website of the Israeli ministry of environmental protection, http://www.sviva .gov.il/AboutOffice/Pages/default.aspx, accessed March 10, 2017 [Hebrew].

27.   See the website of the Blaustein Institute for Desert Research, http://www.bgu.ac.il /BIDR/about.html, accessed March 17, 2015; and Amos Richmond, "Founding the Institute for Desert Research," in A. Paul Hare and Gideon Kressel, eds., *The Desert Experience in Israel: Communities, Arts, Science, and Education in the Negev* (Lanham: The University Press of America, 2009), 119–37.

28.   See the press release on the website of Israel's ministry of foreign affairs, "Israel to Host International Conference on Combatting Desertification," December 21, 2005, at http://mfa.gov.il/MFA/PressRoom/2005/Pages/default.aspx, accessed May 2, 2018. See also Dan Bonbida, "The International Convention on Desertification Offers a New Hope," *Scoop*, December 2, 2008, http://archive.scoop.co.il/article.html?id=20857, accessed December 9, 2011 [Hebrew].

29.   The Arava Institute for Environmental Studies, http://arava.org/academics/, accessed March 17, 2015.

30.   On the Sde Boker High School, see Sol Brand, "Environmental High School," in Hare and Kressel, *The Desert Experience in Israel*, 173–75.

31.   See the Mitzpe Ramon yeshiva's website, https://www.torateva.org.il/, accessed May 9, 2018 [Hebrew]. On the religious significance of nature, see also Arieli, "The Cultural Construction of Nature," 196–200.

32.   Bilha Givon, an environmental activist, founded *Negev Bar-Kayma (Sustainable Development for the Negev)* in 1998. See the organization's website, http://www.negev.org .il/ [Hebrew].

33.   Michael Feige, "Midbar, Shmama, and Garbage Can," in Hare and Kressel, *The Desert Experience*, 27–32 (emphasis added).

34.   *Negev Bar-Kayma* newsletter (February 2004): 6 [Hebrew].

35.   "Negev 2015," the 2005 blueprint for the development of the Negev, was available on the website of the prime minister's office, http://www.pmo.gov.il/PMO/Archive /Decisions/2005/11/des4415, accessed on June 20, 2006 [Hebrew]; quote from section on environmental issues. See also Na'ama Teschner, Yaakov Garb, and Alon Tal, "The Environment in Successive Regional Development Plans for Israel's Periphery," *International Planning Studies* 15, 2 (2010): 79–97.

36.   The English term NIMBY comes up in conversations in Hebrew, but also in writing. See, for example, the heading "The Country's NIMBY," referring to the Negev, in Elisha Efrat, *Man and Environment in Israel* (Tel Aviv: Ramot and Tel Aviv University Press, 2004), 185 [Hebrew]. Tal (*Pollution in the Promised Land*, 404), similarly, notes that "in Hebrew, this phenomenon has been dubbed by centralist environmental regulators as 'NIMBY.'"

37.   According to the Israeli Prison Service website, the four prisons that were built largely for "security prisoners" are Naf'ha (1980) and Ramon (2006) near Mitzpe Ramon; and Ketzi'ot (1988) and Saharonim (2007), which were established in response, respectively, to the first Intifada and to the refugees' illegal entry through the border with Egypt. The information on the site, https://www.gov.il/he/Departments/prison_service, accessed December 14, 2011 [Hebrew], also indicated that the southern district holds about half of the national population of security inmates.

38.   Barak Kalir quotes the figure of around sixty thousand asylum seekers, mostly from Eritrea and Sudan, who entered Israel from 2005 to 2015 by crossing the border from Egypt. See his analysis of the policy toward them in Barak Kalir, "The Jewish State of Anxiety: Between Moral Obligation and Fearism in the Treatment of African Asylum Seekers in Israel," *Journal of Ethnic and Migration Studies* 41, 4 (2015): 580–98. See also Maya Kovaliyov-Livi and Sigal Rozen, "'From One Prison to Another': *Holot* Detention Facility," http://hotline.org.il/wp-content/uploads/Report-Holot-061514.pdf, June 2014. On the High Court's ruling that Holot must be closed down and the subsequent amendment of the law by the Knesset, see Ilan Lior, "High Court Orders Closure of Detention Facility for African Asylum Seekers," *Ha'aretz*, September 22, 2014, http://www.haaretz.com/news /national/.premium-1.617143, accessed March 24, 2015; Jonathan Lis and Ilan Lior, "Knesset Passes Controversial Law to Keep African Detention Facility Open," *Ha'aretz*, Dec. 8, 2014, http://www.haaretz.com/news/national/.premium-1.630662, accessed March 24, 2015.

39.   Yaron Zur, "Last Asylum Seekers Released From Holot Detention Center as Mass Deportation Campaign Moves Ahead," *Ha'aretz*, March 14, 2018, https://www.haaretz

.com/israel-news/last-asylum-seekers-leave-holot-as-mass-expulsion-campaign-moves
-ahead-1.5908461, accessed May 3, 2018.

40. The birds that were attracted to the tall mountain of waste became a safety hazard for planes taking off and landing at the airport: Tal, *Pollution in the Promised Land*, 314–15; Daniel Morgenstern, "Environmentalism in the Negev," *Ariel* 150–51 (2001): 95–96 [Hebrew]; quote from Shmuel Meiri and Zafrir Rinat, "Transporting Garbage from Gush Dan to the Duda'im Site in the Negev Has Begun, Transporting by Truck at Night," *Ha'aretz*, January 22, 1998 [Hebrew].

41. See the website of the Dudaim recycling site, http://www.dudaimrecycling.co.il/, accessed March 12, 2017 [Hebrew]; Ganei Hadas, http://mmmcom.co.il/index.php?id _cat=2&p=page, accessed March 12, 2017 [Hebrew].

42. On Israel's nuclear facility in the Negev, see Avner Cohen, *Israel and the Bomb* (New York: Columbia University Press, 1999); Amir Rappoport, "Residents of Dimona, Yeruham and Yavne Will Get Lugol Pills against Radioactive Radiation," *Nrg*, June 25, 2004, http:// www.nrg.co.il/online/1/ART/746/705.html, accessed March 25, 2015 [Hebrew]; Hanan Greenberg, "IDF Distributes Anti-Radioactive Radiation Pills to Residents," *Ynet*, Aug. 8, 2004, http://www.ynet.co.il/articles/0,7340,L-2959692,00.html, accessed March 25, 2015 [Hebrew]; Bennett Ramberg, "Should Israel Close Dimona? The Radiological Consequences of a Military Strike on Israel's Plutonium-Production Reactor," Arms Control Association, May 2008, https://www.armscontrol.org/act/2008_05/Dimona, accessed March 25, 2015. On Hamas's rockets fired in the direction of the nuclear site, see Yoav Zeytoun, Ilana Curiel, and Roi Kayes, "First in Operation: Three Rockets Sent to Dimona, One was Shot Down," *Ynet*, July 9, 2014, http://www.ynet.co.il/articles/0,7340,L-4540584,00.html, accessed March 25, 2015 [Hebrew].

43. Tal, *Pollution in the Promised Land*, 141. The plan, which was initiated by President Ronald Reagan in the mid-1980s, was canceled by President Bill Clinton in 1993. The significance of the Arava for avian migration to Africa was an important argument in this successful campaign (Tal, *Pollution in the Promised Land*, 139–45).

44. See Elisha Efrat, "Plans for the Negev and Its Development in the Second Decade of the State," *Ariel* 152–53 (2002): 59–66 [Hebrew]. The extraction of potash, bromine, and magnesium began in the pre-state period; other industries include the mining of copper, phosphate, ball clay, glass sand, limestone, and natural gas in various parts of the Negev. Companies that were developed by the state in the 1950s were later privatized. For examples of major companies today that evolved from earlier state-owned industries, see the web-sites of Rotem Amfert Negev, http://www.sulphuric-acid.com/sulphuric-acid-on-the-web /acid%20plants/Rotem%20Amfert%20Negev.htm, accessed March 10, 2015; ADAMA Agricultural Solutions, http://www.adama.com/israel-mcw/he/about/adama.html, accessed March 10, 2015; Negev Industrial Minerals Ltd., http://www.nim.co.il/?lang=en, accessed March 10, 2015.

45. Ramat Hovav Industrial Park is located in an extensive area of 5,750 acres (23,000 dunams). In 1989, it was recognized as an independent regional council. See the website of Ramat Hovav, http://www.ramat-hovav.muni.il/content.php?cid=18, accessed December 14, 2011 [Hebrew].

46.   The Bedouins of Wadi al-Na'am, located near Ramat Hovav and the regional electricity station, suffered from higher rates of cancer and health issues, but other Bedouin and Jewish residents of the Beer Sheva area and other settlements in Ramat Negev were also affected. See the report on "the violation of allowed standards of pollution by Ramat Hovav," submitted to the Knesset Committee on Interior and Environmental Issues on May 12, 2003, www.Knesset.gov.il, accessed June 10, 2006 [Hebrew].

47.   Quote from the website of *Negev Bar-Kayma* (Sustainable Development of the Negev), http://www.negev.org.il/index.php?m=text&t=2770, n.d., accessed December 14, 2011 [Hebrew] (page no longer available).

48.   See "Nature Reserves and National Parks in the Negev," *Ariel* 152–53 (2002): 23–32 [no author; Hebrew]. Tal (*Pollution in the Promised Land*, 178–179) indicates that 38% of the land area of the nature reserves overlaps with military zones.

49.   "Negev 2015," 5.

50.   Sagi, "The Preservation of the Negev Landscape," 222.

51.   Givon, "They Are Stealing the Negev," *Teva Va-Aretz* 33 (1991): 18–19 [Hebrew].

52.   Oz, "On the Love of the Country," 16.

53.   Oz, "On the Love of the Country," 16; Eitan Gdalizon, "Hiking in the Negev in the New Reality," *Teva Va-aretz* 24, 2 (1982): 50 [Hebrew]; Idelman, "The Negev Space: Is the Mission Lost?"

54.   Yossi Ben-Hanan, "Primal Landscape or Fire Zones," *Sevivot* 19 (1987): 125–28 [Hebrew]. Ben-Hanan was speaking at a public forum, sponsored by the Nature Reserve Authority, held in Mitzpe Ramon.

55.   Morgenstein, "Environmentalism in the Negev"; Buki Nae, "Bedouins Demand Compensations Similar to the Yamit Residents," *Ma'ariv*, Jan. 19, 1982, 1, 15 [Hebrew]; Buki Nae, "Nevatim: Airplanes Roar and Bedouins Relocated from the Military Air Base," *Ma'ariv*, Dec. 24, 1982, 24, 34 [Hebrew]; "Tel Malhata: The End," *Yediot Ahronot*, 24 Hours, Jan. 3, 1983, 11 [Hebrew].

56.   Data provided at the website of Mabat La-Negev, the company that built and operates BAHAD City, http://www.mabat-lanegev.co.il/, accessed March 13, 2017 [Hebrew]. Slightly different numbers can be found in Uri Gordon, "Olive Green: Environment, Militarism and the Israel Defense Forces," in D. Orenstein, A. Tal, and C. Miller, eds., *Between Ruin and Restoration: An Environmental History of Israel* (Pittsburgh: University of Pittsburgh Press, 2013), 256; and Noam Amir, "The City of Training Bases Is Underway," *Ma'ariv*, May 3, 2015, http://www.maariv.co.il/news/military/Article-473645, accessed June 20, 2015 [Hebrew].

57.   On environmental warnings, see "BAHAD City near Ramat Hovav" on the website of the Knesset's information department, www.knesset.gov.il, January 20, 2004, accessed June 13, 2006 [Hebrew]; Bilha Givon's public letter to the ministry of defense in *Negev Bar-Kayma* newsletter 4 (February 2004): 7 [Hebrew]. On public demonstrations, see Oded Bar-Meir, "The Industries Won, the Public Lost," *Sheva*, Nov. 28, 2006, 24 [Hebrew]; Amos de Winter, "Demonstrations by *Megama Yeruka* and *Adam, Teva, V'Din* against the Negotiated Agreement with Ramat Hovav," *Sheva*, Nov. 28, 2006, 25 [Hebrew]; Oded Bar-Meir, "Suffer Until 2007," *Kol Ha-Negev*, Dec. 3, 2004, 44 [Hebrew]. On the

continuing legal dispute, see Ranit Nahum-Halevi, "An Appeal Filed by the Israel Union for Environmental Defense Delays the Planning Process of BAHAD City," *The Marker*, Dec. 21, 2009, http://www.themarker.com/markets/1.550842, accessed February 18, 2015 [Hebrew]; Yael Darel, "End of Conflict around the Foundation of BAHAD City," *Ynet*, Aug. 5, 2010, http://www.ynet.co.il/articles/0,7340,L-3930848,00.html, accessed December 14, 2011 [Hebrew].

58. See Dan Rabinowitz, "Until the IDF Arrived at Ramat Hovav," *Ha'aretz*, Op-Ed, June 17, 2005 [Hebrew]. See also Uri Gordon, "Olive Green: Environment, Militarism and the Israel Defense Forces," in Orenstein, Tal, and Miller, *Between Ruin and Restoration*, 257.

59. Avi Bareli, "BAHAD City in the Northern Negev Will Serve as a Pilot for Green IDF Bases," *Ha'aretz*, November 19, 2007 [Hebrew]. See also Tamir Libel, "Making the Desert Green," *Airpower and the Environment* (2013): 177–97; Zafrir Rinat, "The IDF Is Mobilized to Protect the Environment after Acknowledging Damages," *Ha'aretz*, April 4, 2014, http://www.haaretz.co.il/news/science/.premium-1.2288409, accessed March 16, 2015 [Hebrew].

60. Orly Harari, "Sanctifying Life against Destruction and Death," *Arutz 7*, February 4, 2015, http://www.inn.co.il/News/News.aspx/292392, accessed June 20, 2015 [Hebrew].

61. On the competing interpretations of the impact of BAHAD City, see Erez Tzfadia, Yagil Levy, and Amiram Oren, "Symbolic Meanings and the Feasibility of Policy Images: Relocating Military Bases to the Periphery in Israel," *Policy Studies Journal* 38, 4 (2010): 723–44; Merav Arlozorov, "Jews Pursue Distributive Justice between Themselves, and the Bedouins Are Left Behind," *Ha'aretz*, May 21, 2014 [Hebrew]; Ora Koren, "The Franchises Given in the City of Training Bases Are for 6, 10 and 22 Years," *The Marker*, May 11, 2014, http://www.themarker.com/news/macro/1.2318010, accessed June 20, 2015 [Hebrew].

62. The section on environmentalism in "Negev 2015" states that "the Negev is the only region in the country where there remained relatively large spaces of 'Genesis Land' (*eretz bereshit*), which is critical for both nature and man."

63. Yehuda Amichai, "Landscape," in *Open Landscape* (Tel Aviv: Schocken, 1992) [trilingual Hebrew/English/German edition].

64. Uzi Paz, "The Uniqueness of the Negev and the Designation of the Nature Reserves," *Teva Va-Aretz*, 18, 3 (1976): 99–100 [Hebrew].

65. Tal, *Pollution in the Promised Land*, 157.

66. Amir Idelman, "The Negev Space: Is the Mission Lost?" 2–3.

67. Iris Han, "The Negev Is Getting Lost," June 1, 2007, accessed at the website of the Open Landscape Institute (*Machon Deshe*), http://www.deshe.org.il/_Uploads/dbs AttachedFiles/Negev.pdf [Hebrew].

68. Han, "The Negev Is Getting Lost."

69. Mazor, "Open Spaces and Sustainable Development," 261.

70. Sagi, "The Preservation of the Negev Landscape," 223; Paz, "The Uniqueness of the Negev," 99.

71. Michael Feige, "Between the Desert and the Desolate Land: In Memory of Hagar," *Al Ha-Rosh, Midreshet Ben-Gurion* Newsletter, 4 (November 2001): 8 [Hebrew].

72. On the SPNI campaigns to protect the last sand dunes in Nitzana and Ashdod, see the Israel Nature and Parks Authority's website for the Nitzanim Dune Nature Reserve, http://www.parks.org.il/ParksAndReserves/nitzanim/Pages/default.aspx, accessed March 10, 2015 [Hebrew]; on the campaign to save "the Great Dune in Ashdod," see Tal, *Pollution in the Promised Land*, 140.

73. On the campaign for the preservation of the sands of Samar, see Zohar, "To the Last Grain of Sand"; Zafrir Rinat, "Greens Fight to Save Samar's Sand from Eilat Building Boom," *Ha'aretz*, Sept. 10, 2010, https://www.haaretz.com/greens-fight-to-save-samar-s-sand-from-eilat-building-boom-1.314256, accessed December 12, 2011; Zafrir Rinat, "After a Decade of Struggle: Samar Sands Approved as a Nature Reserve," *Ha'aretz*, September 19, 2017, https://www.haaretz.co.il/news/science/.premium-1.4456256, accessed May 4, 2018 [Hebrew].

74. "Sand of Gold," Editorial, *Teva Va-Aretz* 26, 1 (1983), quoted in Arieli, "The Cultural Construction of Nature," 198.

75. The geologist Emanuel Mazor ("Open Spaces and Sustainable Development") championed the preservation of the craters in the Negev.

76. PowerPoint for the SPNI campaign against mining in "West Hatzeva," photography by Eyal Bartov and Albatros Co., was available at www.teva.org.il/_Uploads/dbsAttached-Files/bereshit1.pps., accessed December 7, 2011 [Hebrew].

77. "No Mine for Genesis Land," *Jerusalem Post*, March 30, 2006, http://www.jpost.com/Travel/AroundIsrael/Article.aspx?id=17619, accessed December 7, 2011; Shira Wilkof, "Fourteen Thousand Oppositions to the Mining of Genesis Land," *Walla*, Feb. 19, 2006, http://news.walla.co.il/?w=//861890, accessed December 7, 2011 [Hebrew]; "First Step toward the Recognition of 'Genesis Land,'" *Environmental News*, February 22, 2010; "Genesis Land's Victory," *Nrg*, March 20, 2006, http://www.nrg.co.il/online/1/ART1/062/700.html, accessed December 7, 2011 [Hebrew].

78. Moshe Gilad, "South Park, Israel-Style: The Reclaiming of the Ramon Crater," *Ha'aretz*, Oct. 1, 2012, http://www.haaretz.co.il/gallery/trip/1.1832664, accessed March 12, 2015 [Hebrew]; see also "The ERETZ Staff Interviews Gilad Gabbai, Director of the Israel Nature and Parks Authority's Southern Region," *Eretz*, Dec. 23, 2014, http://eretz.com/wordpress/blog/2014/12/23/under-the-stars-in-the-south/, accessed March 12, 2015.

79. de-Shalit, "From the Political to the Objective"; Eilon Schwartz, "Changing Paradigms of Environmentalism," at http://www.heschel.org.il/%D7%A4%D7%A8%D7%93%D7%99%D7%92%D7%9E%D7%95%D7%AA-%D7%9E%D7%A9%D7%AA%D7%A0%D7%95%D7%AA-%D7%91%D7%AA%D7%A4%D7%99%D7%A1%D7%94-%D7%94%D7%A1%D7%91%D7%99%D7%91%D7%AA%D7%99%D7%AA, accessed December 9, 2011 [Hebrew].

80. Sagi, "The Preservation of the Negev Landscape," 4; Arieli, "The Cultural Construction of Nature," 194–96. Tal (*Pollution in the Promised Land*, 129–130) refers to Alon's embrace of "greater Israel" (although the historic base of the SPNI was closer to the Labor movement) and to the New Israel Fund's refusal to support the SPNI because of its perceived

political leanings to the right under Alon's leadership. On the complexity of the SPNI's views, given its various programs, see also Moshe Gilad, "The New Zionism Does Not Conquer Hills," *Ha'aretz,* Weekend Supplement, January 12, 2017, https://www.haaretz.co.il/gallery/trip/.premium-MAGAZINE-1.3231762?=&ts=_1511795563701 [Hebrew].

81.   Alon, "Nature Protection vs. Zionism?" 28.

82.   On the debate over Zionism and environmental positions, see Tsahar Rotem, "The Negev Settlers: The Society for the Protection of Nature is 'Anti-Zionist,'" *Ha'aretz,* April 20, 2003; Yulie Khromchenko, "Who is a Zionist?" *Ha'aretz,* May 5, 2003 [Hebrew]; Elyashiv Reichner, "Those Who Sanctify the Desolate Land" *[Mekadshei ha-shemama], Kipa,* May 1, 2007, http://www.kipa.co.il/now/20065.html, accessed December 8, 2011 [Hebrew]; Gitit Weissblum, "Bnei Akiva Are Green with Envy," *Ma'ariv,* Sept. 15, 2008, http://www.nrg.co.il/online/1/ART1/787/385.html, accessed December 8, 2011. In 2005, residents of Ramat Negev referred to the scars that the conflict over the individual farms had left within their rather small community. See also Ilanit Ben-Dor, "The Experience of Individual Farm Settlers in Ramat-Negev: Between Individualism and Communitarianism" (MA thesis, the Blaustein Institute for Desert Studies, Ben-Gurion University of the Negev, 2004), 101–5 [Hebrew], and the continuing discussion of these issues in *Makor Rishon*'s position supplement on "Green Organizations and the Jewish Question," November 2011, 25 [Hebrew].

83.   See Gvirtzman, *The Zionist Dimension of Nature Preservation*; "Environmental Zionism: An Interview with Bilha Givon," *Sevivot* 32 (1994): 113–22 [Hebrew]; Iris Han, "Green Zionism—Zionism 2008," *Deshe,* The Open Landscape Institute, http://www.deshe.org.il/_Uploads/dbsAttachedFiles/GreenZionism.pdf, accessed March 15, 2017 [Hebrew]; and SPNI's response to its critics in "Green Zionism Protects the Country for All of Us," in *Makor Rishon,* "Green Organizations and the Jewish Question," 26. See also Tal, *Pollution in the Promised Land,* 102; Eran Doron, "Field School," in Hare and Kressel, *The Desert Experience,* 177–79.

84.   Quoted in Gilad, "The New Zionism Does Not Conquer Hills."

85.   Diana K. Davis, *The Arid Lands: History, Power, Knowledge* (Cambridge: MIT Press, 2016), 5–10; Jeannie Sowers, "Remapping the Nation, Critique of the State: Environmental Narratives and Desert Land Reclamation in Egypt," in Diana K. Davis and Edmund Burke III, eds., *Environmental Imaginaries of the Middle East and North Africa* (Athens: Ohio University Press, 2011), 158–91.

86.   See *Savannization: An Ecological Answer to Desertification* (Jerusalem: Jewish National Fund, 1994) [Hebrew]; Ahuva Bar-Lev and Eli Schiller, "The Jewish National Fund's Projects for the Development and Settlement of the Negev," *Ariel* 152–53 (2002): 123–34 [Hebrew]; Zafrir Rinat, "The Negev on the Way to Savannization," *Ha'aretz,* March 5, 1993, B4 [Hebrew]; KKl-JNF Staff, "Afforestation in Israel: An Ancient Land with New Ideas for Reclaiming Ecosystem Services and Combating Desertification," in *Jerusalem Post,* Nov. 28, 2011, https://www.jpost.com/green-israel/people-and-the-environment/afforestation-in-israel, accessed May 4, 2018.

87.   Tal, *Pollution in the Promised Land,* 100–107. Zafrir Rinat, "Are the Efforts to Save the Negev Damaging?" *Ha'aretz,* July 3, 2014, http://www.haaretz.co.il/news/science/zafrir/.premium-1.2365055, accessed March 16, 2015 [Hebrew]. See also my discussion in chapter 5

on the critiques by human rights and environmental activists of the JNF's forestation projects in the desert as a strategy to stake out state ownership over contested land.

88.   Barbara Kreiger, *The Dead Sea and the Jordan River* (Bloomington: Indiana University Press [1988], 2016), 219–34. The Dead Sea has shrunk by one third in the past half century and is about a hundred feet lower than it was a century ago (229). The evidence of this is highly visible in the expanding beach that was previously covered by water.

89.   Nir Hasson, "In a Few More Holidays There Will Be Nothing to See," *Ha'aretz*, April 12, 2006, 1 [Hebrew]; Shlomo Adler, "Urgent Steps to Save the Dead Sea," Letters to the Editor, *Ha'aretz*, April 21, 2006 [Hebrew]. See also Joshua Hammer, "The Dying of the Dead Sea," *Smithsonian Magazine*, October 2005, http://www.smithsonianmag.com /science-nature/the-dying-of-the-dead-sea-70079351/.

90.   Nir Hasson, "The Death of the Dead Sea: Once a Wonder, Today a Sinkhole," *Ha'aretz*, April 9, 2015; Nir Hasson, "Forty Years after the Construction of the Dead Sea Road, Nature Threatens to Destroy It," *Ha'aretz*, April 10, 2015, http://www.haaretz.co.il /misc/1.1198422 [Hebrew].

91.   Kreiger, *The Dead Sea*, 232–33; Zafrir Rinat, "Dead Sea, Rising and Falling, Poses Engineering Challenge," *Ha'aretz*, Jan. 17, 2016, https://www.haaretz.com/israel-news /science/.premium-1.697584.

92.   The website of EcoPeace Middle East, http://ecopeaceme.org/ecopeace/about-us/, accessed March 15, 2017.

93.   Sami Peretz, "The True Challenge of the Red Sea–Dead Sea Canal," *Ha'aretz, The Marker*, June 13, 2008 [Hebrew]; Zafrir Rinat, "The Green Organizations: The Red Sea– Dead Sea Canal Will Damage the Environment," *Ha'aretz*, June 15, 2008 [Hebrew]. The idea of reflooding an area that had dried up had been tried in Huleh Lake, as discussed earlier, and, on a much smaller scale, in the Einot Tzukim Nature Reserve (*Ein Feshkha*) on the western shore of the Dead Sea. See Zafrir Rinat, "As Dead Sea Shrinks, Israel Attempts Damage Control," *Ha'aretz*, Oct. 28, 2013, http://www.haaretz.com/news/national/1.554802, accessed March 26, 2015.

94.   "Dead Sea Neighbours Agree to Pipeline to Pump Water from Red Sea," *The Guardian*, Dec. 9, 2013, http://www.theguardian.com/world/2013/dec/09/dead-sea-pipeline-water-red-sea, accessed March 12, 2015; Sharon Udasin, "Israel, Jordan Sign Historic Plan to Save Dead Sea," *Jerusalem Post*, Feb. 27, 2015, http://www.jpost.com/Israel-News/New-Tech/ Israel-Jordan-sign-historic-plan-to-save-Dead-Sea-392390, accessed March 12, 2015; Ora Coren, "Israel, Jordan Sign Red–Dead Canal Agreement: Project Will Provide Potable Water to Aqaba and Eilat and Sea Water to Raise the Level of the Dead Sea," *Ha'aretz*, Feb. 27, 2015.

95.   See the report on Israeli-Palestinian collaboration over water, prepared by the Knesset's Center for Research and Information, Feb. 2, 2011, https://www.knesset.gov.il/mmm/ data/pdf/m02767.pdf, accessed March 15, 2017 [Hebrew]; Sarah Lazar-Ozacky and Shahar Sadeh, "Environment and Peace: Theory, Politics, and Activism," Van Leer Forum on Environment and Sustainability, 2009, available at the Van Leer website, http://www.vanleer. org.il/he/search_vl/Environment%20and%20Peace, accessed March 15, 2017 [Hebrew].

96.   See the discussion of cross-border civic collaboration between Aqaba and Eilat in

Tamar Arieli, "Borders and Policy: Local Interests and National Security Perspectives—Policy Making in the Southern Arava Valley," *Ha-Merchav Ha-Tsiburi* 8 (2014): 101–23 [Hebrew].

97. The "Long-Range Population Projections for Israel, 2009-2059," submitted by Israel's Central Bureau of Statistics (CBS) on March 21, 2012, indicates that Israel (which averaged 43.1 people per square kilometer in 1948) had 329 people for square kilometer in 2009. The projections of population growth reveal that this number will soar, reaching a number somewhere between 501 and 800 people per square kilometer by 2059, which will position Israel as having a higher population congestion than that of any other developed country except for small island countries such as Singapore and Bermuda. The report, written by Ari Paltiel et al., of the CBS's Demography and Census Department, was found at http://www.cbs.gov.il/publications/tec27.pdf, accessed on May 8, 2018 [Hebrew]. See also Daniel Ziri, "Israeli Population Density on the Rise, CBS Report Shows," *Jerusalem Post*, September 17, 2013, at https://www.jpost.com/National-News/Israeli-population-density -on-the-rise-CBS-report-shows-326322, accessed May 4, 2018.

98. Shaul Cohen, "Environmentalism Deferred Nationalism and Israeli/Palestinian Imaginaries," in Davis and Burke, *Environmental Imaginaries of the Middle East*, 246–64.

Chapter 7

1. Idith Zaharoni, "Water Is Not Everything in Life," *Ba-Mahane*, 38 (June 20, 1979): 26–29 [Hebrew].

2. On the association of the desert with wars and the military, see Yael Zerubavel, "Passages, Wars, and Encounters with Death: The Desert as a Site of Memory in Israeli Film," in Raz Yosef and Boaz Hagin, eds., *Trauma and Memory in Israeli Cinema* (New York: Bloomsbury, 2013), 299–327; Avivit Agam Dali, *The Place that Lacks Locality* [*Mehozot hefetz*]: *Ad Landscapes in Israel* (Tel Aviv: Resling, 2010), 82–90 [Hebrew].

3. Itamar Levi, "A Visit to Ze'elim," *Ha'aretz*, November 27, 1992 [Hebrew].

4. Israelis' archetypical fantasy of the "Swiss landscape" was also the subject of an ironic painting by the Israeli artist Shai Zurim, exhibited at the Tel Aviv Museum of Art in April 2004.

5. Yitzhak Ben-Ner, *A Distant Land* (Jerusalem: Keter, 1981), 173, 181 [Hebrew].

6. Aharon Megged, *Journey in the Month of Av* [*Masa be-av*] (Tel Aviv: Am Oved, 1980), 7, 14 [Hebrew].

7. The best-known trips for young Israelis until then had been trips to South and Central America or the Far East, typically following the completion of their military service. See Dalit Simchai, *This Track Begins Here: Israeli Backpacking in the Far East* (Tel Aviv: Prague, 2000) [Hebrew]; Chaim Noy and Erik Cohen, eds., *Israeli Backpackers: From Tourism to Rite of Passage* (Albany: SUNY Press, 2005).

8. Shahar Sadeh, "To Leave Paradise: Environmentalism and the Advancement of Peace," *Israeli Sociology* 18, 2 (2017): 77–100, quote on p. 80 [Hebrew]. Three field schools were established in Sinai, the most famous of them in the area of the Santa Katerina Monastery (77).

9. The visible flow of Israeli tourists to Sinai following its return to Egypt has continued even through the periods of tension in the Middle East in the early 2000s. According to available government statistics, 1999 and 2004 were peak years, with an estimated four hundred

thousand departures for Sinai in each. Even in 2001, which was a slump year, approximately a hundred thousand Israelis traveled to Sinai. These statistics were available at the website of the Central Bureau of Statistics, http://www1.cbs.gov.il/www/statistical/touris2011e.pdf, accessed February, 2016 [Hebrew]. For comparisons of the Negev to Sinai long after the latter's return to Egypt, see Raz Shahar, "Substitute for Sinai," *Nrg*, Apr. 14, 2009, http://www.nrg .co.il/online/55/ART1/878/928.html, accessed February 2, 2015 [Hebrew].

10. Natan Uriely, Darya Maoz, and Arie Reichel, "Israeli Guests and Egyptian Hosts in Sinai: A Bubble of Serenity," *Journal of Travel Research* 47, 4 (2009): 508–22. Bedouins and local service providers in the Sinai talked about "going to Egypt" as if the peninsula were an "ex-territory," and Israeli tourists reported experiencing the resorts as an extension of Israel, where they were "surrounded by other Israelis," and could "speak Hebrew to the Egyptian staff, and order Israeli food from menus written in Hebrew" (514). Egypt's diverging visa requirements for Israelis—requiring them to get a visa for entering other parts of Egypt, but not for Sinai—reinforced Sinai's liminal status.

11. Chaim Noy and Ayelet Kohn, "'Avoid Traveling to Sinai': Analysis of Journey Warnings in Israeli Media," *Ofakim Be-Geografia* 75 (2010): 206–22 [Hebrew]; Uriely, Maoz, and Reichel, "Israeli Guests and Egyptian Hosts," 508–22.

12. Noy and Kohn, "'Avoid Traveling to Sinai'," 218–19.

13. Sadeh, "To Leave Paradise"; Moshe Gilad, "Ignoring Travel Warnings, 20,000 Israelis Flood Egypt's Sinai over Holidays," *Ha'aretz*, October 25, 2016, http://www .haaretz.com/israel-news/1.749166; Assaf Kamar, "Israelis Flocked to Sinai in the Holidays: It is More Dangerous in Jerusalem," *Ynet*, October 22, 2016, https://www.ynet.co.il /articles/0,7340,L-4868371,00.html, accessed May 4, 2018 [Hebrew]. According to a January 9, 2018 news release by the Central Bureau of Statistics, two hundred thousand Israelis crossed the border with Egypt on their way into Sinai in 2017, an increase of 4% relative to 2016: http://www.cbs.gov.il/www/hodaot2018n/28_18_005b.docx, 2, accessed May 8, 2018 [Hebrew].

14. Maoz Azaryahu, "The Beach at the End of the World: Eilat in Israeli Popular Culture," *Social and Cultural Geography* 6, 1 (2005): 117–33.

15. Over Passover of 1958, about fifty thousand Israelis "invaded" Eilat and populated its beaches (Azaryahu, "The Beach at the End of the World," 126).

16. During the 1990s, the number of hotel rooms in Eilat more than doubled, from 4,036 in 1989 to 9,341 in 1999, further increasing to 11,136 in 2009: see Israel Bureau of Statistics, Statistical Abstracts 1990, table 17.5; 2000, table 17.6; and 2010, table 23.11. Avni notes that at the end of the 1980s, Israeli visitors made up about eighty percent of Eilat tourism. See Ron Avni, "The Development of Tourism in the Negev," *Ariel* 150–51 (2001): 36. In 2014, Eilat attracted more foreign tourists and Israeli visitors than any other tourist destination in Israel. The ministry of tourism's September 2015 report indicates a slight rise in Eilat's popularity among Israelis but a reverse trend among foreign tourists, according to occupancy statistics, perhaps due to an overall decline in tourism: http://www.tour ism.gov.il/GOVheb/Ministry%20of%20Tourism/Statistics/Documents/Tayarut_Statistic _Report_2014.pdf, 9–10, accessed Mar. 4, 2016 [Hebrew]. A special tax shelter was designed to further enhance Eilat's appeal.

17.   See the guide to Timna Valley Park at the website of Tourist Israel, at https://www
.touristisrael.com/timna-park/2984/, accessed December 21, 2017; and Timna Park's own
website, at http://www.parktimna.co.il/?langId=2, accessed February 6, 2016 [Hebrew].

18.   According to Avni, "The Development of Tourism in the Negev," 35–37, the development of the Dead Sea resort area, with fifteen hundred hotel rooms, attracted both Israeli and
foreign tourists during the 1980s and 1990s. According to government statistics (http://www
.tourism.gov.il/GOVheb/Ministry%20of%20Tourism/Statistics/Documents/Incoming_Tou
rism_Survey_2015.pdf, 9, accessed March 4, 2016 [Hebrew]), during the first half of 2015,
about 48% of foreign tourists to Israel visited the Dead Sea area, though only 10% of those
stayed overnight there. The SPNI website cites the number of thirty thousand visitors to the
Ein Gedi Field School hostel: http://natureisrael.org/EinGedi, accessed January 24, 2016.

19.   Rinat Zafrir, "Dagger to the Heart of the Negev?" *Ha'aretz*, March 8, 2002, http://
www.haaretz.com/dagger-to-the-heart-of-the-negev-1.50991, accessed September 11, 2014;
Elisha Efrat, *Man and Environment in Israel* (Tel Aviv: Ramot and Tel Aviv University Press,
2004), 202–3 [Hebrew]. See also Amir Shani, "The Feasibility of Ecologically Themed Tourism in the Negev and the Dead Sea Regions," PhD diss., Department of Hotel and Tourism
Management, Ben-Gurion University of the Negev, 2005 [Hebrew].

20.   See "The Society for the Protection of Nature and the Negev Settlements Oppose the Heart of the Negev Project," *Globes*, Dec. 31, 2001, http://www.globes.co.il/
news/article.aspx?did=549341, accessed December 27, 2011 [Hebrew]; Moshe Gilad,
"Landscape with a Camel and Four-Wheel Drive," *Ha'aretz*, May 4, 2003, http://www.
haaretz.co.il/captain/1.879805, accessed June 17, 2007; Merav Fleischer Levi, "Every
One According to Their Needs," *Ha'aretz*, Special Negev Supplement, Feb. 2004,
18–19 [Hebrew]; Iris Han, "The Negev is Getting Lost," June 1, 2007, at the website
of the Open Landscape Institute (*Machon Deshe*), http://www.deshe.org.il/_Uploads
/dbsAttachedFiles/Negev.pdf, accessed May 4, 2018 [Hebrew].

21.   Avni, "The Development of Tourism in the Negev," 42; Eli Schiller, "Tourism, Trips,
and Hiking Tracks in the Negev," *Ariel* 152–53 (2002): 34; see also chapter 6.

22.   On "frontier experience" in nature, see Erve Chambers, *Native Tours: The Anthropology of Travel and Tourism* (Long Grove: Waveland Press, 2000), 74; see also Avni, "The
Development of Tourism in the Negev," 40, 42; Schiller, "Tourism, Trips, and Hiking
Tracks," 34; Daniel Morgenstein, "Environmentalism in the Negev," *Ariel* 152–53 (2002):
98 [Hebrew]; Gilad, "Landscape with a Camel."

23.   The jeep may also have become a status symbol, given the cost of its advanced
models. On the discussion of the changing symbolism of the jeep in the desert landscape in
Israeli advertisements of the 1980s and 1990s see Dali, *The Place that Lacks Locality*, 95–97;
and Ze'ev Shavit, "The Return of the Rural Place," in Ze'ev Shavit, Orna Sasson-Levy and
Guy Ben-Porat, eds., *Points of Reference: Changing Identities and Social Positioning in Israel*
(Jerusalem: Van Leer and Hakibbutz Hameuchad, 2013), 336–38 [Hebrew]. The mastery
of four-wheel driving is also an important theme in Tsur Shezaf's novel *The Storm Is a Calm
Place for Us* (Tel Aviv: Hakibbutz Hameuchad, 2000) [Hebrew]. Shezaf uses this theme,
commonly associated with male drivers, to highlight the bold and free-spirited character of
the key protagonist, a desert-loving female war journalist.

24. "Travel, Travel to the Desert," *Yediot Ahronot, Maslul* Magazine, Oct. 17, 2005, 34 [Hebrew].

25. The lyrics for the song were written by Haim Hefer and the music composed by Sasha Argov in 1948; see the website of Zemereshet, a website of Hebrew songs, at http://www.zemereshet.co.il/song.asp?id=630, accessed December 27, 2011 [Hebrew].

26. "Travel, Travel to the Desert," and "Poliker, Raichel, and Moonlit Tours," in *Yediot Ahronot, Maslul* Magazine, Oct. 17, 2005, 6, 34 [Hebrew].

27. "Israel by Bike" is one of the tour options that "Birthright Israel" offers to young Jews whose trips to Israel it organizes and funds. See its website, Israel Outdoors, at http://www.israeloutdoors.com/the-trips/israel-by-bike/, accessed February 5, 2015; see also the annual Israel Ride, organized by the Arava Institute and Hazon organization for sustainable communities, which begins in Jerusalem and leads through the desert to Eilat. See Hazon's website at http://hazon.org/israel-ride/arava-institute-hazon-israel-ride/, accessed February 5, 2015. For biking experiences in the desert see also the website of Israel Bike Trails, http://www.israelbiketrails.com/ServiceProviders/Geofun/tabid/63/Default.aspx., accessed February 5, 2015.

28. See also David E. Nye, "Visualizing Eternity: Photographic Constructions of the Grand Canyon," in Joan M. Schwartz and James R. Ryan, eds., *Picturing Place: Photography and the Geographical Imagination* (London: Tauris, 2003), 74–95.

29. *Ha'aretz*, "Negev: A Special Supplement," February 2002, 24. The advertisement was sponsored by the Negev Tourism Forum, the Negev Development Authority, and the Jewish Agency for Israel.

30. An advertisement for kibbutz Mashabei Sade Resort Village, n.d.

31. *Ha'aretz*, "Negev: A Special Supplement," 24. See also Fleischer Levi, "Every One According to Their Needs."

32. The official website of Negev tourism, https://gonegev.co.il/, accessed December 21, 2017 [Hebrew].

33. Yafa Raziel, "A Green Weekend: Festival and Surprises in the Negev," *Ynet*, July 17, 2008, http://www.ynet.co.il/articles/0,7340,L-3569493,00.html, accessed December 26, 2011 [Hebrew]; Ronit Swirski, "The Dvira Forest: Seeing Green in the Negev Is Not a Mirage," *Ynet*, Apr 13, 2011, http://www.ynet.co.il/articles/0,7340,L-4054768,00.html; accessed April 13, 2011 [Hebrew].

34. Amir Rappoport, Yuval Peleg, and David Regev, "The Sucker Is the One Who Travels Abroad," *Yediot Ahronot, 24 Hours*, July 4, 1996, 16–17 [Hebrew].

35. Quote from the website of the Darom Adom festival, sponsored by Negev residents, at http://www.daromadom.co.il/, accessed January 28, 2015 [Hebrew].

36. The official Darom Adom festival website, at http://www.habsor.co.il/daromadom/, carries information about various sites in the northern Negev and special programs scheduled at this time. Private tours similarly advertise their offerings. See, for example, a special supplement, "A Southern Celebration," included in *Yediot Ahronot, Maslul* Magazine, Feb. 5, 2007 [Hebrew], and the residents' Darom Adom website, mentioned above, at http://www.daromadom.co.il/ [Hebrew].

37. These flowers include the Yerucham Iris and the Negev Iris. See, for example, Sara Gold, "Purim Party in Nature," *Ynet*, Mar. 20, 2008, http://www.ynet.co.il /articles/0,7340,L-3521428,00.html, accessed December 26, 2008 [Hebrew].

38. See the online *Arava* newsletter of the southeastern part of the Negev, with a column entitled "Green in the Eyes" that features garden photographs from that desert area. The text next to a photo of blossoming plants refers to the garden as "a sort of *fata morgana* in the heart of the desert": *Kol Ha-Arava* 17, Aug. 10, 2005, www.arava.co.il, accessed October 17, 2005 [Hebrew].

39. Valdimar T. Hafstein, "Cultural Heritage," in Regina F. Bendix and Galit Hasan-Rokem, eds., *A Companion to Folklore* (Oxford: Blackwell, 2012), 500–519; quote on p. 508.

40. Tahel Parush, "The Desert Generation," *Ha'aretz*, Feb. 18, 2008, http://www.haaretz .co.il/gallery/1.1305855, accessed December 30, 2011 [Hebrew].

41. Hotel Beresheet website, http://www.isrotelexclusivecollection.com/beresheet/, accessed December 22, 2017.

42. Chambers (*Native Tours*, 73–74) points out the distinction between "nostalgic nature tourism," which distances the tourist from nature, and the "embedded experience" of nature.

43. On the Galilean rural style, see Ze'ev Shavit, "The Bourgeois Construction of the Rural: An Israeli Case," *Israel Studies Review* 28, 1 (Summer 2013): 98–119.

44. Quote from the website of Beerotyim, https://www.beerotayim.co.il/index.php /en, accessed May 5, 2018.

45. See the website for Tzell Midbar (Desert Shade), http://desert-shade.com/, accessed February 13, 2016 [Hebrew].

46. See the website for Succah Ba-Midbar (Succah in the Desert), https://www.succah. co.il/homepage, accessed May 7, 2018.

47. Ezra Orion, a sculptor, poet, and Negev resident whose environmental works are displayed in various locations in the Negev, describes the creative process in "Park for Desert Sculpture on the Ramon Crater's Edge," *Sevivot* 21 (1988), reprinted on the website of Midreshet Sde Boker, http://www.boker.org.il/info/negev/orion/park/psramon.htm., accessed January 22, 2012 [Hebrew]. For a list of Orion's works on the website, see http:// orion.boker.org.il/about/e-bio.htm, accessed January 22, 2012 [Hebrew].

48. On the Negev Brigade Memorial for 1948, see Shany Littman, "Iconic Israeli Memorial Celebrates 50 Years: Negev Brigade Memorial Is Renowned Sculptor Dani Karavan's 'Most Important Work' and Symbol of Beer Sheva," *Ha'aretz*, October 30, 2014, http:// www.haaretz.com/life/arts-leisure/.premium-1.623437, accessed February 6, 2015. Karavan's installation "Way of Peace" consists of a hundred columns that carry the term "peace" in different languages and form a line stretching over three kilometers, creating a symbolic path from a 1948 battle site to the border with Egypt. See the website of Peace Monuments around the World, http://peace.maripo.com/m_karavan.htm, accessed February 6, 2015. For other war memorials in the Negev, see Ze'ev Zivan, "Memorials and Memory in the Negev and the South," *Ariel* 152–53 (2002), 67–78 [Hebrew].

49. Orion's large-scale sculptures have a particular dialogue with the open space of the desert, although they are not limited to that region. For photos of these works, see Wikime-

dia Commons under "Sculptures by Ezra Orion" at https://commons.wikimedia.org/wiki /Category:Sculptures_by_Ezra_Orion, accessed December 25, 2017.

50. Arad was founded with the idea of attracting artists and writers, while the older town, Mitzpe Ramon, only developed its artists' quarter (renamed the "Incense Route Quarter") in recent decades. On Neot Semadar, established in 1989, and its distinctly designed art center and programs, see Neot Semadar's YouTube video at https://www.youtube .com/watch?v=tH6oTunlTOo, accessed December 25, 2017; and Hagai Amit, "The People Who Built a Temple in the Desert and Do Not Own Television," *The Marker*, April 4, 2015, https://www.themarker.com/markerweek/1.2606600, accessed December 25, 2017 [Hebrew].

51. The Negev Museum of Art in Beer Sheva has held several exhibits that focused on local art, such as "Southern Breeze (*rua'h dromit)*: Views of the Negev in Contemporary Israeli Art," curated by Dalia Manor, and a "contemporary arts in the Negev" project entitled *Dvarim Ba-Midbar* (Matters in the Desert) in 2014 that coordinated nine exhibits devoted to the desert in various locations across the Negev. For the museum's official website, see http://www.negev-museum.org.il/index_e.php, accessed May 6, 2018.

52. The site Desert Time (Zman Midbar) offers a desert experience that includes spirituality, closeness to nature, and encounters with Bedouins. See its website at http://zmanmidbar.net /home, accessed January 18, 2012.

53. The Vipassana Center at Hatzeva, for example, offers meditation and spiritual retreats, and Ashram Ba-Midbar (Desert Ashram), which draws on the broader appeal of India to Israelis, offers a variety of workshops, although it may be better known for its large rock and trance music festivals; see the ashram's website at http://www.desertashram.co.il/, accessed February 2, 2015 [Hebrew]; Gilad, "Landscape with a Camel"; Fleischer Levi, "Every One According to Their Needs."

54. On the popularity of new-age trends among Israelis, see Benjamin Beit-Hallahmi, *Despair and Deliverance: Private Salvation in Contemporary Israel* (Albany: SUNY Press, 1992); Dalit Simchai, *Flowing against the Flow: Paradoxes in Realizing New-Age Vision in Israel* (Haifa: Pardes, 2009), 135–36 [Hebrew]; Rachel Werczberger and Boaz Huss, "Introduction," special issue on "New Age Culture in Israel," *Israel Studies Review* 29, 2 (2014): 1–16; Rachel Werczberger, *Jews in the Age of Authenticity: Jewish Spritual Renewal in Israel* (New York: Peter Lang, 2017).

55. See Ze'ev Shavit's analysis of the development of post-rural tourism on the Galilean periphery in "The Bourgeois Construction of the Rural"; Shavit further compares the Galilee and the Negev in "The Return of the Rural Place."

56. For an analysis of post-rural tourism, see Jonathan Murdoch and Andy C. Pratt, "Rural Studies: Modernism, Postmodernism and the 'Post-Rural,'" *Journal of Rural Studies* 9, 4 (1993): 411–27; and Jeffrey Hopkins, "Signs of the Post-Rural: Marketing Myths of a Symbolic Countryside," *Geografiska Annaler* 80, 2 (1998): 65–81.

57. See also the discussion of individual farms in chapter 4. A more recent addition is an ecological site near Mitzpe Ramon, owned by the writer Tsur Shezaf, that combines agriculture with hospitality. See Tsur Shezaf's Mivdad Ramon (Ramon Retreat) homepage at http://shezaf.net/english/Trips/Israel/Mivdad-Ramon.html, accessed July 22, 2018.

58. The Alpaca Farm website, https://www.alpacas-farm.com/our-story, accessed May 6, 2018.

59. The shift from the desert's association with the military to its portrayal as a site of refuge and transformation is apparent in Israeli advertisements. See Dali, *The Place that Lacks Locality*, 80–81, 110.

60. See the ad for the Ramon Inn hotel in a brochure published by the Mitzpe Ramon municipality, "In the Desert: The Complete Attraction Guide to Mitzpe Ramon and Its Surroundings," 2013, p. 24 [Hebrew].

61. Hotel Beresheet website, http://www.isrotelexclusivecollection.com/beresheet/, accessed December 22, 2017.

62. The Neve Midbar spa opened in December 1999 and caters to groups and individuals. The quote was taken from its publicity dated January 8, 2012, currently no longer available.

63. Website of Neve Midbar, http://www.neve-midbar.co.il, accessed December 23, 2017 [Hebrew].

64. Rutie Kenan, "Desert Gourmet," *Yediot Ahronot*, Modern Times Supplement, Aug. 22, 2001 [Hebrew]. See also the themes of indulgence, relaxation, and gourmet food in "In the Path of the Nabbatean Incense Route in the Negev," a promotional brochure (Ministry of Tourism and the Negev Development Authority, n.d.)[Hebrew].

65. This trend is obviously not limited to desert tourism. See Efrat Stiglietz, "The Board of Directors Goes Outdoors," *Ha'aretz*, Weekend Supplement, Nov. 26, 1999, 58–64 [Hebrew]. I first encountered this kind of surprise gourmet meal set in the natural desert landscape at a post-conference tour of the Ramon Crater in the mid-1990s.

66. See David Hillel, Yaniv Belhassen, and Amir Shani, "What Makes a Gastronomic Destination Attractive? Evidence from the Israeli Negev," *Tourism Management* 36 (2013): 200–209.

67. See, for example, the website devoted to "zimmer" lodging, http://www.zimmer .co.il; and Gilad, "Landscape with a Camel."

68. See Danit Nitzan, "Almost Like Tuscany," *Ha'aretz*, Galeria section, May 27, 2007 [Hebrew], http://www.haaretz.co.il/gallery/1.1412864, accessed February 4, 2016; and Ofer Dagan, "'Tuscany Is Here': Elite Tourism and the Formation of Ethno-National Space in Individual Farms in the South," MA thesis, Department of Sociology and Anthropology, Ben-Gurion University, 2014 [Hebrew]. Advertisements may even introduce Negev hospitality as being more appealing than European hospitality, highlighting "the intimacy and the special touch of an Israeli *zimmer*" that Israeli desert tourism offers. See quote in Shavit, "The Return of the Rural Place," 324.

69. Such festivals have included the early Arad Festival of Hebrew Songs, later transformed into a rock festival, before it closed when a fatal incident occurred in 1995; the Tamar Festival, in the Dead Sea area, featuring prominent Israeli singers; and the more recent Indie-Negev Festival in the western Negev; special musical productions are offered on top of Masada, and an annual jazz festival takes place in Eilat. Other annual cultural events include the "Sounds in the Desert Festival" at kibbutz Sde Boker, featuring original

Israeli music, and the "Days of Poetry in the Desert" Festival at the Ben-Gurion Center in Sde Boker and local venues in its vicinity.

70.   Anat Rosenberg, "Tourist Tip #352, InDNegev Music Festival," *Ha'aretz*, October 7, 2013, https://www.haaretz.com/israel-news/travel/tourist-tip-of-the-day/.premium -1.550852, accessed December 28, 2017. The Midburn Festival draws its name from a combination of the Hebrew word *midbar* (desert) and the English word "burn," alluding to its inspiration, Burning Man. In its second year, Midburn attracted nearly seven thousand attendees to its giant art installations and various happenings. See "Thousands Descend on Negev for Midburn," *Times of Israel*, May 25, 2015, https://www.timesofisrael.com /thousands-descend-on-negev-for-midburn/, accessed December 28, 2017.

71.   Quote from the website of *Achbar Ha-Ir*, http://www.mouse.co.il/CM.articles _item,636,209,41095,.aspx, accessed October 14, 2009 [Hebrew].

72.   Almog Ben Zichri, "Residents of the Negev against Midburn Festival," *Ha'aretz*, May 3, 2018, https://www.haaretz.co.il/news/local/.premium-1.6053953 [Hebrew].

73.   See the ad for "A House in the Desert" (Bayit Ba-Midbar), in "In the Desert: The Complete Attraction Guide to Mitzpe Ramon and Its Surroundings," 29.

74.   Josephus, *The Wars of the Jews*, 2.8.6–7.9.2, in Josephus, *Complete Works*, trans. W. Whiston (Grand Rapids, MI: Kregel, 1960), 600–603.

75.   A different version of the last stand at Masada appears in the tenth-century *Book of Jossipon*, ed. David Flusser (Jerusalem: Bialik Institute, 1978), 423–31 [Hebrew]. Yet the rise of Masada as a heroic national myth was connected to Josephus's text, reinterpreting the collective suicide within the framework of resistance and readiness to fight "to the bitter end." On the rise of the Masada myth in Israeli culture, see Yael Zerubavel, *Recovered Roots: Collective Memory and the Making of Israeli National Tradition* (Chicago: University of Chicago Press, 1995), 67–73.

76.   Zerubavel, *Recovered Roots*, 114–44, 192–213. See also Nachman Ben-Yehuda, *The Masada Myth: Collective Memory and Mythmaking in Israel* (Madison: University of Wisconsin Press, 1995).

77.   Masada, on the UNESCO World Heritage List, http://whc.unesco.org/en/list/1040, accessed January 30, 2015.

78.   On the transformations at the site following the archeological excavations, see Yael Zerubavel, "The Politics of Remembrance and the Consumption of Space: Masada in Israeli Memory," in Daniel Walkowitz and Lisa Maya Knauer, eds., *Narrating the Nation in Public Space: Memory and the Impact of Political Transformation* (Durham: Duke University Press, 2004), 233–52. According to Masada National Park information from February 2012, about eight hundred thousand individuals visited the site during 2011. A ministry of tourism survey indicates that in the first half of 2015, 27% of tourists to Israel visited Masada: http://www.tourism.gov.il/GOVheb/Ministry%20of%20Tourism /Statistics/Documents/Incoming_Tourism_Survey_2015.pdf, 10 [Hebrew].

79.   On the polemics over the definition of suicide versus martyrdom (*kiddush hashem*), see Zerubavel, *Recovered Roots*, 192–97. On the Dead Sea Chabad's sponsorship of a Torah scribe and bar mitzvah and bat mitzvah rituals at Masada, see the website of the Dead Sea Chabad, at http://www.deadsea-chabad.com/templates/articlecco_cdo/aid/687085

/jewish/bar-bat-mitzvah-on-masada.htm and http://www.deadsea-chabad.com/templates
/articlecco_cdo/aid/1225546 [Hebrew], respectively, accessed January 30, 2015.

80. Zerubavel, "The Politics of Remembrance"; Uri Ram, "Glocommodification: How
the Global Consumes the Local—McDonald's in Israel," *Current Sociology* 52, 1 (2004):
11–31; Roy Arad, "McDonald's at Masada Not Worth Killing Yourself For," *Ha'aretz*, Sept.
23, 2011, http://www.haaretz.com/print-edition/news/mcdonald-s-at-masada-not-worth
-killing-yourself-for-1.386158, accessed September 11, 2014.

81. The Qumran National Park, located in the West Bank territory under Israeli control,
is run by the Israel Nature and Parks Authority. The park's website can be found at https://
en.parks.org.il/ParksAndReserves/qumran/Pages/default.aspx, accessed May 8, 2018.

82. On the scholarly debate regarding the identification of the Quran community
with the Essene sect, see Lawrence H. Schiffman, Emanuel Tov, and James VanderKam,
eds., *The Dead Sea Scrolls: Fifty Years after Their Discovery, 1947–1997* (Jerusalem: Israel
Exploration Society and Israel Museum, 2000); Yizhar Hirschfeld, *Qumran in Context:
Reassessing the Archaeological Evidence* (Peabody: Hendrickson, 2004); Katharina Galor,
Jean-Baptiste Humbert, and Jürgen Zangenberg, eds., *The Site of the Dead Sea Scrolls:
Archaeological Interpretations and Debates*; *Studies on the Texts of the Desert of Judah*, vol.
57 (Leiden: Brill, 2006).

83. For a summary of the archeological excavations and their findings, see archeologist
Emmanuel Anati, "Karkom Mountain in Light of Recent Discoveries," *Ariel* 149 (April
2001): 11–86; the same issue includes information for travelers to the site, *Ariel* 149 (April
2001): 87–95 [Hebrew]. See also Robin Ngo, "Searching for Biblical Mt. Sinai," Bible History Daily, Biblical Archeology Society, http://www.biblicalarchaeology.org/daily/biblical-
topics/exodus/searching-for-biblical-mt-sinai//, February 14, 2014.

84. UNESCO's website for "Incense Route—Desert Cities in the Negev," http://whc
.unesco.org/en/list/1107, accessed May 8, 2018. See also Zafrir Rinat, "The Incense Route
and Three Biblical Sites Were Recognized by UNESCO as World Heritage Sites," *Ha'aretz*,
July 17, 2005 [Hebrew]; Ezra Orion and Avner Goren, eds., *The Incense Routes: Essays* (Jerusalem: Ariel, 2000) [Hebrew].

85. The archeologist Avraham Negev pursued the excavation of Mamshit and Shivta
from 1957 to 1959. He later extended his work to Haluza, and then returned again to
Mamshit. The botanist Michael Evenari, who explored the Nabbateans' agricultural methods, engaged in the excavation and restoration of Avdat and Shivta. See Avraham Negev,
"Survey and Trial Excavations at Haluza (Elusa), 1973," *Israel Exploration Journal* 26, 2/3
(1976): 89–95; and Michael Evenari, *The Awakening Desert* (Jerusalem: Magnes Press, 1988),
172–205 [Hebrew].

86. Avni, "The Development of Tourism in the Negev," 40; Schiller, "Tourism, Trips,
and Hiking Tracks," 37–38. See also Gilad, "Landscape with a Camel."

87. "In the path of the Nabatean Incense Route in the Negev," a promotional brochure
(Ministry of Tourism and the Negev Development Authority, n.d.)[Hebrew]; quote is from
"The Incense Road," on the website of "Go Israel," the official website of tourism to Israel,
https://new.goisrael.com/article/2124, accessed May 8, 2018.

88. On the symbolic continuity between the Nabbateans and the Bedouins, see also Nessia Shafran, "The Nabbatean in Israeli Literature," *Ha-Doar* 83, 3 (2004): 28–35 [Hebrew]; Steven A. Rosen, "The Nabbateans as Pastoral Nomads: An Archeological View," in Aharon Meir and Eyal Baruch, eds., *Settlement, Civilization and Culture* (Ramat Gan: The Institute of Archeology, Bar Ilan University, 2001), 151–66 [Hebrew].

89. The advertisement for the Mamshit National Park appeared in the local newspaper *Sheva*, no. 1861 (Sept. 25, 2009): 28 [Hebrew].

90. The website of Succah Ba-Midbar explains that "every *succah* (hut) has a different name, after the names of the biblical fathers and mothers and the rest of Abraham the Patriarch's family." It lists those names at http://www.succah.co.il/#!rooms__rates/c1jh6, accessed December 24, 2017 [Hebrew].

91. Gideon Levy and Alex Levac, "Highway 40 Revisited," *Ha'aretz*, Weekend Supplement, Oct. 14, 2017, https://www.haaretz.com/israel-news/.premium-1.816631.

92. Yael Zerubavel, "The Seed, the Symbol, and the Zionist Renewal Paradigm," in "Israeli Histories, Societies and Cultures," *Frankel Institute Annual* (Ann Arbor: University of Michigan, 2017), 30–32.

93. On the Yotvata Hai-Bar's success in reintroducing the white buffalo and other species, see Zafrir Rinat, "After the Buffaloes and the Wild Donkeys, the Ostriches Too Return to the Negev," *Ha'aretz*, Apr. 17, 2005, 1, accessed February 1, 2015 [Hebrew]; see also the website of Tourist Israel, https://www.touristisrael.com/yotvata-hai-bar-nature-reserve/8806/, accessed May 8, 2018.

94. For further discussion of the different strategies of representing antiquity in Israeli culture, see Yael Zerubavel, "Antiquity and the Renewal Paradigm: Strategies of Representation and Mnemonic Practices in Israeli culture," in Doron Mendels, ed., *On Memory: An Interdisciplinary Approach* (Bern: Peter Lang, 2007), 337–41.

95. "White Nights," *Yediot Ahronot*, *Maslul* Magazine, October 17, 2005, 28–30 [Hebrew].

96. For example, the site Kfar Ha-Nokdim (Shepherds Village) offers overnight stays in Bedouin tents or rooms, some of which are heated in winter, and a diverse menu of Bedouin meals. See its website, https://www.kfarhanokdim.co.il/en/, accessed May 8, 2018. Khan Ha-Shayarot (The Caravans' Station) offers Bedouin tents or rooms, kosher Bedouin meals, and camel rides, among other attractions. See its website, http://www.shayarot.co.il/, accessed February 10, 2015 [Hebrew]. Khan Beerotayim offers camel rides and Bedouin meals. See its website, https://www.beerotayim.co.il/index.php/en, accessed May 5, 2018.

97. Bob McKercher and Hilary du Cros, *Cultural Tourism: The Partnership between Tourism and Cultural Heritage Management* (New York: The Haworth Press, 2002), 8; see also Dennison Nasj, "Tourism as a Form of Imperialism," in Varlene L. Smith, ed., *Hosts and Guests: The Anthropology of Tourism* (Philadelphia: University of Pennsylvania, 1977), 35–47; Timothy Mitchell, *Colonising Egypt* [1988] (Berkeley: University of California Press, 1991).

98. For the concept of staged authenticity, see Dean MacCannell, *The Tourist: A New Theory of the Leisure Class* (New York: Schocken, 1976), 91–107; John Urry and Jonas

Larsen, *The Tourist Gaze* [1990] (London: Sage, 2011); McKercher and du Cros, *Cultural Tourism*, 28–29, 129; Jane C. Desmond, *Staging Tourism: Bodies on Display from Waikiki to Sea World* (Chicago: University of Chicago Press, 1999); Barbara Kirshenblatt-Gimblett, *Destination Culture: Tourism, Museums, and Heritage* (Berkeley: University of California Press, 1998), 131–76.

99.   Steven Dinero, "Image Is Everything: The Development of the Negev Bedouin as a Tourist Attraction," in *Nomadic Peoples* 6, 1 (2002): 69–94. For a broader discussion of heritage and the impact of tourism, see Hafstein, "Cultural Heritage," 506–8, and Kirshenblatt-Gimblett, *Destination Culture*, respectively.

100.   Barbara Kirshenblatt-Gimblett, "Objects of Ethnography," in Ivan Karp and Steven D. Lavine, eds., *Exhibiting Cultures: The Poetics and Politics of Museum Display* (Washington, DC: Smithsonian Institution Press, 1991), 415.

101.   See the website for the Museum of Bedouin Culture, http://www.joealon.org .il/?page=category&cat=63, accessed February 24, 2016. See also Havatzelet Yahel, Ruth Kark, and Noam Perry, "Multiculturalism and Ethnographic Museums in Israel: The Case of a Regional Bedouin Museum," in Ptanko Pelc and Miha Koderman, eds., *Nature, Tourism and Ethnicity as Drivers of (De)Marginalization* (Charn, Switzerland: Springer, 2018), 179–99. The museum mostly draws Jewish visitors, but about ten percent of its thirty-five thousand visitors in 2016 were Bedouin students (193).

102.   Tamar Katriel, *Performing the Past: A Study of Israeli Settlement Museums* (London: Lawrence Erlbaum Associates, 1997), 29–30, 126–28; quote from p. 126.

103.   The video, produced in 2000, is shown at the site of Abraham's Well. See also the note in a ministry of tourism catalog that "Some people experience their strongest sense of the Bible in the Negev, with its Bedouin encampments that have not changed much since the time of Abraham 4,000 years ago." Catalog no. 166/1: 19, quoted in Dinero, "Image Is Everything," 76.

104.   Quote from the website of Desert Ashram, http://www.desertashram.co.il/, section relating to "Bedouin hospitality," accessed February 2, 2015 [Hebrew].

105.   See, for examples, photos of Israeli desert tour guides and guests wearing a *kaffiyeh* on the websites of Khan Shaharut, http://www.camel-riders.com/, accessed February 2, 2015; Zman Midbar, http://zmanmidbar.net/, accessed February 2, 2015; and Khan Beeortayim http://www.beerotayim.co.il/, accessed February 2, 2015; see also such photos in Kenan, "Desert Gourmet."

106.   For example, the newsletter of *Negev Bar-Kayma* (Sustainable Development for the Negev) first featured the image of a camel walking in the desert (September 2000), which was later replaced by a camel's head (newsletter no. 2, February 2001), which was, in turn, later dropped. The Arad music festival featured a camel for its tenth festival, July 13–16, 1992, and the camel's head still appeared as part of its logo as late as 2014.

107.   A video on the Birthright Israel website featured a young man and woman riding on a camel in the desert, http://www.birthrightisrael, when accessed July 25, 2003 (I thank Muli Brog for pointing this out to me); the video is no longer available on the site. In 2015, camel rides were included among several group-action photos on that same website, http:// www.birthrightisrael.com/letsgo/Documents/globalmainreg.html, accessed February 3, 2015.

108.   Camel rides may range from a half hour (one website presents this option as a photo opportunity) to a few hours or even several days. See, for example, the camel ride offerings as part of "a day in the desert" packages on the websites for Kfar Ha-Nokdim, https://www.kfarhanokdim.co.il/en/, accessed May 8, 2018; The Camel Riders of Shaharut, http://www.camel-riders.com/, accessed February 1, 2015 [Hebrew]; and The Negev Camel Ranch, http://www.cameland.co.il/camel-tours, accessed February 1, 2015.

109.   Orit Ben-David offers similar observations regarding the Jewish guides for the Israeli Society for the Protection of Nature in Orit Ben-David, "*Tiyul* (Hike) as an Act of Consecration of Space," in Eyal Ben-Ari and Yoram Bilu, eds., *Grasping Land: Space and Place in Contemporary Israeli Discourse and Experience* (Albany: SUNY Press, 1997), 132, 136.

110.   Efrat Stiglietz, "Are There Camels in Israel?" *Tslol*, Magazine for Vacation, Trips and Leisure in Israel, March–April 1999, 36–46 [Hebrew]. Dali (*The Place That Lacks Locality*, 99–102) discusses the exotic image of the camel as associated with eroticism in Israeli advertisements, and includes a photo (appendix, photo 15) that features two women wearing bikinis and riding a camel to illustrate this point.

111.   Stiglietz, "Are There Camels in Israel?" 41–42. The daily *Yediot Ahronot* (May 29, 1992, 8) displayed a photo of two well-known singers attempting to ride a camel during the Hebrew Song festival in Arad.

112.   The quote was taken from "The Bedouin Hospitality Experience in *Salamat*," in *Kav Le-Hinuch* (n.d), at http://www.kav-lahinuch.co.il/?pg=indx_entry&CategoryID=329 &ArticleID=5565, accessed February 2, 2015 [Hebrew], emphasis added.

113.   Seffi Hanegbi and Tomer Kahana, both engaged in desert tourism, co-authored a study entitled *Bedouin Tourism: Assessment and Recommendations* for the ministry of tourism, the Negev Development Authority, the Negev Tourism Forum, and the Jewish Agency, in December 2002.

114.   The official website "gonegev," sponsored by the ministry for the development of the peripheries of the Negev and the Galilee and the Negev Development Authority, http://www.gonegev.co.il, has at different times included references to "Bedouin tourism" and the "Bedouin experience" [*havaya beduit*], run both by local Bedouin sites and by tourist projects that offer Bedouin hospitality in the Negev. Another official website for Mount Negev, sponsored by the same agencies, "Har Negev Tourism" at http://www .negevtour.co.il/?p=63, accessed February 9, 2016 [Hebrew], included a reference to "Only Tents—Bedouin Hospitality" in "Bedouin villages along Route 40," without specifying their legal status.

115.   See the website of Sefinat Ha-Midbar, http://www.sfinat-hamidbar.com/, accessed February 13, 2015 [Hebrew]; Sefinat Ha-Midbar was included on a map of tourist sites and individual farms of the Wine Route that appeared on the Ramat Negev website, http://rng .org.il, accessed February 13, 2015 [Hebrew]; Uri Binder, "Individuals But Together: An Optimistic Excursion in the Negev's Individual Farms," *Nrg*, July 21, 2010, http://www.nrg .co.il/online/54/ART2/135/229.html, accessed February 13, 2015 [Hebrew].

116.   See the websites of the two organizations at http://www.desert-embroidery.org/ and http://www.sidreh.org/, accessed May 8, 2018. The associations were formed in 1996 and 1998, respectively.

117. Irit Rosenbloom, "Projects for the Advancement of Bedouin Women Have Been Recognized as Tourist Sites," *Ha'aretz*, Aug. 15, 2007 [Hebrew]. The article refers to about 250 women who are associated with these projects. Some museum shops carry Bedouin craftwork, which has recently received international exposure. See Anat Cygielman, "Will the Bedouin Rugs of the Lakiya Women Become an International Hit?" *Xnet, Ynet*, Aug. 10, 2013, http://xnet.ynet.co.il/design/articles/0,14563,L-3102094,00.html, accessed February 10, 2015 [Hebrew].

118. "Bedouin Experience," http://www.bedouinhospitality.com/#!hospitality/c42f, accessed February 4, 2015.

119. The Desert Charm Festival (*Kesem Ha-Midbar*) was held in Lakiya and the Joe Alon Museum during the Jewish holiday of Sukkoth, in October 2014, and has continued as an annual event. See its website and Facebook page, sponsored by the Authority for Economic Development for the Arab Sector in the Prime Minister's Office, at http://afed.gov.il/Projects /LocalTourism/Pages/DesertCharm.aspx and https://he-il.facebook.com/kesemhamidbar/, respectively, accessed May 8, 2018 [Hebrew].

120. McKee suggests the concept of "truncated image" to describe the effect of the Bedouins' adaptation of Israeli norms in their selective self-representation. See Emily McKee, *Dwelling in Conflict: Negev Landscapes and the Boundaries of Belonging* (Stanford: Stanford University Press, 2016), 39–41, 65.

121. For Drejat's tourist offerings and quote, see http://www.drejat.co.il/english/, accessed May 8, 2018.

122. From the website for "Desert Daughter's Farm," http://www.desertdaughter.com /index.php?dir=site&page=content&cs=3002, accessed February 2, 2015 [Hebrew].

123. See Zafrir Rinat, "Unique Farm Project Offers Sustainable High-Tech for Negev Bedouin," *Ha'aretz*, June 23, 2015, https://www.haaretz.com/israel-news/.premium -1.662360?=&ts=_1514472699341, accessed December 10, 2017.

124. See the Ben-Gurion House website, http://www.bgh.org.il/Web/En/BenGurion Hut/Default.aspx, accessed December 10, 2017.

125. Michael Feige and David Ohana, "Funeral at the Edge of a Cliff: Israel Bids Farewell to David Ben-Gurion," *Journal of Israeli History* 31, 2 (2012): 249–81.

126. Information on the 2014 Ben-Gurion Walk was available on the website of Ramat Negev, at http://rng.org.il, accessed February 10, 2015 [Hebrew].

127. See Tamar Katriel's analysis of educational tours at the settlement museum in *Performing the Past*.

128. See the website of the Museum of Mitzpe Revivim, http://www.mitzpe-revivim .net/english/, accessed May 8, 2018; for a critical ethnography of the narrative it presents to tourists, see Jasmin Habib, *Israel, Diaspora and the Routes of National Belonging* (Toronto: University of Toronto Press, 2004), 84–88.

129. See the website of the Yad Mordechai Museum, http://www.y-m-museum.co.il /info/miclol/miclol-004eng.htm, accessed February 10, 2015.

130. See Maoz Azaryahu, "Water Towers in the Landscape of Memory: Negba, Yad Mordechai, and Be'erot Yitzhak," *Katedra* 79 (1966): 160–73 [Hebrew].

131. For a more detailed comparison of earlier and more recent settlement narratives, see chapter 4. Several farm owners articulated puzzlement over the visitors' surprised response to

the farm owners' lifestyle choice and the visitors' skeptical questions about the implications of that choice for their families.

132. According to a report in *Ha'aretz*, Israel reuses 87% of its treated wastewater for irrigation, compared to 20% reuse by Spain. See Zafrir Rinat, "Israel Leads in Use of Wastewater for Irrigation," *Ha'aretz*, Dec. 12, 2016, updated Apr. 2, 2017, at https://www .haaretz.co.il/news/science/.premium-1.3149818, accessed December 23, 2017 [Hebrew].

133. For example, *Negev Bar Kaima* (Sustainable Development of the Negev) offers various tracks with stops at desert locations where participants can observe and discuss technological methods related to water, electricity, sewage treatments, desert architecture, and similar concerns. See http://www.negev.org.il/index.php?m=text&t=16360, accessed February 14, 2016 [Hebrew].

134. Examples of such websites of the Jewish National Fund (JNF; KKL in Hebrew) include the website for Golda Meir Park, at http://www.kkl-jnf.org/tourism-and-recreation /forests-and-parks/golda-meir-park.aspx, accessed December 26, 2017; and the website of the Yerucham park and lake, at http://www.kkl-jnf.org/tourism/tours/yeruham-park.aspx, accessed December 26, 2017. See also "Sapir Park—An Oasis at the Heart of the Arava," *Jerusalem Post*, July 3, 2007, http://www.jpost.com/Green-Israel/Sapir-Park-An-Oasis-at -the-Heart-of-the-Arava, accessed December 26, 2017.

135. Data from the website of the ministry of tourism, http://www.goisrael.com/evng /Tourist%20Information/attractions/Pages/Tomb%20of%20the%20Baba%20Sali.aspx, accessed May 11, 2017. For further discussion of these developments, see chapter 4.

136. The website "zimmer," providing available lodgings, features a distinct subcategory for religious hospitality within its Negev section: https://www.zimmer.co.il/sSearch .asp?Stype=1&Sreg=16&Ssubtype=1, accessed February 14, 2016 [Hebrew]. The religious kibbutz Saad offers lodging and kosher dining accommodations; and the religious *moshav* Tekuma offers rural hospitality in a "charming religious atmosphere" and appeals to religious tourists coming to Netivot by highlighting its proximity to the grave of the Baba Sali; see the website of the Sedot Negev Regional Council in the northeastern Negev, http://www .sdotnegev.org.il/tour/, accessed February 6, 2015 [Hebrew].

137. Along similar lines, Orvar Löfgren notes that tourists' experiences of the same physical space reveal a diversity of mindscapes, in Orvar Löfgren, "Motion and Emotion: The Microphysics and Metaphysics of Landscape Experiences in Tourism," in Alf Hornborg and Gísli Pálsson, eds., *Negotiating Nature: Culture, Power, and Environment Argument* (Lund: Lund University Press, 2000), 34.

138. Nir Hasson, "Get Up and Walk in the Land, But Not in the Desert," *Ha'aretz*, October 12, 2015, https://www.haaretz.co.il/news/education/.premium-1.2728573, accessed December 26, 2017 [Hebrew].

139. On the importance of access and proximity for the success of a tourist site, see McKercher and du Cros, *Cultural Tourism* , 33.

140. See the promotional brochure *Sculptured Wilderness: Touring the Negev Desert* (Israel Ministry of Tourism and the Negev Tourism Development Administration, n.d.).

141. Moshe Gilad, "Not Just a Sea of Sand," *Ha'aretz*, March 29, 2010 [Hebrew].

142. Hasson, "Get Up and Walk in the Land."

Epilogue

1. The phrase has been attributed to Sheikh Hassan al-Banna, the founder of the Muslim Brothers; to Ahmad Shuqayri, the former chairman of the Palestinian Liberation Organization; and to Egypt's president, Gamal Abdel Nasser. Sheikh Hassan al-Banna is quoted in Dana Adams Schmidt's interview with him ("Aim to Oust Jews Pledged by Sheikh," *New York Times*, Aug. 2, 1948); for the attribution to Shuqayri, see Moshe Shemesh, "Did Shuqayri Call for 'Throwing the Jews into the Sea'?" *Israel Studies* 8, 2 (2003): 70–81.

2. See Yael Zerubavel, *Recovered Roots: Collective Memory and the Making of Israeli National Tradition* (Chicago: University of Chicago Press, 1995). On the shift in the comparison of Masada and the Holocaust, from oppositional to analogous historical events, see Yael Zerubavel, "The Death of Memory and the Memory of Death: Masada and the Holocaust as Historical Metaphors," in *Representations* 45 (Winter 1994): 72–100. On the rise of the Holocaust as a central event in Israeli Jewish memory, and its impact on Israelis' response to the Israeli-Palestinian conflict, see Ian S. Lustick, "The Holocaust in Israeli Political Culture: Four Constructs and Their Consequences," *Contemporary Jewry* 37, 1 (2017): 125–70; see also responses to his essay in the same issue.

3. Gil Eyal, *The Disenchantment of the Orient: Expertise in Arab Affairs and the Israeli State* (Stanford: Stanford University Press, 2006), 152–84; Daniel Monterescu, *Jaffa Shared and Shattered: Contrived Coexistence in Israel/Palestine* (Bloomington: Indiana University Press, 2015), 112.

4. Eyal Weizman and Fazal Sheikh, *The Conflict Shoreline* (Göttingen: Steidl, 2015), 47.

5. Israel's ministry of culture has required Israeli cultural organizations that receive government funding to offer their programs to the "peripheries," including "Judea and Samaria": Yair Ashkenazi, "Israel Asks Culture Institutions to Declare if They Hold Performances in Settlements," *Ha'aretz*, June 15, 2016, http://www.haaretz.com/israel-news/.premium-1.725065, accessed July 27, 2016. On a recent vote by the Likud party to formally annex the West Bank, see Chaim Levinson, "Netanyahu's Party Votes to Annex West Bank, Increase Settlements," *Ha'aretz*, Jan. 1, 2018, https://www.haaretz.com/israel-news/.premium-1.832259, accessed January 15, 2018.

6. The movement "Fence for Life" [*Gader La-Hayim*] was transformed into "Security Fence for Israel" [*Gader Bitahon Le-Israel*] in 2003. See Yeshayahu Folman, *The Story of the Security Fence: Life Repudiation Indeed?* [*Sipura shel gader ha-hafrada: Ha'umnam hafkarat hayim?*] (Jerusalem: Carmel, 2004), 212–15 [Hebrew].

7. See, for example, Chaim Levinson, "Security Coordinator of Bat Ayin Insisted on Building a Fence, Settlement's Leaders Decided to Fire Him," *Ha'aretz*, Aug. 20, 2010, http://www.haaretz.co.il/news/politics/1.1217590, accessed August 27, 2015 [Hebrew]; Mordechai Haimovitch, "Collaborators: Jews and Arabs against a Separation Fence," *Nrg*, Jan. 25, 2014, http://www.nrg.co.il/online/1/ART2/543/771.html, accessed July 25, 2016 [Hebrew]; Folman, *The Story of the Security Fence*, 121–42.

8. According to a 2016 report in *Ha'aretz*, "Around 58,000 Palestinians have permits to work within Israel proper. An estimated 120,000 Palestinians work for Israelis, including over 30,000 who work in Israel illegally and some 27,000 who work in industrial zones in West Bank settlements." See Amos Harel, "Military Wants 30,000 More Palestinians Working in

Israel," *Ha'aretz*, Feb. 8, 2016, http://www.haaretz.com/israel-news/.premium-1.702003, accessed July 31, 2016; James Glanz and Rami Nazzal, "Smugglers in West Bank Open Door to Jobs in Israel and Violence," *New York Times*, June 20, 2016.

9. See for example the reference to the "Apartheid Wall" at the website of The Electronic Intifada, https://electronicintifada.net/content/it-fence-it-wall-no-its-separation-barrier/4715, accessed July 27, 2016; Tamar Katriel and Yifat Gutman, "The Wall Must Fall: Memory Activism, Documentary Filmmaking and the Second Intifada," in Anna Reading and Tamar Katriel, eds., *Cultural Memories of Nonviolent Struggles: Powerful Times* (Basingstoke: Palgrave Macmillan, 2015), 205–25. Yuval Feinstein compares two different movements that opposed the wall, but with opposite outcomes: the "Anti-Wall Movement," which failed to block Israel's security barrier, and a joint legal action by Mevasseret Zion's Jewish residents and Beit Surik's Palestinian residents, which successfully stopped a specific segment near Jerusalem. See Yuval Feinstein, "Between the 'Security Fence' and the 'Apartheid Wall,'" MA thesis, Department of Sociology and Anthropology, University of Haifa, 2006 [Hebrew].

10. See Sam Jones, "Spray Can Prankster Tackles Israel's Security Barrier," *The Guardian*, Aug. 5, 2005, http://www.guardian.co.uk/world/2005/aug/05/israel.artsnews, accessed May 4, 2012. Banksy later returned with a group of about fifteen artists whose art was directed more bluntly at the Israeli occupation: Shahar Smooha, "Art Barrier," *Ha'aretz*, Dec. 13, 2007, http://www.haaretz.com/israel-news/art-barrier-1.235195, accessed May 4, 2012. See also Daniella Peled, "The Art of Politics: How Banksy Inadvertently Created an Israeli-Palestinian Dialogue," *Ha'aretz*, Sep. 15, 2015, http://www.haaretz.com/opinion/.premium-1.676012, accessed July 25, 2016. News featuring the "Walled Off Hotel" that Banksy opened, located across from the separation wall in Bethlehem, publicized its claim to offer "the worst view of any hotel in the world": *The Telegraph News*, March 3, 2017, http://www.telegraph.co.uk/news/2017/03/03/walled-hotel-banksy-opens-dystopian-tourist-attraction-bethlehem/.

11. Eyal Weizman, *Hollow Land: Israel's Architecture of Occupation* (New York: Verso, 2007); Gary Fields, "Enclosure Landscapes: Historical Reflections on Palestinian Geography," *Historical Geography* 39 (2011): 182–207, quote on pp. 196–97; Dan Rabinowitz, "Borders and Their Discontents: Israel's Green Line, Arabness and Unilateral Separation," *European Studies* 19, 1 (2003): 217–31.

12. Yotam Brenner, "The Committee for Legalizing Outposts Offers Legal Tools as Precedents to Sanction Thousands of Structures in the West Bank," *Ha'aretz*, May 4, 2018, https://www.haaretz.co.il/news/politics/1.6054336 [Hebrew]. The article reports that among the problems that the committee addresses is the position of Jewish settlements built on hilltops as "hanging islands" [*iyim teluyim*] surrounded by valleys of land owned by Palestinians.

13. In 1976, the "good fence" between Israel and southern Lebanon opened up the possibility for Lebanese to receive medical aid from Israel and reinforced Israel's ties with the Christian Lebanese militia during the civil war in Lebanon. See Laura Zittrain Eisenberg, "Do Good Fences Make Good Neighbors? Israel and Lebanon after the Withdrawal," *Middle East* 4, 3 (2000): 17–31.

14. The fence Israel had built along the border with the Gaza Strip in the mid-1990s was followed by further protective measures after the "disengagement" from Gaza in August 2005. The construction of a deep subterranean wall to prevent passage through tunnels that

had been dug underneath the security fence followed Israel's military operation against Gaza in the summer of 2014. See Folman, *The Story of the Security Fence*, 94–95, 220; Nahum Barnea, "The Solution for the Tunnels: Concrete Wall Aboveground and Underground," *Ynet*, June 16, 2016, http://www.ynet.co.il/articles/0,7340,L-4816481,00.html, accessed April 13, 2017 [Hebrew]; Isabel Kershner, "New Israeli Wall to Dive Deep to Cut Off Tunnels," *New York Times*, Aug. 11, 2017. In addition, the "Iron Dome" offers a missile-defense system to protect Israeli airspace, thus addressing the inevitably open space through which the country could otherwise be penetrated.

15. See Rony Daniel, "After Three and a Half Years: The Border Fence between Israel and Egypt Was Completed," *Mako*, online news, Dec. 4, 2013, http://www.mako.co.il/news-channel2/Channel-2-Newscast/Article-ebb313933e9b241004.htm, accessed August 4, 2015 [Hebrew].

16. Guy Varon, "The Fence on the Border with Syria Has Been Completed," *Mako*, online news, Oct. 12, 2013, http://www.mako.co.il/news-military/security/Article-291f5f12659 4241004.htm, accessed July 17, 2015 [Hebrew].

17. In 2015 Israel began constructing a security fence along the border with Jordan near the airport accessing Eilat: Zohar Blumenkrantz, "Following 'Protective Edge' Operation: The Airport in Timna Will Be Prepared for International Flights," *Ha'aretz*, Sept. 3, 2014, http://www.themarker.com/news/aviation/1.2423993, accessed July 2, 2015 [Hebrew]; Cobi Ben-Simhon, "Smuggling Weapons through the Dead Sea Is a Matter of Routine," *Ha'aretz*, Dec. 18, 2014, http://www.haaretz.co.il/magazine/.premium-1.2516179, accessed July 2, 2015 [Hebrew]; Na'ama Engel Mishali, "The Cabinet Approved Expanding the Fence on the Egyptian Border to Jordan," *NRG*, June 29, 2015, http://www.nrg.co.il/online/1 /ART2/705/488.html, accessed April 13, 2017 [Hebrew].

18. Quoted in Mishali, "The Cabinet Approved Expanding the Fence"; see also Netanel Leiffer, "Surrounded by Walls: A New Wall Will Be Built against the Tunnels in the Border with Gaza," *Kipa*, June 16, 2016, http://www.kipa.co.il/now/67930.html, accessed April 13, 2017 [Hebrew]; Sylvain Cypel, *Walled: Israeli Society at an Impasse* (New York: Other Press, 2006).

19. The vocabulary of Israeli Hebrew includes the terms checkpoint (*mahsom*), security fence (*gader bitahon*), and separation barrier (*mahsom hafrada* and *michshol hafrada*). The more obscure term *otef* ("enveloping") is used around Gaza and Jerusalem. For the use of these terms, see the Knesset report on "The Project of Constructing a Separation Fence," June 9, 2002, https://www.knesset.gov.il/mmm/data/pdf/m00259.pdf, accessed July 27, 2016 [Hebrew]; Folman, *The Story of the Security Fence*; Shaul Arieli and Michael Sfard, *The Wall of Folly* [*Huma u-mehdal: Gader ha-hafrada—bitahon o hamdanut?*] (Tel Aviv: Aliyat Ha-Gag and Yediot Ahronot, 2008) [Hebrew].

20. For the shift from "wall" to "barbed fence," see Dan Bar-On, *The Rebels against the Desert: Beit Eshel's Story, 1943–1948* (Moshav Yogev, 1984), 24 [Hebrew]. On fences around the kibbutzim in the Jezreel valley, see Hadas Yaron, *Zionist Arabesques: Modern Landscapes, Non-Modern Texts* (Boston: Academic Press, 2010), 135–36.

21. See Isabel Kershner, "Trump Cites Israel's 'Wall' as Model," *New York Times*, Jan. 27, 2017; Ron Nixon, "Official Casts Doubt on a Wall 'From Sea to Shining Sea,'" *New York Times*, April 6, 2017; Luis Sanchez, "Trump Shares Photos Touting 'the Start' of Border Wall," *The Hill*, March 28, 2018, http://thehill.com/homenews/administration/380724-trump

-says-border-wall-construction-has-begun, accessed May 5, 2018; Glenn Kessler, "President Trump Says His 'Beautiful Wall' Is Being Built. Nope," *The Washington Post*, April 5, 2018, https://www.washingtonpost.com/news/fact-checker/wp/2018/04/05/president-trump-say s-his-beautiful-wall-is-being-built-nope/?utm_term=.655584367615, accessed May 5, 2018.

22.   See the title of Jacob Katz's famous study, *Out of the Ghetto: The Social Background of Jewish Emancipation, 1770–1870* (Cambridge, MA: Harvard University Press, 1973).

23.   Avirama Golan, "The Bluff Wins," Opinions, *Ha'aretz*, June 22, 2011, http://www .haaretz.co.il/opinions/1.1177923, accessed July 28, 2016 [Hebrew]; Batia Roded, "Informal Space between a Jewish Ghetto and Fortified Enclave: The Case of the Jewish Settlement in Hebron," *Israeli Sociology* 12, 2 (2011): 303–30 [Hebrew]; Yaron, *Zionist Arabesques*, 145–47. See also the discussions of the impact of the Holocaust and Masada on Israeli politics by Lustick, ("The Holocaust in Israeli Political Culture") and Yael Zerubavel (*Recovered Roots*, 209–13), respectively.

24.   Gideon Levy and Alex Levac, *Ha'aretz*, Weekend Supplement, Oct. 11, 2017, https:// www.haaretz.co.il/magazine/twilightzone/.premium-MAGAZINE-1.4510807 [Hebrew], and its English version, "Highway 40 Revisited," *Ha'aretz*, Oct. 14, 2017, https://www.haaretz .com/israel-news/.premium-1.816631; the quote is from the English edition, except for the text in brackets at the end, which only appeared in the Hebrew edition.

25.   Uri Avnery writes: "Barak himself, in domestic discussions, often used a telling metaphor: Israel is 'a villa in the middle of a jungle.' Meaning, we are an island of civilization surrounded by savage animals": Uri Avnery, "Barak: Villa in the Jungle," July 14, 2002, Gush Shalom website, at http://zope.gush-shalom.org/home/en/channels/avnery/archives_barak/, accessed July 17, 2015; Rubik Rosenthal, "The Linguistic Arena," *Nrg*, Feb. 2, 2012, http:// www.nrg.co.il/online/47/ART2/333/165.html, accessed July 17, 2015 [Hebrew].

26.   Ehud Barak in an interview with the journalist Yigal Ravid, *Kol Israel*, channel 2, Jan. 24, 2012 [Hebrew]. Barak reportedly returned to the "villa in the jungle" metaphor in a speech he gave later the same year at an air force base: Hizki Ezra, "The Minister of Defense: We are a 'Villa in the Jungle,'" *Arutz 7*, Sept. 10, 2012, http://www.inn.co.il /News/News.aspx/243960, accessed July 17, 2015 [Hebrew].

27.   Netanyahu, in a speech for the Israel Defense Forces' high command forum (*Matkal Forum*), reported on Israel Broadcast authority, Channel 2, Sept. 13, 2012; [Hebrew]; Yuval Steinitz, minister of finance, was to present Israel to potential investors as "an island of stability, innovation, and entrepreneurship," and as a solid economy in a volatile global market: Moti Bassok, "On Monday in New York: Steinitz in a Meeting to Encourage Investments in Israel, *TheMarker*, Sept. 5, 2012, http://www.themarker.com/news/macro/1.1817694, accessed July 25, 2015 [Hebrew].

28.   Akiva Eldar, "The Price of a Villa in the Jungle," *Ha'aretz*, Jan. 30, 2006, http://www .haaretz.com/the-price-of-a-villa-in-the-jungle-1.178800, accessed February 2, 2008; Neve Gordon, "A Villa in the Jungle: The Arab Awakening through the Lens of the Israeli Media," *Middle East Law and Governance* 3, 1–2 (2011): 105–17; Menachem Klein, "Accept What Had Been Unthinkable," Op-Ed, *New York Times*, March 9, 2012; Emmanuel Sivan, "Not a Villa, But for Sure a Jungle," *Ha'aretz*, June 11, 2013, http://www.haaretz.co.il/opinions/ .premium-1.2043970 [Hebrew]; Aluf Benn, "The Jewish Majority in Israel Still See Their

Country as 'a Villa in the Jungle,'" *The Guardian*, Aug. 20, 2013, https://www.theguardian.com /commentisfree/2013/aug/20/jewish-majority-israel-villa-in-the-jungle, accessed July 25, 2015.

29.   "Unwarranted Arrogance" [*Hitnasut meyuteret*], *Ha'aretz* editorial, Sept. 27, 2009, http://www.haaretz.co.il/opinions/1.1282516, accessed July 27, 2015 [Hebrew].

30.   Julie Trottier, "A Wall, Water and Power: The Israeli 'Separation Fence,'" *Review of International Studies* 33, 1 (2007): 105–27; Ian S. Lustick, "Abandoning the Iron Wall: Israel and 'the Middle Eastern Muck'," *Middle East Policy* 15, 3 (2008): 30–56; Benn, "The Jewish Majority in Israel"; Avnery, "Ehud Barak: Villa in the Jungle"; Sivan, "Not a Villa, But For Sure a Jungle"; Danny Gutwein, "No More Heroes: Suddenly They Are Our Children," in *Ha-Makom*, May 25, 2015, http://www.ha-makom.co.il/post/gutwein-villa-in-the-jungle, accessed July 27, 2015 [Hebrew].

Index

STANFORD STUDIES IN JEWISH HISTORY AND CULTURE
David Biale and Sarah Abrevaya Stein, Editors

This series features novel approaches to examining the Jewish past in the form of innovative work that brings the field into productive dialogue with the newest scholarly concepts and methods. Open to a range of disciplinary and interdisciplinary approaches, from history to cultural studies, this series publishes exceptional scholarship, balanced by an accessible tone that illustrates histories of difference and addresses issues of current urgency. Books in this list push the boundaries of Jewish Studies and speak compellingly to a wide audience of scholars and students.

For a complete listing of titles in this series, visit the Stanford University Press website, www.sup.org.